12

For your contributions
to those who serve
and sacrifice, we
thank you profusely.
With many
blessings,
Kathy Platoni, Psy.D.
COL/MS/USAR
ODS, OIF, OEFx2

Thank you for your understanding & concern re
our nation's warfighters, returning & their
families.

Blessings & Peace,
Ron (SCURFIELD)
VIETNAM, 1968-69

War Trauma and Its Wake

Decades after Charles Figley's landmark *Trauma and Its Wake* was published, our understanding of trauma has grown and deepened, but we still face considerable challenges when treating trauma survivors. This is especially the case for professionals who work with veterans and active-duty military personnel. *War Trauma and Its Wake*, then, is a vital book. The editors — one a contributor to *Trauma and Its Wake*, the other an army reserve psychologist with four deployments — have produced a book that addresses both the specific needs of particular warrior communities as well as wider issues such as battlemind, guilt, suicide, and much, much more. The editors' and contributors' deep understanding of the issues that warriors face makes *War Trauma and Its Wake* a crucial book for understanding the military experience, and the lessons contained in its pages are essential for anyone committed to healing war trauma.

Raymond Monsour Scurfield, DSW, LCSW is a Vietnam veteran, a professor emeritus of social work, and a former director of the Katrina Research Center at the University of Southern Mississippi, Gulf Coast.

Katherine Theresa Platoni, Psy.D., is a colonel in the Medical Service Corps of the United States Army Reserve and Army Reserve Psychology Consultant to the Chief in the Medical Service Corps.

ROUTLEDGE PSYCHOSOCIAL STRESS SERIES
Charles R. Figley, Ph.D., Series Editor

1. *Stress Disorders Among Vietnam Veterans*, Edited by Charles R. Figley, Ph.D.
2. *Stress and the Family Vol. 1: Coping with Normative Transitions*, Edited by Hamilton I. McCubbin, Ph.D., and Charles R. Figley, Ph.D.
3. *Stress and the Family Vol. 2: Coping with Catastrophe*, Edited by Charles R. Figley, Ph.D., and Hamilton I. McCubbin, Ph.D.
4. *Trauma and Its Wake: The Study and Treatment of Post-Traumatic Stress Disorder*, Edited by Charles R. Figley, Ph.D.
5. *Post-Traumatic Stress Disorder and the War Veteran Patient*, Edited by William E. Kelly, M.D.
6. *The Crime Victim's Book, Second Edition*, By Morton Bard, Ph.D., and Dawn Sangrey.
7. *Stress and Coping in Time of War: Generalizations from the Israeli Experience*, Edited by Norman A. Milgram, Ph.D.
8. *Trauma and Its Wake Vol. 2: Traumatic Stress Theory, Research, and Intervention*, Edited by Charles R. Figley, Ph.D.
9. *Stress and Addiction*, Edited by Edward Gottheil, M.D., Ph.D., Keith A. Druley, Ph.D., Steven Pashko, Ph.D., and Stephen P. Weinsteinn, Ph.D.
10. *Vietnam: A Casebook*, by Jacob D. Lindy, M.D., in collaboration with Bonnie L. Green, Ph.D., Mary C. Grace, M.Ed., M.S., John A. MacLeod, M.D., and Louis Spitz, M.D.
11. *Post-Traumatic Therapy and Victims of Violence*, Edited by Frank M. Ochberg, M.D.
12. *Mental Health Response to Mass Emergencies: Theory and Practice*, Edited by Mary Lystad, Ph.D.
13. *Treating Stress in Families*, Edited by Charles R. Figley, Ph.D.
14. *Trauma, Transformation, and Healing: An Integrative Approach to Theory, Research, and Post-Traumatic Therapy*, By John P. Wilson, Ph.D.
15. *Systemic Treatment of Incest: A Therapeutic Handbook*, By Terry Trepper, Ph.D., and Mary Jo Barrett, M.S.W.
16. *The Crisis of Competence: Transitional Stress and the Displaced Worker*, Edited by Carl A. Maida, Ph.D., Norma S. Gordon, M.A., and Norman L. Farberow, Ph.D.
17. *Stress Management: An Integrated Approach to Therapy*, by Dorothy H. G. Cotton, Ph.D.
18. *Trauma and the Vietnam War Generation: Report of the Findings from the National Vietnam Veterans Readjustment Study*, By Richard A. Kulka, Ph.D., William E. Schlenger, Ph.D., John A. Fairbank, Ph.D., Richard L. Hough, Ph.D., Kathleen Jordan, Ph.D., Charles R. Marmar, M.D., Daniel S. Weiss, Ph.D., and David A. Grady, Psy.D.
19. *Strangers at Home: Vietnam Veterans Since the War*, Edited by Charles R. Figley, Ph.D., and Seymour Leventman, Ph.D.
20. *The National Vietnam Veterans Readjustment Study: Tables of Findings and Technical Appendices*, By Richard A. Kulka, Ph.D., Kathleen Jordan, Ph.D., Charles R. Marmar, M.D., and Daniel S. Weiss, Ph.D.
21. *Psychological Trauma and the Adult Survivor: Theory, Therapy, and Transformation*, By I. Lisa McCann, Ph.D., and Laurie Anne Pearlman, Ph.D.
22. *Coping with Infant or Fetal Loss: The Couple's Healing Process*, By Kathleen R. Gilbert, Ph.D., and Laura S. Smart, Ph.D.
23. *Compassion Fatigue: Coping with Secondary Traumatic Stress Disorder in Those Who Treat the Traumatized*, Edited by Charles R. Figley, Ph.D.
24. *Treating Compassion Fatigue*, Edited by Charles R. Figley, Ph.D.
25. *Handbook of Stress, Trauma and the Family*, Edited by Don R. Catherall, Ph.D.
26. *The Pain of Helping: Psychological Injury of Helping Professionals*, by Patrick J. Morrissette, Ph.D., RMFT, NCC, CCC.
27. *Disaster Mental Health Services: A Primer for Practitioners*, by Diane Myers, R.N., M.S.N., and David Wee, M.S.S.W.
28. *Empathy in the Treatment of Trauma and PTSD*, by John P. Wilson, Ph.D. and Rhiannon B. Thomas, Ph.D.
29. *Family Stressors: Interventions for Stress and Trauma*, Edited by Don. R. Catherall, Ph. D.
30. *Handbook of Women, Stress and Trauma*, Edited by Kathleen Kendall-Tackett, Ph.D.
31. *Mapping Trauma and Its Wake*, Edited by Charles R. Figley, Ph.D.

32. *The Posttraumatic Self: Restoring Meaning and Wholeness to Personality*, Edited by John P. Wilson, Ph.D.
33. *Violent Death: Resilience and Intervention Beyond the Crisis*, Edited by Edward K. Rynearson, M.D.
34. *Combat Stress Injury: Theory, Research, and Management*, Edited by Charles R. Figley, Ph.D. and William P. Nash, M.D.
35. *MindBody Medicine: Foundations and Practical Applications*, by Leo W. Rotan, Ph.D. and Veronika Ospina-Kammerer, Ph.D.
36. *Understanding and Assessing Trauma in Children and Adolescents: Measures, Methods, and Youth in Context*, by Kathleen Nader, D.S.W
38. *When the Past Is Always Present: Emotional Traumatization, Causes, and Cures*, by Ronald A. Ruden, M.D., Ph.D.
39. *Families Under Fire: Systemic Therapy with Military Families*, Edited by R. Blaine Everson, Ph.D. and Charles R. Figley, Ph.D.
40. *Dissociation in Traumatized Children and Adolescents: Theory and Clinical Interventions*, Edited by Sandra Wieland, Ph.D.
41. *Transcending Trauma: Survival, Resilience and Clinical Implications in Survivor Families*, by Bea Hollander-Goldfein, Ph.D., Nancy Isserman, Ph.D., and Jennifer Goldenberg, Ph.D., L.C.S.W
42. *School Rampage Shootings and Other Youth Disturbances: Early Preventative Interventions*, by Kathleen Nader, D.S.W.
43. *The Compassion Fatigue Workbook: Creative Tools for Transforming Compassion Fatigue and Vicarious Traumatization*, by Françoise Mathieu, M.Ed.
44. *War Trauma and Its Wake: Expanding the Circle of Healing*, by Raymond Monsour Scurfield, D.S.W., and Katherine Theresa Platoni, Psy.D.
45. *Healing War Trauma: A Handbook of Creative Approaches*, by Raymond Monsour Scurfield, D.S.W., and Katherine Theresa Platoni, Psy.D.

Editorial Board

War Trauma and Its Wake

Expanding the Circle of Healing

Edited by
Raymond Monsour Scurfield
and
Katherine Theresa Platoni

This book is part of the Psychosocial Stress Series, edited by Charles Figley

First published 2013
by Routledge
711 Third Avenue, New York, NY 10017

Simultaneously published in the UK
by Routledge
27 Church Road, Hove, East Sussex BN3 2FA

Routledge is an imprint of the Taylor & Francis Group, an informa business

Library of Congress Cataloging in Publication Data
War trauma and its wake : expanding the circle of healing / edited by Raymond Monsour Scurfield and Katherine Theresa Platoni. — 1st ed.
p. cm. — (Routledge psychosocial stress series)
Includes bibliographical references and index.
ISBN 978-0-415-50682-3 (hardcover : alk. paper)
1. War—Psychological aspects. 2. Post-traumatic stress disorder. 3. Soldiers—Mental health. 4. Soldiers—Wounds and injuries. 5. Soldiers—Health and hygiene. I. Scurfield, Raymond M. II. Platoni, Katherine Theresa.
RC552.P67W3755 2012
616.85'21—dc23
2012006005

ISBN: 978-0-415-50682-3 (hbk)
ISBN: 978-0-203-12670-7 (ebk)

Typeset in Minion
by EvS Communication Networx, Inc.

Printed and bound in the United States of America by Sheridan Books, Inc. (a Sheridan Group Company

Contents

Foreword by series editor Charles Figley   xi

Preface   xiii

Acknowledgments   xix

1 **An expanding circle of healing: Warriors and civilians impacted
   by war**   1
   RAYMOND MONSOUR SCURFIELD (VIETNAM) AND COL KATHERINE
   THERESA PLATONI (OEF-OIF)

2 **Myths and realities about war, its impact, and healing**   16
   RAYMOND MONSOUR SCURFIELD (VIETNAM) AND
   COL KATHERINE THERESA PLATONI (OEF-OIF)

PART 1
Warriors impacted by war   29

3 **Citizen/warriors: Challenges facing U.S. Army Reserve soldiers
   and their families**   31
   COL DAVID RABB (OIF-OEF) AND LTC (RET) CYNTHIA RASMUSSEN

4 **Army National Guard warriors: A part-time job becomes
   a full-time life**   53
   MAJ CORA COURAGE (OIF-OEF)

5 **Women warriors: From making milestones in the military
   to community reintegration**   69
   MICHELLE WILMOT (ARMY SERGEANT, OIF II-III)

6   The Canadian military and veteran experience   90
    SUSAN BROCK AND LCDR (RET) GREG PASSEY

PART 2
Special populations of wounded warriors   111

7   Traumatic brain injury and post-traumatic stress: The
    "signature wounds" of the Iraq and Afghanistan wars   113
    JOHN L. RIGG

8   Physically wounded and injured warriors and their families:
    The long journey home   134
    LEE LAWRENCE

9   Military suicidality and principles to consider in prevention 156
    RANDI JENSEN

10 Military sexual trauma   172
    LTC (RET) CYNTHIA RASMUSSEN AND CHRIS ZAGLIFA

11 Veterans involved with the criminal justice system:
    Clinical issues, strategies, and interventions   193
    EMILY SIMERLY

PART 3
Civilian populations impacted by war   213

12 Iraqi civilians and the recycling of trauma   215
    ALEXANDER DAWOODY

13 Afghan civilians: Surviving trauma in a failed state   231
    ANNA BADKHEN

PART 4
Military and resiliency initiatives   243

14 U.S. Army combat and operational stress control: From
   battlemind to resiliency, debriefings, and traumatic event
   management   245
   CPT CHRISTIAN HALLMAN (OIF) AND MAJ PATRICK PISCHKE (OIF)

15 Enhancing resiliency through creative outdoor/adventure and
   community-based programs   267
   LTC VALVINCENT REYES, USAR, OEF-A

16 ArtReach: Project America and other innovative models in
   civilian–military partnering   283
   CHRISTOPHER A. MORLEY, SUSAN M. ANDERSON AND
   CHRISTIANE C. O'HARA

17 Military chaplains' roles in healing: "Being here and there"   303
   LTC (RET) CHARLES PURINTON (OEF-OIF)

18 Afterword: A surviving spouse speaks   317
   BEATE MEDINA

   Epilogue   331
   Index   333

Foreword

The U.S. war in Iraq is over. Within a year or so, U.S. troops will be returning from a nearly decade-long war in Afghanistan, and there will be an extraordinary drawdown of active-duty U.S. military personnel. There is a growing concern among mental-health professionals that the Department of Veterans Affairs will be incapable of addressing the needs of war veterans, especially the newly returned warriors. There has never been a better time to publish a comprehensive book on helping those who serve their country in war.

Thus, in this time of great need, I am especially honored to welcome *War Trauma and its Wake* to the Routledge Psychosocial Stress Series. The series began in 1978 with the publication of *Stress Disorders Among Vietnam Veterans*. This book was influential in shaping the modern era of trauma research and practice. *War Trauma and its Wake* is the 43rd book in the series, which has consistently included books focused on war stress and adaptation. It is useful for the reader of this new book to appreciate the other books that came before it:

- The 5th book in the series: *Post-Traumatic Stress Disorder and the War Veteran Patient*;
- The 7th book in the series: *Stress and Coping in Time of War: Generalizations from the Israeli Experience*;
- The 10th book in the series: *Vietnam: A Casebook*;
- The 18th and 20th books in the series, which are the distillation of a government-funded study of Vietnam veterans: *Trauma and the Vietnam War Generation: Report of the Findings from the National Vietnam Veterans Readjustment Study* and *The National Vietnam Veterans Readjustment Study: Tables of Findings and Technical Appendices*;
- The 19th book in the series: *Strangers at Home: Vietnam Veterans Since the War* (winner of the 1980 Waterman Award);
- The 34th book in the series: *Combat Stress Injury: Theory, Research, and Management*, which called for a re-evaluation of the way we assess and treat combatants for stress-related mental disorders and reactions; and, finally,

- The 38th book in the series, *Families Under Fire: Systemic Therapy With Military Families.*

The title of this book, *War Trauma and Its Wake: Expanding the Circle of Healing,* contains the editor's primary premise: that, in war's wake, treating trauma requires circles of support to soften trauma's impact and facilitate growth. The book is co-edited by Raymond Scurfield, a social work scholar and an author of several books focusing on Vietnam veterans' mental health, and Dr. Kathy Platoni, a clinical psychologist. Both co-editors have many years of experience as caregivers in war. Dr. Scurfield served in Vietnam and had a long career directing the first PTSD treatment programs within the U.S. Department of Veterans Affairs. Dr. Platoni, a colonel in the U.S. Army Reserve, recently returned from deployments in the Middle East to continue her private practice as a clinical psychologist.

As the editors note in the first chapter, their book is a compendium of the psychosocial stimulations and reactions that wash over everyone who has survived a traumatic experience. This stimulation can cause PTSD, other traumatic stress reactions, and traumatic dreams, but it can also lead to post-traumatic growth, and a sense of accomplishment. This is the irony of trauma: its effects can lead to fear but also to bravery, accomplishment, and an ability to remain resilient in the face of adversity.

The book's special theme of *expanding the circle of healing* comes through clearly in its discussion of a full spectrum of traumatic stressors and stress reactions associated with war. Here the reader will find, for the first time, a discussion of the distinctive aspects of special populations of warriors (for example, reserve, Guard, women, and Canadian forces), wounded warriors (for example, physically wounded, military sexual trauma, suicides, mTBI), and civilian populations impacted by war (Iraqi and Afghan civilians, and spouses of service members killed in action).

Finally, the *expanding circle of healing* theme suggests that the more we know about how war impacts warriors, their families, and war-impacted civilian populations, the more we understand how we all can be impacted by catastrophic conditions. Moreover, as we understand how best to help those impacted by war, we become more effective in caring for all traumatized people and communities.

Charles R. Figley, Ph.D. Tulane University
New Orleans, Louisiana
Series editor

Preface

Why was this book written? As a Vietnam veteran, I (Scurfield) have been very concerned about and interested in the welfare and fate of our current-day service members who have served their country as part of the Global War on Terror. I have been particularly interested in and concerned about those who have served in the wars in Iraq and Afghanistan—and those who might yet serve.

In addition, I have been dismayed by how little our *country*, our *communities* and our *citizens*, by and large, have been involved. There seems to be little appreciation of the experiences and sacrifices of our service members while they were in uniform and following their discharge from active duty, or of their families. There remains a historic and current dichotomy between those who are familiar and concerned with our military personnel (while on active duty and after becoming veterans) and their families, and those who might not even know what OEF (Operation Enduring Freedom, e.g. deployed to Afghanistan) or OIF (Operation Iraqi Freedom, e.g. deployed to Iraq) stand for and/or who tend to lump together all service members who eventually become veterans into one monolithic and indeed amorphous category.

Expanding the circle of healing

The underlying ethos of *War Trauma and Its Wake* is to expand the circle of healing to incorporate increasingly more persons, institutions, communities and approaches to hopefully optimize contributions to the healing that is so markedly needed. The first two chapters of this book provide the context and backdrop for this ethos: identifying key war and post-war experiences of we, the co-editors (Scurfield in Vietnam and Platoni in Iraq and Afghanistan), that continue to serve as crucial learning points in our own understanding; and formulation of what a creative "expanded circle of healing" looks like, who can and should be involved in ever widening circles of care and support for our nation's service members, veterans and their families.

Myths and realities

The second chapter uncovers and then dispels a number of profound myths about the impact of war that cloud the picture of what is needed to understand the countervailing realities about war's impact and healing. For example, one of the most enduring myths is that "time heals all wounds"; we point out the contrasting belief systems that both fuel and dispel such myths. This is essential information if we are to more fully understand and respond helpfully to war trauma. And it sets the context for the subsequent chapters, which are intended to foster awareness and appreciation of salient, distinctive aspects regarding three different populations impacted by the wars in Iraq and Afghanistan.

Special populations of warriors

It is too easy to group or indeed lump together all service members and veterans into one monolithic catch-all category of people who have served our country in uniform—thus overlooking vital distinguishing characteristics within different populations of warriors. Four such special populations of warriors each has an entire chapter dedicated to delineating and discussing what is unique and distinctive:

- National Guard;
- reserve forces;
- women warriors; and
- Canadian forces.

Each of these chapters is written or co-authored by active duty service members or veterans who are or have been a member of that special warrior population. Hence, each brings both breadth and depth of honesty, understanding and perspective that is grounded in the bedrock reality of those who have been "boots on the ground."

Special populations of wounded warriors

Five populations of wounded warriors each have a chapter written by an author whose exemplary service and expertise reveals an unsurpassed level of depth and insight regarding their experiences, dynamics, challenges (and successes):

- Those who have been impacted by the "signature wounds" of the wars in Iraq and Afghanistan—mild traumatic brain injury (mTBI) and post-combat or traumatic stress;

- Those who were seriously wounded or injured while deployed, requiring medevac (medical evacuation) out of combat, and who went through a series of profound experiences as part of their long journey home;
- Those who suffer from the stigma and critical threat of suicide;
- Those who have suffered from being victims of the perpetration of sexual assault by fellow and sister members of the military; and
- Those veterans whose war and post-war struggles have contributed to their becoming *involved with the criminal justice system.*

Special populations of civilians ("collateral damage") impacted by war

There is profound impact or "collateral damage" during war on two populations of civilians *who need and deserve to have a voice.* In my (Scurfield) initial brainstorming about what populations to include in *War Trauma and Its Wake*, I knew about these from my experiences during and following the Vietnam War and over four decades of working with service members and veterans and their families. These civilian populations *almost never* receive *any* meaningful acknowledgment or recognition in the U.S. And so we are honored that this book is a platform for three extremely emotionally evocative and tragic, yet inspiring, accounts. These are by:

- Beate Medina, the surviving spouse of SSG Oscar Medina, killed in action in Iraq in 2004;
- Alexander Dawoody, a member of the Kurdish population whose family and people suffered horrific trauma. And yet Alexander somehow survived and is thriving as a university faculty member here in the U.S.; and
- Anna Badkhen, a reporter *extraordinaire* who has lived remarkable and in-depth experiences in Afghanistan. She gives an eloquent and searing voice to several Afghan civilians who are surviving decades of widespread trauma.

Military and resiliency initiatives

We were determined that this book would not just document the trials and tribulations of military, veterans and their families. And so, each chapter identifies courage, determination and strength exhibited by the various populations of warriors, wounded warriors and civilians impacted by war. In addition, in the final section, four chapters each describe in depth distinctive or innovative approaches to fostering healing in those sorely impacted by war:

- Two authors describe their boots-on-the-ground experiences and knowledge about combat operational stress control and psychological debriefings in Iraq and Afghanistan;
- An Afghanistan veteran describes exciting and innovative outdoor and adventure-based approaches to healing;
- The founder and two key staff of the private, non-profit ArtReach organization describe their exciting partnership projects with the military, which utilize the creative and expressive arts; and
- An Army Chaplain describes his experiences in both Iraq and Afghanistan.

Choosing a co-editor

My (Scurfield) original intention was to be the sole editor of *War Trauma and Its Wake*, to write a number of the chapters myself and to have several other authors for the topics that I did not have sufficient knowledge about. I also started thinking about the fact that I was in my late sixties and a Vietnam veteran. I had had some meaningful interaction with and knowledge about OEF/OIF service members, including through my wife, Margaret's, several roles as a social worker with the U.S. Navy, especially as the Director of Fleet and Family Service Center programs.

However, I decided that I wanted to have a co-author who was as versed in the OEF/OIF Wars as I was in the Vietnam War. And so I decided to ask my colleague and good friend, Kathy Platoni, if she might be interested in being the co-editor. There was only one small problem—at the time Kathy was deployed to Afghanistan with a combat stress control detachment and was also still impacted by the horrific murders at Fort Hood several months earlier, where five members/friends who were part of her unit getting ready to deploy were killed. Even so, I still emailed Kathy to ask if she was interested. And while we both knew there would be significant challenges, she agreed. This and our next book are the gratifying result of our work together. Kathy's knowledge and ability *par excellence* to multi-task has been invaluable, as has her personal knowledge of several of the authors we have recruited.

One huge book or two "separate but related" books?

Perhaps the major problem that we faced in finalizing our original book proposal to Routledge/Taylor & Francis was the large number of chapters we envisioned (about 35 chapters). Routledge said that any book proposal had to have a maximum length of about 500 pages because of marketing and pricing considerations (a much larger book would require a much higher selling price and take it out of the reach of too many potential readers). On the other hand, we were very invested in the chapter topics we had assembled and felt that all were very worthy and relevant. The outcome was that Routledge agreed to have us resubmit our original book proposal as two different proposals that would be for two "separate but related" books.

We decided to have our second book concentrate on the many exciting and creative approaches to healing that are an extension beyond the innovative approaches contained in the last four chapters of this book. Hence, the title of our separate but related book is *Healing War Trauma: A Handbook of Creative Approaches*. It contains many exciting approaches of which the various authors are the originators, pioneers and trailblazers. These include animal-assisted and outdoor-based approaches; mind–body approaches; social and community-based approaches; technologically based approaches; native pathways to healing; and a Christian-based spiritual approach (see the Epilogue).

Captain Christian Hallman and those killed at Fort Hood, Texas

In closing, we want to acknowledge those who will never have the opportunity to read our books or reap the fruits of the sacrifices of the hundreds of thousands of service members who were deployed to Iraq and/or Afghanistan, and the sacrifices of their families. These are service members killed in action (KIA) or who otherwise lost their lives during service to our country. These include the five colleagues of Kathy murdered at Fort Hood, Texas, while they were preparing to deploy (for more details see Acknowledgments) Further, we wish to pay tribute to Captain Christian Hallman, who tragically died while in the midst of co-writing Chapter 15 of this book.

One of the worst things that can befall service members or veterans is to have their lives and sacrifices forgotten and never fully appreciated. This book is here to shout out loudly: *you are not forgotten—you are remembered, you are appreciated*; and your surviving family members are remembered and appreciated. It is our honor and our privilege to dedicate this book to all who have been impacted by war and to those who care about them. Our mission is to pay it forward, please.

Raymond Monsour Scurfield
Pass Christian, Mississippi

Kathy Theresa Platoni
Beavercreek, Ohio

Acknowledgments

This book is dedicated, first and foremost, to all the men and women who have served and are serving our country as service members, and their families. Also, it is a privilege to have been able to recruit such a gifted and dedicated array of authors to contribute to an expanding circle of healing that each and every service member, veteran and family member so richly deserves.

One of those service members who is so deserving "just happens to be" my co-editor, Kathy Platoni. Kathy is a cherished and invaluable colleague, friend and sister war veteran with whom I have embarked on this incredible journey to produce two major books about war trauma, its impact and healing. Kathy's extensive knowledge of combat operational stress control and the military, her family military history, her courage in facing her ongoing health struggles, which are military-related, and her remarkable network of colleagues/friends around the country, are inspirations to this aging (but not out to pasture yet) Vietnam vet. I wanted this book to be a true collaborative effort "from Vietnam to Iraq and Afghanistan"—and Kathy has been invaluable in having that happen. Hooah!

I would be remiss not to acknowledge Charles Figley, fellow Vietnam vet and my long-time valued colleague and friend since the earliest days of the VA Vet Center Program over 30 years ago. His contributions to the field of post-traumatic stress and especially to war-related traumatic exposure and recovery are legendary. He was very encouraging of my writing this book. Charles even allowed my request to "steal" and incorporate the title of his precedent-setting book, *Trauma and Its Wake* (Volume 1, 1985), which was one of the first major edited works to cover a spectrum of trauma populations (and for which I was privileged to write the overview chapter). Above all, Charles does all that he does with an amazing grace and humility that infuses his wisdom and accomplishments.

Then, there is the amazing Routledge/Taylor & Francis editor, Anna Moore. Anna has been an *absolute delight* to work with and we are indebted to her knowledge and also her incredibly positive attitude.

And to my 30-plus-year soulmate, my wife Margaret, and our three adult children—Helani, Armand and Nick. You are the essence of what makes my life a most precious and joyful journey. You have been with me through the many relocations I put y'all through in moving from one wonderful opportunity to another to serve veterans (mostly with the Department of Veterans Affairs)—from West Los Angeles to Washington, DC to Tacoma, WA to Honolulu, and then to the place where Margaret was raised and I have adopted as my home, the Mississippi Gulf Coast. But through it all, including Hurricane Katrina, we were and are *a family*. And our faith as practicing Catholics has been the life source that underlies everything. Truly, we are blessed.

Ray Scurfield
November 2012

This book is dedicated first to my beloved husband, LTC (RET) John David Hutchinson, whose home front heroism has been my life force for 24 years. Thank you for standing your watch over the American populace, above the clouds, as an Air Force aviator for 25 years. This extraordinary man tolerated my inexplicable commitment to avoid sleep and drink gallons of coffee in order to write and edit this book, without complaint for the last 14 months and since my redeployment from Afghanistan. Never once has he complained about the infinite sacrifices he has made, from managing the house, the bills, the grocery shopping, the snow shoveling, the dog washing … a list as long as the I-70 going west. Waiting 35 years for him was the best decision I ever made. I continue to marvel at all you are and all you do, dear spousal unit!

Second, I wish to dedicate this book to my sister, Lynnette Santolla, and my nephews and nieces, Michael Santolla, Christopher Santolla, Nihad Santolla, and Jennifer Santolla, for waiting for me to find you for more than five decades. You are my touchstones in this life. I must also include in this my dearest cousins of all time, Adelmo Platoni, his wife Patricia, and Janette Platoni, who terminated prejudice and anti-Semitism within my own family, to permit my inclusion within the family fold, despite a lifetime of opposing ethnicities.

I wish to thank Dr. Ray Scurfield, who trusted sufficiently in my abilities to take me on as a partner in the writing of this book. While I worked tirelessly to try to come home from war, he helped me to gather up the pieces of my life, encouraging me when I had nothing left in my addled brain and fortifying my empty soul with the belief that producing this book was well within my capabilities. For "CPT Ray", thanks are but a miniscule token of my colossal gratitude for a debt that has yet to be paid. Thanks to you, my mentor and ultimate teacher for all times, I will come home again and continue to write my war stories. You are no less than a national treasure.

I wish to thank Anna Moore, associate editor at Routledge, profusely not only for believing in the massive undertaking that was the writing of this book, but also for her undying efforts to make this entire project possible …

and with legendary patience. That this has actually come to fruition is largely through her efforts. This calls for eternal gratitude.

Those that I wish to thank for their unceasing support through the writing of this book, and their belief that we would actually see it to its logical conclusion, comprise an elongated list of friends and family members, sometimes one and the same.

I wish to thank the thousands of soldiers and their families who allowed me into their confidences and the trenches of their private wars through the course of my four deployments, particularly those of you assigned to the 3rd Infantry Division (2/69th Armored Regiment), the 4th Infantry Division (Bravo Company, 3rd Platoon, 1–12th Infantry); among them: SGT Ryan Vallery, SSG Matt McIvor, SGT "Tre" Trejo, CPT Dave Seay, CPT Lee Gray, MAJ Steve Gribshaw, CPT Joe Walker, CPT Christopher Preece, Beth Hudson, and SPC Sean Hudson. They willingly overlooked my rank, my gender, and my small stature to allow me entry into the camaraderie and espirit de corps of combat arms, where few outsiders are privileged to go. At the hand of these most extraordinary educators, I have mastered the lesson of the readiness and inclination to lay down one's life for a brother or sister soldier as the most supreme life force. You are my heroes, one and all.

I cannot end without mentioning those extraordinary soldiers and comrades at arms whose unending ministry of presence prevented me from losing faith in humanity, time and time again, and who reminded me that there are some who truly know *what right looks like*—CPT Sean Gargan, MAJ Cora Courage, LTC Val Reyes, LTC Jeffrey Drexler, Dr. Marilyn Shea, Dr. Debra Sowald, Dr. Barry Goldstein, Dr. Ed and Emily Harf, CPT John Fry, SSG Dick Hurtig, former Army SGT Michelle Wilmot, SGT Trey Cole, Victoria Bruner, and CPT Dana Hollywood.

There are a host of others who fall into this category, without whose unceasing support I truly would not have survived a year of austerity, sans the bare minimum of supplies with which to conduct business in Afghanistan, from edible food to the most basic of supplies to run our combat stress control clinic, to—God love you—toilet paper. With the creation of a nationwide supply chain, envisioned and created by my husband (Operation Runtbo), the number of care packages and supplies rivaled a strategic military airlift, making a hell hole livable for the multitudes with their angelic deeds: Mom Bev Peyton of Operation Thank You, Dr. Dan Kirsch, Chaplain Dave Fair, MP Godmother, LTC(RET) Glenda Hull and her merry band of patron saints and "adoptive parents"—Shirley Blayne, Edith Roach, Vicki Snodgrass, Jan Hull, SGM (RET) Joe Attaway, CSM Connie Commenia-Hill, MAJ (RET) Bud Montgomery, COL (RET) Don Franklin, LTC (RET) John Noland, SGT (RET) Monica McCravy, Theresa Ogelsby, and Corrie Ballard—COL (RET) Kathleen Hayes, CPT(RET) Millie Hand-Biawitz, Maria DiMenna, Sally Webster, COL (RET) Dick and Carolyn Redman, Kellie Sharpe, Frank and Sara Jane Lowe, Dr. Ed Rugh and his miracle-working staff, MAJ Linda Bronski, Jay, John, and Trisha Buza, Dr. Judy Green, Dr., Bob Glaser, Mark Collison, Charlotte Davis, Johanna Smith, Alison Lighthall, Ariel Gurvey, Charlotte Davis, Deborah Michalak, Charles Hand, Deb Hatchett, Barbara Hughes, Jamie Keyes, MSG Dave and Kay Johnson, Vicky Snodgrass, John and Margie Baren, Steve Bennett, Terry Borger, Phyl Friend, Hoosiers Helping Heroes, Jacob's Light, the VFW of Turlock, CA, Albertson's Foods, and Ray's Supermarket. I am knee-deep in debt to each of you for a balance that can never be paid.

I wish to thank and bless my extraordinary rescue dogs, Priscilla and Maggie, successors to those beloved pets who died during my last deployment (Suzie and Skippy), whose love and presence during the most difficult of times remains boundless, even at o'dark thirty.

Finally, I wish to pay tribute to my cherished friends and fallen comrades, who lost their lives so tragically during one of the most heinous criminal acts in military history—the Fort Hood Massacre. The enormity of these catastrophic losses has redefined my life:

Major Libardo Eduardo Caraveo, 467th Medical Detachment (CSC)
Captain John Gaffaney, 1908th Medical Detachment (CSC)
Staff Sergeant Amy Krueger, 467th Medical Detachment (CSC)
Captain Russell Seager, 467th Medical Detachment (CSC)
Lieutenant Colonel Juanita Warman, 1908th Medical Detachment (CSC)

Who will go for us. Here I am! Send me.

—Hero bracelet inscription upon which their names are engraved

Kathy Platoni
January 2012

1 An expanding circle of healing: Warriors and civilians impacted by war

Raymond Monsour Scurfield (Vietnam) and
COL Katherine Theresa Platoni (OEF-OIF)

We have been impressed by the challenges in providing services that are evidence-based, timely, relevant and comprehensive for our troops and their families. This was true during and following the war in Vietnam and continues to hold true during and following deployment to Iraq and Afghanistan. And undoubtedly this will be the case for all subsequent wars and conflicts.

I (Scurfield) arrived in Nha Trang, South Vietnam in the spring of 1968. At that time, I was a fresh 2nd LT (also known as a "butter bar") some eight months out of my graduate MSW program and was assigned to be the social work officer on one of the Army's two psychiatric teams in Vietnam. And by the way, a "butter bar" 2nd LT in the Army was the lowest of the low: even a PFC (Private First Class) had more credibility in the Army than did any 2nd LT.

Before arriving in Vietnam, I had two pivotal experiences that have infused my thinking and convictions about the impact of war and recovery from it. These experiences have remained central to some of the principles that I hope we will retain as we continue to forge partnerships to provide necessary assistance to our service members, veterans of prior wars and their families (Scurfield, 2006a).

MSW intern experience with a psychiatrically disabled marine

The first experience occurred during my MSW field placement in 1966–67 at the Sepulveda VA Hospital in the San Fernando Valley north of Los Angeles, where I was a social work intern. One of the psychiatric inpatients assigned to me was a young Marine who had a diagnosis of schizophrenia. In reading through his records, I found out that he had suffered a psychotic break. He had decompensated while on the battlefield and had been medically evacuated out of country. I might note that, later on, I came to realize that it is extremely rare for any troops to break down psychiatrically while in combat in a war zone. Usually, such breakdowns do not occur until some time after the battle is over—perhaps several days or a week or two later when back in base camp or back behind the wire after a mission, or perhaps not until some time after returning from deployment. And that "some time after deployment" can be weeks, months, years or even decades later.

As you might know, the condition of schizophrenia oftentimes is characterized by a waxing in and out of lucidity. It was during one of those lucid times that this Marine said to me, in a conversation that I will never forget: "Ray, you have to help me get back to Vietnam. I 'deserted' my fellow Marines on the battlefield." He continued: "I have got to go back to Vietnam so that I can prove that I am a man." He had seen his having suffered a psychiatric break during battle and being medically evacuated as desertion!

My heart was breaking as I heard this young Marine plead for me to help him return to Vietnam. Of course, he never again would be admitted for active duty into the Marine Corps, let alone be deployed to any war zone. What I learned from that poignant encounter was that *nothing* is more important to a deployed service member than the extraordinarily powerful peer relationships forged in the fire and danger of combat with the other members of his or her operational military unit. *Nothing* exceeds this level of significance. He felt that he had inexcusably let them down; his self-esteem had been sorely damaged and he suffered long-standing guilt over not completing his mission.

I also learned my first lesson about one of the primary mental health axioms of military psychiatry, although I didn't realize it at the time—only as a matter of last resort do you medically evacuate someone out of a war zone. This is not only because the medical mission is to "conserve the fighting strength." It is also because such a medical termination of one's deployment might end up haunting one for years or decades—with no way to "go back and make it right …"

Experience on a civilian airline with a physically disabled combat veteran returning home

The second pivotal life experience happened after I had received my orders for Vietnam and had just come to the end of a stay at home for a couple of weeks prior to being sent off to Vietnam. I boarded a commercial plane in Pittsburgh bound for Philadelphia, and was to catch a connecting flight to Seattle/Tacoma. Because I was traveling on military orders, I was in my uniform. Once I was seated and it seemed like all of the passengers had boarded, the aisle seat next to me still was not occupied. I thought, "Wow, I have caught a break and can stretch out and not have to converse with anyone."

But then, I noticed a late-arriving passenger appear at the front of the plane. He was obviously a veteran, judging by the hat and insignia on his clothing, and he shuffled into full view at the front of the cabin. He slowly moved down the aisle with the assistance of two forearm crutches. I also noticed the patch over one eye and what looked like two prostheses where his legs used to be. As he slowly made his way down the aisle, my gaze was transfixed on him. And then, suddenly, I realized that he was heading, inexorably, toward the empty seat—next to me!

I don't remember a lot about what happened next. I do remember that I felt extremely awkward, thinking "what am I going to say to him?" And I found that I was preoccupied with my own self-centered thoughts about how ironic it was that I was on my way to Vietnam and a blown-up Vietnam vet was going to be seated next to me. He sat down, and we said hello to each other. After we had taken off, I found myself awkwardly silent. And then, I remember that this young soldier turned and *he* started talking to *me*.

What stood out were two comments he made. The first comment was that this was his second trip home from the hospital on convalescent leave, part of the rehabilitation process of adjusting to his prostheses outside of the hospital setting. And I will never forget what he then said to me: "Sir, I am not looking forward to this second visit home. The first time I went home on convalescent leave, several of my high school buddies told me that it was a shame that I had lost my legs and eye for nothing … That really hurt."

I have no recollection of how or if I responded to this intimate revelation. However, I do remember what this brave young Marine then said to me: "But you know, sir, I'm the lucky one. No one else in my foxhole survived …" I didn't realize it at the time, but I had just learned two remarkable lessons. First, that one of the worst things that can befall anyone who has served their country is to be told or to believe themselves that their sacrifices and those of their battle buddies have been in vain—let alone that they are not honored and recognized positively for their service to our country. The second lesson was that this young, severely physically disabled Army veteran had taught me, long before I started reading decades later about "the strengths approach" to mental health and the principle of "post-traumatic growth," that someone who had lost and suffered so very much had somehow been able to reframe that loss and suffering into something celebratory.

Hopefully we are being guided, indeed driven, to be engaged in serving today's military, veterans and their families fueled by some of these very same lessons that I first came to understand through these two fateful encounters even before I had arrived in Vietnam—one with a psychiatrically disabled Marine veteran, and a second with a physically disabled Army veteran.

I had yet to learn that this special population of warriors (those wounded or injured in battle and medically evacuated, and their families) face a remarkable series of additional trauma, stress and challenges. Such challenges occur throughout the medical evacuation process, hospitalization and stabilization Stateside, and continue as a lifelong journey of healing for many. The distinctive experiences of healing for this important special population of warriors is discussed at length in Chapter 8 (see also Scurfield, 2006b).

Colonel Platoni also had two pivotal experiences that have had an indelible and profound impact.

Bringing survival guilt home from Afghanistan

It was almost ten months to the day that my unit redeployed back to the States. I received a surprising call from one of the NCOs in whose platoon we had been embedded within the Taliban stronghold of the Zhari District of southern Afghanistan. We had become brother–sister soldiers early on in our deployment. He had poured his guts, his heart, his soul out to me in the chow hall one day; just one time, but the ministry of presence of our small three-person combat stress control team had become well-established no sooner than our boots hit ground.

These precious moments bond those of us too familiar with the torment of the combat zone together for life. He had reached the end of the line, the end of his rope, battering himself with all the self-blame and guilt he could muster. He survived. The younger soldier, of a lower enlisted rank, did not. His mortal wounds at the hands of the insurgency and their improvised explosive device of the day assured that almost no one would get out of the MRAP (Mine Resistant Ambush-Protected Armored Vehicle, weighing between 32,000 and 38,000 pounds) alive. Their cunning technology often outweighs any armored vehicle we can design, build, and ship overseas in sufficient time to save lives.

He had nowhere to unload his guilt, his blame, or the intrusive piece of information that his buddy had sustained unsurvivable wounds. What outlet would allow him to purge himself of such horrific burdens? He was convinced that those who had not lived in his boots simply could not understand the magnitude or depth of his anguish. He begged me to listen, insisting that no one else could help him. I was "the ma'am" who had been through it with them in real time; all as if I was the only voice that he could hear. And I tried to arrange for him to travel to my home state so that I could treat him pro bono and to set up service for him at his current military installation. Sadly, neither of my offers for assistance ever materialized into an intervention by the time of our last contact. I fear that the cost of his apparent inability to follow through will be far too high for both of us.

This experience has had an overpowering impact on me. It has taught me that if one is willing to provide little more than a brief moment to offer a listening ear, this may very well influence the life of a suffering soul for months or years or even a lifetime. This is also a compelling indication that regardless of rank or training or age or gender, it is possible to offer up the indisputable belief that it is vital to share one's unforgettable and life-altering experience, to be heard, and to be appreciated. This is essential to healing and moving forward in the trauma recovery process.

Immersed in the killing rampage at Fort Hood while preparing to deploy

It is the expectation that those of us on scene during the shooting rampage at Fort Hood, Texas may be steeped in abject horror for the remainder of our lives to one degree or another. Those surreal moments of sheer terror, shock, revulsion and disbelief may diminish in time. However, for many, they are doomed to repeat themselves—the high cost of loss of a fellow soldier produces no less of a reaction.

At the time of writing this book, the (alleged) shooter's court martial has yet to take place. Though the Article 32 investigation hearings (similar to a grand jury in the civilian sector) concluded in the fall of 2010, I (COL Platoni) remain on the witness list and am prohibited from providing specific details of those events that occurred at the soldiers' Readiness Processing (SRP) Site at Fort Hood, Texas on that fateful day of 5 November 2009. Having departed the building shortly before the rampage began and because I am the colonel who refused an escort based solely upon rank in order to move to the head of the line, I was steadfast in insisting that I would wait at the end of lines that were hours long, just as everyone else is required to do. Call it humility or stupidity, my own obstinacy may have saved my life. I bear no shortage of guilt for having removed myself from the line of fire, literally, as there is little doubt in my own mind that there was a round (bullet) with my name on it that day. (I was later informed that I was to have been the shooter's direct supervisor at the first forward operating base to which I was assigned in Afghanistan and that the shooter had marked me for death that day.)

Having completed the medical portion of the SRP after being sent to the overflow building (next to the building where the actual shooting occurred), I reported back to the Soldiers' Dome, the building (built by Elvis Presley many years earlier) in which we both initiated and concluded the SRP process. Subsequent to hearing someone screaming repeatedly that there was a shooting in the other building, I shoved as many people out of a door of the facility as I could push with both hands. Then I ran towards the door and the building in which five of my beloved friends and fellow soldiers had lost their lives. A more likely instinctual survival response ingrained in human behavior would be to move directly for safety. However, soldiers, firefighters, paramedics, emergency medical services and law enforcement are programmed to rush toward danger and straight into whatever fire or line of fire lies ahead.

Before I could exit the door, I witnessed the dying and wounded being carried inside and away from the scene of the rampage by our very own soldiers. To date, there are no adequate or accurate words to describe the impact of the terror and the alarming sights that followed. All of us, in split-second time and on scene, engaged in lifesaving measures in one form or another and became eyewitnesses to the most ruthless killing of soldiers by one of their own in American history.

The night of the massacre, after a day that will be engraved in time for all our days to come, we had been released from "lock down" inside the building, in which many of the wounded and dying were carried to safety, as far from the shooter as possible. Following required interviews with CID (The U.S. Army's Criminal Investigative Command), we were reunited with the remainder of our soldiers at the Iron Horse Dining Facility. Those who were not on scene were directed to this chow hall for accountability purposes and their own protection. It would not be until the next morning that we would be informed of the actual toll of our losses, as many of our soldiers had not yet been accounted for and could not be located.

While waiting to be bussed to this chow hall, I was confronted with waves of near panic. I was realizing that years of sleepless nights would be a continuing blight upon our lives in the face of an event of such catastrophic magnitude, as we waited for the news of the casualty and body counts. There could have been no more devastating a task to face for any and all of us.

I decided that enduring this very night alone and accompanied only by gruesome and sorrowful thoughts and images of the day's events would be conducive to nothing advantageous. I passed the word that everyone was welcome to return to the female barracks in which we were housed at North Fort Hood so that no one would need to be alone or to feel abandoned. Being together, regardless of all else, was essential to recovering from our own trauma. We tossed wall lockers and mattresses on the floor, a living room of sorts created with the bare essentials to provide some modicum of comfort to exquisitely pained souls. Everyone placed what food they had on the tops of lockers for sharing. I made pot after pot of coffee. Pizzas were ordered and the costs shared. There was no agenda, other than to remain together in the face of a tragedy of unparalleled proportions.

It seemed natural not to discuss the events of the day, but rather to forge and solidify bonds based upon the most dreadful of almost all possible life experiences, to guarantee that we would support and bolster and simply be there for one another for the duration of the deployment and perhaps the rest of our lives. No one understands better than someone who has been there in the very trenches of our own experience. It is also quite noteworthy that some of us chose to debrief ourselves many times over in the months that followed, informally and sometimes with no more than two of us at a time, often without planning or forethought. Frequently the only means of doing so was by internet or phone, as we were scattered throughout the combat theater of operations in 13 distinct teams. It would happen time and time again on our own restorative journeys and will no doubt continue well into the future.

This experience impacted my learning that the war accompanies us home in our ruck, our duffel bag, and whatever else we drag home with us. Departure from the wartime theater is geographic in nature only. And no one gets out unscathed (Platoni, 2006). The powerful and enduring bonds among and between those of us who deploy and serve together in times of tremendous adversity and hardship in the combat theater are irreplaceable and, more often, also serve as the most compelling of healing forces.

The development of such extraordinarily powerful and enduring bonds also reinforced my conviction that in order to maximize behavioral health services in the combat theater, mental health and combat operational stress control elements must be deployed as far forward as possible; in other words, they should be on the front lines where their presence is unquestionably most desirable and necessary and where they can do the most good when it is so desperately needed. Also affirmed was what I had learned while deployed to Iraq and Afghanistan: that there are no hard and fast front lines or rear echelons in current combat operations. Indeed, as clinicians we must be very cognizant that exposure to hazardous duty is inherent in being deployed and not limited to the warfighter.

Furthermore, as the Fort Hood killing rampage taught us, trauma occurs both in and out of the war zone. Part of the legacy of the impact of war is that deployment is infused and overlaid with horrific experiences that occur for many of us even before we arrive in the war zone. And for others, trauma occurs following our return back from deployment and becomes enmeshed with our post-deployment readjustment. And many, like me, suffer in and from both venues. Finally, remember that hazardous duty is not confined to deployment overseas. Indeed, risk, serious injuries and deaths are part of the cost of having to participate in dangerous training exercises just to become prepared for combat operations.

I would be remiss, regarding the Fort Hood killing rampage, not to mention our engraved hero bracelets. These are worn by each of us in the 467th and 1908th units, the combat stress control detachments to which we were assigned to deploy in support of Operation Iraqi Freedom and Operation Enduring Freedom. The inscription on our hero bracelets acknowledges the losses suffered and is a means of paying tribute to the five lives sacrificed. It tells the tale most poignantly:

467th and 1908th—'Who will go for us. Here I am! Send me.' 11/05/2009.

MAJ Caraveo, CPT Gaffaney, SSG Krueger, CPT Seager, LTC Warman

Lessons unlearned between 1991 and today

The above described pivotal experiences during the Vietnam, Iraq and Afghanistan wars have been coupled with many others over the past four plus decades. These have contributed to our thinking about an expanded circle of healing that is vital to the post-war readjustment and enhancement of the lives of those who have served our country, and who now need and deserve the recognition and help that they have so richly earned.

In many ways (for Scurfield), writing this chapter today is an ironic déjà vu of a national presentation that I gave two decades ago—back in September 1991. This presentation was part of joint trainings by the Department of Veteran Affairs and the Department of Defense to gear up for the anticipated casualties returning from the Persian Gulf War. One of my presentations, entitled "Where Do We Go from Here?" was given on a joint VA and DOD Satellite Teleconference with VA and DOD care providers (Scurfield, 1991).[1]

I am very sad and frustrated to say that much of what I discussed then has only relatively recently been implemented on a national basis to any degree. In fact, the still remaining issues are just one illustration of the many lessons unlearned regarding war and its impact that led to the title of my third war trauma book, *War Trauma: Lessons Unlearned From Vietnam to Iraq* (Scurfield, 2006a; see also Scurfield, 2004 and 2006b).

We would like to briefly mention some of the main points made during this 1991 teleconference as they remain crucial to our mission of serving those who have served our country, and their families. Many of these recommendations have only relatively recently been made, let alone fully implemented.

1. There should be an established, ongoing systemic liaison and dialogue between the U.S. Department of Veterans Affairs and the DOD. This linkage would focus on traumatic stress and other adjustment/readjustment challenges, both acute and chronic, facing returning veterans and their families. Such linkages must exist whether or not we are in the midst of a war; otherwise, those lessons learned will continue to be forgotten and may or may not be rediscovered years or decades later. Such standing associations or linkages should be implemented at the national or departmental level, at the regional or state level, and at the local level. For example: one or two designated mental health liaison persons from each VA medical facility and from each VA Vet Center should be appointed to coordinate with the nearest military installations; in turn, there should be designated contact persons from each local DOD facility with nearby VA facilities. Further, all such liaison positions should be far more than in name only, with policies in place for enforcement.

2. Perhaps the most efficient and influential local or area activity may be to help facilitate ongoing networking meetings among various providers in various geographic areas. It was our experience in the Pacific Northwest (back in 1991), for instance, that many DOD and civilian service providers at the time felt very isolated and overwhelmed by the debriefing task at hand. Regular networking meetings might well serve the primary needs of the local providers and would undoubtedly include the sharing of strategies, information, referral facilitations, in-service trainings and care-giver support.

---

1   Some readers might not know that the VA is the medical back-up system for the DOD. Hence, prior to the Persian Gulf War I, contingency plans were being made to discharge or transfer VA hospitalized veterans to civilian hospitals to free up VA hospital beds. This resulted in extremely conflicted reactions from the hospitalized vets: "Of course our country needed to be ready for the anticipated mass casualties ... and yet, 'what about us—here we are being pushed aside and forgotten once again.'"

3. There is a significant need for expert provision of critical incident type debriefings. Please note that the use of the term "debriefings" in this 1991 presentation is not relegated only to CISD-formatted interventions, but to a wide range of psychological and counseling interventions that are oriented to assist participants in talking about and reflecting upon what might be troubling aspects of their active duty experiences. Many returnees are very likely not to have had adequate or any type of critical incident debriefings, on either an individual, group or unit basis. One problem is the essential need to differentiate between an operational type debrief that reviews military operations, tactics utilized and operational lessons learned and a critical incident type debrief which attends to the cognitive, attitudinal and emotional aspects of participation in stressful military-related activities. The operational principle and policy that seems missing at all levels is that *anyone* who has served in a war zone has both the *right* and in all probability the *need* to undergo a critical incident type debriefing process. Chapter 14 in this book describes debriefings and resiliency initiatives conducted by the military today.

   However, even if adequate debriefings were offered to all regular military and reserve and National Guard personnel during trainings—and that certainly is a major if—this still leaves unattended all those returnees who now are civilians and who did not receive an adequate debriefing, or any debriefing at all. Who has taken responsibility and been given adequate and ongoing resources to reach out in a systematic way to these returnees and their families to conduct adequate needs assessments and provide debriefings? A continuing national mandate to provide this service is essential—even though a number of returnees will refuse any debrief services offered and will remain isolated and avoidant concerning possible war-zone-related issues for months, years or decades. That the existence of and full implementation of such formal written policies is lacking within the various branches of the military remains a stunning fact.

4. Also identified in 1991 was that linkages or ties with military alcohol and drug treatment programs, as well as community substance abuse programs, are essential. These are primary sites where Gulf War returnees and veteran of previous wars with undiagnosed traumatic stress often find themselves in treatment. Other primary sites include military and community family advocacy programs that deal with domestic violence, child abuse and neglect. These sites require cross-training in war-related traumatic stress and critical diagnostic and treatment indicators.

5. If realistic traumatic-stress information is not being disseminated or allowed by various unit commanders, then one can assume that this is not being passed on to many returnees previously or still on active duty. We must establish an active presence with various military and other service providers, such as chaplains, social workers, psychiatrists,

psychologists, and family service and community service centers. Sharing of information, offering to undertake collaborative trainings and developing partnership relationships with such military and other providers are essential. In addition, such relationships may readily facilitate access to key officers and non-commissioned military unit personnel within the chain of command.

We must make mention of a few of the other key issues and dynamics identified by Scurfield in 1991 which continue to be relevant today. These must be openly addressed as part of any group, family or individual debriefings:

1. There is oftentimes an unspoken lack of trust by the military returnee still on active duty or their family to reveal any "personal problems" to military authorities. This stems from feelings such as betrayal and fear as to what governmental authorities will do with the information received. Also, there is shame, blame and/or guilt over what one has done and/or perhaps not feeling that one's own military experiences "compare" with "heavier duty" war trauma experienced by others.

2. A number of returnees have issues surrounding the fact that "the military did not treat us with honor and dignity," and may feel betrayed. In 1991 this included being forced to take a series of anthrax immunizations prior to and during deployment to the Persian Gulf; in many cases these immunizations were not entered into their military medical records, full disclosure of side effects or longer-term health implications were not provided and every facet of this information was covered up or destroyed with a complete lack of acknowledgement of this publicly (Platoni herself was involved in battling this and directly witnessed some of it). Today, many OEF and OIF veterans are forced to confront equally if not more serious issues. These include, for example, the inexcusable delays in being provided with properly armored and designed vehicles to give the necessary modicum of protection until years after the standard issue humvees were found to be extremely vulnerable to IEDs (improvised explosive devices). OIF and OEF military personnel continued to be issued with defective body armor and Kevlar helmets at least as recently as 2011. These usually are subject to recall only after severe and life-threatening injuries or fatalities occur as the end result of shoddy workmanship or the tendency of the military to accept the lowest bid.

3. There is the widespread myth that "time heals all wounds." We surely wish that this myth were true; it would mean that old folks like us would be paragons of mental health and that mental health services for the elderly could be drastically reduced if not eliminated. "Time heals all wounds" remains a myth that is used by some military and governmental authorities and some clinicians to claim that most returnees or

their families who continue to present readjustment difficulties must have been predisposed to experiencing psychological problems. This is a bogus argument in many cases designed to minimize or prevent recognition of the risks and prolonged impact of combat and deployment. Further, it reinforces the attitude that debriefings for war-related stressors are unnecessary and that it is not the responsibility of any governmental policy, agency or resource to provide relevant services to returnees and their families. Additional myths about war and its impact are discussed in Chapter 2.

4. Military families tend not only to have very strong emotional reactions to what they have perceived to be troublesome changes in their loved ones, but also to maintain the strong need to blame someone for what has happened. Oftentimes, this includes the veterans themselves, the military and/or the government. Further, families have their own reactions to their own personal issues and perceptions about war, violence, physical injury, psychiatric disorders, abandonment and perhaps feeling "used" by the military or the government. And the final and most disenchanting blow is to be forgotten (i.e. to not be remembered as having fought in the war and for the sacrifices one made).

5. Finally, the DOD and the VA have their own organizational cultures that do not necessarily fully trust or understand each other. Each culture is so distinctive that it inevitably complicates if not hinders optimal collaborative efforts—oftentimes in spite of the most well-intentioned motivations of officials and staff from the DOD and the VA. For example, the DOD medical mission is to "conserve the fighting strength" of the military; hence the focus is almost entirely on enhancing service members' performance while they are on active duty—period. On the other hand, the Department of Veterans Affairs' medical mission is to serve and provide care for veterans *after* they have been released from active duty. This necessarily is a longer-term focus.

In addition to the crucial differences in mission, there can be problematic attitudes and perceptions. For example, some DOD personnel believe that VA staff will try to "oversell" the presence of PTSD, imply that any readjustment problems will require years of intensive therapy and help counsel active duty personnel to seek discharge from the military. In turn, VA staff must be aware if they *do* fit any of these perceptions. In addition, they must define what if any are their issues regarding the military and clarify such issues and agendas that pertain to the military and war veterans and their families. For example, it is not unusual for VA staff to perceive that the DOD traditionally has viewed the VA as a "dumping ground" for service members when they no longer are of use to the military.

Recurrent collective amnesia in our society reappears after every war has ended. Please remember that almost all of what has been said above comes directly from Scurfield's presentation to the VA and the DOD back in 1991. This should remind us of the persistence and chronicity of the post-war problems that plague far too many of our war veterans into the present. We exhort everyone to do their part to ensure that the wonderful interventions being planned, developed, researched and implemented today will not dissipate and evaporate once the current wars in Iraq and Afghanistan have come to an end. Of course, in the here and now of 2012, we are once again witnessing the emergence of domestic amnesia by our country to deny or minimize the fact that our troops currently still are deployed to and serving in the wartime theater of Iraq in support of Operation New Dawn. It is as if the war in Iraq is over and we do not have some 50,000 military personnel still serving in harm's way ...

We must do all we can not to let our country relapse to a recurring amnesia, a malady that has afflicted our nation following every war in regard to its human impact and what we have to do to respond adequately. We must be vigilant to ensure that we are doing justice in providing needed services to both military personnel and their families of any current wars being fought, as well as to veterans of all previous wars and their families.

Elements of an expanding circle of healing

This book exemplifies the key elements of the expanded circle of healing that is so sorely needed to more fully and adequately address the readjustment needs and issues that face a substantial number of our nation's service members and veterans and their families. This expanded circle of healing consists of two major elements.

First, there are the various special populations of warriors and civilians impacted by war, each of which has its own distinctive dynamics and healing challenges. A number of these special populations are discussed in this volume in chapters dedicated to each population. These include several military and veteran populations: reserve warriors (Chapter 3), National Guard (Chapter 4), women warriors (Chapter 5) and Canadian forces (Chapter 6) as well as those with PTSD and Traumatic Brain Injury (Chapter 7), those involved with the legal system (Chapter 11), those who have issues of suicidality (Chapter 9), those who have been exposed to military sexual trauma (Chapter 10) and the seriously physically wounded and injured (Chapter 8). And there are three civilian populations impacted by the wars in Iraq and Afghanistan that rarely are written about in U.S. publications about the impact of war: the surviving spouses of service members killed in action (KIA) (see Afterword by Beate Medina), and the civilian populations of Iraq (Chapter 12) and Afghanistan (Chapter 13).

We are greatly concerned about healing efforts that focus primarily on the elimination of narrowly defined psychiatric symptoms of PTSD experienced by combat veterans, such as is typical of manualized cognitive-behavioral treatment protocols. On the one hand, impressive research results have shown that such a narrow psychiatric symptom focus offers the strong potential of a significant reduction of various psychiatric symptoms (especially re-experiencing/intrusive and arousal PTSD symptoms) for a number of participants in such protocols. However, there are two essential conditions to the efficacy of such an exposure-based treatment focus: the service members and veterans must be willing to enter into such exposure-based treatment in the first place; and they must be willing and able to complete the entire protocol and related aftercare.

Typically, such a narrow psychiatric symptom focus does not significantly address the critical contextual and distinctive factors, dynamics and issues that characterize the experiences of the various special military and civilian populations discussed in this book. It is our experience and contention, and that of the authors of the various chapters, that such dynamics and issues are central to a full understanding of the whole person and the military and reintegration picture. Attention to such an in-depth understanding is *essential* if clinicians are to successfully engage therapeutically with service members and veterans.

Military and other intervention strategies and resiliency initiatives

In addition to the chapters on special populations, there is a discussion of special military and other intervention strategies and resiliency initiatives: the military's Combat Operational Stress Control (COSC), which primarily addresses psychiatric casualties in the war zone (Chapter 14); outdoor/adventure-oriented interventions which enhance resiliency and have a special appeal with service members and veterans (Chapter 15); innovative civilian–military partnerships such as ArtReach Project America that utilize the creative and expressive arts for healing (Chapter 16); and the invaluable role of military chaplains in helping to address the religious, spiritual and ethical/moral dimensions that inevitably impact on many deployed service members (Chapter 17).

Where do we go from here?

It is important to note that there have been (1) admirable efforts by the military chain of command at all levels, (2) salutary contributions of military mental health chaplains, (3) advances in recognizing and understanding war trauma and its impact (including the "signature wounds" of Iraq and Afghanistan, PTSD and TBI) and (4) an expansion of the resources of the U.S. Department of Veterans Affairs, the State Departments of Veterans Affairs, Veterans Service Organizations, and so many other public and private resources. In spite of such factors, numerous studies (several conducted by the military) indicate that anywhere from 15 to 30 percent of service members at some time during and/or following deployment have significant mental health and other behavioral and social symptoms (Atkinson, Guetz & Wein, 2009; Bliese *et al.*, 2008; Seal *et al.*, 2007; Tanielian & Jaycox, 2008).

There is one belief that we must never accept—that combat had no impact on the service member deployed to the wartime theater. There is absolutely no truth to such statements. Neither should we believe any service member or veteran who says that "combat had no impact on me." Those of us who have been there and our families know the unmitigated reality: combat *always* has an indelible impact—although not necessarily "disordered"—on all who are exposed to it. This book helps to uncover and elaborate upon the profound and distinctive impacts of war and the post-war recovery that characterize in particular (but by no means exclusively) service members and veterans of the wars in Iraq and Afghanistan.

Having read this book and been fully apprised of and sensitized to (1) the distinctive dynamics and challenges facing the various special populations of warriors and civilians and (2) the several military and resiliency initiatives discussed, readers are encouraged to consider reading our second book, *Healing War Trauma: A Handbook of Creative Approaches* (Scurfield & Platoni, in press). *Healing War Trauma* discusses the limitations of the evidence-based cognitive-behavioral therapy (CBT) treatments that are so much in vogue. More importantly, it also offers in-depth descriptions of a substantial number of innovative healing approaches to be considered as supplemental or alternative to CBT treatment protocols. Such approaches are briefly identified in the Epilogue.

Closing

There is a natural and very powerful relationship between the understanding of and sensitivity to the dynamics and issues of those various special populations discussed in this book and utilizing such knowledge to guide fully informed assessment and treatment planning. This includes consideration of the array of innovative healing approaches described in both this and our second book. We thank you for your interest in and commitment to serving our active duty service members, military veterans and their families.

And we are honored and excited to have such a distinguished array of authors, a number whom are currently on active duty or are military veterans of the wars in Iraq and/or Afghanistan; the remaining authors are civilian clinicians possessing a wealth of experience, along with a sound and in-depth knowledge, who are extremely committed to serving military personnel, veterans and their families. Together, these committed and articulate men and women have intimate knowledge about special warrior and civilian populations impacted by war. They have used this knowledge to design distinctive military and resiliency initiatives to alleviate and/or prevent the devastating impact of exposure to war-related trauma on far too many of our service members, veterans and their families involved in the wars in Vietnam through Iraq and Afghanistan.

References

Atkinson, M. P., Guetz, A. & Wein, L. M. (2009). A dynamic model for posttraumatic stress disorder among U.S. troops in Operation Iraqi Freedom. *Management Science, 55*(9), 1454–1468. Retrived from http://mansci.jurnal.informs.org/content/55/9

Office of the U.S. Army Surgeon General, Mental Health Advisory Team (MHAT) V (2008). Operation Iraqi Freedom 06–08: Iraq Operation Enduring Freedom 8: Afghanistan. Retrieved from www.armymedicine.army.mil/reports/mhat/mhat_v/Redacted1-MHATV-4-FEB-2008-Overview.pdf

Platoni, K. (August, 2006). The war room. *The Ohio Psychologist*, pp. 10–11.

Scurfield, R. M. (1991). Where Do We Go From Here? Joint VA and DOD satellite teleconference with VA and DOD care providers about the VA and DOD Continuing Response to our Returning Veterans.

Scurfield, R. M. (2004). *A Vietnam Trilogy: Veterans and Post-Traumatic Stress, 1968, 1989 and 2000.* New York, NY: Algora Publishing.

Scurfield, R. M. (2006a). *War Trauma. Lessons Unlearned From Vietnam to Iraq.* New York, NY: Algora Publishing.

Scurfield, R. M. (2006b). *Healing Journeys: Study Abroad with Vietnam Veterans.* New York, NY: Algora Publishing.

Scurfield, R. M. & Platoni, K. (in press). *Healing War Trauma: A Handbook of Creative Approaches.* New York, NY: Routledge.

Seal, K. H., Bertenthal, D., Miner, C. R., Sen, S. & Marmar, C. (2007). Bringing the war back home: Mental health disorders among 103,788 U.S. veterans returning from Iraq and Afghanistan seen at Department of Veterans Affairs facilities. *Archives of Internnal Medicine, 167*, 476–482.

Tanielian, T. & Jaycox, L. H. (Eds.) (2008). *Invisible Wounds of War: Psychological and Cognitive Injuries, Their Consequences, and Services to Assist Recovery.* Santa Barbara, CA: RAND Corporation.

2 Myths and realities about war, its impact, and healing

Raymond Monsour Scurfield (Vietnam) and COL Katherine Theresa Platoni (OEF-OIF)

There are many myths about people who are exposed to trauma and their post-trauma reactions. This also is the case with military personnel who are exposed to trauma, particularly in the wartime theater or while otherwise serving on active duty, such as during basic training or while on dangerous realistic training exercises to maintain operational readiness. These myths have a profound impact on understanding and our ability to assist our service members, our veterans and their families to heal from the unceasing impact of war.

Myths and realities

Holding to such myths is profoundly related to the ability of service members, veterans and other trauma survivors to subsequently be able to honestly face and deal with their trauma experiences and the myriad of issues related to these. Unfortunately, clinicians themselves may also embrace some of these myths or may not be fully cognizant of them and the power that they exert against ultimate healing. It is our experience that helping service members and veterans to understand the various myths and their corresponding realities is essential to promoting optimal resolution of war trauma during the course of mental health treatment.

The following myths and realities speak to the issues of war's impact on active duty military personnel (including members of the Reserve and Guard forces and all branches of the Armed Forces) and veterans. Much of this information also applies to survivors of other types of trauma, such as natural and man-made disasters (many of these myths and realities are identified in Scurfield, 2004, 2006a and 2006b). Finally, it is our experience that providing written information to our clients about these several myths and their corresponding realities can be enormously beneficial. Clinicians are encouraged to copy this list intact and share it with clients, or modify/adapt the wording to best fit with the client population being treated.

Myth: *Time heals all wounds.*

Reality: This is one of the most powerful and widely held myths, seemingly ingrained in our culture as "folk-wisdom." Oh, if only it were true! This would guarantee that older people would be free of the impact of trauma experienced earlier in life. The reality, of course, is that a number of war veterans and other trauma survivors continue to experience profound psychological pain and turmoil years and decades later that are intimately connected to earlier life trauma—and oftentimes in spite of having received years of counseling and other treatments.

Long-term follow-up studies of Second World War, Korea and Vietnam veterans indicate that psychiatric symptoms do not necessarily disappear over time. Indeed, for a significant sub-group, the symptoms become worse. It is hypothesized that this is probably due to the aging process, during which there is a significantly greater likelihood of serious illness and being exposed to the deaths and serious illnesses of significant others, resulting in the reduction or complete loss of one's supportive social network as one grows older. Furthermore, there are age-related stresses such as loss of work, career or significant others and financial hardships that are not uncommon with advancing age, as is the increased realization of one's own mortality (see discussion in Scurfield, 2004 and 2006a).

Scurfield treated a 73-year-old Second World War former prisoner of war for war-related trauma; he had sought PTSD treatment for the first time at age 70 but had been manifesting war-trauma symptoms for decades. These symptoms (anxiety and cardiac related) had been considered by both well-intentioned physicians and the veteran himself as medical in nature. The etiological role of emotional and behavioral trauma related to four years as a prisoner of war, and subsequent post-repatriation social and emotional difficulties, were largely ignored.

Finally, it may also be noted that once the bonds forged with fellow military personnel, and the camaraderie and espirit de corps that sustain them through the worst of times, diminish and ultimately disappear over time (due to military discharge, military retirement, geographic moves, illness and death), veterans face the loss of their most valuable support systems and the foundations that have enabled them to withstand the torment they carry with them.

Myth: *Heroes and "normal" or healthy persons do not have problems after being exposed to a trauma, and if they do the problems will only be for short-lived periods of time. And if they continue to have significant problems purportedly related to the trauma they were exposed to, that means they already had problems prior to the trauma; in other words, "they were 'pre-disposed' to having such problems anyhow. The trauma was merely a 'trigger.'" (Scurfield, 2006a: 58). Or: "This person must be malingering."*

This myth is based on the belief that exposure to an identifiable trauma cannot be a legitimate or sufficient explanation for why someone presents with continuing or protracted psychiatric symptoms following exposure to combat- or military-related trauma. In effect, the impact of the nature and severity of the trauma is discounted, denied or grossly minimized.

Hence, the prejudicial conclusion is that presenting post-trauma symptoms are much less likely to be related to the nature, severity and duration of the trauma that the service member was exposed to, and much more likely to be related to problems "within" the individual. These include "internal deficits" of character, mental instability, malingering to avoid dangerous or otherwise unappealing duties, pre-disposition to have problems due to earlier life issues such as an unstable childhood, or purposeful exaggeration or prolonging of psychiatric symptoms for the ulterior motives of receiving a medical discharge and medical/psychiatric disability compensation.

Reality: Trauma *always* has a significant impact on all who experience it, although this does not necessarily result in Post-traumatic Stress Disorder (PTSD) or other psychological disorders. In other words, exposure to trauma is so catastrophic that it will evoke symptoms in almost everyone, regardless of one's background or pre-morbid factors. It is abnormal *not* to have strong reactions to trauma" (Scurfield, 2006a: 58). Viktor Frankl (1959), who survived the Nazi death camps in the Second World War and who founded logotherapy, stated: "An abnormal reaction to an abnormal situation is normal behavior." A common description of Second World War veterans who returned from the war with obvious psychiatric problems was: "Nervous from the service." A not uncommon experience of an OIF service member following return from deployment is: "My body's here, but my mind is there [in Iraq]" (Corbett, 2004).

Myth: *If service members truly are traumatized by what they were exposed to in combat, it would have been evident at the time. To "break down" months or years after such exposure means that they are not truly suffering from something that happened long ago in the war zone.*

Reality: Active duty military personnel *rarely* break down psychologically or behaviorally while in the midst of an emergency or trauma. Rather, there is typically a delay until later—after returning to a more secure area, or hours or days or weeks later, or in a number of cases months, years or even decades after leaving the war zone or being discharged from the military.

And so, just because a service member or veteran is feeling "okay" and in control of him- or herself during or soon after deployment, this does not necessarily mean that this will be the case months or years from now. For many veterans, even though they are far from traumatic exposure in time and distance, festering memories can be expected to come back to haunt, eating away at the soul from the inside out.

Myth: *Being exposed to death, maiming and threat from the enemy are the worst experiences a service member will face while deployed.*

Reality: Yes, such exposure can be and is highly stressful if not traumatizing to a significant number of deployed military personnel. However, in addition, there are other at least equally traumatic threats that "come from within our own ranks"—from fellow and sister U.S. military personnel. These include military sexual trauma (committed against both men and women) (see Chapter 10), other gender-based, as well as race-based trauma (see Chapter 5) and command-perpetrated abuse of subordinates. Yes, sometimes the enemy resides within the gates (Platoni, 2006). Any assessment of possible trauma experienced while deployed is significantly lacking if all of these potential sources of trauma inflicted by U.S. military perpetrators against other American troops are not explored.

Myth: *"My trauma was not as bad as what others suffered, so I should not be feeling as badly as I do. Or, I should feel guilty because I was spared what others suffered" (Scurfield, 2006a: 59).*

Reality: Contrasting one's own trauma with "more severe" traumas suffered by others is a no-win proposition. There is no magic yardstick that gauges which trauma experiences "should" have an impact on someone and which should not. Indeed, trauma experiences *always* have an impact—it is just a question of the extent and duration of the impact. And you can have empathy for what others have suffered without also comparatively "putting yourself down" for what you are experiencing.

Your trauma is your trauma. Period.

In order to be able to heal from the indelible impact of trauma, it is essential that you be willing to face it and to admit the truth to yourself about how your trauma experience has impacted you personally. If you continue to deny the full reality of the impact of a trauma on yourself, then it will *always* continue to have a hold on you (Scurfield, 2006a). In other words, because you are denying or minimizing the actual impact of your trauma experience, you will not admit to yourself how deeply you have been wounded psychologically and/or socially. Thus, you will resist looking meaningfully at your own trauma experience and at what you must do to heal.

Myth: *I am to blame for what happened to me; and if it is not me, it must be someone else who is to blame. In other words, there is a reason why this trauma happened to me—or to a loved one.*

Reality: Bad things can and do happen to good people—and sometimes it is no fault of their own (Scurfield, 2006a). However, most survivors do not accept that trauma is a "random" event; rather, they tend to search and lay blame on someone for their trauma, and/or they blame themselves. This is, of course, because all of us are human. We have shortcomings, faults, have done or avoided things in our past that we might not yet have forgiven ourselves for having done or not done. In the face of being exposed to a traumatic experience, we may well have had a pause or delay in reacting, or may not have responded "perfectly"—and with disastrous consequences. If we joined or volunteered to be in the military, this is yet another reason to blame ourselves for what happened. Any of these are potential sources of self-blame; "reasons" for why the trauma happened to me.

Humans are logical creatures who seek to make sense out of the nonsensical and to apply rational thought to that which defies any basis in things reasonable. Of course, some survivors do not self-blame, instead absolving themselves of any blame or responsibility and instead blaming others for what happened. This could be the enemy who killed our comrades or wounded us. It could be our chain of command who did not exert perfect leadership and made enormous errors in commanding their troops. It could be our government for getting us involved in this war in the first place. And it could be our country for how it has forgotten about us or mistreated us after our war was over.

Finally, if no other person or persons or institutions are to blame for what happened, there are survivors who will blame God or a higher power. How could there be a loving God who would allow this happen to me or to my battle buddies? Where was God when I was in the war zone and called out for his help and needed him—and he did not respond? Where has God been when I have been suffering all these years?

Myth: *"I can never trust myself or anyone else again" (Scurfield, 2006a: 60). I didn't react well or my judgment was bad (during the war) and the environment was dangerous. So, I need to isolate myself and be constantly wary of everyone and everything, be vigilant and careful of my surroundings.*

Reality: Trusting in yourself or trusting in others "is not an all-or-nothing proposition" (Scurfield, 2006a: 60). And yes, developing appropriate degrees of trust in your own decision making and ability to function, and being willing to trust to some degree in others, does involve risks. Yet are not some risks essential for a fulfilling life? After all, what are the options otherwise? Is living a life of isolation and constant wariness what you want—because that is what one receives if they have little or no trust in themselves or others.

Myth: *The war is the cause of all the problems I am experiencing. Or: "I'm behaving or feeling this way just because of the war" (Scurfield, 2006a: 60).*

Reality: "No one was a 'blank tablet' before entering the military and war" (Scurfield, 2006a: 60). We all went as somebody. We were persons who had strengths as well as being persons who had weaknesses, we had positives and we had negatives, likeable and not so likeable traits. Furthermore, trauma, unfortunately, is such a common occurrence in life today that many of us suffered one or several traumas before we ever entered the military—and were not healed from those trauma experiences when we entered the military. Hence, your having problems now may have little or nothing to do with being in the military; these problems may have existed beforehand and been carried with you into the military.

In addition, a number of veterans have suffered serious traumas after leaving the military. This might be related to their veteran status (receiving an "unwelcome home" or no welcome home; being discriminated against in job searches because they were in the military; having traumatic experiences in trying to obtain needed service-related services or benefits) or have nothing to do with being a military veteran (being assaulted or in a severe auto accident, for example).

In other words, current or presenting problems and issues in life might be attributable completely, primarily or somewhat to life experiences before, during and/or following military service; or military service experiences might have aggravated a "pre-existing" condition, so that both pre-military and military issues need to be addressed. Hence, it is essential to be truthful about the cause(s) of presenting problems; otherwise blame and responsibility will be placed where they do not belong and addressing the "true causes" of presenting difficulties will be avoided.

Myth: *No one else can possibly understand what I have been through.*

Reality: Most war veterans initially feel that no one but other combat vets who were in the same war could possibly understand what they have been through and what they are experiencing now. This belief is too frequently aggravated by clinicians or others who are not veterans who say or assume the attitude, "I understand what you are going through." No, most war veterans do not believe that anyone who is not a war veteran themselves can fully understand what they have experienced.

It is not verbalizing how understanding one is about another's military service or coming across as all-knowing that will convince a veteran that you truly can and do understand. Rather, such validation of one's sensitivity, understanding and knowledge comes about through earning the therapeutic trust of veterans. And such trust comes through willingness to truly listen and to be genuinely open and receptive to learning from the veteran what his or her experiences have been and continue to be.

Truly helpful clinicians are also able to demonstrate that they may well understand, from their own life experiences, how it feels to not have the desire to talk to anyone or to believe that no one will be able to understand the nature or magnitude or depth of their experiences. Clinicians must come to appreciate the fact that many service members and veterans live with the hope that if they could just ignore something festering inside, it would eventually go away. Finally, it is true that many clinicians may, in fact, have developed a deep compassion and familiarity with veteran-related issues and dynamics through close therapeutic relationships with various veteran clients or through being from a military family.

Myth: *I did okay during the trauma(s) that happened while I was deployed in the war zone and for a while afterwards, so I shouldn't be having all of these negative feelings and reactions now.*

Reality: People seldom "break down" psychologically or become overwhelmed while in the midst of war (or while in the middle of any trauma) or in the immediate aftermath. Most survivors are able to "bury" painful feelings and thoughts and learn how to "detach" from emotions in order to continue functioning and to survive. In fact, typically, there is a delay in the onset of problematic emotions and thoughts until sometime after the danger has passed—the battlefield is no place to fall apart or spiral down into a state of emotional dyscontrol. This "sometime after" could be hours, days, weeks or possibly months, years or decades later (Scurfield, 2006a).

Myth: *If I can just forget about the traumatic war memories, I can move on with my life.*

Reality: War trauma is unforgettable (except in those rare instances where someone develops complete amnesia). But that does not necessarily mean that life cannot go on pretty much as it did previously. Indeed, most trauma survivors remember aspects of the trauma forever—and yet they are able to move on with their lives to varying degrees. They learn to "co-exist" with unforgettable traumatic memories (Scurfield, 2006a).

On the other hand, there are dysfunctional adaptations that can occur:

- To ease the pain and as a temporary way to forget, some survivors resort to abuse of prescribed or illicit substances, expose themselves to danger and engage in high-risk behaviors; for example driving extremely fast, "living on the edge," and/or becoming workaholics who "have to" channel their energies and thoughts into their jobs.
- Most survivors of trauma that happened quite a while ago will become "experts at detachment, denial, minimization, avoidance" in "an attempt to forget the unforgettable" and to avoid feeling the pain associated with the unforgettable (Scurfield, 2006a: 60).

For most survivors who have become experts at detachment or denial, typically at some point this stops working well. They have become exhausted or the detachment/denial is so severe that it now begins to cause other problems in life, such as not being emotionally accessible to significant others, or having a blunt affect becomes the norm, along with the continuing unresolved emotional pain from the original traumatic experience(s). The dilemma is that as one allows strong feelings and emotions (in addition to anger) to arise, it is not unusual for an inrush of accompanying traumatic memories associated with those feelings to occur.

Myth: *"I must be crazy or weak to still keep remembering and still be bothered by the war after all this time.*

Reality: Trauma is unforgettable (unless one has psychic amnesia). It is absolutely normal not to be able to totally eradicate the memories of trauma, and to be bothered to at least some degree by the trauma—for months, years or decades afterwards. Therefore, "a war survivor will not be able to totally forget salient memories of the war unless they resort to artificial means such as substance abuse, psychotropic medications, constant exposure to current danger, etc." (Scurfield, 2006a: 59). In essence, there is nowhere to permanently or completely file away the memories of events so catastrophic, and thus there is the constant threat that they will overwhelm the senses, the soul, and the spirit.

Myth: *"Most trauma survivors are highly motivated to eliminate or reduce PTSD-related symptoms such as isolation, numbing and physical arousal/ hyper-alertness to the environment.*

Reality: "A number of PTSD symptoms are also survival modes that were learned during or following the war trauma, and many war survivors are very reluctant, ambivalent or not interested in giving them up" (Scurfield, 2006a: 61; see also Murphy *et al.*, 2004). Survivors may:

- feel that it is quite necessary as a self-protective stance to remain removed and isolated from and wary of others because they see themselves as "different" from those who have not been at war, believe that neither they nor others are able to relate to each other, and do not feel comfortable in many social situations;
- believe that they need to continue to detach from their emotions as a means of self-protection from the painful reliving of traumatic memories; and/or
- believe it is wise and indeed necessary, as a protection from and a defense against a dangerous and threatening world, not to trust and to

remain wary of the environment; being constantly on alert and highly reactive are necessary safeguards against unexpected external threats (Scurfield, 2006a).

Myth: *If I fully remember and re-experience aspects of my original trauma (through talking about it, thinking about it, focusing on it), I will "lose control" and "go crazy." I will either be pulled back down into that abyss containing those traumatic memories and never be able to come back out again, or I will become so caught up in extremely strong emotions connected to the traumatic experience that I will begin to cry and never be able to stop or become so enraged that I will lose control and hurt myself or someone else.*

Reality: Trauma survivors almost never "go crazy" from remembering and talking about their traumas. On the other hand, they might well "go crazy" trying desperately to deny the undeniable—that the trauma happened, that it hurt then and it hurts now, that it has not gone away and that it needs to be dealt with directly and straightforwardly. An enormous amount of energy is often expended in trying to keep these emotions simmering below the surface or buried to the point of inaccessibility (Scurfield, 2004).

Myth: *The impact of war on most combat veterans is mostly negative; most veterans are damaged much more than they are positively impacted by their war experiences.*

Reality: Typically, war has both significant "positive" and "negative" outcomes, with positive impact while deployed and post-deployment often outweighing the negatives (Scurfield, 2006a). For example, one study demonstrated that only 11 percent of veterans surveyed reported that their war experiences had had a mostly a negative impact on their lives. By contrast, over half (56 percent) of the veterans surveyed indicated that their war and military experiences had an entirely or mostly positive effect on their lives. The remaining third (33 percent) described the impact as equally positive and negative (Card, 1983).

Positives from war include: an increased or enhanced sense of pride in serving one's country, the development of patience, self-confidence and maturity, and the extraordinarily powerful bonds of comradeship with other service members and veterans. Negatives include: a loss of civic pride, a loss of faith in America, increased cynicism, the inability to make new friends, and unresolved grief or anger from exposure to repeated death and suffering (Scurfield, 2006a).

It should be noted that the same kind of outcomes were found during one of the author's (Scurfield, 2006c and 2008) experiences living and working on the Mississippi Gulf Coast before, during and after Hurricane Katrina. Of course there was widespread dismay, grief and loss of property, entire neighborhoods and communities destroyed, and anger at the inadequate federal disaster response and the attempts of insurance companies to deny damage and grossly minimize claims by those insured. And yet, positive outcomes from Katrina were many and quite profound. These have included: (1) reaffirmation of what is really important in life—not material possessions but family, friends, faith; (2) a remarkable bringing together of neighbors and communities to an extent never experienced previously; and (3) a shared sense of enhanced connections through the amazing numbers (tens of thousands) of volunteers who over several years donated their time, effort and money to the recovery efforts.

Part of the healing process is developing the ability to better understand, acknowledge and accept both the negatives and the positives that are forthcoming in the face of tremendous tragedy and traumatic experiences. And relief is possible and can be enhanced significantly if one is able to find someone they truly and wholly can trust and who understands their experiences, such as a qualified counselor or chaplain/minister.

Our troops and their families deserve to know the full truth

Partly because the myths described above are so profound and widespread, and the realities so obscured or denied, there is a critical need for a series of truths to be clearly, unequivocally, and fully communicated to our troops and their families (Scurfield, 2006a). Historically, this has not occurred either before service members are deployed or after they have returned from deployment.

We contend that the only ethical stance is to communicate these truths fully and unequivocally to our troops and their families both before and following deployment. It is important to note that there have been innovative approaches instituted since the wars in Iraq and Afghanistan that help to address this issue, including the military development of battlemind and resiliency initiatives (see Chapters 14 and 15).

There are several truths that our troops and their families especially deserve to be told about, unequivocally and fully, prior to and following deployment:

- It is both helpful and necessary, while on deployment, to be able to suppress or "bury" painful memories, to learn how to "detach" from emotions while in the war zone and to maintain a mission focus. This will facilitate the ability to survive deployment.
- On the other hand, there is absolutely no evidence that such behaviors, which are conducive, indeed essential, to survival while in the war zone, will have a positive impact on functioning after returning from deployment—either in the short or long term (Scurfield, 2006a).

The experiences of service members returning from deployment to a war zone reveal that the mindset and behaviors ingrained to survive during war can be very problematic to a positive readjustment back in the civilian world. Furthermore, there is compelling evidence (including that from surveys conducted by the military) that for a substantial sub-group of service members, there will be longer-term war-related mental health problems (Hoge *et al.*, 2006; Kulka *et al.*, 1990; Seal *et al.*, 2007; Solomon & Mikulincer, 2006).

It is well documented that the more someone is exposed to the stressors of war, the greater the risk of developing war-related post-traumatic stress or PTSD and other mental health problems, such as mood (depression) and other anxiety disorders. This means that the more deployments, and the longer the length of deployment, the higher the risk is for developing PTSD and other mental health problems. This is the very real long-term risk of being willing to repeatedly put yourself into harm's way—and all military personnel have the right to informed consent about this risk. If you still choose to go into harm's way in service to your country, you are doing so with your eyes wide open as to the potential risks to you in the long term.

By communicating the above truths before deployment to a war zone, the military would be practicing that which is required in all federally funded research projects that involve human subjects: full disclosure of the risks involved for those participating. If such "full disclosure" of the risks is required to be provided to research subjects before they are allowed to participate in a research project, then surely such should be required for service members before they are allowed to be deployed to a war zone (Scurfield, 2006a).

It is our belief that such full disclosure of the risks would promote more trust among our troops that they are being honestly informed of important information. This, in turn, would facilitate a more open, above-board discussion, enhance awareness, and encourage willingness to discuss the impact of military service.

The information, issues and perspectives described by the various authors in this book are consistent with the principle of full disclosure of the risks, dynamics and stressors that our service members face before, during and following deployment. Our military personnel, our veterans, and their families deserve no less.

Closing

These myths and realities are important information for service members, veterans, their families and their providers. They help to provide the context for appreciating the multiple beliefs and facts that are relevant to the impact of being deployed to a war zone. In an ideal world, these would be discussed fully, openly and honestly with all service members and their families by military providers and command before and following deployment, and would be information that all clinicians and other providers are versed in and are comfortable and willing to share with service members, veterans and their families.

It is our hope and intention that these first two chapters have provided an informative overview of an expanding circle of healing and information crucial to understanding more about war trauma and its impact. The remaining chapters go into much more depth about specific military and civilian populations impacted by war, and military and resiliency initiatives to address that impact. Thank you for your interest in better understanding and serving those who have put themselves in harm's way to serve us.

References

Card, J. (1983). *Lives After Vietnam: The Personal Impact of Military Service.* Washington, DC: Lexington Books.

Corbett, S. (2004, February). The permanent scars of Iraq. *New York Times Magazine,* p. 34.

Frankl, V. (1959). *Man's Search For Meaning.* Boston, MA: Beacon.

Hoge, C., Auchterlonia, J. & Milliken, C. S. (2006). Mental health problems, use of mental health services, and attrition from military services after returning from Iraq and Afghanistan. *Journal of the American Medical Association, 295*(9), 1023–1032.

Kulka, R. A., Schlenger, W. E., Fairbank, J. A., Hough, R. L., Jordan, B. K., Marmar, C. R. & Weiss, D. S. (1990). *Trauma and the Vietnam War Generation: Report of Findings from the National Vietnam Veterans Readjustment Study.* New York, NY: Brunner/Mazel.

Murphy, R. T., Cameron, R. P., Sharp, L., Ramirez, G., Rosen, C., Dreshler, K. & Gusman, D. F. (2004). Readiness to change PTSD symptoms and related behaviors among veterans participating in a motivation-enhancement group. *The Behavior Therapist, 27*(4), 33–66.

Platoni, K. (2006, August). The war room. *The Ohio Psychologist, 53,* 10–11.

Scurfield, R. M. (2004). *A Vietnam Trilogy: 1968, 1989 & 2000. Veterans and Post-Traumatic Stress.* New York, NY: Algora Publishing.

Scurfield, R. M. (2006a). *War Trauma: Lessons Unlearned From Vietnam to Iraq. Volume 3 of A Vietnam Trilogy.* New York, NY: Algora Publishing.

Scurfield, R. M. (2006b). *Journeys of Healing: Study Abroad with Vietnam Veterans.* New York, NY: Algora Publishing.

Scurfield, R. M. (2006c). Post-Katrina aftermath and helpful interventions on the Mississippi Gulf Coast. *Traumatology, 12*(2), 104–120.

Scurfield, R. M. (2008). Post-Katrina storm disorder and recovery more than two years later. *Traumatology. The International Journal, 14* (2), 88–106.

Seal, K. H., Bertenthal, D., Miner, C. R., Saunak, S. & Marmar, C. (2007). Mental health disorders among 103,788 U.S. veterans returning from Iraq and Afghanistan seen at Department of Veterans Affairs facilities. *Archives of Internal Medicine, 167,* 476–482.

Solomon, Z. & Mikulincer, M. (2006). Trajectories of PTSD: A 20-year longitudinal study. *American Journal of Psychiatry, 163*(4), 659–666.

Part 1

Warriors impacted by war

3 Citizen/warriors: Challenges facing U.S. Army Reserve Soldiers and their families

COL David Rabb (OIF-OEF) and
LTC (RET) Cynthia Rasmussen

Since the American Revolutionary War, the role of citizen/warriors has been vital to national security. As of 1908, the U.S. Army Reserve's mission has been essential and complementary to the U.S. Army's mission of defending and protecting the United States from external threats and responding to national emergencies. In this current era of America at war, army reserve soldiers and their families have carried heavy burdens and have made significant sacrifices.

This chapter will examine the impact that the wars in Afghanistan and Iraq have had on army reserve soldiers, their families and their communities. While the emphasis is on the army reserve, most of the distinctive features and characteristics described apply to reserve units in the other military branches; notable differences will be mentioned when applicable.

To understand the major challenges reserve soldiers and their families face, one must understand military culture, recent war era history, and the transformation that the reserve components are experiencing. It is our intent to show readers the unique role that army reserve soldiers have played since 2001 in accomplishing the tenets of Title 10 of the U.S. Code ("provide trained units and qualified persons available for active duty in time of war or national emergency"). In addition, there is an elaboration of the distinctive stresses and challenges faced by reserve soldiers and their families, with suggested intervention strategies for mental health clinicians and other providers.

Army reserve composition and culture

In general, U.S. military culture has many similarities to subcultures within the United States. Language, values, traditions, rules of behavior, history, customs, dress, norms and other attributes help to shape the core of a culture and distinguish it from the "majority" culture. The U.S. military has it own cultural characteristics and norms that set it apart. This culture is necessary to support the command and control that protects America's national interests and safeguards its security. As an instrument of power, the U.S. military serves as a micro-subculture that enforces America's strength when diplomacy, and economic and informational alternatives have failed.

What sets U.S. military culture apart from other military cultures around the world is its diversity in organizational structures, operations, and personnel. The Army, Navy, Marine Corps, Air Force and Coast Guard possess their own distinct missions and are configured to meet specific strategic goals and contingencies. Within each branch of service, there are reserve components that augment active duty operations. Furthermore, diversity is reflected in rank; multiple military occupational skills, roles and responsibilities; and the ethnic, racial, gender and religious preferences of service members themselves.

The army reserve is the most diverse component of the U.S. Army. It is a community-based operational force that provides complementary capabilities that augment the Army in joint expeditionary and domestic operations. In 2009, 80 percent of army reserve personnel were enlisted soldiers; 20 percent were officers. There are more minorities and women represented in the army reserves than there are in the entirety of the Army Active Component and Army National Guard. Approximately 40 percent of army reserve soldiers come from ethnic minorities, the highest of any branch in the military. Women represent 24 percent of the force.

The average age of an officer in the army reserve is 42; the average age of enlisted soldiers is 31. Because army reserve soldiers tend to be older than their counterparts in the regular Army, many of them are married (45 percent), and 9.6 percent are single with children. (U.S. Army Reserve, 2009). As the U.S. demographics continue to become more diverse, the army reserve's demographics will certainly follow.

Since 2001, more than two million troops have been deployed in support of Operation Iraqi Freedom (OIF), Operation Enduring Freedom (OEF—military operations in Joint Task Force Guantanamo Bay, Cuba and Afghanistan), Operation New Dawn (OND—military operations in Iraq since September 2010) and many other areas of the world in the Global War on Terrorism. The army reserve role in supporting Army operations cannot be overstated. More than 184,000 Army Reservists have been mobilized for the war effort—and approximately 50 percent have mobilized more than once. The army reserve contributes up to 100 percent of legal and medical support, as well as training and field exercise divisions that provide realistic training to help soldiers advance their military education or military skill set, as well as their combat readiness. More than two thirds of the Army's civil affairs units, psychological operations units, transportation units and theater signal commands, as well as many other combat support services, are assigned exclusively to the army reserves.

The types of reserve unit are listed below with the percentage of provision by the reserves for the Army in brackets (statistics retrieved from www.globalsecurity.org/military/agency/army/usar.htm):

Type of reserve unit (and percentage of total Army provision)

- Training and Exercise Divisions (100%)
- Railway Units (100%)
- Enemy Prisoner of War Brigades (100%)
- Civil Affairs Units (97%)
- Psychological Operations Units (85%)
- Judge Advocate General Units (81%)
- Medical Brigades (80%)
- Transportation Groups (80%)
- Chemical Brigades (75%)
- Petroleum Supply Battalions (69%)
- Medical Groups (66%)
- Theater Signal Commands (66%)
- Chemical Battalions (64%)
- Motor Battalions (60%)
- Hospitals (54%)
- Petroleum Groups (50%)
- Terminal Battalions (50%)
- Transportation Commands (50%)
- Public Affairs (42%)
- Theater Area Army Commands (40%)
- Water Supply Battalions (33%)

Not since the Vietnam War have reserve soldiers and units been called into action to support the U.S. military's total efforts. Less than 1 percent of the American population serves in uniform today (2.2 million), but those who do serve bear 100 percent of the burden of defending our nation, as reported in the White House Report (2011) *Strengthening Our Military Families: Meeting America's Commitment Report*. Therefore, the army reserves are even more marginalized due to their sheer lack of numbers (205,000 soldiers in 2010) and unique role as citizen/warriors. Unlike the Active Duty Components, the reserve components do not benefit from the wide range of social support services and activities provided on active duty bases and in their related communities.

Distinct from National Guard units, which are state-based, but can be federally activated, army reserve units fall under federal government control and do not have the same local or communal connections that support funding and politics at the state and local levels. In the past five years, the army reserves have implemented and expanded programs to assist and support reserve soldiers and their families prior to, during and following deployment. Such programs include the following:

Army Reserve Family Programs

A comprehensive umbrella program focused on educating and empowering members of the military community to develop skills and encourage behaviors that strengthen self-reliance, promote retention and enhance readiness. Programs include Army Family Team Building, Deployment and Homecoming Briefings, Yellow Ribbon Reintegration, Army Strong Bonds, Army Family Readiness Groups, Warrior and Family Center, Army Family Action Plan, Army Strong Community Center, and Fort Family 24/7 Outreach Support (see www.arfp.org).

Yellow Ribbon Reintegration Programs

A series of conferences sponsored by the Army Reserve Family Programs, created to prepare soldiers and families for mobilization, sustain families during mobilization and reintegrate soldiers with families, communities and employers upon redeployment or release from active duty (see www.yellowribbon.mil).

Strong Bonds

Events sponsored by the Army Chaplains which support commanders by strengthening individual soldiers' and family members' readiness through relationship education (i.e. single soldiers, couples and family retreats) (see www.strongbonds.org).

Military OneSource

Part of the Department of Defense Virtual Family Services Program, Military OneSource provides a 24/7 call center where soldiers and their families can obtain help for simple or complex problems such as: finding child care; handling home and vehicle maintenance and repair problems; finding consumer product information, such as electronics, motorcycles, and outdoor gear; finding free recreational activities; and dealing with the emotional challenges of military life and deployment. It also has an interactive website and a non-medical counseling service where soldiers and their families can receive private counseling in their local area (see www.militaryonesource.mil).

Employment Partnership of the Armed Forces

Partnering with over 1000 employers at the national, regional, and local levels, the Employment Partnerships of the Armed Forces provides a direct link to jobs for service members and their families (see www.employerpartnership.org).

Army Ambassadors Program

Appointed by the Chief, Army Reserve (CAR), the Army Ambassadors Program functions at the state and community levels and consists of a group of influential volunteers. Army Ambassadors promote awareness of the army reserve and help to educate the public, community leaders and congressional staff officers about the values of army reserve soldiers and units (see www. usar.army.mil).

Army Reserve Warrior and Family Assistance Center

A program created to assist all members of the army reserve community to work through the challenges of military life. Army reserve soldiers and families can email or call for immediate help (see www.arfp.org).

Army Strong Community Centers

Also known as "Virtual Installations," Army Strong Community Centers provide resources to army reserve soldiers and families that are normally found only on active duty military installations. These centers connect geographically dispersed families with support resources in their own community (see www.usar.army.mil/arweb/NewsAndMedia/stories fromthefront/Pages/ArmyReserveOpensFourthArmyStrongCommunity Center.aspx).

Army Reserve Recovery Care Coordinators

Recovery Care Coordinators have been assigned to army reserves Regional Support Commands to coordinate care for geographically dispersed army reserve soldiers, IRR soldiers, and army reserve Veterans and Retirees who are wounded, injured or ill, and their families. Their job is to assist in the healing process by providing non-medical services that include helping to access medical treatment at civilian military treatment facilities or VA medical centers. They can also assist in locating transition and readjustment resources and filing for VA benefits (see www.usar.army.mil/arweb/soldiers/Pages/RecoveryCare.aspx).

These programs are making major inroads in supporting reserve soldiers and their families. At the time of writing this, however, the army reserve, like other reserve components, is challenged with personal relationship stresses and the breakup of any number of vital relationships; divorce; the interface with law enforcement; involvements in substance and domestic abuse and violence; unemployment and homelessness; and both suicidal intent and completed suicides that are rapidly escalating in number. Finally, army reserve families face a multitude of challenges, ranging from financial problems to devastating emotional strife and strain.

Transformation from a strategic to an operational force: Issues of stability and predictability

To support the transformation of the army reserve from a strategic force to an operational force, army reserve units are being managed under the Army Force Generation (ARFORGEN) cycle (McNeil, 2005). The ARFORGEN cycle is designed to provide units with sufficient time to reset, train and ultimately deploy overseas. In most cases, for active duty units, the cycle ensures that soldiers are granted a two-year dwell time period before they are scheduled to deploy again. For the army reserves, the goal is to provide a five-year dwell time period before soldiers are available to deploy. The ARFORGEN cycle provides predictability and stability for units, soldiers, family members, and employers.

A by-product of the ARFORGEN cycle is that it helps to significantly reduce stress and the many uncertainties and unknowns that might otherwise complicate this process by insuring a substantially longer and more predictable period of dwell time between deployments. Community leaders, educational institutions, employers, health care providers and veteran advocates all need to know that the ARFORGEN cyclical system drives the battle rhythm of the entire U.S. Army and Army reserve components. Programs and prevention and treatment interventions need to be tailored to support reserve soldiers and their families throughout the ARFORGEN cycle. For example, creating a series of three- to four-day retreats that allow for army reserve families to come together before, during and after deployment would significantly reduce the amount of isolation that these families often feel because of geographical distance among them. Interventions that target the improvement of communication, connections and collaboration among families, especially among soldiers and families that are not organic to the deploying unit, could be beneficial to families throughout the emotional cycle of deployment, homecoming and reintegration.

Unlike with past American wars, reserve soldiers are no longer considered supplemental strategic reinforcement for the active duty Army. According to *The Army Reserve 2020 Vision and Strategy 2020* (2011a), now and into the future, the army reserve remains a crucial element of the Army's Total Force and an integral part of the Army's overall deployable strength and war fighting team. As in the past decade, its role in the next decade will be just as vital to the success of our nation in contending with uncertain security environments and persistent conflicts. The army reserve serves as America's primary reservoir of shared military-civilian skills and will continue to be required to transform itself into an enduring operational force that will support the ARFORGEN process in meeting deployment expeditionary and contingency expeditionary requirements.

The distinctive dual role of citizen/warriors

Understanding the culture of the army reserve provides not only basic information necessary for understanding and managing differences between Reserve and Active Components of the Army, but also an appreciation of the thought process and mental conditioning that shapes a citizen/warrior's world view. What significantly distinguishes Army Reservists from their Active Duty counterparts is their dual role and identity as citizen/warriors.

Although reserve soldiers are indoctrinated into the military way of life and value system through their experiences in boot camp or the Basic Training course, their professional conduct, behavior, ethics and attitudes are reinforced and validated by their first line unit leaders. The role assumed by army reserve leaders must model not only what is required to be successful in the role of army soldier, but also what is necessary to be effective in balancing military and civilian life.

The primary factors that shape a soldier's identity are the army values, the Soldier's Creed and the Warrior Ethos. These elements account for the two major responsibilities of a warrior: (1) accomplishing the mission, and (2) taking care of the welfare of troops. Army values are very consistent with Judeo/Christian values and the Puritan work ethic (i.e. loyalty, duty, respect, selfless service, honor, integrity and personal courage). These principles create the conditions in which leadership, mission accomplishment and teamwork thrive. Individuals who embrace the Soldier's Creed are expected to achieve a high level of excellence and be willing to risk their lives in the face of danger. Inherent in the Soldier's Creed is the heart, spirit and soul of a Warrior. Therein lies the dominance of a collective identity over the individual identity and the internal limits and struggles through which soldiers must navigate to make sense of their moral stance and actions during times of peace and war.

The Soldier's Creed

I am an American soldier. I am a Warrior and a member of a team.
I serve the people of the United States and live the Army Values.
I will always place the mission first. I will never accept defeat.
I will never quit. I will never leave a fallen comrade.
I am disciplined, physically and mentally tough, trained
and proficient in my warrior tasks and drills.
I always maintain my arms, my equipment, and
myself. I am an expert and I am a professional.
I stand ready to deploy, engage, and destroy the enemies
of the United States of America in close combat.
I am a guardian of freedom and the American way of life.
I am an American soldier.

Embedded in the Soldier's Creed is the Warrior's Ethos (highlighted above in itals), which requires unyielding discipline and attention to mission accomplishment. This can have major implications for the means by which soldiers strive to manage their personal and professional lives. For the most part, reserve soldiers are driven and goal-directed team players, respectful to orders and authority. Because of their requirement to balance civilian life and their responsibilities, they are often required to be more self-directed than active duty soldiers. Moving from the role of citizen/warrior on a part-time basis to being a full-time Warrior requires mental agility and a shift in priorities—demands that active duty soldiers, understandably, may never face or fully appreciate. Active duty army soldiers are more completely immersed in a militaristic cultural climate and environment in which they operate on a day-to-day basis; by contrast, reserve soldiers must make different transitions and adjustments in order to carry out their military and civilian obligations.

Inherent in the Soldier's Creed is a high level of excellence that can foster soldiers' unwillingness or inability to ask for help or admit that they are not "good to go" (i.e. 100 percent up to their tasks). Crucial to being an effective provider for service members and veterans is an awareness that special attention needs to be paid by health care professionals and veteran advocates to acknowledging and appreciating citizen/warriors' core principles and belief systems. Exploring the unique roles of citizen/warriors can serve as a foundation for providers and others supporting our troops and their families for engaging army reserve soldiers as they journey to and from war.

Reserve and other military families

Distance does to love what wind does to fire; it extinguishes the weak and enkindles the strong

—Author unknown

The impact of war and life in the military on U.S. active duty military families has been well documented. The vast majority of the research has been conducted with Regular Army families and not specifically with Reserve force families. However, because Reserve forces experience many aspects of military life that Regular Army forces and their families face, the following findings comprise vital information for clinicians to be aware of to better understand Reserve families.

Hill's classic 1949 work *Families under stress: Adjustment to the crisis of war separation and reunion* (1971) provides research findings on military-induced separation during the Second World War. It found that military families undergo three phases of adjustment: (1) a state of crisis or disorganization; (2) reorganization into a state of recovery; and (3) settling into a new level of reorganization above, below, or on the same plane as the previous level of stress adaptation. Hunter (1982) reported that military families endure a lifestyle that is unmatched by other population groups due to frequent moves, the uncertainty of being deployed in hostile environments, frequent periods of family separation, geographic isolation from extended family, low pay, younger age as compared to the general civilian population, and a high incidence of young children living in the home. (Interestingly, each of these military family lifestyle elements can be a significant source of stress.)

Hill (1971) suggests that good marital adjustment prior to separation predicts a healthier adjustment and reunion. Baker *et al.* (1967) documented the effects separation had on children's developmental level. Boys between the ages of 5 and 8 who had fathers serving in the military who were on unaccompanied family tours and were away from the family for at least a year in a non-combat zone exhibited increased masculine striving (i.e. aggression) and poor social adjustment. Steiner & Neuman (1978), Nice (1981) and Wickham (1983) proposed that family adjustment directly influences the soldier's combat readiness, retention and overall combat effectiveness. Bell (1991) believed that family adaptation to deployment is a dynamic process which is influenced by both internal and external forces and that families may require different types of support, information and resources at various stages of their emotional cycle of deployment. Black (1993) suggested that the foremost stressor that military families may have to confront is the very real threat that their loved ones may be killed or wounded in combat or military-related accidents.

Hutchinson & Banks-Williams (2006) found that medical and non-medical staff, civilians and non-civilians alike, do not and cannot fully recognize or appreciate the tremendous physical and emotional toll that war takes on soldiers, nor the impact war has upon the family. Mutual readjustment difficulties occur as both soldier and family member experience the other from a different prism. Lesser *et al.* (2010) found that mental health diagnoses among military spouses and emotional difficulties among children are associated with multiple deployments. For the Reserve families who typically never "signed up" for the role of a military family and have never lived on or near any military installation or within close range of other military families, this becomes especially complicated.

Although the above findings reflect the abundance of professional literature and research on the significant movement towards supporting active duty military families, there is a paucity of literature and research on the topic of supporting Reserve families specifically. For example, a recent American Psychological Association Presidential Task Force on Military Deployment Services for Youth, Families and Service Members (2007) found a striking absence of research examining the unique needs of special populations, including the army reserves.

What has been reported highlights important areas of functioning of which clinicians must be aware. Rabb, Baumer & Wieseler (1993) reported that during Operation Desert Storm, army reserve soldiers experienced many of the same stressors that active duty soldiers experience during mobilization.

However, due to their dual role of warrior/citizen, reserve soldiers and their families faced unique challenges and barriers that, if not resolved, placed them at higher risk for dysfunction. Counseling support for Reserve families during pre-deployment, deployment, and reunification and sustainment phases were identified. Counseling efforts with Reserve families during the pre-deployment phase were designed to be preventive in nature and were aimed at providing families with information to help survive separation, reinforcing the perception that families would be taken care of by the military and civilians in their local communities. Contact with Reserve families during the deployment phase strengthened military commitment to the needs of families. Counseling services offered during the reunification and sustainment phase for reserve soldiers and their families provided information to reduce the stress and tension associated with reunion and readjustment to civilian life.

Hammelman (1995), in her study of army reserve soldiers mobilized for the Persian Gulf Conflict, found that married soldiers suffered from greater stress than single soldiers; lower ranking soldiers and their families experienced less stress than higher ranking soldiers; female soldiers fared better in coping with stress than male soldiers; single-parent families handled stressors better than two-parent families; and families with three or more school-age children responded better to stress than families with no children. Varda *et al.* (2009) in a study of 600 army reserve and National Guard families found that 60 percent of soldiers and spouses felt that their families were "ready" or "very ready" for their most recent deployment. The study also found that four out of five families had some type of deployment-related challenge; however, the challenges varied significantly, ranging from emotional and mental health problems to problems with children and employment difficulties.

The above findings suggest that army reserve families, like their Active Duty counterparts, experience significant family system changes and challenges brought on by interpersonal and external stressors when soldiers are deployed. Furthermore, on a closer examination of army reserve families, it was found that their challenges reflect even more complexity and variance during periods of readjustment and transition. It is important that health care providers and counselors do not make the assumption that army reserve families and Active Duty Families are alike. Although there are many similar stressors (family disequilibrium, fear of loved one dying, childrearing challenges), clearly reserve soldiers who are married without children and reserve soldiers who are older, married and higher ranking, may be faced with yet more stress and anxiety during deployments that may go unnoticed or ignored.

"Going inside the box"—Pre-deployment

When going to war and preparing to "go inside the box" (enter the war zone), soldiers' cognitive and psychological coping mechanisms are aligned with three major impulses: (1) surviving the unknown under arduous and some-time hostile and austere conditions, (2) accomplishing the mission, and (3) sustaining connections with family and friends. Soldiers must maintain a realistic emotional armament that will allow them to withstand the strain of separation from loved ones and the threat of being injured or killed when going into harm's way.

Going inside the box requires considerable energy and focus for soldiers to create boundaries and some type of order as they approach the tasks of deployment (this process is described in detail in Scurfield, Platoni & Rabb, 2012). There must be a demarcation from civilian life and a process to capture the spirit, sense of purpose and other qualities and preparations required of soldiers embarking on their wartime journeys. This includes physical stamina, a positive attitude, mission-essential training, self-confidence, and the ability to function while in harm's way in spite of the fear factor—a constellation of qualities and factors essential in order to make the adjustments from "home zone" to "war zone."

Because reserve soldiers are part-time—having one foot in civilian life and the other in military life—they tend to experience a higher level of uncertainty and worry than their active duty counterparts when heading for war. Reserve soldiers may not experience the same community support in departing for war due to the likelihood of widely differing opinions and viewpoints in the civilian community about the war(s) being fought. For example, when the first author (Rabb) deployed to Iraq in 2004, the majority of his closest friends, work colleagues and relatives were opposed to the war and questioned whether it was justified. This is not to infer that all active duty communities are in lockstep about going to war. On active duty military installations, however, the decision to go to war remains in step with the rhythm and pace of activities involved in equipping, preparing and sending units off to war. In the reserve components, deployment can be a very isolating event for reserve soldiers in TPUs (Troop Program Units—soldiers are assigned and participate in monthly "drills" or battle assemblies). This is even more likely to be the case for Individual Ready Reserve (IRR) soldiers who are likely to be augmenting deploying units located many states away from their state of residence and home of record. IRR soldiers are considered to have inactive status, are not required to attend monthly battle assemblies and receive no military pay while on IRR status, but they are subject to recall to active duty status for deployment.

The emotional aspects of "going into the box" for reserve soldiers is similar to that of active duty soldiers. Both experience pre-separation grief and loss for their loved ones, their surroundings and the activities of daily life. Both are typically preoccupied with preparations for war to the extent that there may be little time for responding to the needs of those that depend upon them or to be able to bring domestic matters to some sense of closure. Guilt over perceived abandonment of loved ones and the relinquishment of responsibilities at home can become problematic. In turn, families are often in crisis at this point, and typically experience shock, disbelief and anger over the approaching disruption of security and order in their lives.

For army reserve soldiers and their families, there are other aspects that are more distinctive in the experience of going off to war, which are related to such factors as the dual role of citizen/warriors and the fact that many reserve soldiers and their families had not expected that there would be such a shift to becoming part of an operational (versus strategic) force. Reserve soldiers are more likely to have loose ends to tie up with regard to work, school, civic and religious obligations than their active duty counterparts. Active duty soldiers may not carry guilt about leaving work behind and the impact that this will have on their place of work as their future work is a continuation of their work before deployment.

Both Reserve families and active duty families will undergo the emotional cycle of deployment, i.e. anger and protest, emotional detachment, family stress and marital disagreements (Pincus *et al.*, 2005). Emotional distancing frequently occurs in relationships in order to preserve them. Weeks and days prior to the deployment, a couple may feel like they are "walking on egg shells" in a minefield. Arguments and heated debates, especially those related to finances, jealousy and childrearing, can be exhausting and cut deeply into the bonds of the relationship. Reserve soldiers and their significant others may subconsciously exhibit "testing" behavior in order to see just how far their love goes or to validate that they are still needed and wanted once separated by the deployment. A significant number of relationships disintegrate within weeks into unit deployments because of unresolved emotional spillage stemming from such pre-deployment dynamics and issues. And Reserve families (and a number of reserve soldiers) may be more likely to question or become less committed to a life that has become much less "citizen" and much more "warrior" than originally envisioned when entering the reserves.

Young, unmarried reserve soldiers "going into the box" must renegotiate ties with their family and friends. Emotionally, this process is somewhat different to what active duty single soldiers will experience in that the majority of the latter do not reside in the same state or household as their parents. Their independence from their parents will have been established when they entered boot camp (Basic Training) and moved on to their first full-time active duty Army job. At this point, a healthy psychological distance will have been established as the young warrior was fully initiated into adulthood. On the other hand, reserve soldiers, after completing Basic Training, typically return home or attend college. Establishment of independence and adulthood may not carry the same weight as if they were on active duty full-time. Parents of reserve soldiers, after learning that their child is being deployed, may experience a variety of feelings associated with the emotional cycle of deployment, as well as exhibiting overprotective behavior that might be interpreted by the reserve soldier as clinging behavior or an intrusion into their (personal and "adult") life. Likewise, the young reserve single soldier must necessarily struggle with emotions involving separation from loved ones when his or her unit is about to deploy. Hence, "going into the box" can be fraught with stress and parental skirmishes for young, single soldiers.

Separation from friends may be a lesser problem for active duty soldiers than for reserve soldiers, as unit cohesion and peer-to-peer support in active duty units are characteristically well established prior to deployment. Unlike reserve soldiers, active duty soldiers usually live, train and engage in social activities together on a continual basis. And so, when preparing to go "inside the box," they take their main support group with them. Conversely, reserve soldiers only get to know each another through their much less frequent and less sustained battle assemblies and annual trainings. In fact, most reserve soldiers who transfer into another unit that is being deployed will not become acquainted with their new comrades until the deploying unit is in the process of pre-mobilization training or at their mobilization site. And their families may never get to know or even meet one other or the other soldiers in their respective units, further exacerbating isolation.

"Going outside the box"—Reunification and sustainment post-deployment

It is well known that coming back from war ("going outside the box") is even more difficult than leaving for war. Everything one left behind has changed. Soldiers going "outside the box" must now contend with the effects of surviving a lengthy deployment and adapting to the physical rigors and emotional strain of the battlefield, as well as the uncertainty and chaos that accompany it. Their ways of thinking and being are likely to have shifted and appear "out of sync" with their family, friends and co-workers. Unlike their active duty counterparts, who will have begun their reintegration with dedicated and full-time social and community support on active duty installations, reserve soldiers do not have the support services or social resource infrastructure to sustain them through the reintegration process.

The reserve soldier will also find that their family has changed. Family members will have learned new ways to cope, having had no choice but to become more independent or mature in order to overcome struggle and survive (conversely, some are unable to adapt and function well, resulting in serious adjustment issues and problems). Common thoughts and feelings that we have heard from soldiers who have gone "outside the box" include: "I already feel like I don't belong;" "They don't understand what I have been through;" "My family survived without me;" "I don't want to be around civilians;" "I feel blessed;" "I wish I was back there." In turn, common thoughts and feelings that we have heard from family members/significant others include: "It's great to have him/her back home;" "He/she has changed for the worse/best;" "He/she can't really appreciate what I have been through;" "In some ways it was/is easier for me/us when he/she was away."

It can be argued that cultural shock during reintegration is more prevalent among reserve soldiers because they have to come into contact more often with civilian populations that do not always share their frame of reference or world view. A rapid immersion back into civilian culture can be challenging for reserve soldiers who must resume or find new (civilian) employment in a struggling economy.

Transitioning reserve soldiers home from war is one thing; transitioning them to a college or university is quite another. A warrior's readjustment to private and public space has its challenges, but readjustment to a college campus—with its rich vastness of individual lifestyles, diversity of thought, and age groups—can be daunting and arduous for a person with a military background. Furthermore, veteran students compared with the general college population tend to be older, more mature and more disciplined, and have more life experience, leadership experience and skills. Because of their wartime experiences, they tend to have a different frame of reference. These attributes can create barriers for them in connecting with regular college students.

"Little things" are difficult for returning reserve soldiers, such as the absence of Armed Forces Network (AFN) or TV and radio programming, which is found on active duty installations and/or forward operating bases in the war zone; instead, the reserve soldier is faced with a multitude of civilian TV and radio stations that can be quite overwhelming. Having to navigate through the reintegration process not as a team or a unit, but alone—in one's individual community on one's individual terms—may be tremendously isolating for reserve soldiers, more so than for their active duty counterparts who return to the U.S. as a unit shaped by their wartime experiences and who typically remain as a unit for months or years after deployment.

It is important that reserve soldiers and their families are educated as to the common reactions to reintegration and returning to civilian life so that they are more able to avoid the mistaken belief that they are "going crazy" because of the thoughts that pass through their minds. Transition may require considerable time, and no one is on the same timeline. For most soldiers going "outside the box," several months may be required for them to fully readjust to civilian life. For many, 12 or more months may be necessary for the reintegration process—if we accept the rule of thumb that reserve soldiers must experience a full cycle of events that was missed during deployment (e.g. birthdays, holidays) before they can come full circle and feel more completely reconnected with their previous lives. The transition may take longer, depending on the experiences a soldier had "in the box" and their ability to find meaning and balance on the home front. Finally, based on our work in the VA with Second World War, Vietnam Era and Persian Gulf Era veterans, it may take years, if not a lifetime, before some combat veterans are able to fully return home in the truest sense. And some never do.

Stigma, stress and anger

One of the major obstacles to supporting reserve soldiers during reunion and reintegration is the stigma related to seeking help in the form of combat stress/ psychological services. Although significant efforts have been made to change the culture of the active Army and army reserves, traditional ingrained negative attitudes and fear about seeking behavioral health persist. Hoge *et al.* (2004) surveyed 894 soldiers and cited the principal reasons that they avoid seeking mental/behavioral health assistance. Among such barriers, the most prevalent include fear of being seen as "weak" (63 percent of respondents), that treatment from unit leaders would be different (59 percent) and that unit members would have less confidence in them (59 percent).

Asking for help requires that soldiers admit that they have problems. As mentioned earlier, seeking help or assistance runs against the grain of the Soldier's Creed in terms of exhibiting excellence and refusing to admit defeat. While "in the box," soldiers survived insurmountable challenges and ordeals by pushing through their discomfort and pain, all the while not demonstrating any signs of weakness. The emotional armor they wore "in the box," unfortunately, often follows them during their reunion and reintegration phases (see Scurfield, Platoni & Rabb, 2012). It can be frightening to remove or expose their raw emotions and anguish. Many soldiers going "outside the box" carry with them a good deal of anger and agony that simmers below the surface. They will do whatever they can to suppress it and to force it to remain dormant. On the other hand, they may truly believe that they do not need help in any form, believing that they have conducted themselves exactly as they should have and will survive and be the best soldier/ warrior regardless.

Typically, the people most likely to be able to help—and even more so while they still have active military status—detach suppressed anger, depression or suicidal thoughts in a reserve soldier are his/her battle buddies, who have come to know and to bond with them over the course of a long deployment. For active duty soldiers, the ability to detect individuals who are struggling is more probable because of "gate keeping" strategies they have learned to increase unit members' and leaders' vigilance for the prevention of negative outcomes. This is more difficult to accomplish with reserve soldiers because of long monthly periods between battle assemblies, so leaders and peers do not have the opportunity to watch for signs of mental health concerns (Harrell & Berglass, 2011).

The first author (Rabb) was involved in the treatment of a 25-year-old single reserve soldier who attempted suicide and was subsequently hospitalized on an inpatient psychiatric ward. The soldier had been home from war for four years and had secured a high-paying administrative government position. He also had perfect attendance at his monthly Reserve battle assemblies. This soldier was intelligent and industrious, and was well liked by his friends and co-workers. He maintained a professional, organized and orderly demeanor. His persona, however, would change when he socialized and "went out partying" with his colleagues and friends. He would consume one drink after another and become increasingly agitated, with extreme angry outbursts. Examination of medical records and an initial interview with the soldier revealed that he had been diagnosed with severe PTSD three years earlier, but had not sought treatment for this.

During a follow-up visit, the soldier was asked to provide the "bottom line" reason for his excessive alcohol intake and at this point his anger erupted. He stated that he honestly could not explain why his drinking was out of control and this was followed by unrestrained hostility. He believed the root cause to be somehow related to his tour in Iraq, but he feared and resisted looking back into his past. The soldier was honest and sincere in his responses—factors that we have found to be strong indicators of positive progression towards confronting and resolving one's problems. After the inpatient psychiatric hospitalization, the soldier was referred to a VA Medical Center dual disorder chemical dependency/PTSD program. He has come to find balance in his life by seeking counseling services at his local Vet Center and by attending AA meetings regularly. With a release of information granted by the soldier, his military leader was informed of the hospitalization to garner additional support.

In male-dominated, hierarchical, mission-focused organizations such as the Army and army reserve, expressing anger is far more acceptable than shedding tears. Anger is considered to be beneficial in terms of the fight or flight response, which supports the physical and mental requirements prescribed for the warrior (Scurfield, Platoni & Rabb, 2012). Release of tension, stress, disappointment, emotional hurt and physical pain are often more acceptably expressed through anger than through emotional release. For soldiers to make sense of their experiences "inside the box," they will clearly require psychological support in order to become acquainted with their anger and to learn to release it in an appropriate and safe way. Health care professionals and veterans' advocates will need to become accustomed to and accepting of the unquestionable fact that for warriors, anger is a necessary benefit in order to bear witness to the pain and anguish of war and the place from where it stems. Helping soldiers and combat veterans to understand their own anger and rage will go a long way towards helping them learn to manage it. The next time you observe a soldier expressing extreme anger, consider that this may be an unmistakable indication that this individual is crying for help or stuck in warrior mode.

Challenges in navigating back to the home front

Navigating back to the home front after "leaving the box" is akin to feeling lost in space. The repetitive daily routines, keen focus, collaborative teamwork and intense emotional connections that soldiers grew accustomed to while deployed are no longer present. There are no grid coordinates or navigational devices to orient them as they re-enter civilian life. Reserve soldiers need time to "reboot" and "recharge" as they obtain support in finding their path once again. The vast majority of reserve soldiers going "outside the box" will be able to build the bridge to cross the turbulent waters of change and readjustment. From our experiences and observations, returning reserve soldiers have had difficulties in readjustment primarily due to physical and mental health issues, changes in support structure, relationship problems, financial concerns, the inability to secure employment, lack of housing, substance use and/or abuse, or a combination of these challenges. There is also a tendency among some returning reserve soldiers to be excessively driven to catch up with their civilian peer group and/or to resent having to do this, perceiving that they have lost out on many opportunities or are behind schedule in their educational or career pursuits.

Reserve soldiers who are not capable of reconciling their wartime experience through their reintegration experiences risk becoming disjointed (a sense of feeling awkward and uncomfortable with themselves and with others); disconnected (unable to fit into civilian society and therefore becoming socially isolated and alienated); and/or "dead" (an internal/spiritual sense of hopelessness or giving up and wanting to check out).

Interventions to support reserve soldiers and the tasks of reintegration include a myriad of medical, behavioral and alternative care approaches, and community and faith-based network initiatives. There are no silver bullets for re-establishing good health and maintaining a productive life. Returning soldiers need support in finding their way, but should remain in the driver's seat in setting a course that makes sense to them and has goodness of fit for their lives. Likewise, there is no one agency, organization or program that can provide for all the needs of reserve soldiers and combat veterans. In light of this fact, a true expansion of the circle of healing is required so that more adequate resources from the public and private sectors can be made available (Scurfield & Platoni, 2012). Finally, it is worth noting that when governmental and private resources and communities do not step up to provide adequate services, the impact is profound.

> The willingness with which our young people are likely to serve in any war, no matter how justified, shall be directly proportional to how they perceive the veterans of earlier wars were treated and appreciated by their Nation.
>
> —President George Washington

Positives of being citizen/warriors

Being a citizen/warrior has it challenges, as well as it rewards. Unlike the military in the Vietnam War era, today's military is made up of an all-volunteer force. Today's reserve soldiers are quite aware that they are part of an enduring operational force that has been called up at a time during which our nation has required them to support foreign and domestic contingencies. There are many reasons why people join the army reserves, including learning new skills, traveling to new places, advancing education (GI Bill), earning a second income and the potential for retirement income, or securing future VA benefits, such as home and business loans. However, by far the main reason is the same as why people join other branches of the U.S. Armed Forces—to serve their country and to be of service in time of greatest need. Many of the citizen/ warriors who serve in the ranks of the army reserve joined following the 11 September 2001 terrorist attacks. They felt a need to respond and to do something that would make a difference in the defense and protection of our Great Nation. Perhaps this is the same type of patriotism, drive and call to duty that distinguished Second World War veterans after the bombing of Pearl Harbor.

Over the past ten years, army reserve soldiers and their families have made the rapid transformation and adaptation that is required to sustain and achieve agility to protect our national interests and security. Reserve soldiers have come from being considered "Weekend Warriors" to becoming Warfighters. They have replaced going to drills with going to battle assemblies. They and their families have had to cope with going from two weeks of annual training to 12- to 16-month or longer deployments and multiple deployments in short periods of time. The American public and senior military leaders have asked a lot from them and they have given their all. On a personal level, many reserve soldiers who have been to war have matured through increased responsibilities and interpersonal growth, improved social skills, conflict negotiation, the ability to cope or compromise, and the ability to push through fear and take calculated risks, all of which are inherent in being a member of the Reserve forces. Their families have also grown in their association with the army reserves. The areas of growth for family members include a deeper pride for their loved ones serving in the military; a sense of connection with the military community; having their children learn the value of time, hope and patience as to what is really important in life—life itself; the resiliency that comes with having to learn new things and to take on added responsibilities during temporary duty separations and long deployments; and feeling closer, having gone through an often uncertain shared experience together.

Because of army reserve soldiers' dedication, devotion and duty, the United States has access to trained units and qualified soldiers available to respond to wars and national emergencies. Having army reserve units that are trained and available only when needed benefits the American public in terms of saving millions of dollars in tax payers' money. As part of the 2011 army reserve

Posture Statement (2011b), Lieutenant General Charles Schultz, Chief of the U.S. Army Reserve, stated that

> the army reserve is the best value in that the nation pays for the full cost for a reserve component soldier only when he/she is mobilized. Under the current ARFOGEN process, an active component soldier spends two years in a non-deployed status at a cost of $140K per year, compared with his/her army reserve counterpart, who spends four years in a non-mobilized status costing $47K per year—that's about one third the cost of active component soldiers for train-up over a longer period of time.

Closing

As the army reserve continues its organizational transformation from a strategic to an operational force, it must not lose sight of the quality of services required to support and retain army reserve soldiers and families. Programs that are inadequate in resourcing, staffing and delivery, or that delay pay, orders and promotions and have difficulties providing easy access, cause a tremendous degree of undue stress on army reserve soldiers and their families, who are already challenged by pre-mobilization and/or post-mobilization obligations and demands.

Under the best of circumstances, moving from the role of citizen/warrior on a part-time basis to the role of full-time warrior, and then back again, is very challenging. Such role changes require considerable mental agility to deal with transitions and adjustments between military and civilian obligations. Challenges and stresses particularly relevant for reserve soldiers and their families include separation from friends and unit cohesion and peer-to-peer support prior to deployment that typically are not as developed as they are for active duty units. And Reserve families may never get to know or even meet one other due to their geographic dispersion —thus exacerbating isolation.

It is clear that both military and civilian health care providers must possess a depth of understanding about military culture and operations, including understanding of the differences in soldier versus civilian mentality and the specific challenges and demands that reserve soldiers and their families face. Furthermore, no one agency, organization, or therapeutic approach is the solitary answer to addressing the tsunami of changes and challenges that Reserve service members and their families face in "going in and coming out of the box." Multi-complex readjustment challenges require multiple approaches and solutions. And both military and civilian resources will need to "step outside the box" in order to meet reserve soldiers and their families where they are and be able to establish partnerships that will help create networks that support and sustain them.

Reserve soldiers need to be encouraged to examine how the behaviors that worked for them in the war zone are the same behaviors that can trip them up in the home zone (see Scurfield, Platoni & Rabb, 2012). Finally, because of the distinctive citizen/warrior status of Reserve forces, future surveys and research should specifically investigate the status of Reserve forces and Reserve families in the areas of stress, stigma, and the willingness to seek care in order to better understand the challenges and actions needed to support our citizen/warriors as they continue to serve and to make enormous sacrifices for our country. Both parties deserve no less.

COL David Raab, MSW, LICSW, ACSW started his military career as a Marine infantryman (1976–1980) and completed 23 years in the U.S. Army Reserve, where he was Commander of the 785th Medical Company, Combat Stress Control and Commander of the 113th Medical Detachment, Combat Stress Control. He deployed to Iraq (2004–2005) and currently serves in Afghanistan (2011–2012). He has been employed by the VA since 1985 and currently works at the VA Office of Workforce Management and Consultation (Davidrabb17@aol.com).

LTC (RET) Cynthia Rasmussen, RN, MSN, CANP retired in 2011 from the army reserve having served 23 years as a Mental Health Nurse. She was mobilized for six and a half years to active duty as Director and Psychological Health and Sexual Assault Response Coordinator for the 88th RRC/RSC, serving service members and their families nationwide. She received her bachelor's and master's degrees from Marquette University, Milwaukee, Wisconsin and currently works as an Adult Nurse Practitioner for the Veterans Health Administration (ltcrazz@yahoo.com).

References

American Psychological Association Presidential Task Force in Military Deployment Services for Youth, Families and Service Members (2007). *The psychological needs of U.S. military service members and their families: A preliminary report*. Retrieved from http://www.ptsd.ne.gov/publications/military-deployment-task-force-report.pdf

Baker, S., Fisher, E., Janda, E. & Cave, L. (1967). Impact of father's absence on personality factors of children. *American Journal of Orthopsychiatry, 37*, 269.

Bell, B. (1991, September). *How deployment distress was reduced among families during Operation Desert Shield/Storm*. Paper presented at the Eight User's Stress Workshop, San Antonio, Texas.

Black, W. G. (1993). Military-induced family separation: A stress reduction intervention. *Social Work, 38*(3), 273–280.

Hammelman, T. L. (1995). The Persian Gulf conflict: Impact of stressors as perceived by Army Reservists. *Health and Social Work, 20*(2), 140–145.

Harrell, M. C. & Berglass, N. (2011). *Losing the battle: The challenges of military suicide*. Policy Brief from the Center for a New American Security.

Hill, R. (1971). *Families Under Stress: Adjustment to the Crisis of War Separation and Reunion*. Westport, CT: Greenwood Press.

Hoge, C. W., Castro, C. A., Messer, S. C., McGurk, D., Cotting, D. I. & Koffman, R. L. (2004). Combat duty in Iraq and Afghanistan; Mental health problems and barriers to care. *New England Journal of Medicine,351*, 13–22.

Hunter, E. J. (1982). *Families Under the Flag: A Review of Military Family Literature.* New York, NY: Praeger.

Hutchinson, J. & Banks-Williams, L. (2006). Clinical issues and treatment considerations for new veterans: Soldiers of the wars in Iraq and Afghanistan. *Primary Psychiatry, 13*(3). 66–71.

Lesser, P., Peterson, K., Reeves, J., Knauss, L., Glover, D., Mogil, C. … Beardslee, W. (2010). The long war and parental combat deployment: Effects on military children and at-home spouses. *Journal of the American Academy of Child and Adolescent Psychiatry, 49*(4), 310–320.

McNeil, D. K. (2005). ARFORGEN *Cycle: Reserve Component—Reset Phase/Train Ready Phase/Available Phase Chart.* Part of Army Force Generation Within Joint Force Provider Presentation (Unclassified). Presented by General Dan K. McNeil, Commanding General U.S. Army Forces Command. Remarks to NGAUS, September 19, 2005.

Nice, D. S. (1981). The course of depression affect in Navy wives during separation. *Military Medicine, 148*, 341–343.

Pincus, S. H., House, R., Christensen, J. & Adler, L. E. (2005). The emotional cycle of deployment: A military family perspective. Retrieved from www. hooah4health. com/deployment/familymatters/emotionalcycle.htm.

Rabb, D. D., Baumer, R. J & Wieseler (1993). Counseling Army Reservists and their families during Operation Desert Shield/Storm. *Community Mental Health Journal, 29*(5), 441–447.

Scurfield, R. M. & Platoni, K. T. (2012). An expanding circle of healing: Warriors and civilians impacted by war. In R. M. Scurfield & K. T. Platoni (Eds.), *War Trauma and Its Wake. Expanding the Circle of Healing.* New York, NY: Routledge.

Scurfield, R. M., Platoni, K. T. & Rabb, D. (2012). Survival modes: Coping and bringing the war home: From Vietnam to Iraq and Afghanistan. In R. M. Scurfield & K. T. Platoni (Eds.), *Healing War Trauma. A Handbook of Creative Approaches.* New York, NY: Routledge.

Steiner, M. & Neuman, M. (1978, June). *Traumatic neurosis and social support in the Yom Kippur War returnees.* Paper presented at the Second International Conference on Psychological Stress and Adjustment in Time of War and Peace, Jerusalem, Israel.

U.S. Army Reserve (2009). *The United States Army Reserve 2009 Posture Statement: A Positive Investment for America.* Retrieved from http://armed-services.senate.gov/statemnt/2009/March/Stultz%2003-25-09.pdf

U.S. Army Reserve (2011a). *Army Reserve Vision and Strategy 2020.* Retrieved from www.usar.army.mil/arweb/Documents/AR%20Vision%20and%20Strategy%20 2020.pdf

U.S. Army Reserve (2011b). *The United States Army Reserve 2011 Posture Statement: An Enduring Operational Army Reserve is a Positive Investment for America.* Retrieved from www.armedservices.house.gov/index.cfm/files/serve? File_id=866fb710-2d71-44af-b67c-2629b6e6acd4

Varda, D. M., Hall, K. C., Beckett, M. K. & Stern, S. (2009). Deployment experiences of Guard and Reserve families: Implication for support and retention. RAND National Defense Research Institute. Retrieved from www.rand.org

Wickham, J. A. (1983). *The Army family.* Chief of Staff White Paper. Department of the Army Pamphlet 608–4, Section G–1.

White House Report (2011). *Strengthening our Military Families: Meeting America's Commitment.* Retrieved from http://www.defense.gov/home/features/2011/0111_initiative/strengthening_our_military_january_2011.pdf

4 Army National Guard warriors: A part-time job becomes a full-time life

MAJ Cora Courage (OIF-OEF)

It was 1974, I was 17 years old, and the Vietnam War was coming to an end. I had been raised in a family that considered service for our country a noble profession. I thought the Women's Army Corps (WAC) would be a great place to develop a strong identity and enhance my self-confidence. A year later, the corps disbanded and we were integrated into the Regular Army. We were not a welcomed addition. Despite the hostile environment, the Army decided that having lost so many helicopter pilots during Vietnam, they would open the door for women to attend flight school. I was too short to fly choppers, so instead I became the first female Survival Evasion Resistance and Escape (SERE) Instructor in the Warrant Officer Candidate (WOC) Aviation School at Fort Rucker, Alabama. Sexual harassment was the norm and I found myself struggling to "get along and avoid making waves" in order to survive in a world where men treated women as objects and respect was in short supply. Upon discharge, I transferred to the Army National Guard (ARNG) and lasted three drills (mandatory monthly weekend trainings, now referred to as battle assemblies). The ARNG had the reputation of being a "good old boy" system; something I experienced first-hand before my 21st birthday. Spending annual training in the field with two and a half ton trucks filled with iced kegs of beer and my male counterparts watching 8mm reel-to-reel pornographic films made me reconsider my desire to serve our country in this male-dominated world.

This chapter is designed to provide the reader with an overview of the history of the United States Army National Guard (ARNG) and its involvement in conflicts faced by the nation since the 17th century. In addition, the reader will gain some understanding of the unique challenges experienced by U.S. ARNG warriors over time. Areas of consideration will include preparation for mobilization, deployment, and reintegration concerns. Where pertinent, I will include information from my individual experiences, spanning enlistment in the WAC in 1974, fourteen years in the Minnesota ARNG, and deployments as a psychologist to Iraq in the ARNG and to Afghanistan in the U.S. Army Reserve (USAR). While it is very important to acknowledge the existence of the Air National Guard, my experiences are limited to the ARNG. The opinions expressed here are my own and do not necessarily reflect those of the Department of National Defense or the ARNG.

Historical perspective

Older than our nation, the ARNG has the longest continuous history of any American military organization, its origin dating back to the early 17th century. The initial settlers of that time recognized their obligation to contribute part-time personal service for the protection of the life, liberty, and property they were now free to enjoy. From the homes and farms of individual communities, men voluntarily banded together to form military units and companies. These protective groups, born of necessity, were strictly local and spontaneous—neighbors joining hands for a common cause (e.g. Army National Guard, 2001). The ARNG is the oldest component of the United States Armed Forces. The oldest ARNG unit formed within the Continental United States (CONUS) is the 182nd Infantry of Massachusetts, originally organized as the Middlesex County Militia regiment in 1636. During the First World War, the ARNG made up 40 percent of the U.S. combat divisions positioned in France. One hundred forty thousand Guardsmen were mobilized during the Korean War and it is estimated that of the 12,234 ARNG warriors mobilized during the Vietnam War, more than 7,000 served either in ARNG units or were deployed as individual replacements. More than 63,000 ARNG soldiers were called to serve during Desert Storm and it is estimated that as many as 75 percent of the soldiers serving in the Persian Gulf were Guard or USAR warriors (Allen, Berry & Polmar, 1991).

Guardsmen have seen a greater role than ever before, conducting peacekeeping missions in Somalia, Haiti, Saudi Arabia, Kuwait, Bosnia and Kosovo. In addition, Guardsmen have assisted states during natural disasters, strikes and riots, provided security for the Olympic Games when they have been held in the United States, carried out homeland security missions, and been deployed on multiple Outside Continental United States (OCONUS) missions. Their role has been magnified since the Global War on Terrorism began after 11 September 2001.

Keeping the peace at home

On 24 September 1957 President Dwight D. Eisenhower federalized the entire Arkansas ARNG in order to ensure the safety of the "Little Rock Nine" to attend Little Rock Central High School the following day. Governor Orval Faubus had previously used members of the ARNG to deny these black students entry to the school. The New York NG was ordered by Governor Nelson A. Rockefeller to respond to the Rochester 1964 race riot in July of that year, the first such use of the Guard in a northern city. The California ARNG was mobilized by the then Governor of California Edmund Gerald Brown, Sr. to provide security and help restore order during the Watts Riots in August 1965. Elements of the Ohio ARNG were ordered to Kent State University by the Ohio governor Jim Rhodes to quell anti-Vietnam War protests, culminating in their shooting into a crowd of students on 4 May 1970, killing four and injuring nine. During the LA Riots in 1992, when portions of south central Los Angeles erupted in chaos, overwhelming the Los Angeles Police Department's ability to contain the violence, the California ARNG was mobilized to keep the peace and help restore order.

Although the ARNG involvement was primarily for defensive purposes, during the Waco Siege in 1993, the Texas ARNG was called in to assist the Bureau of Alcohol, Tobacco, Firearms (ATF) and Explosives in overthrowing the Branch Davidians. The ATF suspected that the Branch Davidians could be armed with powerful weapons and called for M1A1 Abrams tanks to be used to protect the ATF's retreat area. Air NG helicopters were used to conduct reconnaissance work and an unknown number of ARNG snipers assisted the ATF in the final assault on the encampment. When a labor strike among Minnesota's workforce in 2000 jeopardized the stability of state-run institutions, the MNARNG was activated for nearly a year to fill positions at the state-employee-staffed institutions. Several of my MNARNG friends were activated to fill positions at the Brainerd and Willmar state hospitals to ensure that their patients were cared for while labor negotiations were completed.

ARNG units played a major role in providing security and assisting recovery efforts in the aftermath of Hurricane Katrina in September 2005. While I was conducting pre-mobilization training at Camp Shelby, Mississippi, the remaining mental health section members from my unit were activated to provide mental health services to the citizens of Mississippi and to the first responders on the scene. In January and February 2007, ARNG troops from eight states were activated to help shovel snow, drop hay for starving cattle, deliver food and necessities to stranded people in their houses, help control traffic, and rescue motorists in blizzards across the country (Greenhill, 2007). ARNG warriors have provided sustained security and assistance in response to their call to active duty as initiated by the Governors of their assigned states, as well as on federal active duty status at times of war.

Federal Active Duty

Prior to the attacks against the United States on 11 September 2001, the National Guard's general policy regarding mobilization was that Guardsmen would be required to serve no more than one year cumulatively on active duty (with no more than six months overseas) for each five years of regular weekend drill attendance. Due to strains placed on active duty units following the attacks, the potential mobilization time was increased to 18 months (with no more than one year overseas). Additional strains placed on military units as a result of the invasion of Iraq increased the amount of time a Guardsman could be mobilized to 24 months. Current Department of Defense policy is that no Guardsman will be involuntarily activated for more than 24 months (cumulatively) within one six-year enlistment period. In 2005, however, members of the ARNG and USAR were said to comprise a larger percentage of frontline fighting forces than in any war in U.S. history—approximately 43 percent in Iraq and 55 percent in Afghanistan. ARNG and USAR members constituted nearly 28 percent of total U.S. forces in Iraq and Afghanistan by the end of 2007.

In the first quarter of 2007, the United States Secretary of Defense, Robert M. Gates, announced changes to the Guard deployment policy aimed at shorter and more predictable deployments for ARNG troops. "Gates said his goal was for Guard members to serve a one-year deployment no more than every five years. [He] imposed a one-year limit to the length of deployment tours for National Guard soldiers, effective immediately" (Baker, 2007). Prior to this time, Guard troops deployed for a standard one-year deployment to Iraq or Afghanistan would serve for 18 months or more, including training and transit time. During the transition to the new policy for all troops in the pipeline, deployed or soon to be deployed, some will continue to deploy more frequently than every five years. "The one-to-five year cycle does not include activations for state emergencies" (Baker, 2007). In 2011, General George W. Casey, Jr., the Army Chief of Staff, stated: "Every Guard brigade has deployed to Iraq or Afghanistan, and over 300,000 Guardsmen have deployed in support of the Global War on Terror" (Salzer, 2011).

The challenge of serving at both the state and federal levels while maintaining a civilian life

The ARNG organization has evolved over the years since its inception as a militia. ARNG warriors are especially challenged, as they serve two functions, being called upon to serve at both state and federal levels by virtue of the fact they fall under the control of the governor of the state in which the unit is assigned to provide emergency assistance in the aftermath of local disasters, as well as federal jurisdiction to support other wartime missions. This may include back filling of positions in CONUS at various military installations, providing homeland security, and activation and deployment to foreign countries (OCONUS) in supportive roles such as peacekeeping missions like those in the Balkans. In addition, the ARNG has been activated on an uninterrupted basis since the commencement of Operation Desert Storm in 1991. Since September 2001, the ARNG has also deployed repeatedly in support of the Global War on Terrorism, including to Operation Enduring Freedom (OEF) in Afghanistan and Operation Iraqi Freedom (OIF) in Iraq.

In essence, those soldiers assigned to National Guard units serve a particular state's needs—as well as those of the entire nation—while also maintaining a civilian life. In the event of flooding of the Red River in 2007 in southeastern Minnesota, the MN ARNG provided soldiers to sandbag levies, provide security to thwart looting, and protect citizens and their property. These citizen soldiers left their civilian jobs and said goodbye to their families and homes at a moment's notice to provide support to communities at risk. The MN ARNG rose to the occasion in their flood fighting efforts in Minnesota and other states several times in 2009, 2010 and 2011, each time assisting communities in preparation for flood control and restoration in the wake of the river's path. In August 2005, more than 50,000 National Guard Soldiers and Airmen from 26 states were mobilized prior to Hurricane Katrina to evacuate and rescue flood victims and brace for the impact. In the aftermath, they worked to restore power, clean and refurbish schools, businesses and homes, and repair and restore public utilities. Homeland security, state needs and wartime missions remain ongoing and place ARNG warriors in the role of carrying multiple burdens.

Despite the difficulties of having to answer to the call of two masters, both state and federal, this aspect of life is hardly the most difficult aspect of the warrior/citizen lifestyle for most ARNG warriors to manage. The reality that ARNG warriors may be called upon to mobilize at a moment's notice is often the most stressful aspect of serving in the ARNG. In the past, there was a sense of respect and admiration for the citizen soldier, willing to take up arms in defense of our country. In current times, the civilian world has not really been prepared for this and due to the multiple deployments they are forced to endure, soldiers are often faced with job loss, divorce and feelings of estrangement when they return home (MSNBC, 2008).

The Army National Guard goes to war

In 1990, an ARNG military police (MP) battalion in Rochester, Minnesota was activated to deploy during Desert Shield-Desert Storm. At that time, the concept of a Family Readiness Group (FRG), or any sort of program to support the families left at home, was non-existent. The war in the Persian Gulf had everyone reeling, as the Guard and Reserve prepared to send sons, daughters, husbands, wives, etc. to war. Any assistance to families members was provided through volunteers who wished help children and spouses prepare for the deployments of their loved ones for the first war in which our country had engaged since Vietnam.

This is not to say that many warriors had not engaged in action against an armed enemy prior to this formal declaration of war. But frankly, the Persian Gulf War seemed to take America by surprise. During the Cold War, most warriors had enlisted in the ARNG as a part-time job. Plans to attend Basic Training, followed by Advanced Individual Training (AIT), to acquire a specific skill that might be utilized in the civilian sector, were motivators for enlistment, as well as the educational financial assistance and other veterans' benefits provided. Many truly believed they would only be required to attend a weekend of training each month and a 15-day extended training period, usually held during the summer months, for completion of their contract obligations. When warriors began to deploy for Desert Storm, photographs were posted on the internet of two and a half ton trucks with chalk-scribbled graffiti written on tailgates that read: "One weekend a month, two weeks a year—My Ass!" After a 14-year break in service, my re-enlistment in 1991 came as a result of volunteering to provide counseling and support to family members of the deploying Military Police Battalion from Minnesota and speaking with a recruiter who suggested that I should undertake mental health service provision in the ARNG.

Growth and change in the ARNG

The ARNG has evolved over the years to become an organization invoking greater professionalism among those who enlist. Once referred to as "Summer Camp," the fifteen days of annual training typically scheduled during the summer is now called "Extended Combat Training" and the term "Battle Assembly weekend" is used in place of "Drill weekend." The ARNG has forged new ground in concert with its theme of "Adding Value to America" by establishing programs for youths at risk. About Face is a program designed to assist youths at risk to develop interpersonal relationship skills and critical thinking. Forward March teaches young adults job search and business skills in real life settings. Youth Challenge is designed to instill discipline, leadership, confidence and self-esteem. The STARBASE program helps students apply the principles of math, science and technology, and personal growth skills into their daily lives.

The ARNG also plays a significant role in many communities, sponsoring drug demand reduction programs and supporting communities to address continuing floods, snowstorms and hurricanes. During the past several years, nearly every state has activated ARNG members to assist their neighbors by providing food, shelter, security and, in many cases, efforts to assist law enforcement agencies in the seizure of illegal drugs. The ARNG continues to play a major role in assisting civil authorities during natural disasters such as earthquakes, tornadoes, wildfires, and by performing lifesaving missions. It is divided into units stationed in each of the 50 states and U.S. territories, and operates under the state governor or territorial adjutant general. The Guard warrior motto is "Always Ready, Always There," yet the ARNG is also required to respond to the pressure and demands of being called to service to deploy in support of other operations outside the United States.

The National Defense Act of 1916 guaranteed state militias as the primary reserve force, gave the President the authority to mobilize the Guard during war or national emergency, made use of the term "National Guard" mandatory, changed the number of monthly drills from 24 to 48, extended annual training from five to 15 days, and authorized drill pay for the first time. With the passage of this act, approximately half of the United States Army's available combat forces and approximately a third of its support organizations were comprised of National Guard units (e.g. Army National Guard, 2001). The ARNG is organized as an operational force that is fully capable of accomplishing state, national and international missions during war and peace. To meet these requirements, it maintains a balanced mix of combat arms, combat support and combat service support units. These units are structured to integrate seamlessly with active component units as needed, and are located in nearly 3,000 communities throughout the United States.

The role of a female Army National Guard behavioral health provider

The terrorist attacks of 11 September 2001 changed the lives of many Guard warriors. On that Tuesday, when I returned home from work, my daughter had lowered the flag in our front yard to half-mast. Her question to me as I entered our home was: "When do you have to go, Mom?" I had 14 messages on my answering machine from my ARNG sisters and brothers who were asking to deploy and soliciting me to go with them to exact retribution. I had been in the MN ARNG for 14 years and had not deployed, but was eager to do my part.

Repositioning roles from civilian life to the upheaval of multiple deployments in order to respond to the attack and potential future threats to the U.S. created not only an increase in pride and a feeling of responsibility to country and service, but also stress to Guard warriors' personal life at home. It was a call to arms for thousands of military service members, resulting in pervasive reactions of fear and anxiety for those left at home. Active duty units then began preparing to deploy to Afghanistan and, later, Iraq.

The PA ARNG had deployed the 28th Infantry Division to support the mission in Kosovo so that active duty warriors could be diverted to Iraq in 2003. This division had deployed without a psychologist, resulting in the demand for a behavioral health provider to be rotated from Landstuhl Regional Medical Center in Germany to fill the position until someone could be assigned. Task Force Associator, a small group of about 500 warriors from the PA ARNG, was responsible for 75 percent of the area of operations for Operation Joint Guardian, a peacekeeping mission in Kosovo.

There were no female officers and only a couple of female lower enlisted soldier medics assigned to this task force. I volunteered to support the PA ARNG as the behavioral health officer for the remainder of their rotation and was advised that the MN ARNG would be assigned the next rotation of Operation Joint Guardian. I deployed to Kosovo on 1 July 2003. While keeping an office at the base camp, I conducted numerous trips to the more remote locations, where handfuls of young men were struggling with home-front issues and deployment stressors. In February 2004, the MN ARNG arrived, providing familiar faces and friends upon whom to lean. Weekly staff consultations with the division psychiatrist at the larger camp, and much needed support from three female senior NCOs, who participated in "girl's nights" together, were essential to sustaining mental health support to a lone female psychologist. A strong friendship with the Kosovo Force (KFOR)/United Nations (UN)

Liaison, who was also female, was invaluable. Whether walking laps around the FOB (Forward Operating Base) to process and debrief, or providing support through a ministry of presence and shared experience, the connection permitted some feelings of isolation to be alleviated. As a high ranking female in a position of authority, with minimal support in this male-dominated domain, the isolation and feelings of estrangement, coupled with the resistance of many male soldiers to seek out mental health or combat and operational stress control services, could have created a sense of separation that would have been greatly detrimental to unit cohesion and morale. Additionally, the disdain for behavioral health providers that many warriors still possess can swiftly cripple the psychological well-being of everyone concerned.

This deployment proved to be an excellent training opportunity as a first-time tour, but along with the expected demands of deployment, there were unexpected ones as well. Unfortunately, one of the PA ARNG warriors, who struggled with depression and who had comrades debating whether or not to take him to see the behavioral health officer, ended his torment in suicide. In early 2004, three weeks of rioting began in Gjilan, Kosovo and spread to Pristina. The barely-below-the-surface sweltering hatred between Albanian, Serbian and Kosovar peoples fueled the anger and aggression that incited rioting, evoked by the misperception that an ethnically motivated incident had caused an accident in which a small child drowned while playing with other children from differing backgrounds. These riots eventually turned toward the peacekeepers and several coalition forces were wounded and killed. Additionally, a terrorist attack during the first week of training for several new UN Police Officers from the U.S. in preparation for working in a detention facility (March of 2004) resulted in 12 UN officers being wounded and three killed. These experiences provided ample experience of debriefing and counseling skills as an Army psychologist.

A common misperception about a deployed psychologist's duty is that they are never exposed to danger. The reality is that they also treat the wounded and dying, recover remains to send home to families, and comfort the war weary, as well as those who struggle with a plethora of significant and often critical issues. Frequently being placed in harm's way, and carrying the burden of the traumas that soldiers address in counseling, make compassion fatigue and burnout dangerous red flags which need to be monitored in mental health service providers (U.S. Department of the Army, 1994). Behavioral health providers may log thousands of miles on the road, traveling to FOBs and COPs (Combat Outposts) and conducting hundreds of debriefings and providing follow-up care for soldiers exposed to critical or catastrophic events. This can afford the opportunity to spend time with convoy escort teams, security patrols and route clearance packages, and to conduct some of the most essential and timely clinical work soldiers may need in the wartime theater. Wearing full "battle rattle:" weapon and ammunition, Individual Body Armor (IBA), Personal Protective Equipment (PPE) such as gloves, eye protection, etc., the Army Combat Helmet (ACH), and a small back pack or large ruck sack can result in an individual carrying an additional hundred pounds of gear on their person.

During OIF, I was often strapped into the back seat of a Humvee in full "battle rattle" and sometimes took the driver's seat to relieve exhausted warriors or served as the Truck/Tank Commander (TC). When traveling for hours through IED-laden areas or ambush sites, in hundred-degree-plus temperatures (even at night), without air conditioning or field sanitation, and with very limited communication vehicle to vehicle, or sitting alongside a road waiting for the Explosive Ordinance Disposal teams to clear the route, prevention and intervention work is frequently conducted in very non-conventional ways. Home front issues, battle fatigue, combat stress and numerous warrior concerns can be addressed during hours and days of extended missions. Long talks in the darkness, leaning over the hood of a truck with only the glow of a lit cigarette to illuminate faces, provided some of the most memorable experiences of this military psychologist's career.

The ARNG is the most versatile Department of Defense force available to the federal government for homeland security, homeland defense and military assistance and support to civilian authorities. ARNG warriors serve on State Active Duty under Title 10 of the United States Code (USC) status. Within 24 hours of the attack on the World Trade Center, 8,500 Army and Air National Guard warriors were on the streets of New York City. Under Title 32 USC orders, within 72 hours of President Bush's summons, Guard warriors were assisting in protecting airports across the U.S.

ARNG warriors are expected to adhere to the same moral and physical standards as their active duty counterparts. The original attitude of "one weekend per month and two weeks a year" is long gone, and it is becoming increasingly more difficult to describe any ARNG member as a "part-time" soldier. I have worked at the same agency since November 2000 (eleven years) but, due to deployments, I have actually only been present for six and a half years. Additionally, I have been deployed for three of the seven years my spouse and I have been together.

Train as you will fight

ARNG units are trained and equipped as parts of the U.S. Army. However, over the years, there have been massive discrepancies in how well-equipped and prepared active duty warriors are, compared with the ARNG. Members of the MN ARNG deployed to Kosovo in 2003 were issued Vietnam-era flak vests. During deployment to Afghanistan in 2009, the night vision goggles issued were sufficiently obsolete to appear as if they were something from the Dark Ages: a fully mounted head set, with two lenses mounted upon a three pound albatross that was supposed to sit on the face. This was clearly not the standard issue one lens/scope that is held by a bracket on Soldiers' Army combat helmets, readily able to be utilized while keeping one eye available for regular vision/sight. This clearly illustrates the substandard equipping of ARNG and USAR soldiers.

"Train as you will fight" is the training motto for all service members. Publius Flavious Vegetius Renatus (commonly referred to as Vegetius), who was a military author during the later years of the Roman Empire, is known for his chastisement of the decadence of the Roman Empire and its lack of discipline in the military forces. He is quoted as saying: "If you want peace, prepare for war." The more current English translations of his *De Re Militari* (Vegetius, 1993, 1996) suggest the continued relevance of his work in our current times. Guard warriors must maintain their readiness and fitness to deploy at all times. When deployed, they learn to develop strong relationships with active duty counterparts in the units they support in order to obtain the mission-essential equipment to remain combat effective.

Combat/operational stress control (COSC) for ARNG warriors

Despite the strain deployments can place on families, individuals, practices, employment and relationships, most warriors long for the opportunity to put themselves to the test of going to war (Yerkes, 1918). When deployed as the sole psychologist for a brigade combat team, the behavioral health provider often becomes the consultant and liaison to the Combat Stress Control (CSC) teams located throughout the theater of operations, as well as providing services to the brigade combat team to which they are assigned. The military doctrine of CSC is to treat as far forward as possible (U.S. Department of the Army, 2006). It is also important to acknowledge that ARNG Brigade Combat Teams usually consist of a behavioral health provider and a technician. Conversely, the Active Duty Army and the USAR utilize Combat Stress Control Detachments, usually comprised of 40+ personnel. During a six-month mobilization at Camp Shelby, Mississippi, the 1st Brigade Combat Team of the 34th Infantry Division (1/34 BCT) used the opportunity to teach basic peer support and defusing models to the medics, personal security details and numerous front-line leaders as a means of encouraging and promoting effective and time-tested strategies for coping with adversity and enlisting each soldier to act as a first responder.

Prior to redeployment, while in Iraq, the 1/34 BCT created a Warrior Transition Program which incorporated debriefings and battlemind training (e.g. Adler *et al.*, 2007; Adler *et al.*, 2009; Castro, Thomas & Adler, 2006) to help facilitate the transition back to the U.S. and to "citizen soldier" lives. President Bush's surging of the troops plan caused 1/34 BCT to be extended in theater for an additional six months, resulting in numerous personal problems in country and at home, which took a vast toll on the psychological well-being of many of these warriors. Depression, anxiety, marital conflicts and divorce were only some of the consequences of the emotional duress and combat/

operational stress issues suffered by these soldiers, ultimately contributing to the many documented suicides the Army has experienced in country (e.g. Hoge *et al.*, 2004).

Unique aspects of Guard (and Reserve) mobilizations: Part-time job becomes full-time life

Often, the Guard warrior receives a telephone call from their assigned unit giving them a verbal warning order, a "heads up," so to speak. This is followed by the receipt of written orders mobilizing them within the next few weeks for the duty they have been assigned to perform. The orders include an estimate of the number of days they are expected to be on Active Duty status and an explanation of travel arrangements. While citizen soldiers strive to maintain a sense of stability and consistency within their civilian lives, they are always aware, perhaps to the point of what might be described as hyper-vigilance, that at any moment they may be required to depart with a very short amount of time between being called to alert status and being required to report for duty.

Units may mobilize at the unit, battalion or division level. When this happens, the soldiers are usually trained for several months in CONUS to prepare them for the mission they will undertake. As they transition through various stages of their deployment, they complete exercises at various bases—both CONUS and OCONUS—before "pushing out" to the installations to which they will be assigned. The time spent together in preparation to deploy is fundamental to building unit cohesion and readiness for the mission. However, some warriors are not permitted this bonding/training experience. Weapons qualification, which develops a healthy competitive spirit, completing " lanes training" for convoy operations, and close quarter marksmanship drills build familiarity between warriors and facilitate bonding, as well as much needed awareness of each other's warrior strengths and areas that call for further training. Frequently, ARNG warriors are sent to war with other warriors who have had minimal, if any, opportunity to train shoulder-to-shoulder in preparation for combat. The reality is that if you are in the National Guard, it is not a case of *if* you will deploy, but *when* the next deployment will happen, and *with whom* you will go to war.

A high ranking officer in the USAR recently stated: "This is not my full-time job—I have a real life and I am going back to it as soon as I finish with this command duty." For many National Guard members, especially those in critical shortage fields, a part-time job has become the reality of their lives for years on end. On a more personal note, since 11 September 2001, I have been mobilized three times and have served OCONUS for 43 months. This service included deployments to Kosovo for 15 months and being mobilized a year later with the MN ARNG, 1/34 BCT for 28 months in support of OIF, which included 17 months in Iraq due to President Bush's troop surging in 2006. My last deployment is the shortest to date: 11 months in Afghanistan. One must acknowledge that the defining line between the ARNG warrior's "real" life versus their role in the Army becomes blurred with so many mobilizations and deployments. The process of transitioning back to "citizen soldier" can be very difficult when it is uncertain how quickly the citizen will be required to reactivate the battle mindset.

ARNG warrior reintegration issues

The 467th Combat Stress Control Medical Detachment suffered a severe blow on 5 November 2009 at Fort Hood, Texas, when a gunman entered the Soldier Readiness Processing site and opened fire, wounding 31 and killing 13 warriors and civilians. As a result, the deploying detachment of 43 personnel included several "replacements" who were mobilized to fill the positions of the deceased and wounded. Numerous others had been cross leveled from other units, while the 467th MED DET (CSC) was still training in CONUS in preparation for the OEF mission and in order to bring the detachment to the necessary strength level to deploy. Cross leveling occurs when an individual or individuals is/are taken from their home unit of assignment and placed in a new group of soldiers as individual augmentees or replacements in order to attain unit readiness and a full battle roster to complete the mission. Due to the small number of combat stress control detachments and companies—in addition to the areas of expertise they comprise, many of which are considered critical wartime shortage areas—the five-year mobilization plan referred to earlier in this chapter is often difficult to sustain. For example, my current unit of assignment, the 1972nd CSC Detachment, based at Joint Base Lewis-McChord, Washington, was mobilized for OIF from 2005 to 2006 and is scheduled to deploy for OEF in 2012. However, more than half of the unit membership is made up of soldiers who have deployed two to three times since 2005.

The average timeframe from the frontline of a combat zone in Vietnam to a soldier's living room was 24 to 72 hours, and thousands of them suffered because they were not identified as at risk or due to their inability to navigate the Veterans Administration (VA) system. While many warriors may experience some difficulty with the tasks of deployment and/or reintegration, today's military is trying to ease this transition from the war zone to the home zone more effectively. To the credit of many states which have been trying to facilitate more effective reintegration, there are a number of Yellow Ribbon or Beyond the Yellow Ribbon events that have been established to assist warriors in the transition home. ARNG and USAR units have hired full-time personnel to facilitate regular telephone contact with the warriors when they return and continue to monitor each service member during that first year home— at least in theory. In the past, ARNG warriors were not required to attend a Battle Assembly for the first 90 days after deployment. Some units held Yellow Ribbon events (reintegration training) at 30-, 60- and 90-day intervals following a return to CONUS, but attendance was optional.

Unless deployed or mobilized, ARNG and USAR members only have scheduled contact with each other for approximately 40 days in the course of a year. The 467th CSC Medical Detachment mandated that each warrior who deployed to Afghanistan be required to attend the Yellow Ribbon event scheduled two weeks shy of the 90-day guideline, remain assigned to that unit for the following year, and attend two more Yellow Ribbon events. It is important to note that more than half of the members of the 467th CSC Medical Detachment, which deployed to Afghanistan in 2009, were replacements or cross-leveled warriors who were not organic to the unit located in Madison, Wisconsin. Such a unit composition seriously impacts unit cohesion.

It is easy to lose sight of one other when individuals come from so many different states. In the year following our return, however, we were to schedule the second Yellow Ribbon event on our own. This meant that many of us attended with people we did not know and who would therefore be unlikely to notice if a fellow veteran was experiencing any degree of difficulties. Additionally, some members of the unit were excused from attending the seventh Yellow Ribbon event in the spring of 2011. Unfortunately, one warrior had maintained minimal contact with the military after we redeployed. Apparently, he was struggling with issues yet to be determined and subsequently committed suicide in the fall. Perhaps if he had been more engaged, a battle buddy would have noticed the changes in his demeanor and possible indicators of his psychological distress.

Critical support role of family, friends and military peers

The sacrifices that families make in supporting ARNG warriors are often greater than many will ever realize (e.g. Park, 2011; Sheppard, Malatras & Israel, 2010; Adler *et al.*, 2005). For example, family members can become ill and the soldier is often unable to be available to assist in relieving the burdens of care; in such situations, children may react to feelings of abandonment and experience feelings of depression and behavioral problems that cannot be addressed by the deployed service member. Financial distress frequently causes problems, as many enlisted soldiers are paid below poverty level. A myriad of home-front issues plague the deployed warrior, who may feel helpless to tackle and resolve them when they are thousands of miles away.

One of the greatest blessings in my life has been the unwavering support of my family and friends. My difficulties with reintegration after the Kosovo Forces NATO campaign came as the result of a long-term relationship ending. It has been said that deployments do not destroy marriages—but they do not fix them either (e.g. Adler *et al.*, 2005; U.S. Army Surgeon General, 2008). It was only a year later, during my deployment for OIF, that I became "an orphan," losing my last parent. Four months later, my teenage daughter graduated from high school and gave birth to a son. All of these changes, coupled with the demands of an extended tour, took a huge toll on me psychologically. I struggled significantly after OIF and one of the most wonderful things that could have transpired was the arrival of several of my battle buddies at our home to share experiences. Their visit, coupled with horseback riding and poker nights, resulted in many hours of "debriefing." Also, I received help from friends and family, who encouraged me to maintain contact with professionals for treatment; this allowed my next deployment for OEF to be much more manageable.

The importance of sharing stories with those we trust can not be stressed enough; it is necessary and invaluable in terms of coming all the way home. If units have hired individuals to keep track of the members after returning home, follow-through is critical. Of utmost importance is the responsibility of leaders to know their soldiers, extend concern always, and step in to provide help when needed. Warriors who struggle often fail to lean on family members for a variety of reasons. The most often expressed reason for refusal to talk openly with friends and family members is the perception that they will not and cannot understand because they were not there, or the warrior does not want to burden those they love and feels a need to protect them from the horrors they have witnessed. I dread the thought of the path my life would have taken without the intervention and undying support of my Army and civilian families.

Post-traumatic stress versus post-traumatic growth

Much of this chapter has focused on the challenges, stressors and trauma experienced by ARNG warriors and their families. However, there is another phenomenon—post-traumatic growth—which deserves some discussion, for it can be a powerful element in post-deployment healing and readjustment. Despite the stresses that deployments place on warriors' lives, they also serve to strengthen them in ways that perhaps only another warrior can fully understand.

Not all exposure to traumatic stress results in the development of PTSD, although the dual role of citizen/soldier unfortunately provides ample opportunity to be exposed to traumas both at home and on deployment. My deployment to Kosovo ended with returning home to discover that the person I had shared the past 11 years with had become involved with another and left my financial status in ruins. During my deployment to Iraq, I experienced a traumatic event that was personally difficult to assuage because of the similarities to an earlier incident in my life. The death of my mother and the significant issues my daughter experienced were losses that required attention during reintegration. Though I returned home from Iraq in 2007, unfortunately, as was and is the case with numerous returning military personnel, it took more than a year for me to locate and become connected with the help I needed to truly heal. In my case, such help consisted of Prolonged Exposure Therapy with a VA psychologist in the PTSD Clinic. After accomplishing the psychological work that was necessary to heal from the wounds of war, I deployed to Afghanistan in 2009 and returned home stronger than I was when I left, despite being exposed to many graphic injuries, participating in the recovery of the remains of deceased warriors and witnessing, first-hand, horrific events, trauma and death on a greater scale than OIF. Additionally, I found the love of my life before I deployed to Iraq, who has been my rock and supported me throughout my recovery. Without this unwavering support, I know I would not have been able to successfully navigate my way home.

Closing: The citizen soldier's life

ARNG warriors and their families face a variety of demands, as they serve both the state to which they are assigned and the federal government in times of war. Originally a community-based organization, ARNG now trains warriors with soldiers assigned to units that are comprised of military members spanning the continent. Frequently mobilized since 11 September 2001, we have been a large faction of the fighting force in numerous war zones. The citizen soldier, who once enlisted as a part-time job, now faces multiple deployments and the stressors that are derived from leaving work and home in order to fulfill the oath they swore to uphold and to defend our state and nation against disasters and enemy forces, both foreign and domestic.

While most NG warriors will tell you they are proud to stand up for America, they have paid a high price in doing so and have sacrificed much to fulfill that promise. We must do a better job in assisting these individuals in reintegration and provide the support they need to make the transition back to citizen status. I continue to serve in the army reserve and look forward to the future, which is destined to include another deployment. As in many other military families, my marriage is strengthened and our commitment is deepened as a result of our time apart. Thus far, I have no regrets, and I would not change any of it. My life, both personally and professionally, is better for the experience. What has been stated in many ways—"that which does not kill us makes us stronger"—is testament to the traumatic growth often achieved when citizen warriors go to war.

MAJ Cora Courage, Psy.D., enlisted in the Women's Army Corps in 1974, transferred to the Alabama ARNG in 1976 and has had an extensive career in the ARNG and the NG, rising through the ranks to her commission as a psychologist officer. Her deployments include Desert Storm, Kosovo, Iraq and Afghanistan. Currently, she is the Clinical Director of the 1972nd Combat Stress Control Detachment, scheduled to deploy to Afghanistan in 2012 (cora. courage@gmail.com).

References

Adler, A. B., Huffman, A. H, Bliese, P. D. & Castro, C. A. (2005). The impact of deployment length and experience on the well-being of male and female soldiers. *Journal of Occupational Health Psychology, 10*(2), 121–137.

Adler, A. B., Castro, C. A., Bliese, P. D., McGurk, D. & Milliken, C. (2007, August). The efficacy of battlemind training at 3-6 months post-deployment. In C. A. Castro (Chair), *The Battlemind Training System: Supporting soldiers throughout the deployment cycle.* Symposium conducted at the meeting of the American Psychological Association, San Francisco, CA.

Adler, A. B., Bliese, P. D., McGurk, D., Hoge, C. W. & Castro, C. A. (2009). Battlemind Debriefing and Battlemind Training as early interventions with soldiers returning from Iraq: Randomization by platoon. *Journal of Consulting and Clinical Psychology, 77,* 928–940. doi: 10.1037/a0016877

Allen, T. B., Berry, F. C. & Polmar, N. (1991). *War in the Gulf.* Atlanta, GA: Turner Publishing.

Army National Guard (2001). Army Regulation 130-5/Air Force Mission Directive 10. *Organization and Functions of National Guard Bureau.* Retrieved from http://www.apd.army.mil/pdffiles/r130_5.pdf

Baker, F. W. (2007, April). Gates promises predictable deployments. *GX: The Guard Experience, 4*(3), 22.

Castro, C. A., Thomas, J. L. & Adler, A. B. (2006). Toward a liberal theory of military leadership. In A. B. Adler, C. A. Castro & T. W. Britt (Eds.), *Military Life: The Psychology of Serving in Peace and Combat: Vol 2. Operational stress* (pp. 192–212). Westport, CT: Praeger Security International.

Greenhill, J. (2007). *National Guard rescues people, cattle after severe storms.* U.S. Army. Retrieved from www.army.mil/article/1257/National_Guard_rescues_people__cattle_after_severe_storms

Hoge, C. W., Castro, C. A., Messer, S. C., McGurk, D., Cotting, D. I. & Koffman, M. D. (2004). Combat duty in Iraq and Afghanistan, mental health problems, and barriers to care. *New England Medical Journal, 351*(1), 13–22.

MSNBC (2008, February 12). *Most vet suicides among Guard, Reserve troops. New government report raises alarm, calls for long-term mental health services.* Associated Press.

Park, N. (2001). Military children and families: Strengths and challenges during peace and war. *American Psychologist, 66,* 65–72. doi: 10.1037/a0021249

Salzer, D. (2011). *Casey: National Guard very different than 30 years ago.* National Guard Bureau. Retrieved from www.army.mil/article/52919/casey-guard-very-different-from-30-years-ago

Sheppard, S. C., Malatras, J. W. & Israel, A. C. (2010). The impact of deployment on military families. *American Psychologist, 65,* 599–609. doi: 10.1037/a0020332

U.S. Army Surgeon General (2008). *Mental Health Advisory Team (MHAT-V): Report.* Washington, DC. Retrieved from *http://www.armymedicine.army.mil*

U.S. Department of the Army (1994). *Field Manual 22-51: Leaders Manual for Combat Stress Control.* Washington, DC.

U.S. Department of the Army (2006). *Field Manual 4-02-51. Combat and Operational Stress Control.* Washington, DC.

Vegetius (1993 and 1996 [383]). *Vegetius: Epitome of Military Science* (M. P. Milner, Trans). Liverpool, England: Liverpool University Press.

Yerkes, R. M. (1918). Psychology in relation to war. *Psychological Review, 25,* 85–115. doi: 10.1037/h0069904

5 Women warriors: From making milestones in the military to community reintegration

Michelle Wilmot (Army Sergeant, OIF II-III)

It was three months since I had returned from Ramadi, Iraq, and two months since I'd started a full college course load to keep my mind off all that I had endured the previous year. It wasn't long before I discovered that school wasn't distraction enough from the images playing in my head. A montage of carnage was constantly on display in my mind's eye, while at the same time I was listening to 19-year-olds yammer on about their opinion on the war—even though most of them had never left the United States, with the exception of perhaps Mazatlan for spring break, or the comfort of their parents' pockets.

I had reached a point after just one and a half months of that spring semester where my studies began to take a nosedive. It was then that I reached out to the regional VA office in Atlanta, Georgia. After a few minutes of explaining that I wasn't looking for benefits, but just wanting to get screened for mild traumatic brain injury and possibly PTSD, as the signs and symptoms were blaringly present, I was told by the woman on the line to "prove" I was ever in the military, let alone Iraq. Oddly enough, she had pulled my records over the phone by using my Social Security number, so I inquired about this, only to have her also demand my DD214. The requested document was mailed and I waited three weeks before making contact again with the regional VA office. I was met with the voice of a different woman, who, like the one before her, had the audacity to question my military service and my service in combat as a female. When I argued the point that I had used some of my GI Bill money and that as she had pulled up my information with my Social Security number, she had to have known my military service record existed, she hung up on me.

It took me years to get beyond that alienation, by not only my fellow Americans, but an institution that was supposed to take care of me as a veteran. While I had begun making VA contact over the course of several months, this was followed by a lapse in contact that lasted several years and proved to be one of the most difficult periods in my life outside of serving in Iraq.

It should go without saying that women have not only been making historical strides, but also paying dearly for their bravery. It is important to note not only the history of oppression of and discrimination against women in the military and the necessary steps towards breaking down these barriers as well as seemingly myriad socio-cultural hurdles, but also that we must help pave the way to a less tumultuous future. This chapter will discuss women veterans' history as well as military sexual trauma, combat service, benefits and barriers, discrimination, and progress. The topic of women veterans alone could fill volumes of books. Here I will attempt to address many sensitive subjects which can act as a springboard to activate a discussion of even more critical and essential points for service providers and women veterans in general.

A historical perspective

Throughout world history, women have served their countries courageously in times of war and peace. Women have served throughout various periods of American military history and changes in military strategy reflect the growing need to have women present in some of the most dangerous situations in modern warfare; and women are now serving in direct combat operations. However, despite progress and doors opening for women in general, women veterans remain invisible. Every single day, female service members make the sacrifices necessary to serve our nation, some going above and beyond the call of duty to create vital historical leaps. But when they return home, they often find that benefits and recognition have taken a leave of absence. This chapter will describe the obstacles that women veterans face and address the enormous need for communities and health care providers to aid and promote successful community reintegration.

Women are an integral part of the Armed Forces and the veteran community. They have served in times of war throughout history, seemingly hundreds of years ahead of their time, due to the amount of time required for women to be accepted into the military at all. Yet in contemporary American culture, the struggle to give women credit for their bravery and steadfastness under fire remains. From Lozen, the Apache woman warrior (St. Clair Robson, 2008), to Molly Pitcher of the Revolutionary War (Berkin, 2006), to Vernice Armour in Operation Iraqi Freedom (Holmstedt, 2007), the list of women who have demonstrated remarkable courage does not just comprise a historical chapter. Indeed, there is a continuously expanding list of women who are willing to step forward and risk their lives for the sake of their loved ones and their country.

From the American Revolution through the Spanish–American War

During the American Revolution, some women served in support roles, accompanying spouses and loved ones onto the battlefield. Women such as Molly Pitcher, however, served in direct combat (Berkin, 2006). In the Civil War, approximately 400 women disguised themselves as men and fought alongside men. But despite the roles women have played, credit in the average grade school history textbook remains *in absentia*. Nevertheless, the milestones are undoubtedly there. While the roles of women in the line of fire were still unrecognized and undefined—and unaccepted—the Spanish–American War ushered in the inception of the Army Nurse Corps, which established the first clear roles for women in the military in 1901. This was followed by the Navy's acceptance of women in 1908, which saw the establishment of the Navy Nurse Corps (Bureau of Medicine and Surgery, 1945).

The First World War to Vietnam

During the First World War, 34,000 women served in nearly all military branches but were offered no recognition, as evidenced by the absence of any rank or military benefits. During the Second World War, there was a dramatic rise in the number of women veterans, with 350,000 serving throughout the war, primarily in the Nurse Corps. By 1943, women were recognized as members of the military, giving rise to the Women's Army Corps (WAC); this was preceded by the Women's Army Auxiliary Corps (WAAC), Women Air Force Service Pilots (WASPS), Women Accepted for Volunteer Emergency Service (WAVES), and other women's reserve units (New Mexico Department of Veterans Services, 2011).

In 1948, the Women's Armed Services Integration Act established women as permanent members of the Armed Forces (U.S. Marine Corps, 1948). This was yet another step closer to United States entry into the Korean War. At the onset of this conflict, 22,000 women were serving in the military, rising to approximately 48,700 at its most active period. At this time, the Defense Department Advisory Committee on Women in the Services (DACOWITS) (U.S Department of Defense, n.d.) was created to address issues surrounding women and retention, recruitment and integration; this, in turn, allowed outdated policies and regulations to be reviewed and amended for the benefit of women veterans.

The Vietnam War

During the Vietnam War, the demand for women to serve in the wartime theater rose once again. This time, however, additional roles were created for women as a result of societal changes. This included a greater momentum towards gender equality. After years of confronting obstacles in achieving higher military rank, regulations began to change, allowing officers such as Brigadier General Anna Mae Hays to become the first female one-star general in the U.S. Army in 1970 (U.S. Army Medical Department, Office of Military History, n.d.). In 1972, Rear Admiral Alene B. Duerk (McDaniel, 2003) became the first woman to be promoted to the rank of admiral, followed by the first one-star general for the Air Force, Brigadier General E. Ann Hoefly, that same year (U.S. Air Force web site, n.d.).

Post-Vietnam

Throughout the 1970s, the gradual promotion of female officers continued. And while archaic barriers still remained, women continued to break through the glass ceiling. During the Gulf War of 1990–1991, we saw yet another milestone of achievement when a great number of women were deployed in time of war. Almost 41,000 women served in roles that placed them directly in harm's way (Maupin, 2011). Bans on women serving in combat-related roles were lifted in 1994 after female service members demonstrated to promote change of their roles (New Mexico Department of Veterans Services, 2011).

Iraq and Afghanistan

The commencement of the Global War on Terrorism in 2001 launched an era of women serving in direct combat operations in both Afghanistan and in Iraq (Bowman & Dale, 2009). By 2005, the Army had created the Combat Action Badge (U.S. Army website, 2011), designed for non-infantry soldiers—including women—who were exposed to direct combat operations but were still barred from direct combat by Department of Defense policies.

Team Lioness

The needs on the ground in Iraq and Afghanistan resulted in the incorporation of women into ground combat operations in what was coined "Team Lioness." These were female soldiers, initially attached to Marine infantry units, who trained to conduct house raids, personnel searches and checkpoint operations—all of which often resulted in direct contact with insurgents and other enemy forces. Such teams were not officially "assigned," which made it quite difficult for women to prove their service in direct combat upon returning home and attempting to acquire benefits. Attachments such as Team Lioness were expanded into other branches of the Armed Forces, but the Marine Corps quickly adopted the program and made it an official enterprise, with extensive training and preparation, incorporating Marine Corps martial arts techniques and language classes (Aranda, 2008).

Female Engagement Teams (FETs)

FETs (Kelleher, 2011) were utilized in similar capacity as Team Lioness, thereby creating another milestone for women in terms of surpassing barriers and addressing a much needed policy update on women serving in combat (the policy update is still uncertain and the DOD missed the deadline for the report submission in October of 2011 [Bacon, 2011b]).

The number of women serving in our Armed Forces today is unprecedented. After years of struggle, we have finally witnessed the lifting of the ban on women serving in combat, a change long overdue after the demonstrated need for women in combat roles and their capacity to serve—let alone the fact that women have already been serving in direct combat operations, but without acknowledgement. Certainly the evidence for this has been unmistakable, as shown by the sustained performance of women on the battlefields of both Iraq and Afghanistan. Approximately 200,000 women have been deployed in support of Operations Iraqi Freedom and Enduring Freedom (Afghanistan) (Foster & Vince, 2009b).

Facing the facts and figures today

One can continue to look back not only on the past few decades, but for centuries to take stock of the large magnitude of historical contributions made by women. It is also important to bear in mind DOD figures and VA reports on women's service to become acutely aware of the absolute need to prepare our women veterans to properly reintegrate. The debates on whether or not women should serve in combat are now moot. We have a new generation of women veterans who have served in direct combat, a feat that was made possible by women veterans who paved the way through multiple battlefields in numerous conflicts throughout American history. Therefore, the military, the VA and civilian health professionals must both understand and be responsive to the specialized mental health needs of the women who have served in the wartime theater and in combat.

According to the U.S. Department of Veterans Affairs (VA), the number of female veterans is expected to grow to 2.1 million (15.2 percent) in 2036 (Foster & Vince, 2009b). As of 2011, women veterans represent 14 percent of active duty forces and 18 percent of the National Guard and Reserve forces (ibid.). Twenty percent of new recruits are women, 11 percent are single parents (compared to four percent of their male counterparts), and the numbers of women deployed in time of war increased from 41,000 in the Gulf War to 200,000 during Operation Iraqi Freedom, Operation Enduring Freedom, and Operation New Dawn. The average age of female veterans is 47 (ibid.), as compared with the male average age of 61, bringing a younger veteran cohort to veteran service facilities. Women represent the fastest growing veteran population segment. However, various public and private institutions still maintain programs with male-centered treatment and lack facilities and trained professionals who are prepared to meet the distinct needs of women veterans.

Employment and opportunities

A major part of one's reintegration into the community following service in the military is the ability to acquire and maintain employment. The average income for female veterans is $31,925, compared to $42,416 for male veterans (U.S. Department of Labor, Women's Bureau (2010). This is a significant gap, but the root causes have yet to be explained. While one might believe that service to our country would be an excellent point on a résumé, there remains considerable reluctance on the part of employers to incorporate veterans into the workplace, let alone address the topic of recruiting women veterans. With such a discrepancy in income between male and female veterans, one could extrapolate that the same is true for opportunities in general, including military service opportunities that remain closed to women.

Case example: A disturbing employment interview

During an interview I undertook with a particular agency, which conducted a thorough background investigation, including a polygraph test, I heard one of the most offensive questions yet posed to me since returning from Iraq. The polygraph specialist, a former long-time field agent himself, did not ask the dreaded "Did you kill anyone?" question, but very plainly asked something I deemed to be quite inappropriate. He inquired about my activities in Iraq, the missions I had performed while I was on Team Lioness, and my familiarity with Middle Eastern culture. I had been at ease and confident that the job I was aiming for—a position in the Middle Eastern sector of this agency—was going to work out. However, after we had a long discussion about my military background, he paused, looked at me, and said, "I just don't know how to feel about hiring you. Can you imagine how threatening your service would be to the experience of others around you? Perhaps even be detrimental to office morale?" I was beginning to think, "So I'm good enough to die on a battlefield for this country, but not good enough to work in your office?"

Needless to say, my motivation and desire to work for this agency dissipated rapidly. The last I heard, this agency ended up hiring someone I knew who was male. He had only been outside the country twice, knew no other languages aside from some rudimentary Russian, and was still very much "wet behind the ears" in terms of life and professional experience. No wonder our nation's intelligence assets are constantly under fire. They would sooner take an inexperienced "yes man" than an experienced female combat veteran who has traveled to more than 20 countries and speaks several languages.

Female veterans and employment obstacles

Unfortunately, my experience with this agency was not an uncommon story. Female veterans between the ages of 18 and 24 have an unemployment rate of 16 percent, twice the average of non-veterans and significantly higher than their male veteran counterparts of the same age group (U.S. Department of Labor, 2011). While I have asked both male and female veterans about the hurdles they face in obtaining employment, there is a common thread that is still not discussed openly or reported. "Who wants to hire a veteran with PTSD? They'll flip out in the office, won't they?" It is truly a sad commentary that this is the prevailing ignorance veterans are forced to tolerate. I have heard this personally, even from people with whom I was working. That this stems from a lack of education is only a small portion of the problem in various places of employment, from federal government agencies to nonprofit organizations. After all, who is to say that a veteran seeking employment even suffers from PTSD or that they don't have their symptoms under control? Any non-veteran looking for employment could very well be less functional as an employee and could suffer from some form of severe mental illness. To discriminate on the basis of one's military service, regardless of gender, is an egregious act.

Women veterans, despite the historical facts and figures, are still new or perhaps even absent in the psyche of the general American public. Perhaps such members of our communities, including employers, fear and/or are prejudiced about that which they do not know with respect to women in combat roles or as veterans. Again, this is another symptom of the categorical ignorance of the American public at large. This leaves a marked lack of exposure to and awareness of all that women veterans bring to the table and ultimately bars or severely handicaps them from potential opportunities for professional development, growth and proper community reintegration.

Homelessness

When addressing the issue of unemployment and the potential repercussions for women veterans, particularly those with children, the question of homelessness is another important factor to consider. Out of 136,334 homeless veterans (National Coalition for Homeless Veterans, 2011), who comprise 33 percent of our nation's total homeless population, women comprise 13,100 (Service Women's Action Network, 2011). Female veterans have a greater risk of homelessness than male veterans and since the wars in Iraq and Afghanistan, those figures are steadily climbing (Agha, 2011).

Traumatic experiences prior to, during and following military service appear to be a common factor in adding to these figures. Many women join the military to escape physically, sexually, and/or emotionally abusive situations and an unstable home life. This appears to be reflective of general problems in our society, as opposed to an overrepresentation of such women in the military (SAMSHA, 2011). If one adds Military Sexual Trauma (MST) to this experience, the risk for Post-Traumatic Stress Disorder (PTSD) is increased ninefold, leading to an increase in the potential for problems with substance abuse, lower economical and educational achievements, difficulties in interpersonal relationships and maintaining safe and secure housing.

As female veterans readjust to civilian life, it is vital to take these factors into consideration. Adequate medical and mental health care is of the utmost importance in order to address psychological symptom management, especially in terms of readjustment to civilian life and the ability both to maintain employment and secure safe housing. Since homelessness among female veterans is a growing issue of concern, community resources and healthcare providers would do well to maintain the most up-to-date information in order to address this population and to provide appropriate care and treatment of trauma and gender-specific issues by educated direct service providers.

Marriage, relationships and family

Relationship Struggles

In a videotaping session about the positive effects of combat veteran peer support, I had the privilege of sitting with a female Iraq War veteran, with whom I shared one of the more enlightening conversations regarding relationship struggles as a female veteran. We were surrounded by cameras and production-crew members, while we took turns discussing the problems we had faced. We could have discussed anything in our 45-minute session, but we chose to go straight for the "relationship jugular." In a matter of a few minutes, we discovered that we had considerable and startling experiences in common.

Since returning from Iraq, we had both dealt with a significant number of situations where men seemed intimidated by our combat experiences—seemingly to the point where they felt emasculated or determined to devalue our experience as some sort of "defense mechanism." Both of us had met men who seemed to be fond of us until they found out about our combat tours of duty in Iraq. Some even sought to physically or emotionally abuse us as a result.

Is it that women serving in the military are quite threatening to a number of men because of the prescribed roles women are "expected" to serve in society? I have found that my duty in Iraq is intimidating to most men and leaves them believing that women veterans who have been in combat "have nothing to teach us." (This belief or attitude is quite problematic for women veterans who are seeking a partner, not a teacher or a master!) In short, our experiences seemed to demonstrate that most men, in one way or another, did not handle our résumés very well.

Another point was that we ourselves were disinterested in their military experiences or lack thereof—all we wanted was to engage in happy, fulfilling relationships. From co-dependent types, to sociopaths, to abusers and users— we had seen them all and we were waiting patiently for someone who seemed somewhat more normal and genuine.

Near the end of the interaction, and after a few zany and sometimes tragic stories of love gone wrong that left the crew giggling or shaking their heads, this fellow female veteran said something that has always remained with me as a personal truth: "I don't want a father in a partner. I've got a father. I don't want to look after my partner like a son. I'd like a son one day, but my own. I want an equal to walk beside me, not in front of me or behind me. And I won't accept anyone who I can't look in the eyes and not feel that way."

The statistics on women veterans and marriage

After hearing that morsel of truthful goodness, I have kept what my fellow woman veteran said in mind. Yet when observing the growing number of broken homes and families of women veterans, I believe this subject needs much further elucidation. Statistics reveal a clear pattern. Women veterans are more likely to be single parents than male veterans (11 percent versus 4 percent) and are less likely to be married than their civilian counterparts by the age of 44 (51.5 percent versus 69.9 percent—a pattern that begins after age 33). Statistics reveal that the overall divorce rate among female military personnel is markedly higher than for their male counterparts, as well as their civilian counterparts (Associated Press, 2011). By the age of 27, 65.3 percent of active duty males were married, compared with 33.3 percent of male civilians—a 32 percent difference (U.S. Department of Defense, 2009). By the age of 44, the percentage difference between married active duty males and civilian males decreases to 19.7 percent. By the age of 44, 69.9 percent of civilian females were married, versus 51.5 percent of active duty females (ibid.). Beginning at age 18, active duty females are more likely to be married than civilian counterparts through the age of 33. Yet from age 33 on, active duty females are less likely to be married than female civilians counterparts (ibid.). What causes the rift after age 33 for these active duty females, and enlisted women especially? This raises the question of why female veterans are more likely to be divorced than male veterans.

Distinctive family stressors facing women in the military

Female service members and veterans face stresses and challenges that are similar to their male counterparts, such as relocations, frequent separations, overseas deployments, home life pressures and heavy occupational demands. The statistics on broken relationships and homes need to be addressed in a much broader context, one which can be addressed only superficially here.

Military life is filled with stressors that impact both men and women, but for women service members married to military personnel, the challenge of separate duty assignments and differing career goals and demands adds a significant amount of pressure, in addition to the expected challenges faced in non-military marriages or relationships. For women service members who are married to civilian men, the challenges that stem from being the spouse of a service member as a male and being able to adjust to military-dependent life should be thoroughly examined. More research is needed on the topic of higher divorce rates and relationship struggles amongst female veterans; speculation on this subject matter alone could readily encompass an additional chapter to this volume.

Finding a partner

And so, within the context of the issues discussed above, and from personal experience and after sharing ideas with other female veterans for years, I hypothesize that women service members and women veterans may have significant difficulties in finding a partner who is secure enough in who they are as an individual to accept us as we would accept them. There are a number of men who appear uncomfortable with women veterans who have been able to succeed in the male-dominated military system; they seem to find this troubling or challenging to their own sense of self. I have been proud of what I have accomplished, both personally and professionally, and have no desire to pick someone apart for their achievements in life—or the absence of them. Like other women veterans, I simply wish to find a partner who I could consider an equal and who would reciprocate this sentiment.

Female veterans and children

The issue of having children raises another concern when addressing interpersonal relationships; the breakdown of family structures and support networks becomes even more complicated for female veterans with children who are minors. More than 40 percent of female veterans have children (Pellerin, 2011) and approximately 30,000 single mothers have been deployed (Glantz, 2009). Because women veterans who have the need for childcare and other support services comprise a smaller population within the military, a lack of access to programs can be problematic, making it difficult for them to properly address other aspects of reintegration because these very basic needs are unmet. Homeless female veterans face a further barrier in finding shelters that are safe for both them and their minor children.

And so, family dynamics, relationship difficulties and obstacles in obtaining adequate childcare continue to be major challenges for female veterans and another of a series of struggles that demand further investigation.

Military Sexual Trauma (MST)

There is an entire chapter in this book dedicated to the subject of MST (Chapter 10). However, MST is so prevalent, and the harm caused by it so severe, that it would be a gross oversight not to at least briefly discuss it here (or in any writings regarding women service members and women veterans). In addition, the trauma of MST is often problematic for many women veterans who experience some of the other issues and challenges described here, such as homelessness, employment problems, marriage and relationship difficulties, war-related PTSD, mTBI, and other service-related conditions—all of which may be further complicated by being the member of an ethnic or racial minority.

The statistics are sobering. Of all female veterans of all eras, *one in three* has reported the experience of sexual assault. This is in comparison to one in six within the female civilian population (Maze, 2011). Sexual harassment and assault of women in the military have become emphasized and elucidated in recent years. And while this problem is in dire need of attention, it is also important to highlight the plight of male veterans who have fallen victim to MST.

Under U.S. Code 1720D of Title 38, Military Sexual Trauma is defined as "psychological trauma, which in the judgment of a VA mental health professional, resulted from a physical assault of a sexual nature, battery of a sexual nature, or sexual harassment which occurred while the veteran was serving on active duty or active duty for training."[1] MST affects both female and male veterans. Some 22 percent of females and 1.2 percent of males have reported incidences of MST, according to the Veterans Health Administration (Kimerling *et al.*, 2007). Out of 2,212 MST cases in 2007, only 8 percent (181) of these reported incidents have gone to trial. In 2009, there were 3,230 MST cases reported, according to the Service Women's Action Network (Stalzberg, 2010). Only 20 percent of assaults are ever reported, with a 64 percent increase of incidents from 2008 to 2009. Only 8 percent of perpetrators ever face prosecution (ibid.).

The number of cases that have been "swept under the rug" by corrupt military commands or others with questionable leadership capabilities severely hinders justice. Many cases are still being investigated following military service and organizations such as Service Women's Action Network (SWAN), a New York-based national nonprofit association, offer services to women service members and veterans needing advocacy. According to SWAN, one in three female veterans faces some form of sexual assault, while 66 percent face harassment. MST includes any sexual activity in which someone is involved against their will (ibid.).

Based upon the statistics, it is safe to say that the annual mandatory check-the-box briefings instilled by the military to cover MST are simply not enough to drive the point home that MST is a crime. Military legal authorities must also *enforce* these regulations; however, judging by the numbers of cases that go to trial, there appears to be a great lack of oversight.

Not only are women veterans forced to deal with the deleterious effects of combat stress, PTSD, Traumatic Brain Injury (TBI) and numerous other issues that stem from military service (including MST), they also have to face an appallingly inadequate response to MST. According to VA mental health statistics in 2010, 54.4 percent of female veterans reported a MST-related encounter; and while not nearly as high, more than a third of male veterans (37.6 percent) reported an MST-related encounter. These figures are even

---

1   This is what the U.S. code states, but it should apply to the DOD as well.

higher for OIF/OEF/OND female and male veterans—MST incidents were reported at 58.4 percent and 48.3 percent respectively. When examining the rates for homeless veterans, the figures are even more disturbing: 87.2 percent of female veterans and 77.5 percent of male veterans reported MST incidents that occurred at least once in the span of their military service (Stalzberg, 2011).

While much more attention needs to be paid to MST, there is one issue concerning MST and media outlets that I have found to be incompatible in promoting gender equality in the military. When observing the achievements of women veterans, it is usually the case that MST dominates and overshadows anything else we have experienced or contributed as women veterans. For example, it can be overlooked that we might have experienced significant combat-related trauma, been subject to prejudice as women in the male-dominated military culture, been discriminated against in receiving fair performance appraisals, and been denied promotion opportunities because of our gender.

Of course, MST is a subject that should be investigated and discussed at much greater depth. However, this should not be at the expense of recognizing and attending to other types of military-related trauma exposure, gender and racial discrimination, or appreciating the tremendous contributions and historical milestones that are the credit of women in uniform. When studying the impact of MST, let none of us forget that we are so impacted, female and male veterans alike, because we are "victims" of this crime of aggression and violence and it occurs in a culture and system that much too frequently allows the perpetrators to escape any justice. Also, we are all survivors. With the promotion of MST awareness and the proper legal follow-up of both civilian and military legal entities, MST survivors can become leaders and continue making tremendous contributions as they have throughout their military service and after their re-entry to the civilian world—if we intervene legally, educationally, and therapeutically.

Cultural diversity

Many people have asked why I chose to leave the Army. I have to admit that there were plenty of times when I enjoyed my military service, made meaningful and lasting friendships in training and on the battlefield, and experienced both positive and negative events that have shaped the person I am today. However, there is a main reason why I left the military as soon as my ETS (discharge) date arrived, snubbing thousands of dollars in re-enlistment bonuses without a second thought. It was not the issue of combat exposure or the possibility of multiple deployments that deterred me from staying. It was racial discrimination.[2]

Being someone from a diverse cultural background, others often mistake my ethnicity for another. From Chinese to Mexican, Iraqi to Roma—you name it, I probably have been mistaken for it at one point or another. I have heard people instantly scoff at this reason for their own personal prejudices or ignorance, sometimes labeling me as a "sensitive minority" or citing their adherence to the notion that we live in a "post-racial society." Post-racial for whom? And when did having a promotion packet thrown away seven times, without cause, by a predominantly white, female command, and facing false UCMJ (Uniform Code of Military Justice) accusations after reporting discrimination and slurs make one merely sensitive? Calling me a "sensitive minority" was calling me *over*-sensitive to race-based remarks and related acts of bigotry. It was an attitude that reflected the belief that anyone of non-Anglo Saxon descent is *over*-sensitive and should just accept racist comments and related acts of bigotry.

Racism in Iraq

My deployment to Iraq involved quite a significant amount of bigotry by a command that was based in the Baghdad International Zone or "Green Zone," while I was serving on far more dangerous missions with Marines in the Al Anbar Province. The combination of not only being an ethnic minority but also a woman was not the main issue that my former command had constantly targeted—it was the fact that I was a minority female who was tactically and technically proficient, a fully capable soldier. Due to their limited views on minority women, my command felt threatened not only by me, but also by other personnel who fit a similar description, including an officer whom they had also persecuted along eerily similar grounds. There were no reasons to punish women like us, but the fact that we were capable soldiers who happened to be minority women was "offensive" to this bigoted command.

Without going into every painful detail of what transpired, let us just say that the treatment I received and the persecution I faced, based on my physical traits as a minority, were ruthless enough for me to leave a military I once loved. Race remains a "hot" issue but it is often pushed aside, not only in the

---

2   There has been one study of racism experienced in the military and the relationship to war-related PTSD. This was a study of Asian American Vietnam veterans (Loo *et al.*, 2001). Note-worthy about the findings is that experiencing racism from fellow service members while deployed to Vietnam *was the most significant stressor* associated with the development of PTSD—even more so than exposure to combat stressors, hence revealing how damaging racism by American Soldiers against fellow American Soldiers is to date. For diagnostic and treatment strategies and suggestions when working with racial minority veterans exposed to race-related stressors, see Loo *et al.*, 1998).

military, but in society as a whole. This is evidenced by an evasion of the topic whenever I have addressed this traumatic part of my overseas experience with individuals working with VA, nonprofit, or media resources.

The statistics

Fourteen percent of women veterans describe themselves as multi-racial and the highest enlisting ethnic groups per capita for women veterans are Native Americans and Pacific Islanders (Department of the Interior, Office of Insular Affairs, 2010; Department of Veteran Affairs, Rural Health, 2011). As a Pacific Islander (Pacific Islanders' Cultural Association, 2009) myself (Chamorro—indigenous to the Mariana Islands), I am often erroneously grouped in with Asians—a completely different ethnicity. But this is still unbeknownst to what seems like the majority of those I encounter—and calling someone something they are not is certainly not the best way to build rapport. Being culturally aware is something that would behoove any provider, regardless of their experience with veterans, as it can make or break trust and rapport instantly. There have been instances where others don the "Pacific Islander" ethnicity until they are otherwise discovered. This characteristically ends in the type of embarrassment experienced by those with no Native American ancestry who falsely claim Pocahontas or Sitting Bull as an ancestor in front of someone who actually is Native American.

In terms of overall ethnic diversity, 36 percent of active duty forces and 30.2 percent of Reserve forces originate from racial/ethnic minorities (America's Promise Alliance, 2011). African Americans account for 19.8 percent of active duty minorities, followed by Hispanics at 13.5 percent (U.S. Army Corps of Engineers, 2011) and other racial categories account for more than 5 percent. African Americans make up 22 percent of the reserve component forces, followed by Hispanics at 9.8 percent and all other minorities at 5 percent (ibid.). When examining racial categories, it often becomes difficult to further assess after Caucasians, African Americans and Hispanics have been accounted for without leaving room for error in addressing minority female veteran issues. Non-white female vets are expected to increase to 44 percent in 2020, compared to 37 percent for male counterparts (Foster & Vince, 2009b). Thus, there is an ever increasing need for awareness of cultural diversity within the female veteran population. If someone seems fixated on placing me (or many other ethnic minority service members or veterans) into a checkbox that has nothing to do with me, you can forget and disregard any and all discussion about what happened in Iraq.

LGBTQ and repeal of "Don't Ask, Don't Tell"

Similar hurdles and struggles in diversifying care and focusing on individualized treatment can be identified with the LGBTQ (Lesbian, Gay, Bisexual,

Transgender/Transsexual/Two-Spirited, Queer/Questioning) community of veterans who have a sexual orientation other than heterosexual. With the recent repeal of "Don't Ask, Don't Tell" (DADT), at last we are witnessing an end to at least one form of institutional discrimination. Of course, DADT in and of itself may or may not actually impact significantly those discriminatory attitudes and behaviors that are more subtle. Even so, DADT certainly denotes promise for those of us seeking justice who have endured racial discrimination. While LGBTQ veterans will continue to face issues involving prejudice and discrimination, hopefully this change in policy will help to give attention to the multitude of challenges surrounding everyone who has faced injustice at the hands of bigoted and/or racist commands and prejudiced personnel. Organizations such as SWAN have committed themselves to monitoring progress and policy changes with LGBTQ veterans and offer services involving peer support and legal counseling.

Reintegration and challenges

The military experiences of each individual are vastly different, with a huge range of variation in exposure to emotional and/or physical trauma. In turn, not everyone is ready to share their experiences and may need time to process difficulties in accordance with their individual needs. Furthermore, it may be difficult to share experiences with those who may not understand—this refers to both VA healthcare professionals and civilian providers. Vulnerability, loneliness, interpersonal difficulties, financial problems, instability and a lack of a sense of belonging are just a few of the things one could be facing in the reintegration process. Separation from military service and re-entry into civilian life and work present many difficulties for female veterans, and it can potentially take years before economic, emotional and interpersonal stability can be achieved.

Reintegration undeniably carries with it a variety of challenges that families, loved ones and communities must prepare for, but addressing the individual's needs and aiding in the transition process may require a more holistic approach. Female veterans clearly require assistance at different times in their lives beyond military service and depend greatly on their economic, educational, interpersonal and dependent status. Access to gender-specific and family-oriented care is of the utmost importance for female veterans. Living within a community that is prepared to meet those challenges through proper training and educational awareness is far more likely to ensure the success of a female veteran transitioning into civilian life.

Benefits and VA access for female veterans

Other possible barriers that have come to light in recent years include the question of benefits and VA access for female veterans. From requiring MST counselors on site at VA healthcare facilities to establishing women's clinics, such responses certainly have been a long time in coming, considering how long women have been contributing to the security of this country by serving in the Armed Forces. This is just the beginning, and constantly aiming towards improved and effective treatment options should be of great interest and concern to both public and private providers if female veterans are to gain full access to proper care.

According to the VA Office of the Inspector General, The Veterans Benefits Administration (VBA) is more likely to deny female veterans' disability claims for PTSD than male veterans' claims, while they often deny male veterans' disability claims for other mental health conditions (excluding PTSD) (Department of Veterans Affairs, Office of the Inspector General, 2011). Unfortunately, the VBA does not retain historical data on its denial decisions and many female MST cases have not been addressed when filing for PSTD. One may ask when the VA Office of the Inspector General will begin requiring reasons for the greater denial of PTSD and MST-related claims for women?

Whose concern is it?

Reintegration is not just a matter of concern for the military, VA or any civilian organization providing medical and/or mental health care. It is everyone's business. A successful veteran is also a successful citizen who can contribute to making a community stronger and more vibrant. Facing the challenges surrounding female veterans, including those who have actively engaged in direct combat operations, is vital to this success. With the necessary and appropriate education, attitudes and methodology for addressing individual needs, we may all be successful in these endeavors.

We can continue to rely on studies conducted by private institutions or government agencies that will tell us the facts and figures on suicide, homelessness, MST or any other issues a veteran may have faced. Or, we can take a far more proactive stance and directly involve ourselves in helping veterans. The main factor that aids in the steady climb of women veterans continuing to face discrimination, isolation and sub-par care is the citizens of the United States doing nothing. If the aforementioned topics and statistics bother you, *do something about it.* Do not wait for someone to ask you; do not wait for a friend, family member or co-worker to become a statistic. Get involved.

Remember, the emotions female service members and veterans experience during the cycles of deployment and military service are normal reactions to abnormal situations, unique to military personnel. If a female service member or veteran experiences combat stress, MST, or gender, employment and/or racial/ethnic/sexual orientation discrimination and these remain untreated, this will surely and seriously interfere with community reintegration and rehabilitation. No veteran, female or male, should have to go it alone.

Closing

Discussing women veterans' history, MST, homelessness, diversity, family issues and so much more in terms of the special challenges this population must confront, we can elicit far more conversation than this chapter permits, extending a brief page or two into volumes of intensive studies and an examination of the difficulties female veterans face. Understanding trauma and its impact on the female veteran population is essential to properly educate any entity providing support services, from psychosocial rehabilitation to education to benefits access.

Female veterans require female-specific services and providers could greatly benefit from using peer support programs among other female veterans in order to build a sense of community and a stronger support network. Understanding military culture is also key for non-veteran and non-military providers in any community. Trauma-informed care is essential in any community-based treatment and bearing military service-related challenges in mind is crucial in discovering how a female veteran may overcome her personal set of challenges. If you have noticed the increased use of the word "understanding" in the past few lines, I commend you. Just keep in mind that anything you take away from this chapter involves just that in successful female veteran reintegration.

If there is anything I might leave with a provider, loved one or family member of a returning female service member or veteran in terms of advice, this would be it:

DON'T
- Judge them entirely or predominantly based upon their military service. Like diagnoses, keep things in first-person language. There is more to female veterans than their military experiences.
- Ask them if they've killed anyone.
- Be flippant in your personal views on current events, politics, etc. Avoid it.
- Ask them to explain the basics of military structure and facts. There are many resources that anyone can access online and educating yourself is a great step in understanding.

DO
- Be patient with female service members and veterans.
- Respect them if they do not want to talk about traumatic events right away.
- Let them know they are respected and valued.
- Become familiar with female-friendly veterans' resources in your area.
- Keep up-to-date on military and veterans' mental health initiatives.

Much of this information was not as accessible, or so I had thought, when I returned from Iraq in 2005. I have come to realize that, like a lot of other combat veterans, I was far less focused on "proper veteran reintegration and rehabilitation" and far more centered on how alone I felt. There was such an enormous amount of survivor's guilt, anger and frustration with adjusting to civilian life; consequently, it was difficult to process any new information, or to connect with anyone personally who had not served in combat with me. Even so, for the most part, I have to say that I feel lucky; lucky that I had a strong cultural foundation to support me, an inclination towards fine arts and writing that served as a pressure valve to express myself, and people who never stopped believing in me.

However, there are plenty of veterans out there who are not so fortunate. Without the proper social support, basic necessities and anything else one can allude to in Maslow's hierarchy of needs, veterans will continue to slip through the cracks. This is, without question, a tragedy that our country must no longer turn a blind eye to—it requires action from all of us. It is essential for all of us to become more aware of effective coping mechanisms, various networking channels and veterans' assistance resources in our communities and geographic areas. As a community, we are all needed to help "expand the circle" to ensure the successful transition of female service members and veterans from any form of trauma or experience to becoming effective leaders and contributors to our society as a whole.

Michelle Wilmot was an Army medic, mental health sergeant and retention NCO for eight years. She was a member of Team Lioness while deployed (Iraq, 2004–2005). She received the 2009 Outstanding Woman Veteran Award, State of Massachusetts, for her service in the military and veteran community. Of Chamorro descent, Michelle speaks several languages and has a political science degree with a specialty in Middle Eastern studies. She is writing a book about her experiences (MichelleWilmot@yahoo.com).

Bibliography

Agha, M. (2011). Transition to civilian life challenging for homeless female veterans. *The Sacramento Bee*. Retrieved from www.sacbee.com/2011/03/06/3452876/transition-to-civilian-life-challenging.html

America's Promise Alliance (2011). *U.S. Military Demographics*. Retrieved from www.americaspromise.org/Our-Work/Military-Families/Military-Families-by-the-Numbers.aspx

Aranda, J. (2008). Lioness Program trains, maintains female search team. Operation New Dawn website. Retrieved from www.usf-iraq.com/?option=com_content&task=view&id=20372&Itemid=128

Associated Press (2011). Females in military struggle with higher divorce rate. *USA Today*. Retrieved from *www.usatoday.com/news/military/2011-03-08-Female-military-divorce_N.htm*

Bacon, L. (2011a). Odierno backs expanding role of women in combat. *Army Times*. Retrieved from www.armytimes.com/news/2011/10/army-ray-odierno-endorses-expanding-women-role-in-combat-102211w

Bacon, L. (2011b). DOD misses deadline for women-in-combat report. *Army Times*. Retrieved from www.armytimes.com/news/2011/11/army-dod-misses-deadline-for-women-in-combat-report-111711w

Berkin, C. (2006). *Revolutionary Mothers: Women in the Struggle for America's Independence*. New York, NY: Vintage Books.

Bowman, S. & Dale, C. (2009). *War in Afghanistan: Strategy, Military Operations, and Issues for Congress*. Congressional Research Service. Washington, DC. Retrieved from www.fas.org/sgp/crs/row/R40156.pdf

Bureau of Medicine and Surgery (1945). White task force: The story of the Nurse Corps, United States Navy. *NAVMED 939*. U.S. Navy.

Department of the Interior, Office of Insular Affairs (2010). *U.S. Military Veterans Honored in Micronesia—FSM citizen and other Pacific Islanders Serve in U.S. military at higher per-capita rate than U.S. citizens*. Retrieved from www.doi.gov/oia/Firstpginfo/islanders_in_the_military/111810.html

Department of Veterans Affairs, National Center for PTSD (n.d.). *Military Culture*. Retrieved from www.ptsd.va.gov/professional/ ptsd101/course-modules/military_culture.asp

Department of Veterans Affairs, Office of the Inspector General (2011). *Review of Combat Stress in Women Veterans Receiving VA Health Care and Disability Benefits*. Retrieved from www.va.gov/oig/52/reports/2011/VAOIG-10-01640-45.pdf

Department of Veterans Affairs, Rural Health (2011). *Frequently Asked Questions*. Retrieved from www.ruralhealth.va.gov/native/frequent.asp#who

Foster, L. & Vince, S. (2009a). *California's Women Veterans: The Challenges and Needs of Those Who Served*. California Research Bureau. Sacramento, CA. Retrieved from www.library.ca.gov/crb/09/09-009.pdf

Foster, L. & Vince, S. (2009b). *Women Veterans by the Numbers*. California Research Bureau. Sacramento, CA. Retrieved from www.library.ca.gov/crb/09/WomenVeteransBreiflyStated.pdf

Glantz, A. (2009). Report: 30,000 Single mothers deployed to Iraq, Afghanistan. *The Huffington Post*. Retrieved from www.huffingtonpost.com/aaron-glantz/report-30000-single-mothe_b_322185.html

Holmstedt, K. (2007). *Band of Sisters: American Women at War in Iraq*. Mechanicsburg, PA: Stackpole Books.

Keleher, K. (2011). Female engagement team leads the way in Afghanistan. *DOD Live*. Retrieved from www.dodlive.mil/index.php/2011/07/female-engagement-team-lead-the-way-in-afghanistan

Kimerling, R., Gima, K., Smith, M. W., Street, A. & Frayne, S. (2007). The Veterans Health Administration and Military Sexual Trauma. *American Journal of Public Health, 97*(12), 2160–2166.

Loo, C., Singh, K., Scurfield, R. M. & Kilauano, B. (1998). Race-related stress among Asian American veterans: A model to enhance diagnosis and treatment. *Cultural Diversity and Mental Health, 4*(2), 75–90.

Loo, C., Fairbank, J., Scurfield, R., Ruch, L., King, D., Adams, L. & Chemtob, C. (2001). Measuring exposure to racism: Development and validation of a race-related stressor scale (RRSS) for Asian American Vietnam veterans. *Psychological Assessment, 13*(4), 503–520.

McCutcheon, S. & Pavao, J. (2011). *Resources for Military Sexual Trauma (MST) survivors.* Presentation to the National Training Summit on Women Veterans. Retrieved from www.va.gov/WOMENVET/2011Summit/Breakout-ResourcesforMSTSurvivors2011.pdf

McDaniel, E. (2003). *Registered Nurse to Rear Admiral.* Waco, TX: Eakin Press.

McMichael, W. (2009). Military struggles to recruit Hispanics. *Army Times.* Retrieved from www.armytimes.com/news/2009/01/army_hispanics_020209w

Maupin, L. (2011). Military women: Critical analysis. *News Hour Extra, PBS.* Retrieved from www.pbs.org/newshour/extra/teachers/lessonplans/iraq/women_4-2.html

Maze, R. (2011). VA revising sexual assault claims process. *Army Times.* Retrieved from www.armytimes.com/news/2011/10/military-va-revising-sexual-assault-claims-process-101811

National Coalition for Homeless Veterans (2011). *HUD, VA Release Supplemental Report on Veteran Homelessness.* Washington, DC. Retrieved from www.nchv.org/news_article.cfm?id=863

New Mexico Department of Veterans Services (2011). A brief history of women in the Armed Forces. Retrieved from www.dvs.state.nm.us/womenvets.html

Pacific Islanders' Cultural Association (2009). *The Pacific Islands.* Retrieved from www.pica-org.org/Terms/terms.htm

Pellerin, C. (2011). *New guide helps communities aid homeless women vets.* American Forces Press Service. Retrieved from www.af.mil/news/story.asp?id=123264751

SAMSHA (2011). *Co-occurring disorders and military justice: Women veterans With co-occurring disorders.* Retrieved from www.samhsa.gov/co-occurring/topics/military-justice/women-veterans.aspx

Service Women's Action Network (2011). *Homeless women veterans: The facts.* Retrieved from http://servicewomen.org/wp-content/uploads/2011/09/HWVfactsheet.pdf

St. Clair Robson, L. (2008). *Ghost Warrior.* New York, NY: Forge Books.

Stalzberg, B. L. (2010). *Military Sexual Trauma (MST): The quick facts.* Service Women's National Network. Retrieved from www.vawnet.org/Assoc_Files_VAWnet/SWAN-MSTFactSheet.pdf

U.S. Air Force website (n.d.) *Brigadier General E. Ann Hoefly.* Retrieved from www.af.mil/information/bios/bio.asp?bioID=5823

U.S. Army Center of Military History (2011). *First female General in the U.S. Army.* Retrieved from www.history.army.mil/faq/FAQ-FemGO.htm

U.S. Army website (2011). Combat Action Badge. Retrieved from www.army.mil/symbols/CombatBadges/action.html

U.S. Army Corps of Engineers website (2011). *Building strong as one team.* Retrieved from *http://usace.armylive.dodlive.mil/index.php/2011/02*

U.S. Army Medical Department, Office of Military History (n.d.). *Embracing the past: First Chief, Army Nurse Corps turns 90! Brigadier General Anna Mae. V. McCabe Hayes.* Retrieved from http://history.amedd.army.mil/HaysBio/HayesBio.html

U.S. Congress (1948). Public Law 625: The Women's Armed Services Integration Act of 1948. United States Marine Corps History Division. Retrieved from www.tecom.usmc.mil/HD/Docs_Speeches/Publiclaw625.htm

U.S. Department of Defense (n.d.). DACOWITS: Defense Advisory Committee on Women in the Services. Retrieved from http://dacowits.defense.gov

U.S. Department of Defense (2009). *Population Representation in the Military Services: Fiscal Year Report 2009.* Retrieved from http://prhome.defense.gov/MPP/ACCESSION%20POLICY/PopRep2009/summary/PopRep09Summ.pdf

U.S. Department of Labor, Women's Bureau (2010). *CA female veterans by the numbers.* The National Center on Family Homelessness. Retrieved from www.family-homelessness.org/media/175.pdf

U.S. Department of Labor, Women's Bureau (2011). *Trauma informed care for women veterans experiencing homelessness.* Retrieved from www.dol.gov/wb/trauma/WBTraumaGuide2011.pdf

U.S. Navy, Bureau of Medicine and Surgery (1945). *White Task Force: The Story of the Nurse Corps, United States Navy.* Washington, DC: Government Printing Office.

U.S. Marine Corps (1948). Public Law 625: The Women's Armed Services Integration Act of 1948. Retrieved from www.tecom.usmc.mil/HD/Docs_Speeches/Publiclaw625.htm

6   The Canadian military and veteran experience

Susan Brock & LCDR (RET) Greg Passey

This chapter is designed to provide the reader with an overview of Canada's military involvement in international conflicts, the psychological impact upon those involved and the development and adaptation of programs designed to address the needs of those injured as a result of their military service. Included are descriptions of Canada's Operational Stress Injury Social Support Program; the Third Location Decompression Program (TLD), which was developed in 2002 by the Department of National Defence to provide soldiers departing theatre with a rest and relaxation period prior to returning home to family; the CF (Canadian Forces) Member Assistance Program; and Military Family Resource Centres. Finally, two distinctive treatment approaches and illustrative clinical vignettes are described: Neurofeedback (NFB) and the Canadian Veteran Adventure Foundation, which has applied wilderness therapy programs to mentally and physically injured Canadian forces and veterans.

Military-related trauma and Canadian forces

Since 1956, over 120,000 Canadians have served in more than 50 operations mandated by the UN Security Council (United Nations, 2010). These deployments have occurred in many countries all around the world including, Cyprus, the Belgian Congo and Cambodia, and, more recently, East Timor, Haiti and the Sudan. Canada's commitment to peacekeeping has not been without sacrifice. As of 2008, Canada retains the second highest fatality rate among peacekeepers, having lost 114 soldiers. Fifty-three soldiers died during the mission to Egypt (UN Emergency Force in Egypt [UNEF]) between 1956 and 1967, and 11 died between 1974 and 1979. Twenty-eight soldiers died during the mission to Cypress (UN Force in Cyprus [UNFICYP]) between 1964 and 1993, and 11 died during the mission to the former Yugoslavia (UN Protection Force [UNPROFOR]) between 1992 and 1995 (United Nations Association in Canada, 2011).

Currently, more than 3,050 Canadian Army, Navy, and Air Force personnel are deployed overseas on operational missions, which typically last six months. More than 95 percent of the Canadian Forces personnel deployed are participating in the Afghanistan phase of Operation Enduring Freedom.

On any given day, about 8,000 Canadian Forces members—one third of our deployable force—are preparing for, engaged in, or returning from an overseas mission (Department of National Defence, 2011b). Since Canada's involvement in Afghanistan began in 2002, 159 Canadian Forces members have been killed (December, 2009) and as many as 65,000 Canadian soldiers will have served in Afghanistan by the time this current mission comes to an end (Department of National Defence, 2011b). Of those who have died, 130 were killed in enemy action and the remaining 24 perished in non-enemy actions, which included six friendly fire deaths, two suicides and three unspecified causes of death (Department of National Defence, 2011b).

The number of Canadian soldiers injured from the time the military deployed to Afghanistan in April of 2002 until 31 December 2009 was 1,442. Of these, 529 were wounded in action and 913 were considered non-battle injuries (those occurring as a result of traffic accidents, the accidental discharge of a weapon, any other accidental injuries unrelated to combat, such as illness or other medical reasons) (Department of National Defence, 2011b). There were no specific data regarding the percentage of those who were sent home for reasons of mental illness.

The rate of suicide in military members who served in Afghanistan or on other overseas missions is more difficult to determine, as is that of Reservists and veterans who also served overseas. There were 16 recorded suicides by Canadian Forces personnel in 2009, the highest annual number since tracking began in 1995. It is unknown, however, how many of these are linked to overseas deployments (O'Neill, 2010).

Discussion on treatment specific to military-related trauma was reborn in Canada in the 1990s, after having been nearly non-existent since the aftermath of the Second World War and the Korean War. By and large, the "treatment" for military personnel still took the form of shaming and/or tough-love types of philosophies. If an individual's symptoms were severe, he or she tended to be "fast tracked" for medical release.

Canada was involved in the tragic UN mission in Rwanda from 1993 to 1994, where civil war erupted and resulted in the genocide of 800,000 Tutsi and moderate Hutu civilians by the Hutu military and militia forces. Canadian General Romeo Dallaire served as Force Commander of the UN forces in Rwanda during this period. Despite obvious evidence and desperate pleading from Dallaire, the UN and the rest of the world offered no assistance. Furthermore, UN forces were ordered not to confiscate weapons caches or otherwise intervene. This was the worst case scenario of soldiers being ordered to remain helpless and passive observers of what could only be considered evil (Dallaire, 2003).

By the mid 1990s, due to increased United Nations peacekeeping deployments to the former Yugoslavia, Somalia and Rwanda, the number of individuals seeking support for their symptoms was mounting, while the number of medical releases also grew. Many soldiers returned home from their United Nations tours struggling with psychological difficulties, only to find a wall of silence. Not only did the military fail to address these issues, but the Canadian public was also largely oblivious to the realities of soldiers' trauma exposure while in theatre. The limited availability of assessment and treatment resources (only four military psychiatrists and a handful of social workers), coupled with the ongoing stigma associated with mental health issues, severely limited the number of military personnel willing to come forward for help. Many soldiers submitted requests for release during their tours or immediately after returning, rather than risk falling apart in front of their peers.

In 1995, it became apparent to General Dallaire that he and his UN Military Observers were struggling emotionally with the aftermath of their experiences in Rwanda. He made the unprecedented request that he, his UN Military Observer officers, and their spouses or significant partners be provided with mental health assistance. In July of 1995, LCDR Passey (psychiatrist) and Major LaMontigny (social worker)—both of whom had deployed to Rwanda in September of 1994 as part of a mental health team established to assess the mental health impact of the UN mission—conducted two days of debriefing, education about stress disorders, and brief cognitive-behavioural therapy sessions at Canadian Forces Base (CFB) St. Jean. These sessions with General Dallaire's officers and their spouses comprised the first Canadian Forces mental health initiative specifically designed to address PTSD and its effects, not only upon soldiers, but also on family members.

There were no further mental health initiatives for PTSD until 1997, when Lieutenant General Romeo Dallaire stepped forward and disclosed his own battle with PTSD, his subsequent alcohol dependence, and his struggles dealing with the stigma and difficulties accessing treatment. It was only at this point that the country and its military began to address this age-old illness in a serious manner (Canadian Forces, 1998).

In November 1998, the CF announced the establishment of multidisciplinary treatment sites. The facilities were implemented late in 1999 and named Operational Traumatic Stress Support Centres, which consisted of at least one military psychiatrist, a military mental health nurse, a military social worker, a military padre (chaplain) and one or more civilian psychologists. Centres were established at CFB Halifax and CFB Esquimalt naval bases, CFB Valcartier and CFB Edmonton army bases, and Ottawa CF Headquarters (which is within two hours of travel from CFB Petawawa, a large army base). Until the Centres opened, there had been an increasing reliance on the very limited number of civilian psychologists and psychiatrists who had some degree of experience in this field.

Operational Stress Injury Social Support (OSISS) is born

From 1999 to 2000, a CF board of inquiry was convened to address the large number of members who served in Croatia and developed significant physical and psychological problems (Department of National Defence, 1999). It was after this that Major Stéphane Grenier proposed a peer support initiative. This arose following his contact with a soldier who had been medically released from the Canadian Forces, but was suffering such severe psychological problems that he became homeless. He intervened and helped the soldier such that he was able to obtain the assistance needed. The realization that a fellow soldier was able to help another recover his life, when both the military and the VAC had effectively abandoned him, demonstrated the enormous potential of peer support (Richardson et al., 2008).

Lieutenant Colonel Grenier developed the term Operational Stress Injury (OSI) to describe a collection of psychological injuries that stem from military duty. It was an attempt to reduce the stigma associated with psychiatric diagnoses and to emphasize that, like visible physical injuries, these psychological and physiological symptoms resulted from injuries to the brain and psyche, caused by exposure to military-related trauma.

In May of 2001, the Operational Stress Injury Social Support (OSISS) program was launched. OSISS, which comprises a partnership between the Department of National Defence and Veterans Affairs Canada, was created to support military and veteran personnel suffering from serious stress-related injuries as a result of their tours of duty. OSISS was founded to address the social, educational and leadership deficits associated with Operational Stress Injuries (OSIs), such as PTSD, anxiety and depression. The mission of the OSISS program is, first, to establish, develop and improve social support programs for current and former members of the Canadian Forces and their families affected by operational stress; second, to address the needs of bereaved families of military members and veterans; and third, to create an atmosphere that leads to a better understanding and acceptance of operational stress injuries (Richardson *et al.*, 2008).

The OSISS program hires Peer Support Coordinators who have been diagnosed with an OSI, but are deemed by their psychiatrist and/or psychologist to be at a stage in their own recovery where they are able to manage this type of work. It is important to note that these Peer Support Coordinators are neither replacing nor acting as health professionals. Instead, they offer non-clinical assistance and support based upon shared experiences to current and former Canadian Forces members suffering with an OSI. The main activities of the OSISS Peer Support Coordinator are one-on-one assistance (listen, assess and refer); organization and facilitation of peer support groups; recruiting, training, and managing volunteers; and conducting outreach briefings/activities (Richardson *et al.*, 2008).

Family Peer Support Coordinators are family members who have had the experience of living with a Canadian Forces member or veteran diagnosed with an OSI. They provide one-on-one assistance to families of military members and veterans suffering from an OSI and going through similar experiences to their own. They also provide outreach briefings, conduct psycho-educational groups, and select, train and manage volunteers.

The most recent addition to the OSISS program is the bereavement component, which is comprised of volunteers who have experienced the loss of a loved one due to military service and who are able to offer support to those who have recently suffered the same.

Social support is a crucial element in decreasing the feeling of stigma and facilitating the recovery of soldiers and veterans suffering from psychological trauma. The benefit of trained peer support personnel lies within the peer's ability to readily identify with the suffering member, to convey acceptance, to demonstrate resourcefulness, and to maintain a special credibility in the eyes of the soldier, the veteran and their families. The ongoing collaboration between clinicians working with soldiers and veterans who have operational stress disorders and the national peer support program has been successful not only in providing treatment and support, but also in decreasing the stigma of OSIs.

Development of Operational and Traumatic Stress Support Centres and Operational Stress Injury Clinics

In 2002, Veterans Affairs Canada (VAC) and the Department of National Defence (DND) jointly announced a mental health strategy to enhance the service and support provided to the growing number of clients diagnosed with an OSI. The CF's five Operational and Traumatic Stress Support Centres (OTSSC) provided assistance to members of the Canadian Forces who were dealing with an OSI resulting from military operations, however they were not capable of providing treatment to veterans or their families. Unlike U.S. Veterans Affairs, VAC did not have medical outpatient facilities and only had one inpatient hospital for veterans—typically chronically ill elderly Second World War or Korean War veterans. There was an ongoing expectation that civilian community medical services would provide full care for Canadian veterans. However, it rapidly became clear at this point that there was insufficient capacity within the civilian community to provide the necessary services for veterans and their families.

By March 2003, VAC had 3,501 psychiatric cases, with 1,802 having PTSD (51.5 percent). By March 2007, there were 10,272 psychiatric cases with 6,500 (63.3 percent) having been diagnosed with PTSD (Veterans Affairs Canada, 2010). As a result, in 2007 VAC developed an initial network of five OSI clinics and subsequently expanded this network to ten OSI clinics across Canada. In March of 2010, VAC psychiatric cases increased to 12,689, with 8,758 PTSD cases (69 percent). The OSI Clinics' clinical staff typically consists of a psychiatrist, three psychologists, one mental health nurse and one social worker. They provide outpatient clinical assessments, as well as individual, family and group therapy (including telehealth treatment via a secure videoconference line).

Assessment and treatment modalities

The Canadian military now provides a continuum of post-deployment treatment that begins with Third Location Decompression (TLD) in Cyprus and post-deployment screening upon returning home. Specific treatment programs include the Canadian Forces OTSSC clinics for currently serving members and the Veterans Affairs Operational Stress Injury Clinics, which are available to veterans, currently serving military members, and their families. When these services are not available to members, either because of their location or because of waiting lists, they are referred to private practitioners within their local communities.

Third Location Decompression Program

The Third Location Decompression Program (TLD) was developed in 2002 by the Department of National Defence to provide soldiers departing theatre with a rest and relaxation period prior to returning home to family. The five-day TLD program was developed as a means of easing reintegration, rather than as a medical intervention to prevent PTSD. The most recent version of the program is called the "Road to Mental Readiness—Transition and Reintegration". Since 2006, this has been conducted at a resort on the island of Cyprus. This five-day decompression period consists of individual free time, structured recreational activities and educational programs. Soldiers take part in two two-hour education sessions that cover a variety of topics, including decompression and physiological functioning, responses to deployment transition challenges, reintegration techniques, warning signs, barriers to seeking care, peer support, spirituality, and mental health resources.

A Department of National Defence survey measured satisfaction in more than 3000 participants both at the end of the program and four to six months later. Ninety-five percent strongly agreed that some form of TLD was good, 85 percent found the program valuable, and 83 percent recommended it for future deployments to Afghanistan (Garbor & Zamorski, 2010).

It is not surprising that the overall assessment of the TLD by soldiers is positive, considering they have come straight from Afghanistan to a resort in Cyprus where they can effectively "cut loose" with few restrictions. However, whether the majority of soldiers are gaining anything meaningful from the education portion of the TLD has yet to be determined, as there have been no clinical outcome studies specifically to assess these factors. The following vignette was written by a soldier who completed the TLD following his tour in Afghanistan:

> We arrived around supper time from Dubai UAE. We went through an in-clearance that included room assignments, ground rules, lecture locations and timings etc. Our first night curfew was midnight and the last

two were at 02:00. The first two mornings we had mandatory lectures; some topics were elective and some were not. The third day was all ours, no lectures. The day after that was our trip home. The afternoons were ours to do what we wanted. There were a number of organized activities like deep sea fishing, golf, island tours etc. It was strongly suggested we partake in these, but it was up to us if we wanted to or not. I think/know it was to keep us busy so we didn't just sit around the pool and drink all day. We were given wristbands for drinking purposes; you were not allowed to consume alcohol without one. Violation of the rules or curfew would result in loss of the wristband.

The lectures dealt with reintegration back to the family, drug and alcohol abuse, PTSD symptoms and where and how to get help, etc. I personally did not get much out of these and neither did most of the people I spoke to. We had just left Afghanistan, the last thing we wanted was to sit through lectures, some of which were given by civvies (civilians) who, by their own admission, had no idea what we just went through or what it was like there. I personally feel these lectures should have taken place in KAF [Kandahar Air Field]; there was time while we turned in "kit" [i.e. weapons, body armour, helmets].

Although I did not get much from the lectures, the four days in Cyprus were a perfect way to decompress and reflect, briefly, on the last seven months. It was great to "unwind" with the men and women we went to war with. Back to the lectures; I would have paid a lot more attention if the speakers were ex-military who gave examples of their return home, etc., as opposed to a civvies who could not even relate to us. It's always the same; people think or imagine what it's like, but unless you actually experience it you can never think or imagine what it's like to spend every day outside the wire, wondering if your next step is going to be your last. Then these same people are going to tell me how I am going to reintegrate with my family etc. Have someone tell me who has actually done it, then I will listen. Overall, I think those people who just completed their first tour may have gotten some good info, but this being my sixth tour, I did not get anything out of the lectures. The rest of the decompression, on the other hand, was great.

There is also a transition and reintegration program offered to families back in Canada in preparation for their loved ones' return home (see the Department of National Defence website for more detailed information [Department of National Defence, 2011a]).

Enhanced post-deployment screening questionnaire

In an attempt to identify and deal with potential health care problems more proactively, the CF has developed and implemented an enhanced post-deployment screening questionnaire. In addition to having soldiers complete three standard, validated post-deployment health questionnaires, a mandatory health screening interview with a mental health professional is administered four to six months later. Based upon questionnaire data and interviews, recommendations are generated for further evaluation and care. By January 2008, detailed follow-up screenings indicated that 27 percent of people returning from Afghanistan experienced post-war difficulties and that approximately 16 percent of those individuals engaged in hazardous drinking activities. In addition, a number of people were struggling with more serious mental health issues, depression and PTSD being the most commonplace (Jaeger, 2008).

Outcome data reported by the CF as of 7 January 2011 from screenings of 12,717 soldiers showed that 3.9 percent reported symptoms suggestive of PTSD and 4.5 percent reported symptoms of Major Depressive Disorder (MDD). Thirteen percent reported symptoms of one or more common mental health disorders and those with a prior history of mental health care were three times more likely to report post-deployment symptoms. Mental health professionals conducting these interviews identified one or more "major concerns" in 17 percent of the total number of soldiers screened. Soldiers were screened an average of five months post-tour and more than 50 percent of those identified with symptoms of PTSD or MDD were already receiving treatment. Follow-up care was recommended for 22 percent of the total screened. The CF deemed this process to be more effective in identifying individuals with unmet mental health care needs than previous methods (Zamorski, 2010). The reader is referred to the DND website for a more detailed discussion of this process (Department of National Defence, 2011a).

CF Member Assistance Program

The creation of the CF Member Assistance Program was announced in January 1999 (Canadian Forces, 1999). This offers a 24/7 toll-free telephone service that provides confidential short-term problem-solving counselling services to assist service members and their families with personal concerns that affect their well-being or work performance. If long-term interventions or more specialized services are needed, referrals to appropriate professional resources can be made.

Military Family Resource Centres

Military Family Resource Centres were established in 1991 to provide support resources for military family members. They are located on or near bases across Canada. This is a community-based non-profit organization, established to provide information, support and programs to meet the needs of military families. Crisis intervention coordinators and staff are available to assist soldiers and their families to find a variety of support services in times of stress and crisis. They work in collaboration with psychosocial and spiritual wellness services on various military bases and are mandated to provide short-term individual counselling for family members.

Treatment access following release from the military

Under the new Veterans' Charter, veterans with service-connected physical or mental health injuries are entitled to medical and vocational rehabilitation. Medical rehabilitation includes an initial assessment for determination of diagnoses and whether conditions qualify as service-related. Once veterans are successful in their application for service-related entitlements, their psychological and medical rehabilitation is coordinated through their treatment providers and VAC. Depending upon their location and preferences, they may receive treatment from an OSI clinic where they can access individual as well as family therapy, or elect to seek treatment from a private practitioner.

Inpatient treatment programs

Inpatient treatment programs specific to military and police-related trauma were non-existent in Canada until 2001, when Dr. Janice Hambley, director of Bellwood Health Services in Toronto, Ontario, crafted a proposal to DND and VAC for a concurrent PTSD and addictions treatment program for military and veteran personnel. Bellwood, a private, fee-for-service inpatient addictions treatment centre, had been receiving increasingly more military and veteran referrals since the early 1990s and subsequent to increased numbers of UN peacekeeping tours. In treating these soldiers and veterans, staff found that symptoms related to trauma exposure played a significant role in their addiction profiles. Consequently, Bellwood has been routinely developing individualized components to meet the specific needs of this population.

Bellwood's 59-day trauma treatment program currently accepts new referrals every two weeks. As a referring psychologist to this program, the benefits to be obtained are twofold: (1) provision of a safe place to begin to address their trauma symptoms for those clients who are too symptomatic for once-weekly outpatient treatment and (2) continued involvement between the referring professional and the inpatient program to provide for more comprehensive outpatient treatment planning and an easier transition back to outpatient treatment. From the client's perspective, one of the major benefits offered with this type of program is safety in terms of being able to speak freely with people who have a shared understanding of military culture and the knowledge that they are able to speak freely without traumatizing civilians who may have difficulty understanding their experiences.

While in the program, veterans undergo eight to ten hours of treatment per week, which includes individual therapy, group therapy, an intensive four-week anger management workshop, nightmare re-scripting, and various somatic processing components such as progressive muscle relaxation, massage therapy, acupuncture and exercise programs. In addition to this program, they take part in the substance abuse treatment program in an open group, which allows the opportunity to work on social skills development within a civilian population. Bellwood also offers a one-week family component, where family members are provided with information related both to addiction and trauma recovery.

The most recent pre- and post-treatment (six months after treatment) outcome statistics available from Bellwood demonstrate a number of significant improvements in clients who completed the program. These include improved quality of life ratings, reduced number of drinking days out of a six-month period, no relapse in drug use, reduced suicidal thoughts and improved management of trauma symptoms (J. Hambley, personal communication, 2011).

Canada now has several other inpatient treatment programs with a combined focus on addiction and military and/or police trauma available across Canada, which range from one to three months of treatment time. The following vignette was provided by a soldier who participated in a combined trauma and addiction inpatient treatment:

> I underwent a 60-day inpatient trauma treatment program, which was the first step of many that has helped to turn my life around for the better. Being part of a military group of eight allowed us to work on our individual traumas in a way that none of us had been able to communicate or share before. We underwent this group therapy for two hours a day, Monday through Thursday, and it was, in my opinion, even more beneficial than our individual therapies while in the program.

Outpatient treatment

As in the United States, cognitive-behavioural therapy and, more specifically, prolonged exposure therapy (PE) or cognitive processing therapy (CPT), are the treatments of choice in Canada, due to the large body of outcome research demonstrating efficacy in the treatment of patients with PTSD and MDD, and the willingness of insurance companies to fund such treatments (Foa, Hembree & Rothbaum, 2007; Resnick, Monsoon & Chard, 2007). However, as effective as these treatments are, they are frequently insufficient for many and too overwhelming for some. In particular, PE has not been found to be helpful for those soldiers and veterans whose traumatic memories involve predominant feelings of shame or guilt or for those who have uncontrolled rage around their traumatic memories. Often those with significant dissociation or full-blown flashbacks are also poor candidates for PE until such time as these symptoms are better controlled.

A fundamental aspect of treating trauma is the rebuilding of trust and the re-establishment of a sense of community and collaboration. To achieve this, trust must be built in the therapeutic relationship and must also exist in a broader treatment team that may consist of, but is not restricted to, family physicians, physical fitness trainers, massage therapists, physical and cognitive rehabilitation specialists, family, peers, vocational rehabilitation personnel and employers. To truly assist in helping military personnel to transition and adjust to civilian life, an ongoing team approach is required. The composition of the team will change over the course of recovery according to need, providing continuous opportunities for the veteran to gradually rebuild trust within a safe and supportive environment, which can then be generalized into the larger world.

There is considerable work to be done toward making this collaborative approach a standard, fully funded aspect of all treatment programs, but the process has at least begun. Inpatient treatment programs have always recognized the need for multidisciplinary treatment, but until very recently there has been a strong disconnect between what veterans had access to during an inpatient treatment program and what they had access to following discharge.

Over the past few years, there has been an increasing awareness and commitment to a more holistic approach to treatment. For example, it is not unusual for treatment recommendations to include a supervised physical fitness program, massage therapy, group therapy, and marital and/or family therapy in addition to psychological and pharmacological treatment. This type of holistic program is currently supported by VAC for members identified as having an OSI. More recently, there has also been support provided for neurofeedback and recreational therapies, which are discussed below.

Two distinctive treatment approaches

Two distinctive treatment approaches being utilized in Canada in the treatment of military-related trauma will be very briefly described here: Neurofeedback (NFB) and recreational therapies used by the Canadian Veteran Adventure Foundation.

Neurofeedback (NFB)

NFB is an old-new-again method of treatment that originated in the 1970s with Sternman's landmark discovery and subsequent research on its use in the treatment of epilepsy (Sternman, 1972). NFB is a form of biofeedback that utilizes electroencephalography (EEG) to provide information that can then be utilized as feedback regarding brain activity. Like other forms of biofeedback, neurofeedback training (NFB) uses monitoring devices to provide moment-to-moment information to an individual on the state of their physiological functioning. The characteristic that distinguishes NFB from other biofeedback is a focus on the central nervous system and the brain. NFB has its foundations in basic and applied neuroscience, as well as in data-based clinical practice. Ongoing research, particularly in the area of Attention Deficit Hyperactivity Disorder treatment, has re-ignited the interest in this treatment modality.

Over the years, there have been a number of studies demonstrating the efficacy of NFB in the treatment of PTSD (c.f. Graap & Feides, 1998; Peniston & Kulkosky, 1991; Peniston *et al.*, 1993; Peniston, 1998; Kelly, 1997; Saxby & Peniston, 1995), but these were overshadowed by the psychopharmacological revolution that took place around the same time. In addition, there have been methodological criticisms of these studies due to the lack of norms and the individual nature of the response patterns. However, these studies, in addition to a strong body of clinical case studies, are propelling the field toward the development of more empirically rigorous research designs (van der Kolk, 2010). To date, in Canada, there are growing numbers of certified NFB practitioners working in the area of trauma and several research projects underway examining the efficacy of NFB.

A clinical perspective by Dr. Susan Brock

As a new practitioner of NFB, but also someone who has worked almost exclusively in the area of military and police-related trauma for 13 years, I began using NFB as an adjunct to more traditional talk therapy with a small group of five clients suffering with chronic PTSD and addiction. These individuals have all had long-term (three months) inpatient drug/alcohol and PTSD treatment in addition to talk therapy (CBT and exposure therapy) over a period of at least five years. They had experienced ongoing difficulties with relapse, typically stemming from an inability to manage stress without significant increases in their PTSD symptoms.

At the time of writing, the five clients each had between 40 and 45 sessions of neuro feedback. The most notable changes to date are in their relative state of arousal. They have all shown improvements in being able to manage stress without the overreaction and subsequent decompensation experienced previously. The changes in these individuals have been observed and commented on by members of their therapy groups, by family members and by the individuals themselves. Two of the five have remained abstinent from alcohol since beginning treatment, one quit a one and a half packs per day smoking habit cold turkey (stating he just found it "tasted funny") and all five have reported improved ability to manage interpersonal interactions, both at home and at work.

It is acknowledged that there are numerous potential explanations for these outcomes. The individual who quit smoking had been trying unsuccessfully to quit smoking for two years (he has also reduced the frequency of his binge drinking); the two individuals who have maintained their sobriety were abstinent at the start of treatment, however, both of them suffered from chronic alcoholism and, in spite of multiple types of treatment, both inpatient and outpatient, had continued to relapse. For both individuals, this is their longest period of uninterrupted sobriety outside of a treatment facility in the past five years. In addition, the remaining three have had fewer relapses and their periods of relapse were much briefer than in the past. As for the improvement in this group's overall level of calm and in their ability to pay attention, although one could argue for a placebo effect, it should be remembered that these individuals have had numerous types of treatment over the years that they have not found consistently helpful and were quite willing to say so. Their treatment team (psychologist, psychiatrist, family doctor and peer support coordinator), their fellow therapy group members, and their families have all noticed improvements in overall functioning.

The novelty of NFB treatment©, and the perception that it is more "scientifically objective" than traditional talk therapies, may also contribute to the more positive assessment of the reported changes. However, when NFB was added to Pat's treatment protocol (name used with permission), he used some instructive imagery in describing its effect on his brain. He stated:

> Before NFB it was like I had four TVs in my head that were always on and the volume was always turned all the way up. Now, I can control the volume and focus in on one at a time and on a good day, I can even turn the others off. I feel calmer and I feel like I have time to think about how I want to react rather than just losing it and thinking about what I should have done after it is too late.

Although it remains to be seen what will occur as the treatment continues, the attentional improvements alone suggest that NFB should be considered as an adjunct to more traditional talk therapy methods which, for some individuals, either do not work or are insufficient.

Canadian Veteran Adventure Foundation

Another innovative treatment program, developed from one veteran's personal struggle and his acute awareness of the needs of others, is the Canadian Veteran Adventure Foundation© (CVAF). CVAF is a non-profit corporation that aims to take the proven effectiveness of wilderness therapy programs and apply it to mentally and physically injured Canadian Forces and RCMP veterans (see Hyer et al., 1996 and Scurfield, 2004 for a description of an Outward Bound adventure-based program with U.S. veterans; and Chapter 15 of this volume for a description of an outdoor-based intervention utilized with U.S. military personnel).

Former MCpl (RET) Christian McEachern created the CVAF, which is now in its fourth year of operation, located in Calgary, Alberta. Christian developed a program of activities that includes low-impact group pursuits, such as white water rafting, equestrian development courses, golfing, light hiking, biking, fishing and winter ski resort programs. The focus during the activities is upon the interpretive and the experiential to assist veterans in refocusing outside of their ingrained tactical thinking processes so that they can have more relaxed and enjoyable learning experiences. By combining these outdoor leadership methods and others, such as discussion of the goals and support for each activity, with regular group debriefings of the experience with the group's usual trauma psychologist, McEachern believed that the result would be a powerful, constructive and positive group experience for all involved (personal communication, 2010).

We were able to experience this first hand when the Saskatoon military trauma group was invited to be the first group to participate in McEachern's new program. Dr. Brock invited McEachern to attend one of our regular monthly group sessions to outline the program and invite participation. The general consensus was one of support and well wishes; however, commitment to participate was much more difficult to obtain. To understand this, one must first understand that the majority of group members suffer from severe chronic PTSD, with many also meeting criteria for Major Depressive Disorder and Alcohol and/or Drug Dependence in various stages of recovery. Further, most of these individuals were deployed on so-called peacekeeping missions (truly a misnomer for the deployments in the early to mid 90s) and returned home to loss of career and little or no support. Many never received any form of treatment for an average of five years post-tour, during which time they developed multiple maladaptive coping mechanisms that were highly resistant to change.

In particular, avoidance and isolation were primary. For many of these individuals, the only social interaction that they had outside of family, if they had any familial relationships still intact, was the once-monthly group gathering. The group was time-limited (two hours) and predictable in terms of structure and participation. The thought of embarking on a four-day outing to an unfamiliar place and engaging in team-based activities, even with the familiarity of group and having two of their treatment providers there, was overwhelming. Between the initial invitation and the actual leave date, members signed on then backed out repeatedly. In the end, with lots of discussion and support, nine veterans (out of a potential 12), two treatment providers, McEachern and three other CVAF team members participated.

The anxiety in the parking lot prior to leaving was palpable, but when the group connected again in Kananaskis later that day, it had settled somewhat. After setting up camp and preparing and enjoying a meal together, they settled in for a largely sleepless night. The next morning, their anxiety was extreme and several were not sure that they were going to take part in the day's activities. With some one-on-one reassurance from the treatment team, as well as from McEachern, everyone climbed into the two rafts and we were off on our journey. Several hours, a group lunch and two river runs later, I was profoundly moved by what I observed. Smiles and laughter replaced anxiety and fear. There was lots of joking and pats on the back—the ability to physically connect through caring gestures was, in my mind, a major change. Individual members came up to me to express how good they felt, saying that they could not remember the last time they felt so relaxed. One member had tears in his eyes, telling me how good he felt and asking if we could do something like this where the group members' children could take part. The day ended with a group barbeque and lots of stories and laughter, without the need for alcohol or drugs. After another day of activity, we conducted a group session that was extremely productive. The participants were open and interactive and there was a calmness to their energy.

Two members detailed their experience in the program:

> The trip was planned and executed with several challenges in mind, but the logistics of just driving there was an emotional trigger in itself for many of us. The majority took part in the first day's white water rafting trip, which meant surrendering control to someone else, which for most soldiers or anyone suffering from PTSD is extremely difficult. I truly believe the bonding at the campfire the night before and on the drive there helped each of us gain a certain trust in each other that was lost when we were injured, and afterwards when people doubted or condemned us. Not for a long time for me, and even longer for others, did we feel like we belonged to a team, with confidence in ourselves and others. There were smiles, anticipation, laughter and a sense of accomplishment. It helped having our docs there, who monitored and guided us when they sensed or we let them know things were beginning to feel intense. Feeling like you belong, an identity, is something that is missed the most when you have known what it is like to truly belong.

Figure 6.1 Teamwork. Used with permission.

Figure 6.2. Perseverance. Used with permission.

Figure 6.3 Trust. Used with permission.

Those of us in the military, especially the Army, had come to know "camping" as work or part of our job and so the thought of camping didn't appeal to many of us. With a little bit of positive motivation, we were able to get most of us from our veteran's group out of our comfort zones and taking a chance on something that had many negative connotations associated with the activity. The weekend started out with a bit of a tense six-hour drive to get us to our destination; but it quickly led to some laughs and the constant chatter of a road trip. Once we got to the mountains and to our campsites, the strangest thing took place! Everyone unloaded the vehicles and immediately, without orders being called out, we set up our campsites before anyone sat down to relax! Funny how some positive camaraderie could motivate even the most disgruntled soldier! The rest of the day and evening was spent with some campfire "war" stories followed by a surprisingly good night's sleep.

The next morning, we all set out for a whole day of white water rafting with a few members among us with some major water issues. White water rafting that day brought smiles to the faces of some of our guys that I swear hadn't been seen for years. That night, more stories and good food were shared by all, leading us to another incredible night's sleep. The weather this weekend tried to ruin our event by pouring rain on us from the time we had left home for the mountains. So on our last day, we, as a group, visited the town of Banff and enjoyed the hot springs before packing up and staying the last night at our

Figure 6.4 CVAF Rafting Day, Saskatchewan OSI Group, August, 2009. Used with permission.

Sponsor's home, staying inside out of the rain and enjoying a fantastic supper with some really uplifted people! We conducted a "group" therapy session with our doctors starting things up and then sat back and watched and shared the experience of all of our weekends' fun and shared in some tears of joy and some heartfelt laughs.

The program that was offered to our group was the first major positive experience for so many of us in years. The worst part of the weekend was having to pack up the vehicles and head back home to reality.

Closing

Looking towards the future, we would like to see a continued emphasis and expansion of the multidisciplinary approach to treatment. As noted previously, VAC is already beginning to endorse such an approach in that it provides funding for various types of treatment and programming (e.g., individual and group therapy, physical rehabilitation, and educational and/or vocational programming). However, at present, it is often done on an ad hoc basis, with little or no interaction between the various professionals involved. That is, unless one or more of them takes on the responsibility for developing and maintaining a team-based approach.

From a treatment perspective we are excited about the possibilities that new treatments, such as neurofeedback, bring to the field. As much as CBT, and in particular exposure therapy, works for many, we now recognize that the cumulative and intense nature of military trauma (over months at a time) can cause profound changes in functioning such that talk therapy on its own is simply not enough.

The new Veterans Charter requires further modification so that the needs of families are more thoroughly addressed in both the short and long term. There also needs to be a quality assurance program instituted that is external to Veterans Affairs Canada and staffed by veterans and professionals from various disciplines involved in soldiers' and veterans' care. Such a program would provide soldiers, veterans and their families with an opportunity to voice their concerns and feedback, ensuring that this information could then be utilized in a timely fashion to address areas of perceived suboptimal service delivery.

In conclusion, over the past ten years, there has been significant progress in Canada toward recognizing the impact of military trauma exposure on both soldiers and their families, and developing various forms of support in terms of reintegration and access to treatment. However, there are still a number of areas that need to be addressed in order to assist veterans and their families as they move through the various stages of the reintegration and recovery process.

Postscript

Although those of us who work in the field of trauma and/or live with war trauma do not need to be reminded how devastating this illness can be, we were tragically reminded of that fact in the midst of writing this chapter. Corporal Michael Priddell (retired) had served Canada with pride in Croatia during the civil war in the former Yugoslavia. Like many veterans before him, he chose a permanent solution to end his physical and psychological pain by taking his own life. Mike was a quiet man who was a dedicated father and spouse, but his severe avoidance and hypervigilance symptoms limited his life and that of his family. He was an infrequent participant in our PTSD support group, but we know that he tried in the best way he could to maintain some connection. His biggest accomplishment with us had been the inaugural CVAF trip to Kananaskis, Alberta. The strength and courage it took for him to commit to this trip was immense and I know that our group will always remember the smiles and the heartfelt expressions of calm that he shared in the group session that Sunday evening. Mike's name will be added to the list of the fallen that is honoured each year at our local memorial. Regardless of the way in which he died, like so many others, he was a casualty of war. He joined a burgeoning list of often invisible and unknown fallen who have died of their military injuries long after a safe return home.

Figure 6.5 Cpl. Michael Priddell, Princess Patricia's Canadian Light Infantry II, January 6, 1972–January 21, 2011. Used with permission.

Dr. Susan Brock, Ph.D., is a clinical psychologist working in Saskatoon, Canada. In 1999 she participated in an international delegation to South Africa and attended the inaugural South African Conference on Post-Traumatic Stress: Working Toward Solutions. Her area of expertise is the assessment and treatment of trauma in military and veteran personnel, police officers and other front line workers. She has been a presenter/speaker on PTSD at numerous local, national and international conferences and teaches professionals, military and police services about PTSD (brocks@sasktel.net).

Dr. Greg Passey, M.D., is a psychiatrist whose area of expertise is in stress disorders in military members, veterans and police officers. He served 22 years in the Canadian military and deployed to Rwanda in 1994 to assess and treat mental health issues in Canadian Forces Personnel. He was awarded the ISTSS Sarah Haley Memorial Award in 2004 for clinical excellence in the field of PTSD. He works in private practice and at the British Columbia OSI Clinic (gpassey@telus.net).

References

Canadian Forces (Producer) (1998). *Witness the Evil* [Film].

Canadian Forces (1999, January 26). *Canadian Forces Medical Services briefing.* Paper presented to the CF Medical Personnel on the Canadian Forces Member Assistance Program (CFMAP).

Dallaire, R. (2003). *Shake Hands With The Devil.* Toronto: Random House Canada.

Department of National Defence (1999). *Croatia Board of Inquiry—Provisional Report.* Retrieved from www.forces.gc.ca/boi/engraph/home_e.asp[1]

Department of National Defence (2011a). Operations. Retrieved from www.forces.gc.ca/site/operations/current-ops-courante-eng.asp

Department of National Defence (2011b). Retrieved from http://www.forces.gc.ca/site/index.asp

Foa, E., Hembree, E. & Rothbaum, B. (2007). *Prolonged Exposure Therapy for PTSD—Emotional Processing of Traumatic Experiences. A Therapist's Guide.* New York, NY: Oxford University Press.

Garbor, B. & Zamorski, M. (2010). *Evaluation of a third-location decompression program for Canadian Forces members returning from Afghanistan.* Paper presented at the International Society for Post-Traumatic Stress Studies, Montreal.

Graap, K. & Freides, D. (1998). Regarding the database for the Peniston alpha-theta EEG biofeedback protocol. *Applied Psychophysiology and Biofeedback, 23*(4), 265–272.

---

1   Note that the Board's Report was on the DND website for some time after its release. It was removed for a number of years, and only recently have selected parts of the Board's work been made available on the DND website. References here are to a copy of the report in one of the authors' possession.

Hyer, L., Boyd, S., Scurfield, R., Smith, D. & Burke, J. (l996). Effects of Outward Bound experience as an adjunct to inpatient treatment of war veterans. *Journal of Clinical Psychology, 52*(3), 263–278.

Jaeger, H. F. (2008, January 31). Brigadier General H. F. Jaeger, Surgeon General, Canadian Forces. *Appearance before the Standing Committee on Public Accounts.*

Kelly, M. J. (1997). Native Americans, neurofeedback, and substance abuse theory: Three year outcome of alpha/theta neurofeedback training in the treatment of problem drinking among Dine' (Navajo) people. *Journal of Neurotherapy, 2*, 24–60.

O'Neill, J. (2010, April 13). Suicide third leading cause of death in Canadian Forces: Study. *Montreal Gazette.*

Peniston, E. (1998). Comments by Penison. *Applied Psychophysiology and Biofeedback, 23*, 273–275.

Peniston, E. & Kulkosky, P. (1991). Alpha-Theta brainwaive neurofeedback for Vietnam veterans with combat-related post-traumatic stress disorder. *Medical Psychotherapy, 4*, 47–60.

Peniston, E., Marrinan, D., Deming, W. & Kulkosky, P. (1993). EEG alpha-theta brainwave synchronization in Vietnam theater veterans with combat-related posttraumatic stress disorder and alcohol abuse. *Advances in Medical Psychotherapy, 6*, 37–50.

Resnick, P., Monsoon, C. & Chard, K. (2007). *Cognitive Processing Therapy.* U.S. Department of Veterans' Affairs.

Richardson, J. D., Darte, K., Grenier, S., English, A. & Sharpe, J. (2008). Operational stress injury social support: A Canadian innovation in professional peer support. *National Defence and the Canadian Forces, 9*(1), 57–64.

Saxby, E. & Peniston, E. (1995). Alpha-theta brainwave neurofeedback training: An effective treatment for male and female alcoholics with depressive symptoms. *Journal of Clinical Psychology, 51*, 685–693.

Scurfield, R. M. (2004). *A Vietnam Trilogy. War Trauma and Post Traumatic Stress, 1968, 1989 & 2000.* New York, NY: Algora Publishing.

Sternman, M. B. (1972). Studies of EEG biofeedback training in man and cats. Highlights of 17th Annual conference. *VA Cooperative Studies in Mental Health and Behavioral Sciences,* 50–60.

United Nations (2010). United Nations Peacekeeping Factsheet. Retrieved from www.un.org/en/peacekeeping/resources/statistics/factsheet

United Nations Association in Canada (2011). The UN and Peacekeeping. Retrieved from www.unac.org/en/link_learn/fact_sheets/peacekeeping.asp

van der Kolk, B. (2010). *Opening address.* Paper presented at the 21st Annual International Trauma Conference, Boston, MA.

Veterans Affairs Canada (2010). Mental health quarterly statistical report: Data to March 31, 2010. Retrieved from www.rcmpvetsnational.ca/DidYouKnow/VACReport/VAC%20MHP%20-%202009_10%204th%20Quarter%20MHQSR%20EN%20.pdf

Zamorski, M. (2010). *Findings of enhanced post-deployment screening of Canadian Forces (CF) members deployed in support of the mission in Afghanistan.* Paper presented at the International Society for Traumatic Stress Studies, Montreal, QC.

Part 2

Special populations of wounded warriors

Leave no comrades behind!
[signature] Nov 9, 2012

7 Traumatic brain injury and post-traumatic stress: The "signature wounds" of the Iraq and Afghanistan wars

John L. Rigg

Veterans are the light at the tip of the candle, illuminating the way for the whole nation. If veterans can achieve awareness, transformation, understanding and peace, they can share with the rest of society the realities of war.

—Thich Nhat Hanh (Veteran's Heart Georgia, 2009).

There has been considerable interest in concussion injuries in the news media over the last few years, particularly in the world of contact sports. Rules and regulations pertaining to the means by which concussions are dealt with at the time of the injury, as well as concern and speculation about the long-term consequences of concussion, particularly with respect to cognition and long-term mental health, have been raised. It is an area of medicine that still has a long way to go in understanding the molecular and structural details of the injury. The Global War on Terrorism, which is now the longest-running war in American history, has produced a large number of concussion patients due to the nature of warfare in this conflict. What I believe to be a significant detail impacting not only the injury in the acute phase, but also maintenance of symptoms well past the period of time when patients are normally expected to recover, is the fact that these military concussions occurred as the direct result of someone trying to kill them.

In this chapter, I will discuss the facts concerning concussion, also known as mild Traumatic Brain Injury (mTBI); its symptoms and etiology; the physiological, psychological and social dynamics as they impact service members; and the interrelationship of traumatic brain injuries with PTSD. There is a description of insights and ideas discovered in my work with Army soldiers over the course of the last three and a half years that are relevant to understanding how post-concussive symptoms originate and are maintained. Finally, best practice interventions will be described. These involve a holistic approach, offering insight and understanding of strategies that can be utilized to improve post-concussive symptoms and the lives of service members and their families. The opinions expressed here are my own and do not necessarily reflect those of the United States Army or the Department of Defense.

Mild Traumatic Brain Injury (mTBI)

Nearly two million American service members have deployed to Iraq and Afghanistan during the Global War on Terrorism (Hosek, Kavanagh & Miller, 2008). During this time, service members have faced multiple deployments and redeployments, increased length of deployments, and decreased breaks between deployments (ibid.). Our troops have also been exposed to a new kind of warfare in which the weapons of choice used by the insurgency are explosive devices, including improvised explosive devices (IEDs), mortars and rocket-propelled grenades (RPGs). Service members have been exposed to blasts in staggering numbers, resulting in significant numbers of them returning home having experienced one or more concussions. It has been estimated that as many as five to 35 percent of U.S. troops who have been exposed to combat in the Global War on Terrorism may have sustained a concussion during deployments to Iraq or Afghanistan (Hosek, Kavanagh & Miller, 2008; Hoge *et al.*, 2008; Schneiderman, Braver & Kang, 2008) [AQCh7.1] and that approximately 80 percent of these concussions are secondary to blast exposures (Hoge *et al.*, 2008).

Initial experiences

After experiencing a concussion, many service members begin to experience headaches, insomnia, memory problems and neuropsychiatric issues that may include depression, anxiety, irritability and anger (Hoge *et al.*, 2008; Brenner *et al.*, 2010). Frequently, these symptoms will span the remainder of their deployments, yet often they will resolve or service members will adapt to their symptoms and the ensuing problems in order to complete their tours of duty. Additional factors also experienced in combat and in the wartime theater that may contribute to the development and maintenance of symptoms after returning home may include: combat involvement and traumatic experiences leading to chronic hyper arousal, in-theater physical stress due to intense physical challenges, musculoskeletal injuries, prolonged sleep deprivation, separation from and disruption of family and other interpersonal relationships, and possible exposure to toxins.

Upon redeployment from the wartime theater, physical symptoms may or may not be present immediately. The excitement of homecoming, rekindling relationships with family and friends, and finding safety from life threatening experiences may allow the service member to be relatively symptom free. Symptoms may not be apparent and may initially be well tolerated. Currently, service members are routinely tested twice via medical screening evaluations. The Post Deployment Health Assessment (PDHA) is completed at the demobilization site and a second test, the Post Deployment Health Reassessment (PDHRA), is given within three to six months after returning from deployment. Service members are asked to report the occurrence of any injury-producing events and are asked questions about alterations in or loss of consciousness, feeling dazed or confused, "seeing stars," or loss of memory. The questions are designed to distinguish between concussions and acute stress reactions. Tinnitus (abnormally loud sounds occurring in the ear canal, commonly referred to as "ringing in the ears"), balance problems and headaches are associated more with concussions, whereas palpitations, rapid heartbeat and anxiety are more reflective of an acute stress reaction.

Admitting to having any type of physical or psychological symptomatology as a result of having sustained a concussion(s) in theater on the PDHA may lead to delays in homecoming, reuniting with families and loved ones, and obtaining a well-deserved break from duty. Consequently a service member may deny any history or symptoms of concussion in order to guarantee that he/she will be able to return home quickly. But after the initial thrill of returning home has subsided, reintegrating with families and non-combat social structures can easily create a high degree of stress, contributing to an exacerbation of symptoms. Eventually, of course, service members must return to their duty assignments and the symptoms, including headaches, insomnia, memory problems and neuropsychiatric issues that may include depression, anxiety, irritability and anger begin to flare up and worsen. Being separated from one's family or the assigned unit with whom one deployed also leads to loss of support systems that offer significant comfort.

Service members may begin to experience symptoms and not know what to do. Initially, insomnia, mood issues, memory problems and headaches may not seem severe enough to schedule an appointment with a medical provider. It is also important to consider how reluctant many dedicated service members are to admitting the significance of the impact of these symptoms on day-to-day life. "Sucking it up" and moving forward is a most admirable quality in service members, but this can impact and significantly delay recovery. Eventually, these symptoms will be too great to bear, resulting in the service member presenting to his/her medical provider, and it is at this point that the recovery from the physical and emotional violence of war begins.

Post-concussion symptoms, post-traumatic/combat stress and brain functioning

Headaches, cognitive/memory problems, insomnia and mood issues (typically depression, anxiety, irritability, changes in libido), commonly known as post-concussion symptoms, are the most familiar symptoms service members experience that drive them to seek help. Many of them will also present with musculoskeletal pain issues (typically back, shoulder or knee pain) that originated after an injury in theater, or balance problems, dizziness, vertigo or visual disturbances.

The typical first-line treatment that these service members will receive is symptomatic management using pharmacological agents. Medications prescribed may include preventative (prophylactic) and abortive headache treatments; sleep medications addressing difficulties in falling and staying asleep; psychiatric medications for depression, anxiety or irritability; and pain medications that may include narcotic analgesics to manage pain secondary to musculoskeletal injuries sustained during combat. Unfortunately, resolution of symptoms may not be achieved. A service member may obtain temporary relief with symptomatic management, but this route of treatment does not result in resolution of symptoms unless the body naturally recovers from injuries. It is not unusual for a service member to be sent to multiple providers, including specialists, all of whom attempt to treat the symptoms in their particular area of expertise. Service members may find themselves being prescribed multiple medications that may have significant side effects, negatively affecting their cognition and causing fatigue and problems with sexual functioning.

Persistence of post-concussion symptoms

A review of the medical literature on how long post-concussion symptoms last in civilians reveals that the majority of patients recover completely from within a few hours to up to 90 days (Holm *et al.*, 2005; McCrea, 2008). It is also reported that there are a number of patients who do not spontaneously recover and have post-concussion symptoms that persist. In civilian populations, it has been reported that anywhere from 11 to 64 percent of concussion patients may experience subjective cognitive difficulties, along with a continuation of physical symptoms including headache, dizziness, insomnia and mood issues (Boake *et al.*, 2005; Shaw, 2002). Data regarding the typical time course of recovery and the numbers of military personnel with persistent post-concussion symptoms that do not naturally resolve within 90 days remain unknown.

The initial symptoms of headache, insomnia, cognitive problems and mood issues can be due to the neurometabolic/physiological changes that the brain sustains in a concussion, but it is important to consider what factors may be responsible for the prolongation/maintenance of these symptoms. Of course, symptoms may be prolonged due to actual physiological damage to the brain. But in addition, it has been postulated that the maintenance of post-concussion symptoms is brought about by stress factors that originated during combat (Hoge *et al.*, 2008). This post-combat/deployment/traumatic stress may or may not meet the criteria for PTSD as per the *Diagnostic and Statistical Manual of Mental Disorders (DSM-IV)* (American Psychiatric Association, 2000), but a heightened stress level, often accompanied by depression and anxiety, is typical of patients being evaluated for mTBI. It has also been reported that service members who have not experienced a brain injury during deployment, but who show significant post-combat stress issues, also experience post-concussive-type symptoms more often than expected (Hoge *et al.*, 2008). Service members who present with a history of concussion and PTSD have been found to be more likely to experience post-concussive symptoms, including headache, memory problems, balance problems, dizziness and mood issues (Brenner *et al.*, 2010).

Post-combat stress factors

At the most basic level, most concussions sustained by service members in the highly stressful environment of the combat theater are a direct result of someone trying to kill them. Service members "going outside the wire" on missions or even in the supposed safe haven of their Forward Operating Bases (FOBs) are always aware of the fact that at any moment, incoming mortars, rockets, rocket-propelled grenades or small arms fire attacks may occur. When going out on missions, every inch of the roadway presents an opportunity to be blasted by an IED. These service members are constantly facing life and death situations—that is the very nature of warfare. As a result there is hyperactivation of primitive animal survival instincts—the fight or flight reaction. This is actually very advantageous to the soldier while in theater, keeping him or her hyperalert, quick to respond to potentially life-threatening situations and therefore more likely to survive. Evolution has indeed prepared animals, including humans, with lightning fast responses to dangerous threatening situations. In order to understand how the fight or flight reaction is triggered and the significance of its hyperarousal, we need to understand some basic brain anatomy.

Introduction to brain anatomy and the mechanism of hyperarousal

The brain can be simplified into two structures, the brainstem and the cortex. Each of these structures has a very specific role to play in the functioning of a human being. All animals possess some type of a brainstem structure that is responsible for operating the basic biological activity/machinery of the body—respiration, circulation and digestion. This is accomplished via the autonomic nervous system. The brainstem is also where basic instincts such as safety, food, sleep, reproduction, emotions of love, pleasure, anger, fear and survival are programmed.

The strongest instinct that all animals have is that of survival. Animals and humans will respond to dangerous threatening situations with the fight or flight response in order to protect themselves or run away from dangerous threatening situations in order to stay alive. This response is activated by the brainstem structure called the amygdala. The amygdala's role is to ask the question "Is this dangerous?" If yes, it will trigger the fight or flight response. On the other hand, we have the cortex, which takes up most of the mass of the brain in humans. It is responsible for our higher intelligent thinking, memory, reasoning powers, language, reading/writing skills and higher cognitive functioning, allowing us to build computers, hospitals, cars, etc. It is where our consciousness, our thoughts and personalities exist. It is the cortex that makes us human. Let us now consider what happens when the soldier returns home.

Returning home: Perseverance of hyperarousal

When a service member returns home, his or her conscious cortical mind knows he/she is back in the United States. However—and here is a key point— the understanding of geography, the recognition that the soldier has returned home and is no longer in combat, is a thought that exists in the cortex. Remember that the hyperactivated fight or flight response is located in the brainstem, the amygdala, which does not understand geography. It does not make decisions based on the individual's geographic location. Its only concern is whether or not current sensory data is signaling danger. Consequently, the service member remains in a state of hyperarousal, a hyperactivated fight or flight mode, due to the fact that the hyperaroused survival instinct does not shut down after returning home.

The fight or flight response

Unfortunately, the cortex cannot shut off primitive instincts. We cannot, for example, control/stop our heartbeat, change our digestion or kill ourselves by holding our breath. The fight or flight response, fine-tuned by the experiences of war, remains active, even though the service member is no longer in a combat zone. The unfortunate result of this is that the amygdala will trigger the fight or flight response readily and often in response to non-threatening situations. There is no rational, conscious decision-making process involved in the reactions of the amygdala. The highly evolved intelligent human cortex is not involved in the activation of the flight or fight response. In the same way that the birds and squirrels in your backyard will run away when you show up without any intention to harm them, the human amygdala can and often does respond with the fight or flight reaction to situations that may be perceived as threatening, even though they are not. Service members may believe that they are involved in actually making a choice in these matters. However, I believe it is important to understand that they are simply reacting—not engaging in a conscious action—to a situation that is being interpreted by the amygdala as perilous.

Brain processing of sensory information

Let us now look at how our brain processes sensory information. Information from four of the five senses—vision, hearing, taste, touch—is sent to the thalamus, the brain structure that serves as a relay station, forwarding the signal to be processed to both the brainstem and the cortex. Our sense of smell, the olfactory sensation, has a more direct route into the brain. All sensory information is ultimately sent to the cortex and brain stem for analysis. The cortex, the "thinking" part of our brains, spends time identifying, categorizing and analyzing objects/situations in whatever form the sensory information was received in order to determine how to respond or react to the situation at hand.

For example, imagine a service member with combat experience attends a rock concert. During the show, fireworks explode. The service member's reaction to the explosion is likely to be one of diving to the floor for cover. Let us consider exactly how that reaction (not consciously determined) was triggered by the brain. The incoming sensory data—bright flash and loud explosion—are sent to the cortex and the amygdala via the thalamus. The cortex, which is our intelligent thinking brain, will analyze the sensory data: "What was that? It sounded like a bomb. But wait, I'm not in theater anymore. Wow, is it a terrorist bomb? No one is running for cover, doesn't seem that anyone is hurt or concerned, the band is still playing. Phew, it was a fireworks explosion—I am safe!" Simultaneously, however, the thalamus sends the sensory data to the amygdala in the brainstem. The role of the amygdala is actually very simple—it simply asks the question: is this situation dangerous? If the answer is yes, the fight or flight reaction is triggered. In this example, the amygdala asks: "Is an explosion dangerous to a service member?" and concludes: "Of course it is!" Previous explosions have been recorded in the amygdala as traumatic—death, dismemberment, bodies blown apart, blood splattered everywhere. Consequently, the amygdala will react by triggering the fight or flight response—in this case flight, with the service member reacting to the fireworks explosion by diving to the ground.

A very important key point here is that the amygdala processes information much faster than the cortex. As a result, a reaction—a non-thinking response—is generated before a conscious and deliberate action/response is produced. Before the cortex has the opportunity to use its intelligent reasoning power to determine that the explosion is not a dangerous bomb, but simply fireworks, the amygdala interprets the sensory data as life threatening and triggers the flight reaction without any conscious thought process occurring. It is only after the service member has already hit the floor in a dive for cover that his or her cortex responds and he or she then realizes that the explosion involved fireworks, causing great embarrassment over his or her reaction to the situation. The amygdala triggers primitive survival instincts, an involuntary non-thinking reaction to real or misinterpreted sensory data. The fight or flight response is reaction, not a conscious action.

Irritability

Irritability is one of the core issues that service members report upon returning home from the combat theater. This is typically an overreaction to a situation that may arouse intense anger, fear, etc. When looking back at the event later, the individual realizes that it was indeed an overreaction to a situation that is nowhere near as threatening as the reaction it triggered. Here is an example told to me by a service member: A husband who was a combat veteran and his wife were having a peaceful day at home. The wife asked her husband if he could please take out the garbage. He immediately said yes and took out the trash as requested. Meanwhile, his wife walked into their living room and discovered that their two small children had spilled chocolate milk all over a new white sofa. She became very angry. She then walked back to where her husband was sitting, approaching him with an angry face and fire in her eyes. She was not angry at him at all, but was angry about the large brown stain on their new white sofa. She approached her husband with an angry look on her face and in an aggressive tone of voice asked him: "Did you take out that trash like I asked you to?" He reacted to her question with anger and cursed at her.

Let's look at why he "reacted" with anger/hostility. First, she approached him with an angry look on her face and second, she yelled at him in a mean and aggressive tone of voice. Now let us consider how this sensory information—the angry look on her face and her aggressive voice—are processed by the husband's brain. Recall that sensory information is sent to the amygdala and the cortex for processing, but the amygdala is the swiftest part of the brain to respond. So what the amygdala received to process was an angry face and an aggressive tone of voice.

Can this information be interpreted as dangerous—absolutely yes. So what happens? The fight response is triggered, resulting in an unthinking "reaction," the husband's hostile reaction. The amygdala does not recognize wife versus bad guy versus Taliban, etc. or consider the context of situations. It responds in a very simple, immediate way to a situation that can be interpreted as being potentially life threatening. In this case, the fight response did not actually involve striking the person, although certainly that may happen in some situations. This is often followed by much guilt and remorse, subsequent to the time when the cortex comes into play and the attacker realizes their overreaction to the triggering event.

How personality gets hijacked by the amygdala

Discovery consists of seeing what everybody has seen and thinking what nobody has thought.

—Albert Szent-Györgyi von Nagyrapolt, Hungarian-American biochemist,
1893-1986, awarded the Nobel Prize for Medicine in 1937
for his investigation of biological oxidation processes and
the action of ascorbic acid (vitamin C) (Think Exist website, n.d.)

In 1637, the French philosopher René Descartes, in an attempt to prove the existence or "beingness" of a person, stated, "I think, therefore I am." This philosophical statement attempts to define the existence, the "being," of the person having the thoughts by identifying their existence through the thoughts they experience. The ontological search for undeniable proof of the existence of "being" continued in the world of philosophy until, in the 1960s, the French existentialist philosopher, playwright, novelist, screenwriter, political activist and biographer Jean Paul Sartre, proposed that, "I am not my thoughts; I am the person that sees my thoughts" (Tolle, 2005).

Seeing through the lens of combat experiences

Our service members returning from the war theater have thoughts *that are not of their own conscious creation.* Their thinking and outlook on their lives is seen through the lens of their combat experiences. Much of their lives are not being managed by their consciousness, but rather by unconscious "reactions" to sensory information being interpreted as dangerous by the amygdala. They are often on high alert, in a highly stressed state of mind, so that many normal day-to-day experiences are unconsciously interpreted as dangerous or threatening by their amygdala, which creates a fight or flight response. Hostility and irritability often prohibit normal and healthy social relationships for service members. They are not the "being" that is responsible for many of their thoughts as their thoughts and reactions have been hijacked by primitive animal reflexes that have become hyperaroused as a consequence of exposure to violent, bloody, often catastrophic experiences.

Many of their thoughts are subconsciously triggered "reactions" to experiences that are not formulated by their own conscious decisions, but are actually primitive emotional fight or flight instinctual reaction behaviors to sensory stimuli being interpreted as dangerous. For example, many combat veterans have a strong aversion to going to public places—shopping malls, sporting events, restaurants, amusement parks, grocery stores, etc. In public places, they are often overwhelmed with security concerns. This can obviously have a significant impact on a service member's social life and a profound effect on the family. They may not go to any of these places at all. If they do, they will feel the need to leave quickly as they will have felt very irritable while there. They will be constantly vigilant, always having to know where the exits are, having an escape route planned, never sitting with their back to the wall in a restaurant, etc. I will often ask a combat veteran whether they go out shopping or to restaurants with their family and frequently the answer will be no. I will then ask, "But do you let your wife and children go?" and they will answer, "Yes." I will then ask them if they think it is unusual that they are uncomfortable going, yet they let their wives and children go. I then explain to them that in theater, their primitive survival instincts have been taught that all strangers are dangerous. In theater, the enemy is not wearing a uniform; one never knows who is going to be a suicide bomber or who will pull out and detonate a grenade or who will produce a weapon and begin shooting.

The fact that all strangers are potentially dangerous is imprinted into the survival instinct during deployment. Remember the previous point made about the brainstem not understanding geography; well here is another situation in which this is illustrated. Although the service member is now back in the United States, the survival instinct still becomes hyperactivated when around strangers. Who is at the shopping mall, sporting event, restaurant, amusement park, grocery store? Strangers. The combat veteran's cortex identifies these people as other American citizens shopping for food or clothing, out watching a sporting event or concert, or having dinner, but the survival instinct identifies them as potentially dangerous. They are strangers and the combat veteran has learned in theater that strangers are dangerous. This will create intense feelings of discomfort and irritation as defense mechanisms to protect the service member from the falsely perceived danger. Even after service members become aware of this, they still tend to feel annoyed or agitated in these situations and tend to avoid them altogether.

Importantly, these service members have little conscious choice in how they are "reacting" to sensory input. As this example has shown, often they are not making conscious choice "actions" but are "reacting" to events that are being interpreted by a part of their primitive reptilian brain, the amygdala, as dangerous. These thoughts seem real and have significant impact upon their lives. This hyperactivation of the primitive survival instinct in the brainstem, resulting in easy triggering of the fight or flight response, is a normal reaction to an abnormal situation—the blood-and-guts violence of war. When a human being is exposed to the violence of war, this has an effect on the brain (specifically the amygdala and its primitive animal survival instincts), whether the individual wants this to happen or not. This is simply the way the brain is wired. No matter how "tough" the individual may wish to be, their survival instincts are hyperactivated by the trauma of war.

The complexity of physiological injuries to the brain secondary to concussion blasts and/or trauma

In addition to maintenance of post-concussive symptoms by stress, actual physiological damage to the brain may have occurred during combat. Neuroscientists have not yet accurately determined the exact microscopic/molecular-level changes that occur in the brain during a concussion, causing post-concussive symptoms. It is likely that the eventual development of post-concussive symptoms is due to a multitude of events. These may include changes in the chemical reactions that normally occur in brain cells (neuro-metabolism), alteration and dysregulation of the normal signaling pathways in the brain (neuro-modulation) via changes in the up or down regulation of the chemicals (neurotransmitters) that allow transmission of signals to pass from one nerve cell to the other, or changes in the actual neural pathways (axonal damage) that allow communication and integration of information between different areas of the brain.

Researchers are investigating whether elevated serum levels in stress hormones, caused by the highly stressed combat environment, change the serum chemical milieu and impact the nature and severity of the neurological injury. Also, temperatures of over 120 degrees fahrenheit are not uncommon in Iraq, Afghanistan and the multitude of other Middle Eastern countries to which service members are deployed and where concussions often occur in these hyperthermic conditions. Hyperthermia is considered by some researchers to have a negative effect on the severity of a concussion (Farag, Manno & Kurz, 2011). It is also important to consider that each individual's genetic composition is a significant factor, instrumental in determining individual reactions to the experienced traumas of war.

We must remember that we are dealing with the most complicated entity in the entire universe—the human brain. Neuroscience at this time has a limited knowledge of the workings of the brain, much less an understanding of the neuro-metabolic and structural changes that are triggered by concussive events.

Researchers have found that glucose metabolism in patients who have suffered only mild concussions resembles that of severely brain-injured coma patients. Normally, the quantity of glucose that the brain uses is closely tied to the level of brain activity. Positron Emission Tomography (PET) scans that measured brain glucose utilization were conducted to compare post-traumatic levels of glucose utilization with the level of consciousness (normal versus coma) at the time of the study. It was found that glucose metabolism in patients who suffered only mild concussions surprisingly resembled that of severely brain-injured coma patients and that the reduced brain metabolism may continue for days to weeks after the injury. Research also suggests that reduced brain metabolism may indicate a state of increased vulnerability to further injury (Hovda, cited in Newsweek, 2010).

Overlap of mTBI and PTSD

The perception of post-combat stress/PTSD as a psychological injury, versus TBI as a physical injury, needs to be avoided. The symptoms of post-combat stress are the result of a change in physiological functioning of the brain. Animal models suggest that head trauma can readily make one more susceptible to PTSD. According to David Hovda, Director of the UCLA Brain Injury Research Center, "minor traumatic brain injury does not necessarily cause post-traumatic stress disorder, but it places the brain in biochemical and metabolic states that enhance the chances of acquiring PTSD" (cited in Newsweek, 2010).

Both TBI and post-combat stress/PTSD are physiological injuries[1] which need to be treated within the larger context of symptoms including headaches, insomnia, cognitive issues, mood issues and pain. Effective treatment demands a holistic approach—looking at the entire body and not treating only one symptom—as the severity and resolution of the symptoms depends on their interrelationship. Improvement in one of the symptoms will likely improve the others. For example, improving sleep will likely result in improvement of mood, memory and headaches. Improvement in headaches will likely have a positive impact on memory, mood, and possibly sleep as well. When an individual begins to experience recovery of cognitive deficits, he or she will likely have an improvement in mood, which can then positively influence headaches and sleep, both of which can be challenged by stress.

Stress is caused by a physiological process resulting in dysregualtion of the autonomic nervous system. In animal models, stress has been shown to have a significant effect on physiological and structural changes in the amygdala, hippocampus (the part of the brain most involved in memory formation) and prefrontal cortex. These changes include increased sensitivity to input in the amygdala, remodeling of the brain cells (neurons), a reduced number of connections made by the neurons in the hippocampus, and the inhibition of the growth of new brain cells (neurogenesis) in the hippocampus (Kennedy *et al.*, 2007).

Consider post-concussion/mTBI symptoms and those commonly found in PTSD. Both situations can result in headaches, insomnia, cognitive problems (particularly concentration and attention) and mood issues (irritability, anxiety, depression). They are basically the same, with the exception of headaches, which are more likely to be found in the mTBI population. Following exposure to the life-threatening events of war, a soldier who has returned home walks through life with a hyperactivated survival instinct that can easily be triggered by subconscious assessments of situations as dangerous. Living in this hyperaroused state creates significant stress that is manifested physically.

The relationship between hyperarousal, chronic stress and physical symptoms

One of the primary symptoms experienced following concussion(s) is headache. When treating headaches, it is imperative to consider the actual cause. In the case of service members who have been injured during combat deployments, stress is a significant factor that can manifest physically as muscle tightness, particularly in the neck and back, which can be a significant

---

1   It is important to note that many clinicians consider PTSD to be as much if not more of a "psychological" injury as a physiological one. And, of course, there is the viewpoint that it is both. What I say to that is that all "psychological" injuries are actually physiological—i.e. the psychology is being driven by changes in brain neurochemistry that dictate mood, behavior, etc.

generator of tension-type headaches. These tension headaches can also be a trigger for migraines. Muscle tension is an obvious target for a treatment plan to reduce both the frequency and the severity of headaches. Physical examination will reveal which muscles are tight and tender and a treatment plan utilizing modalities such as application of heat and ice and stretching exercises can be initiated. This can be an effective plan to treat headaches prophylactically, allowing for the decreased usage of medications.

Service members may also present with insomnia, typified by difficulty falling and staying asleep. They frequently have difficulty falling asleep and awaken in the middle of the night with security concerns, feeling compelled to check their doors and locks, inspect the premises, conduct reconnaissance, etc. Their hyperactive survival instinct often denies them the ability to sleep by keeping them on a high security alert, as if they are still in a combat zone—remember the primitive survival instinct does not understand geography and remains activated, even though they are back in the United States. The survival instinct is concerned with immediate safety, not the long-term consequences of stress.

Memory, concentration and attention problems

In many instances, subjective memory problems are reported and suspected to be secondary to concussion(s). However, in reviews of neuropsychological assessments of service members who had sustained at least one concussion and were complaining of subjective memory problems, it was reported that only 14 percent of the patients complaining about memory problems could be diagnosed as having a cognitive disorder consistent with persons still recovering from a mTBI. (Rigg & Mooney, 2011).

We must ask what factors might be involved in the symptoms of those patients who subjectively believe that they are experiencing cognitive problems, in spite of the fact that neuropsychological testing in unable to substantiate any objective findings. Memory can be significantly affected by the typical post-concussive symptoms of insomnia, headaches, pain-related issues and mood. For a service member with a hyperactivated amygdala, concentration and attention may be significantly affected, leading to problems with memory.

Case example 1

Here is an example of how this can occur. One day in the office, after completing a medical appointment, I was having a conversation about sports with a service member who was a combat veteran and suffering from symptoms of mild TBI and post-traumatic stress. As we were discussing his favorite sports team, we got up, left the office and walked down the hallway of the TBI clinic. When we reached the end of the hallway he turned to me and said: "Doc, just like I told you, my memory is terrible—I don't remember a word that you said."

At that point, we retraced our steps in an attempt to figure out what happened. What occurred was that as soon as I opened the door from my office into the hallway, he saw other doors in the hallway. He began to question who might be in those rooms. "What kind of weapons do they have in there?" "Whose footsteps are those coming down the hall?" "What if he throws a grenade down this hall?" The truth is that he did not forget what I said as we walked down the hall together—he never heard it in the first place. His attention/concentration was focused on survival and not the actual conversation at hand. His attention had been hijacked by his hyperactivated amygdala.

Case example 2

Here is another common example of how loss of concentration/attention may result in memory problems. A post-combat service member and their spouse are driving along in their vehicle. The spouse is telling the service member, who is driving, about upcoming events, such as a visit by the family, school meetings, social situations with neighbors, etc. All of a sudden, the service member driving the vehicle spots a box or an abandoned car or a dead animal on the side of the road. In theater, these objects are frequently found to be IEDs placed on the roadside or in the road itself. What characteristically happens next is that the service member begins to think of these objects as possible IEDs, even though their conscious cortical thinking knows they are back in the United States and there are no IEDs being buried in or on the roads. A hyperreactive amygdala is arousing suspicion and activating the survival instinct so that attention and concentration are now directed at the object in the road. In the meantime, the spouse's conversation is being ignored, as attention/ concentration has been hijacked by an aroused survival instinct, focusing attention on the potential life-threatening situation at hand. The details of the spouse's conversation do not register. Once again, the service member does not have a memory problem, but rather a concentration/attention problem that prohibits memories from being formed.

There is a solution: Treatment strategies and implications

> *Imagination is more important than knowledge.*
>
> —Albert Einstein (quoted by Nilsson, 2010)

At this point, we must ask what we can do to actually help resolve these symptoms.

The conventional medical model

The typical medical model—treatment with medications—only provides temporary symptomatic relief. The conventional medical model of treatment in an outpatient involves the patient discussing their ailments with a physician, who then gives a diagnosis, develops a treatment plan and writes a medication prescription to fix the problem. This model certainly works well for treatment of skin infections, for example. A physician examines a wound, suspects a Staphloccocus aureus infection, prescribes an antibiotic to kill the bacteria, which it does effectively, the body heals the wound naturally, and everything is brought to resolution. Unfortunately, this medical model is ineffective in the treatment of either post-concussive symptoms or post-traumatic stress. First of all, there is no easily identifiable lesion to be repaired. It is important to recognize that current pharmacological interventions do not actually cure the injury to the brain, the post-concussive symptoms or the post combat stress— they simply treat the symptoms. Headaches, insomnia and mood issues are not cured by medications. These can offer only symptomatic cover-up while waiting for the brain to heal itself. It is also important to always keep in mind that an injured brain may be more sensitive to side effects; and the effects of medications on an injured brain are often difficult to predict.

The holistic approach

There are no medications that can correct a hyperactivated amygdala. In order to promote the resolution of these symptoms, an holistic approach must be taken. So what do we have at our disposal to facilitate the healing process? The first step is to involve the patient in their own recovery, placing them at the center of the treatment model—rehabilitation is not a passive process.

Patient education is a key component of any treatment and recovery plan. This is absolutely imperative, particularly as many patients may expect their injuries to heal as the result of medications prescribed to treat headaches, sleep disturbances and mood disorders. It is essential for service members to understand for themselves that their primitive survival instincts are being hyperaroused, which is not subject to their conscious control. They must be made aware of the fact that the survival instinct is a triggered reaction, not a conscious action, and that they have no choice in the matter.

When a service member returns to the home front, they certainly do not choose to remain in a hyperactivated state. It is, however, a normal reaction of the amygdala to persist in battle mode. Understanding this physiological fact can make it easier for the service member to admit that the problem exists and, even more importantly, to understand what the target of a treatment plan should be in any given case. Understanding the impact of combat operational stress and post-traumatic stress issues on physical symptomatology is crucial; a history of self-reported concussion, in combination with current combat stress and depressive symptomatology, may result in a three to eightfold increase in the risk for manifestation of continued post-concussion symptoms (Schneiderman, Braver & Kang, 2008; Cooper *et al.*, 2011).

It is imperative that these service members are also evaluated and treated by behavioral health providers. At our facility, the role of behavioral health providers, who are able to offer counseling to help service members become aware of how their physical symptomatology is related to the stress factors that are centered in their minds, is an essential component of their treatment. Patients will see their behavioral health therapists on a regular basis in order to receive a continuity of support and education that can assist in their recovery.

Stress reduction techniques

> *The greatest mistake in the treatment of diseases is that there are physicians for the body and physicians for the soul, although the two cannot be separated.*

—Plato (Philosopher's Notes website, n.d.)

Stress reduction techniques, in particular "mind-body" techniques, can be used to temper the fight or flight response. These techniques include deep breathing, physical exercise and movement, guided imagery, meditation, spiritual practices, mindful and healthy eating, yoga, tai chi, or qigong (Bisson *et al.*, 2007; Bolton *et al.*, 2007; Gordon *et al.*, 2004; Gordon & Staples, 2005; Gordon *et al.*, 2008).

Two simple techniques that can easily be learned are deep breathing and stretching. Our breathing is controlled by the brainstem. In a fight or flight situation, stress hormones are released, triggering an increase in heart rate and blood pressure, dilating the bronchi and altering breathing patterns to short, shallow breaths. These physiological changes provide the muscles in the arms and legs with increased oxygen and nutrients to fight or run. We cannot voluntarily slow down our heart rate or blood pressure, but we can consciously control our breathing. When we force ourselves to take long deep breaths, it triggers a physiological reaction in the brainstem to calm down the fight or flight reaction.

There are several different deep breathing techniques that can be utilized, but a simple technique that can be employed in an immediate situation to reduce a hyperreaction to a perceived but not necessarily valid threat is to intake air for four seconds through the nose and exhale for six seconds through the mouth. An attempt should be made to concentrate on the breath itself, visualizing positive energy, strength, power and peace entering the body on inhalation and letting go of anger, irritability and fear on exhalation. Focusing on breathing throughout the day and "deepening" breathing as one goes about one's routine daily activities can also help to lower the fight or flight reaction trigger.

In a hyperaroused state, the body tenses the muscles as it prepares itself for a fight or flight reaction. Most "stressed" individuals are found on physical exam to have tight, tender muscles in their neck, trapezius and upper, middle or lower back muscles. Stretching exercises can relax those muscles and relieve post-concussive symptoms. Relaxing/loosening of these tensed muscles sends a signal to the brainstem, indicating that the cortex has made a conscious decision that there is no need for the fight or flight reaction to be triggered. Manual massage is a therapeutic course that may also help to reduce muscle tightness, leading to a reduction of post-concussive symptoms.

These techniques have been used throughout history and practiced within many different disciplines to help individuals relax. These are physical skills that anyone can perform—the more they are practiced, the more effective they become. I have found it helpful to use the following analogy with veterans: We can compare these simple skills to swinging a baseball bat. Anyone can stand in their yard and swing a bat, but not many individuals can stand in a batter's box and hit a ball coming at them at 90 mph. In order to improve their skills, they need practice. Practicing with a batting coach would help to become a better hitter. The same is true of these relaxation techniques. As they are practiced and fine-tuned with a therapist/instructor and applied to stressful situations, the individual is empowered to become effective in calming the unthinking fight or flight response. In the same way that a batter does not hit a home run every time he or she steps up to bat, these exercises will not be 100 percent effective every time. Sometimes stressed individuals will, metaphorically speaking, "hit a home run" and their stress levels will diminish immediately, allowing them to remain calm, fall asleep or curtail an angry/irritable feeling in response to situations or other individuals. Other times, they may strike out and nothing will happen when they attempt to employ these stress reduction tools. And sometimes they may not hit a home run, so to speak, but will obtain the equivalent of a single, double or triple, and stress will be decreased, maybe not 100 percent, but it will be reduced, resulting in attenuation of the post-concussion symptoms.

Psychotherapy

It is important to remember that psychotherapy can also provide healing pathways to recovery from the trauma of war, resulting in a lowering of the post-combat hyperarousal, with consequent improvement in symptoms. Transpersonal, cognitive-behavioral, psychodynamic, interpersonal, humanistic-existential, mindfulness and art therapies, and biofeedback, eye movement desensitization and reprocessing are all therapeutic disciplines that can provide significant stress reduction to service members experiencing post-combat stress issues with a resultant improvement in post-concussive symptoms.

Multidisciplinary team intervention

Finally, multidisciplinary teamwork is essential to optimally address the full range of physiological, psychological and social impacts of mTBI and PTSD.

In fact, it is my professional opinion that it is not possible for an "independent or solo practice provider" to give the quality of health care that is required to treat the complexity of post-concussive symptoms in service members returning from war. There needs to be a recognition that patients with post-concussive symptoms, secondary to the intertwined etiologies of concussion/TBI and post-deployment stress, need to be sent to a facility where the full range of proper care is available, as has been described here. Simply stated: if a clinician does not have the resources sufficient to address the medical, psychological, therapeutic and social issues of a service member with post-concussive symptoms, they need to refer the patient on so that they can access such resources.

Once a service member or veteran is engaged with a multidisciplinary team, it is essential that the team works synergistically—together as a team with the patient as an integral member—to amplify the benefits of therapy by using common language and skills to reinforce one another's work. Recovery from these post-concussive and PTSD symptoms is not a passive process. It requires motivation and dedicated work on the part of the service member to recover from these scars of war. Service members who acquire an understanding of how their symptoms develop and are then maintained are empowered to understand them and take appropriate actions to alleviate them.

Closing

Our lives are determined not by what happens to us, but by how we react to what happens; not by what life brings to us, but by the attitude we bring to life

—Anon (Performer's Advantage website, n.d.)

There are many questions about military concussions and how they are impacted by exposure to combat and ongoing stressors that still need to be answered. Exposure to combat stressors, the development of war-related PTSD and exposure to continuing stressors following return from deployment are likely significant factors impacting post-concussion symptoms. How the neurometabolism and anatomy of the brain are damaged in the case of combat-related brain injury, and how that injury then generates and maintains post-concussive symptoms and contributes to the development of PTSD, are still not well understood and warrant further research. Investigators are attempting to determine if the mechanism of injury—i.e. blast versus impact—is relevant to the development of post-concussive symptoms and PTSD. Researchers are also considering what other unique circumstances occur in warfare that may have an impact on the development and maintenance of post-concussive symptoms. Improved knowledge of these factors, leading to a better understanding of etiology, will likely lead to improved treatment strategies.

As mentioned previously, the significance of being in a war zone and facing life-threatening experiences on a daily basis produces a hyperactivated fight or flight response that persists on returning home as post-traumatic stress. I personally do not consider post-traumatic stress to be a "disorder"; rather, it is simply a natural reaction to the daily blood and guts trauma of war. Humans do not have control over the activation of their primitive instincts or when they are activated—this has been programmed by millions of years of evolution. Hence, hyperarousal becomes the lens through which sensory information is first processed.

Headaches, memory problems, insomnia and mood issues can have several etiologies, including both concussion/mTBI and persistent post-combat stress. This is an important factor to consider in understanding the maintenance and/or exacerbation of post-concussive symptoms. Unfortunately, much if not most of the time it is impossible to determine which of these two factors is the most influential. In spite of this fact, treatment must continue.

At this point, there is still much to be done to help service members through a long and difficult recovery. One of the most important facts for them to understand is that they are experiencing normal reactions to the abnormal situation of war; that the survival instinct, activated and ingrained when they are subjected to the type of assault upon their lives on a daily basis that they experience in warfare, continues both during and following deployment. Although some post-concussive symptoms are due to a brain injury itself, there is no doubt that continued functioning in a survival mode following return from deployment and the symptoms of PTSD, along with exposure to continued post-combat stress, are persistent driving forces for these symptoms. The challenges of working with service members with mTBI and PTSD are exceeded only by the daily life struggles of these brave warriors and the satisfaction and privilege that derive from being able to provide them with self-knowledgeable and caring services.

John L. Rigg, M.D., after a 20-year career as a professional musician based in New York City, returned to school to pursue a career in Medicine (City College of New York, Albert Einstein College of Medicine, Kessler Institute/University of Medicine and Dentistry of New Jersey) and a fellowship in traumatic brain injury at the University of Pittsburgh Medical Center. He is currently the Traumatic Brain Injury Program Director at the Dwight D. Eisenhower Army Medical Center, Fort Gordon, Georgia (Jackrigg@yahoo.com).

References

American Psychiatric Association (2000). *Diagnostic and Statistical Manual of Mental Disorders (DSM-IV)*. Washington, DC: American Psychiatric Association.

Bisson, J., Ehlers, A., Matthews, R., Pilling, S., Richards, D. & Turner, S. (2007). Psychological treatments for post-traumatic stress disorder: Systematic Review and Analysis. *British Journal of Psychiatry, 190,* 97–184.

Boake, C., McCauley, S.R., Levin, H. S., Pedroza, C., Contant, C. F., Song, J. X. … Diaz-Marchan, P. J. (2005). Diagnostic criteria for post concessional syndrome after mild to moderate traumatic brain injury. *The Journal of Neuropsychiatry and Clinical Neuroscience, 17*: 350-356.

Bolton, P., Bass, J., Betancourt, T., Speelman, L., Onyango, G., Clougherty, K., Neugerbauer, R., Murray, L. & Verdeli, H. (2007). Interventions for depression symptoms among adolescent survivors of war and displacement in Northern Uganda. *Journal of the American Medical Associatin, 298*(5), 519–527.

Brenner, L. A., Ivins, B. J., Schwab, K., Warden, D., Nelson, L.A., Jaffee, M. & Terrio, H. (2010). Traumatic brain injury, posttraumatic stress disorder, and Postconcussive symptom reporting among troops returning from Iraq. *Journal of Head Trauma Rehabilitation, 25*, 307–312.

Cooper, D. B, Kennedy, J. E., Cullen, M. A., Crithfields, E., Amador, R. R. & Bowles, A. O. (2011). Association between combat stress and post concussive symptom reporting in OEF/OIF service members with mild traumatic brain injuries. *Brain Injury, 25*(1), 1–7.

Farag, E., Manno, E. M. & Kurz, A. (2011). Use of hypothermia for traumatic brain injury: Point of view. Minerva Anestesiol, *77*(3), 366–370.

Gordon, J. S. & Staples, J. K. (2005). Effectiveness of a mind-body skills training program for healthcare professionals. *Alternative Therapies, 11*(4), 36–41.

Gordon, J. S., Staples, J. K., Blyta, A. & Bytqi, M. (2004). Treatment of posttraumatic stress disorder in post-war Kosovo high school students using mind-body skills groups: A pilot study. *Journal of Traumatic Stress, 17*(2), 143–147.

Gordon, J. S., Staples, J. K., Blyta, A., Bytyqi, M. & Wilson, A. (2008). Treatment of post-traumatic stress disorder in post-war Kosovar adolescents using mind-body skills groups: A randomized controlled trial. *Journal of Clinical Psychiatry, 69*, 1469–1476.

Hoge, C. W., McGurk, D., Thomas, J. L., Cox, A. L., Engel, C. C. & Castro, C. A. (2008). Mild traumatic brain injury in U.S. soldiers returning from Iraq. *New England Journal of Medicine, 358*(5), 453–463.

Holm, L., Cassidy, J. D., Carroll, L. J. & Borg, J. (2005). Summary of the WHO collaborating centre for neurotrauma task force on mild traumatic brain injury. *Journal of Rehabilitation Medicine, 37*, 137–141.

Hosek, J., Kavanagh, J. & Miller, L. (2008). *How Deployments Affect Service Members.* Santa Monica, CA: RAND Corporation. Retrieved from www.rand.org/pubs/monographs/MG432

Kennedy, J. K., Jaffee, M., Leskin, G. A., Stokes, J. W., Leal, M. A. & Fitzpatrick, P. J. (2007). Posttraumatic stress disorder and posttraumatic stress disorder-like symptoms and mild traumatic brain injury. *Journal of Rehabilitation Research and Development, 44*(7), 895–920.

McCrea, M. (2008). *Mild Traumatic Brain Injury and Postconcussion Syndrome: The New Evidence Base for Diagnosis and Treatment.* New York, NY: Oxford University Press.

Newsweek (2010, November 11). *Veteran's head injuries confound military doctor.* Retrieved from www.newsweek.com/2010/11/08/veteran-s-head-injuries-confound-military-doctor

Nilsson, J. (2010). *"Imagination is more important than knowledge."* Retrieved from www.saturdayeveningpost.com/2010/03/20/archives/retrospective/imagination-important-knowledge.html

Performer's Advantage website (n.d.). Retrieved from www.performersadvantage. com/pages/More_Quotes

Philosopher's Notes website (n.d.). Retrieved from http://philosophersnotes.com/ quotes/by_teacher/Plato

Rigg, J. L. & Mooney, S. R. (2011). Concussions and the military: Issues specific to service members. *Physical Medicine and Rehabilitation, 3*(10), Suppl 2, S380–386.

Schneiderman, A. I., Braver, E. R. & Kang, H. K. (2008). Understanding sequelae of injury mechanisms and mild traumatic brain injury incurred during the conflicts in Iraq and Afghanistan: Persistent postconcussive symptoms and posttraumatic stress disorder. *American Journal of Epidemiology, 167,* 1446–1452.

Shaw, N. A. (2002). The neurophysiology of concussion. *Progress in Neurobiology, 67,* 281–344.

Tolle, E. (2005). *The New Earth.* New York, NY: Penguin Books Ltd.

Think Exist website (n.d.). Retrieved from http://thinkexist.com/quotation/discovery_consists_of_seeing_what_everybody_has/186385.html

Veteran's Heart Georgia (2009). Quote by Thich Nhat Hanh, originally written in *True Love.* Retrieved from www.veteransheartgeorgia.org

8 Physically wounded and injured warriors and their families: The long journey home

Lee Lawrence

The scene on the air lift was hard to believe. We had row after row of litters stacked three and sometimes four high with patients. . . For them this trip was only the beginning.

—Lt. Col. Frank Correa, medical crew director with the U.S. Air Force's 491ˢᵗ Expeditionary Aeromedical Evacuation Unit in 2003 (Carroll, 2006)

In 2007, I flew on a medevac mission out of Afghanistan, from the Heathe N. Craig Joint Theater Hospital in Bagram to the Landstuhl Regional Medical Center in Germany. Unlike Lt. Col. Correa's flight in 2003, this one was relatively uncrowded: six stretchers and about a dozen walking wounded sitting on flip-seats along one side of the C-17 cargo plane. For some, the six-and-a-half-hour flight to Landstuhl was the third and by no means the last leg of a long journey home. It had started at what the military calls POI—Point of Injury. A patch of ordinary land suddenly churned to dust and blood by the deafening blast of an IED. Or the motor pool on a Forward Operating Base where, one minute, troops are routinely checking equipment and chewing tobacco; the next, they are racing for cables and jacks and crowbars, anything they can find to free a comrade now trapped under an 800-pound tool kit. Or the rooftop of a middle-class house on an empty street where a bullet from a distant window finds soft tissue.

The wounds suffered by American troops since boots first hit the ground in Afghanistan in 2001 are many and varied. At one end of the spectrum are minor injuries—from sprains to uncomplicated bullet wounds and simple fractures that can be treated at the field hospital and do not prevent the warrior from resuming full duties within days or weeks. At the other end are life-altering injuries. This chapter focuses on what happens to warriors when they require more extensive treatment and repatriation. A list of their injuries includes complex fractures, spinal cord injuries, amputations, back and neck injuries, burns, eye injuries, hearing loss, genital injuries and polytrauma injuries—when the warrior suffers one or more physical wounds, often along with Post Traumatic Stress Disorder and/or Traumatic Brain Injury. In such cases, within hours of the injury, the warrior is returning home, a journey that catches both the wounded and the family unprepared. Unlike a unit's scheduled homecoming, this return is unexpected, fraught, complicated and, for too many, seemingly never ending.

This chapter will sketch what that journey looks like for warriors and their families, from the point of injury (POI), through the chain of medical treatments and procedures, to the threshold to life beyond. It is important to note that clinicians and even the wounded and injured service members themselves typically do not fully understand, acknowledge or address the events—often a series of traumatic events—that service members experience between the POI and discharge from a medical facility stateside. This is in spite of the fact that such experiences are fraught with successive traumatic experiences, for both the service member and their family, that should be attended to at some point, but seldom are (Scurfield & Tice, 1992; Scurfield, 2006).

I will draw on a number of sources, including interviews with wounded warriors and their families, current research, published personal blogs, conversations with volunteers and others intimate with the daily rhythms of warrior care, as well as conversations with a variety of people inside non-profit and military organizations. In addition, while making a documentary about military chaplains, I spent three months embedded with U.S. troops in Afghanistan and Iraq in 2007. I will also be drawing on my own experience and that of my film collaborator, Terry Nickelson.

From point of injury to landing stateside

Downrange

> We were driving the same route we'd driven every day ... I heard the boom, and as soon as I heard the boom I was on fire. . . The hatch above me was open, thank God ... My face was on fire so I didn't know where the ground was, all I knew was that I had to get to the ground. So I jumped from the top of the vehicle and when I landed I broke my leg.... I rolled around on the ground, and it was all dead grass and sand and dust so it wasn't putting the fire out, and I was covered in fuel ... I rolled one way and I fell into a canal I had no idea was there. And the canal put the fire out. It also gave me cholera, funguses.
>
> —U.S. Army Sgt. Rick Yarosh (Yarosh, 2010)

> I was trapped underneath the equipment, probably about 800 pounds, for about fifteen minutes, and myself, I didn't think I was going to make it out of there because they were taking so long ... because there was so much blood and it was so painful and so hard to breathe. Some of my fellow soldiers would say, "C'mon Keller, you can make it. You can't let this get you. You're stronger than this. Just hang on." And that's what I needed; I listened to their voices. [Crying] I'm sorry. It's hard to remember that experience because it was such a painful..."
>
> —U.S. Army SFC Mackie Keller (Keller, 2007)

The stories are as varied as the warriors' backgrounds. Often the wounded witness others being killed or dismembered; sometimes they wait with other wounded for a break in the fighting so their comrades can drive them back to camp; one soldier describes the wounded huddled on the bed of a damaged truck bed, while the platoon leader hijacked a civilian truck (Raddatz, 2007). If the unit is far from the base, the way out is via helicopter. At Camp Al Taqaddam in Iraq's Al Anbar province, Terry was covering a medical team when the "POI call" came through. Within minutes, the team was hopping off the Blackhawk helicopter onto an improvised landing zone, rushing with a stretcher to a group of Marines kneeling on the ground. From an overpass, an insurgent had dropped an explosive into the Humvee tower. It exploded under the Marine, tearing off his right leg at the hip. As the medics strapped him onto a stretcher and ran him back to the helicopter, another Marine held out the disembodied leg, offering it to the medics.

The point is that the parade of horrors does not stop at the point of injury. In fact, a new parade often begins, colored by the additional trauma of the wound and the associated fear of death or dismemberment. When they rushed the Marine into the Al Taqaddam hospital, doctors crowded around the wound, while Chaplain Bautista-Rojas stood by his head. "I can't feel my leg," the Marine said. "I need to go to my mom and sister" (Nickelson, 2007).

No sooner is he wheeled into the Operating Room, than the first narcotics flow into his system, enough to keep him unconscious while he travels to the next level of care at Balad (Iraq) or Bagram (Afghanistan) and probably on through to Landstuhl (Germany). It is impossible to know just how much any warrior will remember of the scenes witnessed during this first leg of the journey home. But if some patients under full anesthesia record memories (Bruchas, 2011), then this cannot be ruled out. And even if shock and medications prevent the brain from recording memories, does this mean that the scenes witnessed, sounds heard, smells registered, and panic experienced leave no imprint?

Stateside

For families, the POI comes in the form of a phone call: a disembodied voice informs them that their warrior has been injured in Iraq or Afghanistan and, in many cases, is en route to Germany. Often the call comes within hours of the incident, unless personnel records are incomplete or out of date, in which case it could take long enough that rumors sometimes reach the family before the official call. For some spouses and parents, particularly those from non-military families and not living near or on a base, this can be their first plunge into the world of acronyms. They are now PNOK—Primary Next Of Kin; the voice at the other end is the CACO or CAO, which denotes casualty assistance; and their warrior falls under one of the following classifications:

- *VSI (Very Seriously Injured)*: the warrior may not survive;
- *SI (Seriously Injured)*: a very critical condition, but one that doctors do not believe is imminently life-threatening;
- *III (Incapacitating Injury or Illness)*: while not a serious or life-threatening injury, this nevertheless makes it impossible for the warrior to communicate directly with family; and
- *NSI (Not Seriously Injured)*.

In the case of VSI and SI, the military pays for and assists with travel arrangements so the next of kin can be at the warrior's bedside. This still leaves the spouse, parents or other next of kin with a list of urgent tasks—cancel appointments, notify employers and schools, break the news to the rest of the family, arrange for child-care, find pet-sitters. They have to note down pertinent names and phone numbers from the military, contact the unit's family readiness group to obtain assistance, keep track of travel-related expenses—and all the while processing their own shock, coping with the emotions of relatives, listening out for the next phone call with an update on their warrior.

Finally, there might be the phone call in which the voice on the other end says that there has been an incident and although the information is still sketchy, their warrior is "believed to be injured." The next phone call either floods them with relief or confirms the family's fears, the wait having added yet another layer of anxiety to the process.

Still in theater but headed home

What follows for warriors is a journey, usually by helicopter, to either the U.S. Air Force Theater Hospital at Joint Base Balad or the trauma unit of the hospital in Bagram. This may not be their first wound—many warriors have been wounded, healed and redeployed. For warriors with less serious injuries, this is the time they can most easily call their families and, indeed, sometimes they are the first ones to let their parents or spouse know they have been injured. Some warriors, however, resist making these phone calls. At the Bagram hospital, the chaplain routinely encouraged those who could to call home, telling them that nothing would assuage their families fear as much as hearing their warrior's voice. Most took him up on the offer, but one soldier stubbornly refused. He was afraid, he finally admitted. Afraid his mother might get mad. She had not wanted him to enlist.

Warriors with more serious wounds often transit this hospital in a haze. Doctors treat their wounds, operate if necessary, and stabilize them for the flight to Landstuhl. No sooner do they arrive than a medical team and a chaplain greet them. Although some are unconscious, most are at least semi-aware as medics transport them on gurneys from the landing zone to the hospital by ambulance. "I know you're in there, Dennis," the chaplain told one soldier who, to hide his face from our cameras, pulled a blanket over it. "Welcome to

Germany. God Bless." There were variations on this theme, and occasionally the chaplain did not utter the phrase "God bless." Several things are striking here: the use of the warrior's first name; the care to check the records first and then decide whether or not to say "God bless;" and the immediate reference to Germany. At one level, this speaks directly to observations by Scurfield & Tice (1992) that, during the Vietnam War, little to no attention was paid to the psychological state of wounded warriors, as medical teams shunted them from one facility to another (Scurfield, 2006). Something as simple as the use of a warrior's first name can be powerful. In their unit, last names and nicknames are the order of the day—to hear their first name is to feel that they are seen as if by a family member or close friend. This is also a marker that they are transitioning to a new world, where the first stop is Germany. To state this explicitly is to hand back a small measure of control in the form of information.

While Germany means "out of combat" and "safe," most soldiers are also acutely aware that, if they have been transported to Landstuhl, the likelihood of their returning to combat is virtually nil. Germany is also where the American community at large begins to welcome warriors back, not only through its American staff, but also through such things as clothes donated by a variety of organizations and individuals, quilts made by military wives' groups, and travel kits supplied by such groups as the Wounded Warrior Project and the American Red Cross. It could be weeks before the warrior receives his or her personal belongings back from theater, so these interventions are not only an expression of support, they are practical. This means that when warriors arrive stateside, they will be able to greet their families wearing something besides a hospital gown.

Taking inventory

The nature and severity of the injuries determine how aware warriors are during their stay in Landstuhl. Even those still heavily medicated often regain consciousness and, typically, one of the first things they do is take an inventory of their bodies. Foremost in the minds of young servicemen is the question: "Is my junk (genitals) together?" Given their state of shock and their sedation, this may not be the first time they've asked this and it is often not their last (Brown, 2011). The devastating truth is that, for an increasing number, the answer is not an unequivocal "yes." Already in early 2008, studies showed that servicemen had suffered more genitourinary injuries in Operation Iraqi Freedom (OIF) and Operation Enduring Freedom (OEF) than during any other military conflict (Serkin *et al.*, 2010). Later studies record that the percentage of wounded who suffered genitourinary injuries almost doubled, from 4.8 percent in 2009 to 9.1 percent in 2010, with no sign that this trend is abating (Brown, 2011; Waxman, 2009). Some have called it "the new signature wound" of these wars.

It is useful at this point to develop a sense of the range of injuries warriors confront in Landstuhl. Exact numbers are not easy to come by, because it all depends on just how one defines who is actually wounded. One organization that tracks casualties and fatalities places the total figure of U.S. wounded in OEF and OIF as of July 2011 to more than 45,000 (iCasualties.org, n.d.), and this seems to include warriors who have recovered in theater and returned to their units. The most immediately visible injuries are loss of limbs, burns and injuries that impair mobility, such as those to the spinal cord. The most recent figures are already somewhat dated, but they suggest that burns are on the rise, paralleling the rise of traumatic limb amputations. From 1 October 2001 to 1 June 2006, the military recorded a total of 423 major limb amputations, a rate that was comparable to previous conflicts (Stansbury *et al.*, 2008). But by the end of January 2010, the number of wounded OEF and OIF Service had reached 36,702 (iCasualties.org, n.d.), of which more than 950 had undergone one or more major limb amputations (Pasquina, 2010). This means that the average monthly rate of 7.5 amputations before June of 2006 soared to just over 12 for the period between June 2006 and January 2010. We need to keep in mind that such statistics are only snapshots—they do not include those who will undergo amputations weeks or even years down the road, once all efforts to salvage a wounded limb fail. Of all amputations, 15 percent are performed later (Stinner, 2010). While the numbers for burns remain lower, the rise of IED attacks is taking its toll, along with a number of causes not related to combat. Troops burning waste at a small FOB, working by fuel tanks, handling ammunition, fixing generators, and other similar routine duties account for about 25 percent of burns (Kauvar, 2009).

To bring the statistics up to date, between February 2010 and July 2011, an additional 8,468 U.S. service members were wounded, raising the total numbers of wounded since the launch of OEF in 2001 to more than 45,000 (iCasualties.org, n.d.). Moreover, a significant proportion of these wounded in action also suffer from TBI and PTSD. Among amputees alone, the rates are, respectively, more than one third and one fourth (Pasquina, 2010). This underscores an important point. Burns, spinal cord injuries, loss of limbs and many other injuries are often but one aspect of a complex set of wounds that can also include fractures, infections and eye injuries as well as "invisible" injuries such as TBI, PTSD, chronic pain and injuries involving impairment or loss of hearing.

Indeed, the noise of a blast or repeated blasts can perforate eardrums, cause dizziness, or trigger speech-language disorders (Helfer *et al.*, 2011). In some cases, doctors in theater have diagnosed soldiers suffering from hearing loss as depressed (Zoroya, 2008), a mistake that may have serious consequences. In combat situations, survival can depend on hearing orders and warning sounds, which explains why impaired hearing is a major cause for disability among service members (Ritenour *et al.*, 2008). Equally "invisible" is tinnitus: almost half of all warriors exposed to blasts suffer from a phantom noise that ranges from being a mild nuisance to a screeching so intrusive that it robs them of their ability to focus. It can sometimes drive people to such distraction that they would rather die (Groopman, 2009). Even more debilitating is chronic pain, defined as pain that persists more than three to six months after the underlying disease or injury has been resolved. The most common locations are back, head and shoulders and, according to one study, this kind of persistent pain is often associated with familial discord, work issues, psychological distress and depression. Chronic pain can be as disabling as PTSD (Lew, 2009).

When we visited wards and the Intensive Care Unit in Landstuhl in 2007, it was clear that troops were well informed about their injuries and what courses of treatment doctors expected for each of them. Again, this was a favorable comparison to the unnecessary anxiety many wounded during the Vietnam War experienced from simple lack of information (see Scurfield & Tice, 1992; Scurfield, 2006). Even Mackie Keller, who was heavily medicated, listed the injuries he suffered as a result of being trapped under an 800-pound tool kit. "I broke my leg, and I broke all of my ribs, and I have a laceration on my spleen. I fractured my sternum, and I had 17 fractures on my spine." He also knew he had traveled from his FOB to Balad and Landstuhl and that he was now headed back to the U.S. (Keller, June 2007).

Strong Bonds

What Keller also insisted on telling us, despite severe pain, was equally revealing. He knew from the staff that Terry and I were interested in chaplains, and this Sergeant First Class was going to make sure we knew just how good these members of his band of brothers were. Keller told us how a chaplain had been there at his bedside at Balad hospital, how he woke up about every 15 minutes and always found the chaplain by his side, how a chaplain had told him how much he admired him. And every time we made a move to leave and let him rest, Keller added more, generalizing his praise to all chaplains:

> This ain't the first time in my military career that they've helped me in hard times ... Chaplains are great people. They have long hours; I don't know how they do it. They're up late, sometimes don't get any sleep because there's so many troops in the world, in Iraq, in the States, and in other countries, and there are so few chaplains. And somehow they get to every one of them's needs ..." (ibid.)

What is significant here is not so much the support Keller received from chaplains, but the extent to which his mind and heart were bound up with the military and the effort he made to praise his fellow soldiers. Also in the ICU and suffering from severe burns and injuries to the right side of his body, Marine SGT Leonard Chargualaf kept bringing the conversation back to "my

Marines." When the chaplain asked if he wanted to pray also for his daughter, he said "just for my Marines" (Chargualaf, 2007). It was not because Chargualaf did not love his daughter—one can hear his love for her in his voice when he speaks of her today. It was because in his heart and mind he was still part of his unit, responsible for his Marines.

This is a recurring motif, even for troops like Army SSG Jonathan Mann, whose unit was based in Germany. Mann had set out in a convoy to assist fellow soldiers when his truck hit an IED. In absorbing the shock, some of the armor on the truck fell on his right leg, shattering it. In his case, Landstuhl Regional Medical Center was close to where his family was waiting for him, so his wife was at his bedside when we met him in June 2007. His leg was encased in a scaffold of metal and he was lucid, though he had been placed on strong pain medications. What was foremost on his mind was not his wife or being home. When the chaplain we were shadowing came by to see him, Mann told him about both a young man and a young woman in his platoon. Before they set out on their mission, Mann had been teasing the female soldier about her impending marriage and palling around with the other. Thirty minutes later they were both killed. "And I didn't talk to them about God," he said (Mann, 2007).

At the time, it seemed that his guilt was directed toward the God he believed asked him to bear witness. But I caught up with him recently and he mentioned that, more than four years later, he continues to wrestle with this guilt, now the subject of regular therapy sessions. This indicates, to me, at least, that the primary guilt he bears is directed towards these fellow soldiers. He feels responsible for not "saving" them, in all senses of the word; a form of survivor guilt to be sure, but also a powerful reflection of just how strongly Mann, who remains on active military status, looks first to the needs of his soldiers.

"Strong Bonds" is the name of a program the military has instituted in an effort to help troops strengthen their marriages and family ties. But at this point in their journey home, the strongest bond they feel is to their units. It is a bond forged in war and survival. Their physical pain stemming from injuries is now exacerbated by the experience of being suddenly and forcibly separated from their mates, adding a layer of loss tinged with guilt and failed obligation. "It dawned on me when I got stateside," says SGT Chargualaf, "and I realized that I was thousands of miles away—that was a lot to deal with because my main mission was to take care of my Marines" (Chargualaf, 2011).

Landing stateside

Administratively, wounded warriors who require treatment lasting six months or more are transferred out of their units. In the Air Force, they are attached to the Air Force Wounded Warrior Program, while Marines and soldiers are moved to the Marine Corps Wounded Warrior Regiment and the Army's Wounded Warrior Transition Unit, respectively. These Army and Marine units were established in 2007, in the wake of the Walter Reed Army Medical Center scandal, which exposed a healthcare system that was overwhelmed and coming apart at the seams. Most agree that the system has vastly improved in recent years, but it remains for many a challenging bureaucratic maze whose efficiency depends on the responsiveness and attentiveness of individuals who are often overwhelmed.

Physically, the wounded all travel from Landstuhl to Malcolm Grow USAF Medical Center at Andrews Air Force Base in Maryland. Here, a second triage takes place and a "new normal" begins. This is a phrase heard over and over again—a recognition and acceptance that life has taken a turn and that, at least for the immediate future and perhaps forever, one's activities, roles, expectations, dreams have changed.

Some warriors may spend a night or two at Andrews AFB, while the staff arranges their transfer to a hospital at the military installations to which they were assigned prior to their overseas deployments. The severely wounded, meanwhile, are immediately transported to facilities such as the Burn Center at Brooke Army Medical Center in San Antonio, Texas or the trauma unit at Walter Reed National Military Medical Center in Bethesda, Maryland. There are cases where spouses and parents have traveled to Landstuhl because the doctors felt they could contribute significantly to the warrior's recovery; but for the most part, families and warriors meet stateside.

It is hardly the homecoming they have dreamt of—there is usually no cheering and "hoopla," no rushing into each other's arms for that first hug. Instead, service members and their loved ones approach each other through a cloud of contradictory emotions: longing, dread, hope, fear. Warriors may be reluctant and feel powerless—"I didn't want my mother to see me this way," says Chargualaf. "She didn't need to see me hurt. That was a big thing for me, but I had no control over that" (ibid.). And families steel themselves for fear of breaking down. "They try to prepare you for the worst of the worst and there's just no explaining the actual feeling," says Crystal Nicely, a Marine whose husband, Corporal Todd Nicely, stepped on a pressure plate (type of IED), the explosion leaving him a quadruple amputee. (Nicely, 2011)

At Walter Reed, parents and spouses walk down hallways where men and women are being pushed in wheelchairs and lying on gurneys, where doors left ajar offer a glimpse of IV stands and monitors and life support medical equipment and bandages. Some spouses are young women who had barely come to know their husbands before deployment separated them. Some had partied hard, had an exuberant time of it and, on the eve of deployment, tied the knot; now, overwhelmed by the enormity of life-changing injuries, they leave their marriages. But in a testament to the remarkable resilience of the human psyche, many spouses stay in the marriage, and their responses shift quickly from despair at the news of the injury to gratitude. "When I saw him," says Nicely, "to be honest, all I saw was that he was breathing, whether it was the machines or not, he was breathing … which meant he was alive" (ibid.).

There is always someone who is worse off: their warrior at least has his limbs; the shrapnel could have lodged in his brain; the infections are under control; he could have easily bled out. And always the bottom line: unlike so many others, he is alive. Alive.

A new unit

At this point, the narrative splinters into particularities, and every generality has its exceptions. What follows are some common situations and emotions that warriors and their families experience during this stage of their journey.

Even in its more efficient incarnation, the medical maze is daunting. Under the new system, all warriors are assigned a "Triad of Care," a team charged with coordinating treatment with clinical and non-clinical professionals according to a "Comprehensive Transition Plan" or CTP. These are the warrior's new orders, intended to give him or her a focus and goals. Interestingly, the Army is currently considering adding a review process by which officers would evaluate the "work" of service members while assigned to the Wounded Warriors Transition Unit.

Social cohesion is a key concept in the military, a commitment to putting the interests of the group first, which is enshrined in such mottoes as the Marines' *Semper Fidelis.* A closer look at this concept across different military settings—infantry and all combat arms units versus support units that include all support elements, ranging from medical to administrative—led some researchers to define two types of cohesiveness: "task cohesion," which rallies members around a shared mission and yields high performance, and "social cohesion," which fosters bonds among members and provides more emotional and psychological support (Coulter, 2010).

In a wounded warrior unit, evaluating performance may be a tool by which to foster a hybrid of these two concepts. The task for all wounded warriors is to follow instructions and devote their energy to recovery—even if that differs widely from one person to the next. And though warriors spend time together, their individual trajectory through the healthcare system precludes any lasting form of "social cohesion." This being said, there is much to be gained from recasting the wounded from victim to active agent and instilling the sense that working towards recovery is a valuable contribution to a greater whole: the unit. At the same time, knowing that one's efforts, as well as those of the guy in the next bed or room, will impact evaluation reports may further encourage the "Battle Buddy" phenomenon that already exists on military hospital wards. In one such case, when it was obvious that a brawny serviceman from Texas was frightened of falling asleep at night, a fellow wounded warrior took to singing to him till the Texan relaxed and drifted off.

If instituted, an evaluation process may also affect the emotional and psychological dynamics of future transition. As treatment progresses, a medical board reviews each case to determine whether warriors are able to continue to serve in the military, perhaps in another military occupational specialty, or whether they will be required to leave the military, through the medical evaluation board process, due to the severity of their injuries.

This was the case for Mackie Keller who, months after his injury, was walking with the help of a brace. "I'm almost as good as new," he said during a fishing outing organized for patients at Walter Reed by a volunteer outing group. "The doctors say I'll be fine, but because of my back injury, I won't be good enough to be a soldier anymore. I won't be able to do some of the things a soldier needs to do anymore" (Leibe, 2007). Will a strong evaluation help counter the sense of failure implied in the words "I won't be good enough?" Or might these evaluations lead to an even greater loss of self-worth and hopelessness?

A new normal

The new normal also involves accepting a new appearance, a new set of physical limitations, be they temporary or permanent. "It took me weeks before I was able to look myself in the mirror, before I was able to come to grips with the reality of what my life was going to be, the rest of my life," said Aaron Mankin, a Marine Corporal who was injured in an IED blast that burned more than 25 percent of his body (Mankin, 2011). By the time CPL Mankin held up a mirror, loved ones had already seen his disfigurement and begun accepting this "new normal." But sometimes, warriors and families are not at all "on the same page," making it tougher for both.

While a young wife was trying to absorb the reality that her husband had lost a leg, he kept assuring her that his manhood was intact and that they could have a normal sex life. But what meant so much to him, right then, meant little to her. She was frustrated, angry, upset—she wanted him to stop going on about sex, she wanted to focus on the next treatment, the next evaluation; she wanted time with him to see just how much he had changed inside. Who he was on the inside was far more important to her than his ability to perform sexually.

A caveat

The presumption throughout this chapter is that the wounded warrior is male. Indeed, 98.1 percent of all casualties are sustained by men. But that still leaves 1.9 percent who are women. While some researchers have studied gender differences in terms of combat-related stress and subsequent post-deployment mental health (see Vogt *et al.*, 2011), there seems to be no focused examination of the role that gender plays in the recovery process from physical wounds. The scant research that does exist suggests that gender differences may affect recovery rates (Cross *et al.*, 2011). In this regard, it is useful to keep in mind that certain injuries—such as facial burns, lacerations and other wounds that dramatically alter a warrior's appearance—may take a greater psychological toll on women in our current cultural context. In addition, since relationships, family and community play a key role in the healing and transition process, gender differences may have a significant impact in terms of current cultural perceptions of women in combat and in the military. Joining the military is still viewed as a non-traditional career option for women, so the community may be slow in recognizing their service and extending its welcome and support.

Similarly, the presumption throughout is that the primary caregiver is female—and, 96 percent of all caregivers are indeed women. But that leaves four percent who are men, whose journey can be very different from that of female caregivers. In hospitals, the fathers of wounded warriors often express more anger at the situation than do warriors' mothers. But while fathers can rely on their child's mother to take over as primary caregiver, husbands of wounded warriors often have to shoulder the duty themselves, with little ready-made support. No matter how open a unit's Family Readiness Group (FRG) is to husbands, the reality is that most of their activities are geared to women and male military spouses rarely participate. When disaster strikes, women can rely on relationships they have built during deployment through their FRG, but male spouses have no such immediate recourse. Similarly, although many women caregivers document their experiences in blogs and participate in online communities, it is rare to find their male counterparts blogging or reaching out through online groups. As a result, the community at large has little sense of what these husbands are experiencing—if they even know they exist at all.

The crucial and difficult role of caregivers

The tasks facing the caregiver are formidable. Even as they digest the changes in their partners or children and mourn the visions they had of their own futures, caregivers are faced with providing both emotional and practical support, with the additional need that they act as an advocate to make sure the system does the best it can for their warriors; for the reality is that the CTP is as much their mission as it is the warrior's. Many of the physically injured are also battling psychological wounds or are heavily medicated, rendering them incapable of performing self-assessments, setting realistic goals, or meeting other requirements of the CTP.

This means that for weeks, months, and sometimes years, while the warrior is closely tethered to the hospital, either as an inpatient or an outpatient, the spouse or parents must put their own lives on hold. To accomplish this, they may be forced to take unpaid leave, relinquish jobs and sources of income, or ask others to manage a multitude of issues back home, all of which can readily add another layer of guilt for the warrior:

> From day one, my mom has been with me. She gave up a 20-something year career at the drop of a dime to come take care of her son. And that's something I have to live with the rest of my life. (Chargualaf, 2011)

The caregiver also carries a heavy emotional burden. Within a week of her arrival at the trauma unit to see her husband, the young wife of an OIF warrior found herself working through an unfamiliar system that was transferring her husband to a hospital in their home state. "We are nobody," she told another wife, "we don't have a lot of money. But he's my husband, and I want him to have the best, he deserves the best." Ensuring "the best" means researching rehabilitation centers to determine the one best suited to provide for her husband. If it falls outside the military healthcare system, she needs to research which treatment facilities accept TriCare, the military medical insurance plan. Then there is the transportation piece of the puzzle, and oftentimes the need to set up childcare. What also emerges is the degree to which internal family dynamics can be fraught. In one particular case, the physician stopped by while the injured warrior's mother-in-law was at his bedside. The physician informed the mother-in-law that he had changed the warrior's prescription, but she failed to pass this information along to his spouse. The young woman was scrambling to remain fully informed of her husband's care and prescribed treatments in order to best advocate for him, so she felt undermined by her mother-in-law.

When one considers such additional factors as age and experience, education, concurrent needs of small children, financial worries, and family dynamics, it is easy to understand why many caregivers report increased levels of stress and anxiety, sleep disturbances, and depression over time (Michigan Department of Veterans Affairs, 2011). It is important also to remember that the ranks of parents and spouses include a number who are not native English speakers. For them, the disorientation is even more acute as they try to understand their warrior's prognosis, the nature and aim of treatments, the results of medical diagnostic testing, the possible side effects of medications, the likely progression and course of recovery from injuries, and the like. Unable to communicate with most of the English-speaking spouses and parents on the ward, they may also feel isolated. For the warrior, this gives rise to considerable additional stressors, as the wounded service member attempts to translate for parents or spouses.

Lost in the shuffle

As willing as spouses and parents might be, there are times that their love may be laced with resentments. Many parents, for instance, have reached the stage in their lives when they can look forward to retiring—and instead they have a child who depends on them completely for his or her care as well as for basic survival and sustenance. The mix of emotions is even more complex if the child enlisted without their blessing. A spouse, who looked forward to having her partner back home to share the duties of running a household and raising children, finds herself instead faced with an additional dependent. In many cases, wounded warriors and their families are at a hospital far from home, separated from support systems they have relied upon throughout deployment, juggling home obligations by remote, all the while at the mercy of the hospital's schedule. For those at Walter Reed, for instance, this may be the first time they have been in Washington, DC, confronted by unfamiliar territory and a city and transportation system that overwhelm and frighten them.

So much attention is focused on the warriors themselves that the caregivers are sometimes "lost in the shuffle." Many hospital volunteers offer services ranging from yoga to art therapy to massage, but these are, by and large, geared to the warriors and not to their families. Some grievances might at first blush seem petty. A mother whose white roots are showing because she can't— "not at these DC prices!"—go to the hairdresser; or a spouse who rushed to her husband's side wearing casual, comfortable clothes and, now, is mortified when officers or officials visit the hospital. But behind such laments lies a plea for control in a situation that is, at its best, full of uncertainty. And it is not always at its best. As improved as it may be, the system still does not work smoothly for everyone. Families experience delays in compensation, bureaucratic choke points, and onerous bureaucratic processes.

On 27 July 2011, Crystal Nicely enumerated many of the problems caregivers face when she testified before the Senate Veterans' Affairs Committee:

> I'm not only my husband's caregiver, non-medical attendant, appointment scheduler, cook, driver and groomer, but I'm also his loving wife, faced with my own stresses and frustrations. ... I rely on compensation that is provided to non-medical attendants to maintain my household. With Todd's injury the bills do not stop coming and, in fact, it has gotten more expensive. We are grateful for what assistance we do get from the Marine Corps, but had we not been greeted by people who were able to assist, we would have been lost in the recovery process.
>
> Todd has been a part of an integrated disability evaluation system, which I understand is supposed to be a faster and more efficient way to complete evaluation and transition out of the service. That has not been our experience. At one point, a simple summary of my husband's injuries sat on someone's desk for almost 70 days waiting for approval. I thank Chairman Murray [whom Nicely appealed to for assistance] who helped get this resolved, but it should not take my talking to a United States senator to help my husband. More importantly, what about all the other wounded Marines who have not had the chance to ask for that kind of help?
>
> Coordination of care for Todd has also been a problem. There seem to be so many coordinators that they are actually not all on the same page at this time, doing opposite things. Though she was trying to help, I rarely saw my federal recovery coordinator, who seemed to have too many people she was responsible for.

This lack of communication has also extended to benefits and pro-grams—I have received very little information on how to participate or enroll in what is offered by the VA. From the benefits we know about, we often face problems in actually receiving them.

(Iraq and Afghanistan Veterans of America, n.d.).

Second life

For all that can go wrong for some in the hospitalization phase, this is also a time when warriors experience the gratitude of a nation most distinctly. Vol-unteer groups send gifts ranging from iPods and clothing to laptops and cash. They organize all-paid outings, deliver free snacks, and provide DVDs and books. Officials stop in to express appreciation, cameramen in tow; and to those wounded in combat, high-ranking officers present Purple Heart medals. This is also the time when they are surrounded by warriors who have shared the experience of war and when caregivers can connect.

As much as warriors and families look forward to leaving the hospital, they often find themselves suddenly out of the spotlight and, in the case of those transitioning to the civilian world, entering a culture that feels alien. This dif-ficult shift to civilian life may occur within months of the injury or years later, by which time the warrior may have experienced new traumas—a late ampu-tation, repeated surgeries, acute infections, broken relationships. And the new trauma may not always conform to an outsider's or even a fellow warrior's expectations. In addition to suffering serious burns up and down the right side of his body, Chargualaf lost "a chunk" of his right thigh. Asked whether he had feared losing the limb altogether, he said, "I was kind of disappointed to keep my leg and arm—I would rather have a prosthetic. I always thought that people that have prosthetics look cool. You stand out, you look—futuristic."

You also look like you have been through a war; you're not just a guy with a limp. This, at least, is what research on burn patients suggests might lie behind Chargualaf's words. In a 2008 paper published in the *Journal of Advanced Nursing*, researchers found that burn patients regarded their bodies as telling the story of their experiences, both how they suffered their burn injuries and what surgeries they had subsequently endured (Moi, 2008). If this is the case for civilian burn patients whose goal is to resume their pre-burn life, it is all the more the case for warriors for whom injuries signal both proud service to their country and a radical shift in identity. Scars, prosthetics, and other vis-ible signs of injuries can therefore play a positive role in this population. They are a badge of honor, a distinction, and a way of bringing their former identity as a warrior into their new civilian life.

As warriors and their families move forward in this phase, time and money are the scarcest commodities, and building new identities and a sense of pur-pose their greatest challenge. "This is a whole new battle," says Chargualaf, who was medically discharged in May 2010 and has since been receiving disability, which is "not even close to half" his previous pay. Married with three young children, he is also supporting his mother, who is his primary caregiver. Four years after his injury, Chargualaf has not yet reached the point in his recovery where he can return to school and earn qualifications for a civilian job.

Building a new identity for some warriors also involves engaging with the world through a very changed body; in some cases, a face so disfigured as to be unrecognizable. In order to gain mobility and function, these warriors undergo surgery after surgery after surgery, with all the stress this entails for both themselves and their families. And still, many will never look the same, forced now to interact with the world with a face they themselves were once frightened to see in the mirror. Being accepted by their loved ones is key to being able to step out and seek acceptance in the wider community. Once again, families find themselves providing crucial support, while processing their own grief about the changes in their loved ones. As Chargualaf says about his own situation, "It feels endless."

Welcome interventions

Theory indicates that we learn from our mistakes, but we can learn as much, if not more, from models that work. I will conclude this chapter by highlighting some interventions that benefit our wounded warriors and their families on their long, tortuous journey home.

Housing

Free accommodation for families near military hospitals, provided by such non-profit organizations as Fisher House and Operation Homefront, enables families to remain together while the warrior is being treated. This also lightens the financial burden and, in the best of cases, offers a community of peers, formal counseling services and opportunities for informal mentoring. At a later stage, organizations such as Home for Heroes provide housing adapted to the specific disabilities of severely injured veterans, enabling them to move out of their parents' homes and live independently, empowering them and providing them and their parents with hope. By involving other wounded warriors as volunteers, Home for Heroes is helping a larger community of veterans to find new purpose by helping others.

Mentoring

Spouses and veterans sometimes return to the hospital and informally share their hard-earned knowledge with warriors or spouses who have just begun their journeys. In the hospital, much of this happens ad hoc and may or may not benefit from institutional support. Later, during the transition to life beyond the hospital, this mentoring can take place through storefront, community-based "Vet Centers" (Readjustment Counseling Service, U.S. Department of Veterans Affairs), much to the benefit of both mentor and mentee. While the latter receives valuable information and emotional support from someone who truly understands, the mentor finds meaning and purpose in the offering of support and assistance.

Recognition

Only those warriors injured in combat receive the Purple Heart medal. This leaves many warriors wounded in Iraq and Afghanistan with no concrete recognition of their service. Silver Star Families of America (SSFOA) rectifies this by awarding silver star banners or certificates. These are not to be confused with a Silver Star medal, which is issued by the government for gallantry in action. The SSFOA banner/certificate is an unofficial recognition that expresses the community's appreciation. Similarly, one can submit a request to the SSFOA to honor caregivers, usually relegated to the ranks of unsung heroes.

Financial assistance

Every stage of the wounded warrior's journey involves unexpected expenses. Various veteran, church and other civilian organizations have found creative ways to assist. SSOFA, for example, sends families gift cards for Domino's Pizza or other fast-food outlets while they are at the bedsides of their hospitalized wounded warriors. The Good Guys Marine Fund in California intervenes at a higher level: working with military hospitals in California, this organization furnishes $5,000 grants to severely injured warriors. Operation First Response (OFR), on the other hand, grew out of the realization that there is often a significant lag between the time when a warrior is medically discharged—or "MedBoarded" out—and the point at which VA benefits take effect. Even when physical wounds are stabilized, many still struggle with short-term memory problems, anger issues and other PTSD and/or TBI-related symptoms that prevent them from completing a degree or holding down a job. Transitioning from regular pay to disability payments and compensation (Maynard et al., 2010) can represent a significant reduction in income. OFR, along with a panoply of sports groups, veteran organizations and community activists of all stripes, stage fundraisers to help bridge the gap and to assist warriors on the road to self-sufficiency. In addition, organizations such as the Department of Defense Yellow Ribbon Program helps warriors and their families to budget and gain control over their financial lives.

Recreation

Whether a fishing outing for Walter Reed patients, a weekend hunting trip for veterans, or training in disabled and adapted sports, local and national groups are giving warriors a much-needed break, while at the same time building their confidence and imparting that most elusive and life-enhancing commodity: hope. It seems fair to say that such activities are instrumental in enabling warriors to rebuild their identities, in part through the increasingly recognized power of play.

Reconstructive and plastic surgery

Many warriors require specialized advanced surgery to maximize functionality or restore their features to "normal" proportions. Operation Mend and the Iraq Star Foundation are two organizations that fund such surgeries, covering also the expenses for their families. Such interventions not only impact warriors' view of themselves; they also improve their interaction with the community at large. For although the surgeries do not—indeed typically cannot—erase all scars or restore a warrior's original appearance, they can reduce the disfigurement and restore severely damaged faces to the familiar template of chin, nose, cheeks and forehead. Since our brains are attuned to patterns, this means that when outsiders first encounter them, they recognize the 'pattern' of a human face and therefore respond with less aversion or fear.

Supporting caregivers

We are increasingly recognizing that caregivers require support as well. Whatever form it takes, from Red Cross-sponsored coffee hours at Walter Reed or a weekend retreat organized by the Wounded Warrior Project to dinners hosted by local churches and organizations, these interventions are invaluable for caregivers. They provide them with a sense of community, much-needed respite, recognition for their valuable work, and a reminder that the world is larger than their everyday routines. Hope for the warriors has also launched a Caregiver Scholarship Program that helps caregivers to build their futures.

Education

Among many programs designed to facilitate education, the Army's AW2 Education Initiative is geared to wounded warriors who wish to remain in the military, while the year-long TRACK program offered by the Wounded Warrior Project in Florida and Texas provides a holistic approach that supports veterans as they earn academic credits and pursue personal goals. Many colleges and universities make an effort to reach out to veterans, creating an opportunity for donors to step in at a stage in the wounded warrior's journey time when such gifts as computers would be timely (as opposed to offering these gifts earlier on while the warrior is still hospitalized).

Community building

Participating in a community of some type can develop and expand one's network of relationships, which is key to the well-being of wounded warriors and families. The trick is finding the right community. This can be a geographically based group, such as civic organizations and local churches, or an interest-based group. Many of the organizations mentioned previously foster a sense of community by involving warriors, as well as civilians and families, in those activities they organize. There are also efforts whose primary goal is to establish a community that aims specifically to integrate wounded warriors and their families. These range from blog platforms for caregivers (such as http://veterancaregiver.blogspot.com or http://blog.familyofavet.com) to interventions directed towards breaking down the barriers between civilians and veterans. The latter include speaking engagements organized by Tempered Steel, in which wounded warriors address schools and communities, and Veteran–Civilian Dialogues, in which Intersections International orchestrates evening-long group conversations. On a larger scale, the Minnesota National Guard has launched a Yellow Ribbon Community Campaign that asks towns to engage its residents and institutions in a shared commitment to support their veterans. Hospitals, for example, commit to accepting TriCare so that warriors and families do not have to travel to a distant VA hospital; civic leaders make the time to recognize and publicly welcome returning warriors; and employers reach out to veterans.

The bottom line

As is clear from the plethora of groups that have emerged to assist wounded warriors and their families, their journey does not end with the completion of medical treatment, their medical discharge, or a new job in the civilian world or even the military. The Point of Injury is more than a single traumatic event. It is a turning point that for many marks the death of one identity and the birth of a series of "new normals."

For each wounded warrior, the journey is different, as it is for each family member affected. As they move forward through the stages of adult life, they carry visible and invisible scars, mourn unfulfilled dreams, battle pain. At the same time, many experience deep spiritual and emotional growth, find new purpose, and embrace life in inspiring ways. We have a responsibility to our wounded warriors, and their parents, children, spouses and partners, to listen and respond with respect, appreciation, and care. This will enable us to walk with them and learn from them and make this long journey home a shared one.

Lee Lawrence spent four years working on Chaplains Under Fire, an award-winning documentary she co-directed. This included three months embedded with the military in Iraq and Afghanistan. She remains actively interested in veteran affairs. As a freelance journalist, she writes for the Christian Science Monitor, the Wall Street Journal and other publications (Lalawrence@mac.com).

Bibliography

Ainspan, N. D. (2011). From deployment to employment. *U.S. Naval Institute Proceedings, 137*(2), 44–50.

Brown, D. (2011, March 4). Amputations and genital injuries increase sharply among soldiers in Afghanistan. *The Washington Post*. Retrieved from *www.washingtonpost.com/wp-dyn/content/article/2011/03/04/AR2011030403258.html?sid=ST2011030504659*

Bruchas, R., Kent, C., Wilson, H. & Domino, K. (2011). Anesthesia awareness: Narrative review of psychological sequelae, treatment, and incidence. *Journal of Clinical Psychology in Medical Settings, 18*(3), 257–267.

Caban, A. (2011, January 28). Life of a military spouse: Wayne Perry. *Veteran Journal*. *Retrieved from www.veteranjournal.com/military-spouse-wayne-perry*

Carroll, A. (Ed.) (2006). *Operation Homecoming: Iraq, Afghanistan, and the Home Front in the Words of U.S. Troops and Their Families*. New York, NY: Random House.

Chargualaf, L. (2007, June). Interview with Lee Lawrence and Terry Nickelson. Parts of the interview are available in the documentary *Chaplains Under Fire*. Retrieved from www.chaplainsunderfire.com

Chargualaf, L. (2011). Interviews with Lee Lawrence, August and September 2011. Parts of the interview are available in the documentary *Chaplains Under Fire*. Retrieved from www.chaplainsunderfire.com

Coulter, I., Lester, P. & Yarvis, J. (2010). Social Fitness. *Military Medicine, 175*(8), 88–96.

Cross, J. D., Johnson, A. E., Wenke, J. C., Bosse, M. J., Ficke, J. R. (2011). Mortality in female war veterans of operations Enduring Freedom and Iraqi Freedom. *Clinical Orthopaedics And Related Research, 469*(7), 1956–1961.

Fitzgerald, C. E. (2010). Improving nurse practitioner assessment of woman veterans. *Journal of the American Academy of Nurse Practitioners, 22*, 339–345.

Groopman, J. (2009, February 9). That buzzing sound. *New Yorker, pp.* 42–49.

Helfer, T. M., Jordan, N. N., Lee, R. B, Pietrusiak, P., Cave, K. & Schairer, K. (2011). Noise-induced hearing injury and comorbidities among post-deployment U.S. Army soldiers: April 2003–June 2009. *American Journal of Audiology, 20*, 33–41.

iCasualties.org (n.d.) Statistics on OEF and OIF military fatalities compiled from statistics released by the Department of Defense. Retrieved from http://icasualties.org

Iraq and Afghanistan Veterans of America (n.d.) Testimony of Crystal Nicely [Video file]. Retrieved from http://iava.org/testimonies/iava-founder-and-executive-director-paul-rieckhoff-costs-war

Kauvar, D. S., Wade, C. E. & Baer, D. G. (2009, October). Burn hazards of the deployed environment in wartime: Epidemiology of non-combat burns from ongoing United States military operations. *Journal of American College of Surgeons, 209*, 453–460.

Keller, M. (2007, June). Interview with Lee Lawrence and Terry Nickelson. Parts of interview are available in the documentary *Chaplains Under Fire*. Retrieved from www.chaplainsunderfire.com

Leibe, P. C. (2007, September 21). For injured and their families, a day away from Walter Reed. *The Enterprise*. Retrieved from www2.somdnews.com/stories/092107/entemor170848_32116.shtml

Lew, H. L. (2009). Prevalence of chronic pain, posttraumatic stress disorder, and persistent postconcussive symptoms in OIF/OEF veterans. *Journal of Rehabilitation Research & Development, 46*(6), 697–702.

Mankin, A. (2011, January 27). Operation mend: Reconstructing lives through reconstructive surgery [Video file]. Retrieved from http://homefrontheroes.com/play/19257044

Mann, J. (2007, June). Interview with Lee Lawrence and Terry Nickelson.

Maynard, C., Flohr, B., Guagliardo, T. A., Martin, C. H., McFarland, L. V, Pruden, J. D. & Reiber, G. E. (2010). Department of Veterans Affairs compensation and medical care benefits accorded to veterans with major limb loss. *Journal of Rehabilitation Research & Development, 47*, 403–408.

Michigan Department of Veteran Affairs (2011, October 10). Caregivers of veterans: Serving on the home front. Retrieved from http://michigan.gov

Moi, A., Vindenes Hallvard, A. & Gjengedal, E. (2008). The experience of life after burn injury: A new bodily awareness. *Journal of Advanced Nursing, 64*(3), 278–286.

Murray, C. K. (2008). Epidemiology of infections associated with combat-related injuries in Iraq and Afghanistan. *The Journal Of Trauma, 64*, S232–238.

Nicely, C. (2011, July 13). "He's my best friend." The Crystal Nicely story [Video file]. Retrieved from http://homefrontheroes.com/play/26408221

Nickelson, T. (2007, June 15). TQ POI: Saving our wounded. [Web log message]. Retrieved from http://web.me.com/lalawrence/Add-on_footage/POI.html

Pasquina, P. F. (2010). DOD paradigm shift in care of service members with major limb loss. *Journal of Rehabilitation Research & Development, 47*(4), xi–xiv.

Perry, T. (2011, April 6). U.S. Troops in Afghanistan suffer more catastrophic injuries. *Los Angeles Times*. Retrieved from http://articles.latimes.com/2011/apr/06/world/la-fg-afghanistan-wounds-20110407

Procida, L. (2011, October 1). Third annual Walk for the Wounded along the Ocean City Boardwalk raises money for veterans. *Press of Atlantic City*. Retrieved from www.pressofatlanticcity.com/news/breaking/third-annual-walk-for-the-wounded-along-the-ocean-city/article_5091fff6-ec8a-11e0-8fe8-001cc4c03286.html

Raddatz, M. (2007). *The Long Road Home: A Story of War and Family*. New York, NY: G.P. Putnam's Sons.

Ressner, R. A. (2008, March). Outcomes of bacteremia in burn patients involved in combat operations overseas. *Journal of the American College of Surgeons, 206*, 439–444.

Ritenour, A. E., Wickley, A., Ritenour, J. S., Kriete, B. R., Blackbourne, L. H, Holcomb, J. B. & Wade, C. E. (2008). Tympanic membrane perforation and hearing loss from blast overpressure in Operation Enduring Freedom and Operation Iraqi Freedom wounded. *The Journal Of Trauma, 64*, S174–178.

Scurfield, R. M. (2006). Medical evacuations from the battlefield to stateside: A trail of tribulation. In R. M. Scurfield, *Healing Journeys: Study Abroad with Vietnam Veterans* (pp. 17–39). New York, NY: Algora Publishing.

Scurfield, R. M. & Tice, S. (1992). Interventions with psychiatric and medical casualties from Vietnam to the Gulf War and their families. *Military Medicine, 157*(2), 88–97.

Serkin, F. B., Soderdahl, D. W., Hernandez, J., Patterson, M., Blackbourne, L. & Wade, C. E. (2010). Combat urologic trauma in U.S. military overseas contingency operations. *The Journal Of Trauma, 69*(Suppl 1), S175–178.

Stansbury, L. G., Lliss, S. J., Branstetter, J. G., Bagg, M. R. & Holcomb, J. B. (2008). Amputations in U.S. military personnel in the current conflicts in Afghanistan and Iraq. *Journal of Orthopaedic Trauma, 22*(1), 43–46.

Stinner, D. J., Burns, T. C., Kirk, K. L., Scoville, C. R., Ficke, J. R. & Hsu, J. R. (2010). Prevalence of late amputations during the current conflicts in Afghanistan and Iraq. *Military Medicine, 175*, 1027–1029.

Vogt, D., Vaughn, R., Glickman, M. E., Schultz, M., Drainoni, M.-L., Elwy, R. & Eisen, S. (2011). Gender differences in combat-related stressors and their association with post-deployment mental health in a nationally representative sample of U.S. OEF/OIF veterans. *Journal of Abnormal Psychology, 797*–806.

Waxman, S., Beekley, A., Morey, A. & Soderdahl, D. (2009). Penetrating trauma to the external genitalia in Operation Iraqi Freedom. *International Journal of Impotence Research, 21*, 145–148.

Yarosh, R. (2010, December 20). "I don't have one regret." The story of SGT Rick Yarosh, U.S. Army (ret) [Video file]. Retrieved from http://homefrontheroes.com/play/18032289

Yarosh, R. (2011, January 14). Interview with Sgt. Rick Yarosh, U.S. Army (ret) following the Premiere [Video file]. Retrieved from http://homefrontheroes.com/play/18782449

Zoroya, G. (2008, August 4). Soldier's story illustrates risks of hearing loss in war. *USA Today.* Retrieved from http://www.usatoday.com/news/military/2008-08-03-troops-hearing_N.htm

9 Military suicidality and principles to consider in prevention

Randi Jensen

For years, news services have routinely published freshly calculated statistics showing rising rates of suicide in the military. To date, the U.S. military has lost more troops to suicide than to combat in both Iraq and Afghanistan (Donnelly, 2011). Non-military estimates reveal that a million people worldwide die annually by suicide (World Health Organization, n.d). In the United States, suicide is the fourth leading cause of death in the general population overall, and the third leading cause of death in those aged between 15 and 24 (Centers for Disease Control and Prevention, 2010). Ostensibly, suicide is not strictly a military problem—nor is it purely a civilian problem. Suicide is clearly a human problem.

In this chapter, there is a discussion of various factors essential for the understanding and prevention of suicide per se: the dynamics of suicidality and the psychobiology of suicide. With particular relevance to the problem of suicides in the military, further discussion includes: the prevalence of suicidal ideation, stigma against suicide, combined risk factors for suicide, perfectionism, and current psychopharmacological treatment. Finally, you will be introduced to a suggested peer-support protocol of community involvement that takes suicide prevention methods one step further through engagement of concerned others in order to proactively, purposefully and confidently intervene in ongoing suicidality. This peer-support approach is particularly relevant to service members and veterans and can move us in an innovative way towards solving this devastating problem.

Introduction

In order to outline and fully describe a prevention plan, it is helpful to define the relatively recent term suicidality. In a 2009 publication by the Substance Abuse and Mental Health Services Administration, suicidality is defined as a spectrum of thought patterns and behaviors encompassing thoughts of suicide, plans and attempts to die by suicide and, ultimately, death by suicide (Substance Abuse and Mental Health Services Administration [SAMHSA], 2009).

Since the late 1960s, with the seminal research and publications of suicidologist Edwin Schneidman, Ph.D. and the American Suicidology Association, the American public has struggled with a deep awareness of the problem of suicide among its citizens. In contrast, it was not until the Gulf War on Terror, which began in 2001, that the U.S. military first truly appreciated the onerous magnitude of suicide among its ranks. The small-unit cohesion and bonds among comrades that typify life in the military are such that any deaths—suicide in particular—reverberate powerfully and impose "collateral damage" far and wide within the military community.

For all the sincere and dedicated efforts of the military command, loss of life to suicide has not abated. The fact that eighteen veterans are dying by suicide every day (Army Times, 2010b) urges us to cast our network beyond institutionalized services and towards the problem-solving power of community and extended family. Embarking on proactive interventions instead of relying on nebulous institutions to save lives is empowering.

Compassion surrounds the desperate desire to highlight and end the toll exacted by suicide. Turning the tide and demonstrably saving lives necessarily requires intrinsically motivated, forward thinking, system-oriented pioneers. We can no longer feed prevention research and elegant statistics to this consuming problem and expect a forthcoming solution. Suicidality is a system-oriented human problem that requires a community-oriented collaborative approach.

The dynamics of suicidality

To better understand how suicidality manifests itself, we must first understand that it develops on a continuum and can initiate at any time in someone's life. Acute suicidality constitutes an imminent plan, whether revealed or not, possibly preceded by multiple attempts. Suicidality begins with immediate thoughts of dying by suicide and often immediate options for death by suicide come to mind; it is precipitated by a collection of unresolved stressors with one or more appearing expressly impossible to overcome. Acute suicidality puts one at the highest risk for an attempt that will result in death. At this time, if thoughts of suicide are not vehemently, purposefully and deliberately eliminated, the option of dying by suicide remains subliminal, resurfacing when faced with another similar collection of stressors. It may be days, months, or even years before those precipitating stressors appear; or they may not—no one can predict.

Whether or not revealed to others, the condition of chronic suicidality in an individual encompasses any period of time that he or she has considered the prospect of dying by suicide as a method of coping with the stressors of life. It can include periods of planning for and attempting suicide. During the imminent plan/attempt phase, the condition is upgraded to acute suicidality. If the individual has moved through the acute phase, or has survived a suicide attempt, the existing condition of chronic suicidality does not disappear. It may become subliminal for long periods of time, but always remains a consideration as a uniquely accessible coping mechanism.

In terms of the military as well as the general population, two fundamental aspects of suicidality must be understood. First, suicidal ideation is common; and second, stigma against suicide is real.

Suicidal ideation

Suicidal ideation appears to be much more common than ever suspected. This author has observed that patients, civilian and military alike, reported intermittent yet perpetual suicidal ideation and reveries of "not being" on this earth. Anecdotal research reveals that suicidal patients think about dying by suicide almost daily and attempt it multiple times; yet their suicidal ideation on the whole is only occasionally uncovered. Most reveal conscious but unspoken suicidality spanning years and sometimes entire lifetimes. Indeed the seeds of suicidality are often sown biopsychologically in childhood (Wise, 2004). Biologically, some evidence points to alterations in brain chemicals, such as decreased levels of serotonin, which has been linked with a history of depression, suicide attempts, and impulsive disorders (Arango, Underwood, & Mann, 2003). Psychologically, an individual can acquire from peers and respected others an acceptance of suicide as a problem-solving option (Wise, 2004). Validating this anecdotal research, the 2009 National Survey on Drug Use and Health (NSDUH) revealed staggering statistics on adult suicidal ideation and consequent behaviors in the prior year. In this study, an estimated 8.3 million adults had serious thoughts of suicide, 2.3 million created suicide plans for it and 1.1 million made purposeful attempts on their own lives (SAMHSA, 2009).

David Rudd, Ph.D., the designer of a recent study presented at the 119th American Psychological Association Convention, found that almost half of U.S. military veterans currently attending college has suicidal ideation. Of those surveyed, 20 percent indicated that they at some point have had a suicide plan, with 3.8 percent admitting to a recently planned attempt. Rudd noted that these rates were significantly higher than those of non-military college students (Rudd, 2011). All age groups studied revealed some amount of suicidal ideation: 6.7 percent of young adults ages 18–25; 3.9 percent of those aged 26–49; and 2.3 percent of those aged 50 or older (SAMHSA, 2009). Realization of the disproportionate suicidal ideation among military veterans has prompted a higher degree of awareness and training among campus veteran service providers.

Acknowledgement that suicidal ideation is relatively common in the general population prompts a suggestion that a significant percentage of individuals entering the military might also carry with them established suicide thought patterns. This comprehensive research suggests that thoughts of suicide could endure and possibly span a lifetime. Thus, consequent investigation should be targeting the barriers preventing individuals from divulging their suicidality at critical times and seeking explanations as to why many might fail to receive appropriate and timely care.

Stigma against suicide

Most individuals who have struggled with suicidal thoughts have experienced the guilt and shame surrounding suicide, as well as the internal dissonance that is created during its contemplation. Dissonance is defined as the discomfort one feels while considering two opposing concepts. Applicable to suicidal thought, dissonance involves deliberating the two diametrically opposed concepts of struggling to stay alive, while simultaneously planning to die. Feeling completely "crazy" and beset by uncontrollable suicidal ideation, suicidal individuals very seldom reveal their suicidality. They isolate to protect themselves from the inevitable judgment involved with the disclosure. Because of the stigma involved with suicidality, they generally do not reveal their inner conflicts, thereby receiving little or no help in battling them. The futility these individuals feel is underpinned by the commonly held misconception that suicidal people "choose" suicide. Consequently, the external societal stigma involved with suicidality creates an internal barrier to self-disclosure. Fearing their own inner conflicts and having been failed by numerous prescribed remedies, they conclude that their situation is hopeless. Many active duty military and veterans describe themselves as being "at the end of the road."

Military and civilian patients alike who have revealed their suicidality report losing jobs, promotions, and the respect of family and community. Especially within the military, stigma is keenly felt by those who disclose any psychological health problems. This is attributed to the pervading "suck it up, soldier on" mentality, which requires service members to maintain a tough "in control" exterior, regardless of internal turmoil. Suicidal service members believe that if they divulge their suicidality, they will be perceived as weak and be harassed for seeking help (Hoge *et al.*, 2004). Their own personal guilt and shame can be amplified by social derision and religious ridicule.

A recent account from a Marine corpsman in Basic Training (personal communication, 2010) describes what he perceived as standard treatment of recruits who self-report suicidal thoughts: "They put his [the corpsman with suicidal thoughts] cot in the middle of the barracks, took away his shoestrings, belt, and razor. For a 'safety check' the drill instructor ordered him to be awakened and called to attention every hour, twenty four hours a day." The confidential informant said the recruit was then required to run five miles with his fellow recruits. His pants, too large due to weight loss, slid down, tripping him, and his boots, unsecured, ploddingly flapped on and off, causing bloody blisters. At some point, the drill instructor offered his gun to the faltering recruit "to just get it over with" so they could both "get on with business."

Although this kind of abuse is distressing, the infliction of verbal abuse in Basic Combat Training, as well as triumph over it, is reportedly a source of great pride—exemplifying the necessary toughness of military regimen. This is a rite of passage and a fact of military life. The important thing to remember is not that a particular treatment was inherently inhumane, but that the thoughts of suicide were *not eradicated through intimidation*. They were drummed underground to settle into the subliminal territory of the subconscious, remaining vital and very accessible.

Until recently, the families of active duty service men and women who died by suicide did not receive a condolence letter from the President, a shockingly stigmatizing and shaming practice. Although they had served honorably and had perhaps been highly decorated for valor, many service members who have died by suicide are still deemed unfit for recognition due to their manner of death. Some of those service member families will now receive a condolence letter if their loved one died in a combat zone, but not if the suicide happens stateside or in a non-combat zone (National Journal, 2011). Albeit less than sufficient, this current reversal in presidential policy is one fundamental step towards removing the stigma of suicide in the military.

Suicidality seems simple enough to understand, but if that were the case, we would not continue to spend millions in research dollars trying to understand it. After viewing a film about suicide among veterans, two reviewers described suicidality as "the enemy within." While this poetic license grabs attention, it also inadvertently demonizes and stigmatizes suicidality. The following conversation, which demonstrates a hardcore military mindset concerning the concept of "the enemy within," might shed some light on the attitudes that contributed to the Marines' 2009 record high suicide rate (Military Times, 2010):

An interchange between two experienced Marines was overheard during a break at a mandatory suicide prevention seminar. The first Marine commented, "You know, man, this is bullshit. If you are thinking about f***ing killing yourself, you're not thinking about saving your life or anyone else's. You're gonna get me f***ing killed, too." The second Marine responded by recapping the energy and time spent in training. He summarized his understanding of his charge as a Marine: "You take out the enemy and if the f***ing enemy is yourself, you know what to do, don't you?"

How does a service member avoid the deadly dichotomous feelings of being an honorable patriot invaded by foreign forces when classified as having "an enemy within?" Individuals who are suicidal say they feel "crazy," out of control, like the emotional floodgates are stuck in the wide open position. We must not compound that sensation by blaming the victims, driving them unavoidably further into isolative alienation, using the notion that they are aiding and abetting emotional insurgents. If we can excise the dishonoring notion that there is an enemy inside suicidal individuals, we can convince those same individuals that it is honorable and courageous to ask for help.

The psychobiology of suicide

Eradication of stigma means plucking suicidality from the realm of emotional instability and placing it correctly in the science of psychobiology. Comparison of the psychobiological similarities of suicidality and addictive thinking makes clear the need for this paradigm shift. The noted progression of suicidality follows a precise and predictable addiction continuum. Through research and documentation of the behavioral aspects of the endorphinergic (creating endorphins) release inherent in suicidal thought, the addictive nature of the ideation pattern appears distinct. Considered a vital element in reducing shock, the body's natural morphine system, collectively referred to as "endorphins," actually consists of several different forms of endorphins and enkephalins. Endorphins act as the body's natural painkillers and were discovered to key into the brain's pain relief receptors (Lowinson et al., 1997).

The process initiates with hope and its antithesis, hopelessness. The hopelessness that accompanies suicidal thought is expressed as psychological pain. The brain cannot initially distinguish between physical pain and psychological pain. The messages of both share many of the same neural pathways in the brain (Eisenberger, Lieberman & Williams, 2003). When an individual is coping with hopelessness, the first thought of simply "not being here" creates a sudden rush of relief. That "rush" is exhilaration brought on by pain-relieving endorphins (Eisenberger & Lieberman, 2004). That newfound hope, expressed by the thought of "not being here" temporarily eliminates the psychological pain.

Hope alone can mitigate pain (Groopman, 2004). Patients receiving a nonreactive substance, while believing they are receiving a pain reliever, still report relief from discomfort—this is known as the "placebo effect." That is the power of hope and expectation. Dr. Groopman theorizes that the body is responding to hope by releasing its own pain-relieving endorphins. When an individual feels backed into an emotional corner devoid of options, the thought of removing themselves permanently from the painful situation is expedient and natural. Most psychological challenges are met by concentrated problem solving. If critical thinking is not initiated and solutions are not forthcoming, pain and psychological discomfort mount.

At this juncture, two processes begin. The brain perceives distress and releases endorphins to mitigate the pain level and a neural pathway begins to form. Suicidal thoughts continue to extend the groove; a neural pathway that grows deeper and more indelible over time, fed by the reinforcing action of endorphin-creating thought. The brain necessarily acts on the imperative to balance the neurochemicals (Restak, 2003). In cases of suicidality, this can cause the eventual return to previous states of distress.

Suicidal individuals quickly discover that relief from the initial thoughts of "not being here" gradually diminishes. Pursuit of relief will result in a return to the familiar and fruitful neural pathways, which continue to deepen, becoming increasingly accessible over time. It appears that tolerance to baseline endorphin levels must accrue on an individual timetable, much like addiction to opiates. Increasing tolerance drives the unconscious, unstoppable progression. Each step in the attempt plan brings an added increment of relief-providing endorphins—until the inevitable point of diminishing returns. At this point, it is just as painful to devise the plan as it is to not fulfill it. Most likely because of depleted neurochemical stores and increased tolerance, no sufficient pain relieving endorphin flood is sensed—just unendurable pain.

A sense of hopelessness is concomitant and pervasive in active suicidal ideation. But, there is also within chronic suicidality a desperate grasping for hope. At a Seattle psychiatric hospital, in a group of patients who had attempted suicide, patients being discharged were asked about their hopes. A female patient stated on her discharge day that she had "hope for hope" to stay alive. Unfortunately, that desire was not enough. It faded quickly and she died by hanging only hours after leaving the hospital. Although she had what the medical discharge staff determined was sufficient overall social support, no immediate safety net of concerned, compassionate peers was in place directly after her discharge.

Generally, suicidal individuals try numerous methods to rid themselves of their pain. Marine Clay Hunt, an acclaimed proponent of community service as a method of allaying suicide, sadly died by suicide himself. He reportedly tried everything, including displaying exemplary humanitarian service. After years of battling suicidality, he ultimately surmised that there was no relief—no answer to the pain.

The fundamental behavioral aspects of this well-established pain-relieving neural pathway are threefold: the consequent loss of engagement in problem-solving, the depletion of the individual's self-efficacy or hope and the subjective relegation to social isolation. The solution to suicidality is the reversal of these three manifestations.

The risks of psychopharmacological treatments

Prevention of suicide requires overcoming several roadblocks particular to the military population. Chronic pain carries with it a high risk of suicide, as does depression. Numerous Armed Forces service members are prescribed various drugs for sleep issues, anxiety, depression, flashbacks, nightmares, and chronic pain (Army Times, 2010a). Even though suicidal thought is closely related to depression, many individuals suffering from chronic pain may not be depressed. Yet some service members are being treated for symptoms of pain and depression using combinations of antidepressants, antipsychotics, opiates, and benzodiazepines (ibid.) —all of which are subject to abuse and overdose (SAMHSA, 2009). Antipsychotics are prescribed routinely for off label use in the treatment of insomnia and post-traumatic stress symptoms, and are suspected in some cases to cause suicidality themselves. The U.S. Defense Logistics Agency has reported that military use of psychiatric medications has increased by more than 75 percent since 2001, with some drug prescriptions doubling in that amount of time. The pharmacological price tag was $1.1 billion (Army Times, 2010a).

At least one in six service members is taking psychiatric medications (ibid.). Pain-relieving opiates are and should be available if necessary during a deployment for obvious reasons, but their use is not being monitored for overuse or life threatening or addictive side effects. The Veterans Administration admitted that no adequate monitoring of drug dispensing is in place (Next-Gov, 2010). Sleep aids and antipsychotics prescribed for PTSD are known for their frightening side-effects, including reported suicidal thoughts, suicide attempts and death by suicide (Army Times, 2010a). Bernal *et al.* (2007) reported that compared to normal control subjects, individuals diagnosed with PTSD are at a higher lifetime risk for suicidal ideation (32.9 percent) and suicide attempts (10.7 percent). Unnecessary use and lack of monitoring of continuing use of these prescription drugs can heighten potential suicidality and make lethal means dangerously more accessible.

Perfectionism as a suicide risk

Perfectionism is an identified suicide risk factor (Hewitt, Flett & Turnbull-Donovan, 1992) and an additional behavioral roadblock to recovery. Perfectionism is behavior portraying a propensity for being displeased with anything that is flawed. The more desirable option to the pursuit of perfection is the goal of excellence. Individuals who seek excellence are forgiving of their own mistakes and are satisfied with intrinsic gratification in a job well done (Freedman, 2011). Seeking gratification through the approval of others and engaging in self-criticism or negative talk are hallmarks of perfectionism and can lower self-esteem to the level of suicidal ideation.

Perfectionism coupled with the necessity of making repeated instantaneous life and death decisions are particularly pertinent to both the military and law enforcement professions (Industry Lessons, n.d). In an article written for *Today in the Military*, Elizabeth Freedman (2011) notes that perfectionists are reluctant to ask for help and tend to be hypersensitive to criticism. Fearful of not meeting their own standards of ideal behavior or not maintaining personal control in the eyes of others, perfectionists are reticent to disclose suicidal ideation. Perfectionism places an individual in pursuit of the impossible, in search of illusive control in life and prone to a sentence of self-isolation. It seems to be about control—demand for it and lack of it. Uncontrollable, unfathomable thoughts and emotions could not pose a more untenable situation for a perfectionist.

Common risk factors for suicide

Some common risk factors for suicidality in the general population are: a family history of suicide, depression, previous suicide attempts, substance abuse, uncontrolled anger, hopelessness, isolation, acceptance of suicide as a resolution, loss of significant relationships, disability, chronic pain, or access to lethal means (Centers for Disease Control and Prevention, 2010).

Specific military cultural stressors present unique suicide risks. Colonel John Bradley, Chair of Integrated Health Services at Walter Reed Army Medical Center, Department of Psychiatry, states that survivor guilt (a response to surviving when comrades did not) and unbridled rage lead to deadly consequences for returning combat service members (Osterweil, 2011). Scurfield (2006) adds that unexpended rage is a common legacy of surviving insurgent and counter-insurgency warfare in particular, in that the enemy is very difficult to identify and frequently does not present a ready target to eliminate. This contributes to pent-up frustration and rage that often has limited or no combat outlet.

Unbridled rage often compounds reintegration difficulties and prompts family members and loved ones to allow isolation because of fear for their own safety. Patients have described being confounded by their own inexplicable rage, not comprehending where or when or at what level it will manifest. Patients who have never had any anger issues in their lives report uncontrollable urges to strike out, to break things and to inflict pain. Devastated, a normally kind and compassionate Master Sergeant developed a suicidal fury four years after his last tour in Afghanistan and sorrowfully reported that the only control he felt he had in his life was the ability to inflict pain. Patients report desperate resolutions for protecting family members—one patient locked himself in his basement, another tied himself to his bed, still another installed locks on every room in the house.

Others who are returning with symptoms of post-traumatic stress and traumatic brain injury (TBI) frequently experience alienation upon reintegration. They feel conspicuously out of place in their own communities, desperately struggling with their invisible wounds, while trying to fit back into their stateside jobs and households (Hoge *et al.*, 2004).

Deployment length, combat intensity, family separation, legal and/or financial troubles or a history of misconduct can stretch the normal coping mechanisms to a breaking point (Osterweil, 2011). However, one statistic continues to baffle military command. Most military suicides are committed by those who have never been deployed, many of whom are in the National Guard and Reserve Forces living far distances from military installations (Department of the Army, 2010). Combining the lack of daily unit member support that is usually available to active duty service members at military installations (Pietrzak *et al.*, 2010) and the aforementioned known military stressors with the statistical prevalence of suicide ideation in general could partially explain the suicides of the non-deployed.

In the established suicide treatment protocols, The Department of Defense includes programs for financial management, marriage and family relationship skills, anger management and conflict resolution skills. These programs are expected to increase resiliency and life skills, and improve mental and emotional well-being. However, service members remain distressed over persistent system-related failures. In other words, beyond the military member's control, services designed to mitigate stress have instead become sources of that stress. Problematic areas have been identified in accessing behavioral health services, including poor service delivery for dependents, lack of standardized screening, tracking and intervention, and an immediate leadership climate that engenders stigma (Osterweil, 2011).

Leaving the military provides little protection, as the suicide rate among retired service members continues at eighteen per day. Overall, veterans and active duty service members requesting help do not always find the relief they seek. Many report prescribed cocktails of drugs to be ineffective (NextGov, 2011). Extreme regimens (electro-convulsive treatments, antipsychotic medications) are now becoming more commonplace, but have not been shown to be successful in reducing suicidality on a long-term basis (Prudic & Sackheim, 1999). Even the standard hospitalization, whether voluntary or not, has not proven to be highly successful in preventing eventual death by suicide. Hospital stays are short and the focus is on medication management and discharge planning, with a minimal focus on precipitating stressors (SAMHSA, 2009). In fact, the greatest risk of suicide is during the psychiatric hospitalization itself and in the first week following discharge (Walling, 2000). As a consequence, the psychosocial issues that prompted the admission are still present at discharge.

With the failure of a multitude of institutional treatments, seemingly unsolvable problems prompt thousands of suicidal individuals to see themselves as incurable and burdens to everyone. Their resigned, determined resolution is that the world and their loved ones in particular, would be better off without them in it.

Admittedly, medical and psychological institutional intervention is definitely useful in the right context at the right time. An individual may need an antidepressant to be able to fully and adequately consider their circumstances. An injured service member may need multi-faceted rehabilitation services. The acutely suicidal person in imminent danger requires hospitalization. An individual with substance abuse or addiction problems may need inpatient treatment. However, the operational key to lasting suicide prevention is apparently not found in institutional programs—or the "success" rate of such institutional programs would be much higher.

Peer-to-peer and community support

If the solution does not lie solely in the myriad of research-oriented and manualized treatments, then a countervailing view espoused by this author and others is that it has to be in the heart-to-heart concern of community (Beskow, 2010). The military community is well suited to provide the ongoing social support for an individual at risk. The battle buddy concept imbued with the common military values of trust, honor and service provides the needed foundation for a life-saving protocol.

The Army's Suicide Prevention "ACE" Training instructs service members to "ask" about suicidal intent and listen reflectively; "care" for the suicidal person by not leaving them alone and removing risks; and "escort" the individual to a designated person or facility. This strategy has been somewhat successful in bringing the person at risk temporarily to safety. However, it covers only the first half of the process. Recently, after hearing of their battle buddy's death by suicide only hours after his release from the base hospital psychiatric ward, the following comments from an Army Specialist were recorded: "I asked 'em. I even took 'em, but then, for what? My buddy was released from the psych ward—went home and shot himself. No one told us what to do when he got out." His buddy had no safety net in place. Not one of his friends or family knew what to do after hospitalization or what to do to preserve life, thus avoiding the necessity for hospitalization.

Research has shown that peer-to-peer support can reduce stress-related mental health symptoms (Defence Centers of Excellence, 2011). Indeed, within the social fabric of the extended family and peers, there exist threads of compassion, understanding, dedication and willingness to weave the social support network required to keep individuals alive until they can keep themselves alive. It is this view that underlies the suicide prevention strategies presented here.

Ongoing peer social support protocol

Defining best practice

Social support from peers involves provision of emotional support, information and advice, practical assistance, and help in understanding or interpreting events. Elevated self-esteem, more positive attitudes and feelings of control are benefits realized with mutual social support systems. Support traditionally provided by battle buddies in the military provides protection from isolation and a consequent increase in a sense of well-being (Real Warriors Campaign, 2011). The support of military peers can attenuate common or mutual stressors, help to buffer toxic life events, and reduce isolation, providing opportunities for development of more effective coping strategies (King et al., 1998).

This author postulates that social support for suicidality, augmented by psychotherapy provided by a trained mental health professional, may offer the best prognosis for preventing suicidality. Significant empirical evidence exists suggesting that cognitive-behavioral treatments are successful for reducing suicidality (Brown *et al.*, 2005) and that those actuated by Motivational Interviewing are considerably more efficacious (Britton, Williams & Conner, 2008). Motivational Interviewing, with its non-directive, self-determining techniques, effectively dispatches inherent suicidal ambivalence. Effective treatment involves a combination of problem solving and acknowledging what choices and control can be exercised, while letting go of things that cannot be controlled.

The Jensen Suicide Prevention Peer Protocol (JSP3©), devised and used by this author in civilian counseling practice, is suggested for application to the military battle buddy paradigm. Best practices in peer support as identified by the Defense Centers of Excellence (2011) comprise trusted and concerned persons willing to interact and intervene in a friend's distress in specific ways to problem solve, increase hopefulness and reduce isolation. The JSP3© meets these criteria, in addition to providing specific methods of achieving these goals.

The JSP3© is a coalition consisting of the suicidal person and approximately three trusted individuals bound together by honesty and cooperation in order to provide specific support for the suicidal person. The main purposes of the JSP3© are to prevent suicide through increasing immediate problem identification and resolution and promoting healthy activity in order to build alternate, endorphin-driven neural pathways. The key elements of the JSP3© are:

- The coalition, including the suicidal person, has a thorough understanding of the psychobiological underpinnings of suicidality.
- The support members are non-judgmental, compassionate and willing to get involved proactively in a specific process of suicide prevention. By participating in health-affirming activities, they help the suicidal person retrain his or her brain.
- The suicidal person understands that the purpose of the support, and his or her involvement in it, is to prevent impulsive action that might lead to injury or death by suicide. The suicidal individual agrees to help his or herself by assisting in the development of a personal suicide prevention plan and then following it as established.
- Support responsibility is mutually shared. The suicidal individual and his or her peer support members know it is acceptable to defer to another support member if necessary. It is also healthy to ask the suicidal person to take part in helping others, as well as him or herself.
- The support members are sources of hope and dedicated to increasing the suicidal person's belief in successful problem solving (self-efficacy). They employ simple, easily acquired Motivational Interviewing techniques, such as employing active listening skills, fostering healthy decision making and exercising restraint from argument.

This chapter's space limitations do not allow complete delineation of the peer protocol; a complete explanation and directions for forming a JSP3© can be found at www.JSP3.org.

This coalition of concerned others must keep in mind three major barriers to suicide prevention: unchecked insomnia, chronic pain, and the inability to process information. Overcoming these barriers with peer advocacy is paramount to mental health. Any peer support team must be prepared to leave no stone unturned in pursuing medication evaluations, acupuncture, massage, meditation, etc., in an effort to advocate for their resolution.

An added and essential element of the JSP3© is reciprocity. Research shows that individuals are more likely to ask for help if they know they will be allowed to reciprocate (Wills, 1992). Yet the fear of overburdening or causing more stress often prevents anyone from asking the suicidal person for assistance. However, requesting their help builds satisfaction, hope and self-efficacy, making it easier for the person at risk to ask for help in the future.

Admittedly, peer support for suicidality can be a long and arduous process, but it is also an extremely rewarding one. The military has never shied away from long-term commitment. Indeed, the legacy of battle buddies has been known to transcend generations. Peer support provides a venue for engagement in problem solving, thus resolving incremental stressors. It encourages hope and builds confidence in future endeavors. Finally, and possibly most importantly, it prevents isolation through joining forces to lighten the load of pain and grief. Overall, peer support uses the power and compassion of the human community to solve a human problem. Enriched in a coalition forged by the devotion of battle buddies and dedicated in mutual contribution to a simple life-saving process, each individual can be assured of a transcendent purpose—a noble and worthwhile life is saved.

Closing

This chapter has outlined the psychobiology of suicidality and the existence of long-term subliminal suicidal ideation. Barriers to disclosure that must be overcome so that they may lead to treatment being sought include stigma-induced apprehension and subjective fear of imperfection. Identified military-specific suicide risk factors, combined with unmonitored use of prescription psychoactive drugs, further reinforce a persistent roadblock to suicide prevention in service members and veterans. And finally, a community-based peer protocol has been proffered as one innovative proactive intervention for ongoing suicide prevention.

In closing, it is important to note the words of Navy veteran Jerry Reed, now a civilian suicide preventionist working for the Department of the Army. In his address to the Department of Defense and Veterans Administration 2011 Annual Suicide Prevention Conference, he stated: "Suicide is not just a challenge for the military and the veteran community; it is a challenge for the American community" (Reed, 2011). It is in the community that we find the compassionate healing and daily agency needed to prevent suicide. Ultimately, we know that suicide prevention is everyone's business and everyone's responsibility. Emphasizing that the Unites States military is only one per cent of the national population, it is therefore not only right, but judicious that the remaining 99 per cent come together to preserve the lives of their courageous countrymen.

Randi Jensen is Director of the Soldiers Project Northwest, a nonprofit organization providing free confidential counseling for Afghanistan and Iraq veterans and current service members and their loved ones. Specializing in treating suicidality, she is a Certified Chemical Dependency Counselor and a Licensed Mental Health Counselor with a counseling practice in Shoreline, Washington (rjjjrb@comcast.net).

References

Arango, V., Huang, Y., Underwood, M. & Mann, J. (2003). Genetics of the serotonergic system in suicidal behavior. *Journal of Psychiatric Research, 37,* 375–386.

Army Times (2010a, March 17). Medicating the military. Retrieved from www.armytimes.com/news/2010/03/military_psychiatric_drugs_031710w

Army Times (2010b, April 22). Eighteen veterans commit suicide each day. Retrieved from www.armytimes.com/news/2010/04/military_veterans_suicide_042210w

Bernal, M., Haro, J. M., Bernert, S., Brugha, T., de Graaf, R., Bruffaerts, R. ... Alonso, J. (2007). Risk factors for suicidality in Europe: Results from the ESEMED study. *Journal of Affective Disorders, 101,* 27–34.

Beskow, J. (2010). The meaning of suicidality. In J. Osorno, L. Svaranstrom & J. Beskow (Eds), *Community Suicide Prevention, 2nd Revised Edition* (pp. 37–38). PA Group [Online publication]. Retrieved from www.scribd.com/doc/37485233/Suicide-Prevention-2nd

Britton, P., Williams, G. & Conner, K. (2008). Self-determinism theory, motivational interviewing, and the treatment of clients with acute suicidal ideation. *Journal of Clinical Psychology, 64*(1), 52–66.

Brown, G., Ten Have, T., Henriques, G., Xie, S., Hollander, J. & Beck, A. (2005). Cognitive therapy for the prevention of suicide attempts: A randomized controlled trial. *Journal of the American Medical Association, 94,* 563–570.

Centers for Disease Control and Prevention (2010). *Suicide facts at a glance.* Retrieved from www.cdc.gov/ViolencePrevention/pdf/Suicide_DataSheet-a.pdf

Defense Centers of Excellence (2011). Best practices identified for peer support programs: White paper. Retrieved from www.dco.health.mil/Content/Navigation/Documents/Best_Practices_Identified_for_Peer_Support_Programs_Jan_2011.pdf

Department of the Army (2010). *Army health promotion, risk reduction, suicide prevention report.* Washington, DC: U.S. Department of the Army.

Donnelly, J. (n.d.). More troops lost to suicide. Retrieved from www.congress.org/news/2011/01/24/more_troops_lost_to_suicide

Eisenberger, N. & Lieberman, M. (2004). Why rejection hurts: A common neural alarm system for physical and social pain. *Trends in Cognitive Sciences, 8,* 294–300.

Eisenberger, N., Lieberman, M. & Williams, K. (2003). Does rejection hurt? A fMRI study of social exclusion. *Science, 302,* 290.

Freedman, E. (2011, April 4). Is perfectionism hurting your career? *Today in the Military.* Retrieved from www.military.com/opinion/0,15202,229238,00.html

Groopman, J. (2004). *The Anatomy of Hope: How People Prevail in the face of Illness.* New York, NY: Random House.

Hewitt, P., Flett, G. & Turnbull-Donovan, W. (1992). Perfectionism and suicide potential. *British Journal of Clinical Psychology, 31,* 181–190.

Hoge, C. W., Castro, C. A., Messer, S. C., McGurk, D., Cotting, D. I. & Koffman, R. L. (2004). Combat duty in Iraq and Afghanistan: Mental health problems and barriers to care. *New England Journal of Medicine, 351,* 13–22.

Industry Lessons (n.d.). Perfectionism in professional sports and public safety professions. Retrieved from www.beruly.com/?p=956

King, D., King, L., Fairbank, J., Keane, T. & Adams, G. (1998). Resilience-recovery factors in post-traumatic stress disorder among female and male Vietnam veterans' hardiness, post-war social support, and additional stressful life events. *Journal of Personality and Social Psychology, 74,* 420–434.

Lowinson, J., Ruiz, P., Millman, R. & Langrod, J. (1997). *Substance Abuse: A ComprehensiveTextbook, 3rd Edition.* Hagerstown, MD: Williams & Wilkens.

Military Times (2010, September 13). Marine suicide rate highest in the military, what have you done to curb it? Retrieved from www.militarytimes.com/forum/showthread.php?1587719

National Journal (2011, July 6). President reverses condolences letter policy to include troop suicides in combat zones. Retrieved from wwwnationaljournal.com

NextGov (2001, August 5). Defense panel backs controversial drug treatments, but can't track impact. Retrieved from www.nextgov.com/nextgov/ng_20110805_9592.php?oref=topstory

Osterweil, N. (2011, August 8). Suicides, homicides among military share common features. Internal Medicine News Digital Network. Retrieved from www.internalmedicinenews.com/news/mental-health

Pietrzak, R. H., Goldstein, M. B., Malley, J. C., Rivers, A. J., Johnson, D. J., Morgan, C. A. & Southwick, S. M. (2010). Post-traumatic growth in veterans of Operations Enduring Freedom and Iraqi Freedom. *Journal of Affective Disorders, 126*(1), 230–235.

Prudic, J. & Sackheim, H. (1999). Electroconvulsive therapy and suicide risk. *Journal of Clinical Psychiatry, 60*(Supplement 2), 104–110.

Real Warriors Campaign (n.d.) Five steps veterans can take to support PTSD treatment. Retrieved from www.realwarriors.net/veterans/treatment/ptsdtreatment.php

Reed, J. (2011, March 2). One team, one fight: Learning from military suicide prevention. Retrieved from www2.sprc.org/directorsblog/one-team-one-fight-learning-military- suicide-prevention

Restak, R. (2003). *The New Brain: How the Modern Age is Rewiring Your Mind.* Emmaus, PA: Rodale.

Rudd, D. (2011, August 4). *Student Veterans: A national survey exploring psychological symptoms and suicide risk.* Retrieved from www.apa.org/news/press/releases/2011/08/suicide-veterans.aspx

Scurfield, R. (2006). *Lessons Unlearned from Vietnam to Iraq.* New York, NY: Algora Publishing.

Substance Abuse and Mental Health Services Administration (SAMHSA) (2009, September 17). *The NUSDUH Report: Suicidal Thoughts and Behaviors Among Adults.* Rockville, MD: SAMHSA Office of Applied Studies.

Walling, A. (2000, April 15). Which patients are at greatest risk of committing suicide? *American Family Physician*. Retrieved from http://*aafp.org/afp/20000415/tips/22. html*

Wills, T. (1992). The helping process in the context of personal relationships. In S. Spacapan and S. Oskamp (Eds.), *Helping and Being Helpful: Naturalistic Studies.* Newbury Park, CA: Sage.

Wise, T. (2004). *Waking Up: Climbing Through the Darkness.* Corona de Tuscon, AZ: Pathfinder Publishing.

World Health Organization (n.d.). Suicide prevention (SUPRE). Retrieved from www. who.int/mental_health/prevention/suicide/suicideprevent/en

10 Military sexual trauma

LTC (RET) Cynthia Rasmussen and Chris Zaglifa

Thank - you Art Reach !
I have been personally
touched by your great
work. [Ch...]

It is a Saturday afternoon, Fall, 2008. I (LTC Rasmussen) am sitting in a room in a circle with 30 women veterans from Korea, Vietnam, Iraq, Afghanistan, and all branches of the Armed Forces. I am thinking to myself, "How am I going to keep a conversation on Military Sexual Trauma (MST) going here for two solid hours, especially at the end of a long day of speakers?" I ask them to introduce themselves and tell the group why they chose to attend this session and what they expect to get out of being here. I am thinking, "Whew, this will kill some time!" By the time it is the second veteran's turn to speak, I realize that something is going to happen here that I had never expected, and that I have no control over it. The years and stories begin to flow—time is peeled back as we listen to the story of a Korean War female veteran; how she had been so proud to serve and wear the uniform until she was repeatedly sexually harassed and assaulted by fellow service members. "Breathe," I tell myself, as she admits she has never shared this information in her life.

I think back to the reading that we do each time we train new Sexual Assault Response Coordinators (SARCs) and Unit Victim advocates (UVAs) in our week-long training for the Sexual Assault Prevention and Response Program (SAPR); about how many lives are forever changed by the trauma anyone, including this woman (and each and every victim), has endured at the hands of her "comrades."

The tears and stories continue to flow. At the two-hour point, we have not even moved around the entire circle of participants in the room. I had thought through all of my experience and the knowledge I had regarding the true immensity and impact of sexual trauma on military members—but now I truly knew the road would be winding and emotional and that we had a long way to go. It was also clear that we were beginning a new era.

This chapter is dedicated to all those service members and veterans who have trusted us enough to share their stories, their pain and their anguish, and to all those service members and veterans, both men and women, who have experienced sexual trauma at the hands of their fellow service members. Readers are provided with an overview of Military Sexual Trauma (MST), the psychological impact upon those involved, and an introduction to programs and treatments designed to address the needs of those who have experienced MST while serving their country in some capacity of military service. The authors will provide additional information regarding current programs and treatments available to support and care for MST survivors under the auspices of both the Department of Defense (DOD) and the Department of Veterans' Affairs (VA). This is not necessarily an all-inclusive list.

The opinions expressed here belong to the authors and those service members with whom they have interacted and do not in any way reflect the views or policies of the DOD or the VA. When discussing aspects of MST, unless otherwise stated, we do not differentiate between male versus female, as both genders are at risk for falling prey to sexually abusive perpetrators.

Extent of the problem

Twenty percent of female veterans who have served in Iraq and Afghanistan have been identified as having experienced MST at some point in their military career (U.S. Department of Veterans Affairs, 2010). According to the DOD, approximately one in three military women has been sexually assaulted, in comparison to one in six civilians (Foster & Vince, 2009). The DOD reported 3,158 military sexual assaults—on both male and female service members—in the fiscal year 2010 (Department of Defense, 2011). Finally, as high as these statistics are, it has been documented that as many as 75 percent of sexual assaults go unreported in the military for reasons that will be discussed later. This truly is a critical problem for all concerned and exemplifies how MST should be considered a most significant concern, especially for—but not restricted exclusively to—women who serve in the military.

The prevalence of military sexual assault among female veterans ranges from 20 to 48 percent; 80 percent of female veterans have reported being sexually harassed (Foster & Vince, 2009).

Prior to 9/11 and the beginning of current active military activities in Afghanistan and Iraq, neither the American public or DOD were focused on sexually traumatized service members or MST. In 2004, a task force was initiated and within less than a year, the Sexual Assault Prevention and Response (SAPR) program was unveiled. This program will be detailed later in this chapter.

Military Sexual Trauma (MST)

The DOD and MST

Discussions on MST and care for survivors first began in earnest in early 2004, when the then Secretary of State, Donald Rumsfeld, requested a review of increasing reports of sexual assaults on service members in Kuwait and Iraq. The gathering of information regarding MST, its dynamics and effects, as well as treatment considerations, is still in the evolutionary phase. The term MST was rarely discussed or even mentioned until recently and remains a relatively forbidden subject for most people both inside the military environment and in the civilian community.

The Department of Defense (2008) defines sexual assault as:

> Intentional sexual contact, characterized by use of force, threats, intimidation, abuse of authority, or when the victim does not or cannot consent. Sexual assault includes rape, forcible sodomy (oral or anal sex), and other unwanted sexual contact that is aggravated, abusive, or wrongful (to include unwanted and inappropriate sexual contact), or attempts to commit these acts.
>
> Consent means words or overt acts indicating a freely given agreement to the sexual conduct at issue by a competent person. An expression of lack of consent through words or conduct means there is no consent. Lack of verbal or physical resistance or submission resulting from the accused's use of force, threat of force or placing another person in fear does not constitute consent. A current or previous dating relationship by itself or the manner of dress of the person involved with the accused in the sexual conduct at issue shall not constitute consent.

The VA and MST

The U.S. Department of Veteran Affairs' (VA) definition of MST (U.S. Department of Veterans Affairs, 2010) comes directly from federal law and, in general, is defined as sexual assault or repeated, threatening sexual harassment that occurred while a veteran was on active duty or active duty for training or during some form of in-uniform service. It can occur on or off base, while a veteran is on or off of duty. Perpetrators can be men or women, military personnel or civilians, superiors or subordinates in the chain of command, strangers, friends, or intimate partners. MST includes any sort of sexual activity in which someone is involved against his or her will. They may be pressured into sexual activities (e.g. with threats of consequences), unable to consent to sexual activities (e.g. intoxicated or drugged), and/or physically forced into participation. It may involve unwanted touching, grabbing, oral sex, anal sex, sexual penetration with an object and/or sexual intercourse. Physical force may or may not be used. Other examples include threatening and unwelcome sexual advances, unwanted sexual touching or grabbing, or offensive remarks about a person's body or sexual activities. Veterans of all eras, from all branches of the military, all ranks, ages, races, and genders, have reported being victims of MST.

MST and complex trauma

The particularly damaging effects of MST are reflected in the above defini-
tions, as well as the following descriptive comments regarding military sexual
trauma by some of its victims. MST has been described by its victims in their
own words as "incest," "a violation of military values," and "worse than any
combat." Typical statements include: "I can no longer feel proud of my military career" or "Before this I wanted to be in the military my whole life; now I
cannot even stand looking at my uniform."

Complex trauma

MST is considered one of the traumatic experiences that can be categorized as
complex trauma (American Psychiatric Association, 2000). Complex trauma
refers to traumatic stressors that are interpersonal, pre-meditated, planned
and "caused by other humans, such as violating of another person. Any
trauma that intensifies emotions and the meanings is harder to resolve, makes
the trauma more severe or 'complex'" (Courtois, n.d.). A trauma or disaster
related to unknown or uncontrolled situations, such as an "act of God," is usually less personal and less complicated to resolve. Situations that are relatively
more psychologically complicated and toxic, and which result in significant
psychological adaptations having to be made in order to cope (such as resolution of one's own responsibility in the occurrence, as well as feelings of shame
and significant confusion for life safety) are considered complex.

MST and salient military factors

MST is considerably complicated when military factors are added to the picture. Perpetrators are usually known to the victim and considering that in
military culture service members are taught to "watch each other's backs"
and that "we are all family," MST is a fundamental violation of trust. Military
culture dictates that service members must be interdependent to survive the
demands of military service and of the battlefield, and, most importantly, in
order to stay alive and return home. Significant trust in one's fellow service
member is a necessity. Interdependency within the military requires blind
trust—not only in one's comrades, but in the fact that the system will take
care of you in the face of sacrificing yourself to injury or harm. Interpersonal
trauma such as MST violates that trust at its most basic level. Survivors of
interpersonal trauma may suffer more injury than survivors of natural disasters because of the need to resolve the issues related to another person, let
alone one's buddy, doing this to you.

Other military-specific attributes that contribute to the complex aspects of
MST are the perception of the military as a family, potentially placing MST in
the category of incest or incest-like assault. I remember one victim looking at

me sadly and stating, in a total confusion, "I named his kittens." How could someone who you were so close to that they let you name their kitten do this to you?

Also, the military is a hierarchical and authoritarian system and military culture places a premium on strength, self-sufficiency and loyalty. "Mission first," above all else, is a mainstay of military culture—and that includes one's own health and welfare. This is a driving force that also explains the often confusing behavior of a service member who ignores his/her own needs or moves on without reaching out or getting help. Victims are often stuck in conditions of relative entrapment (restricted freedom of movement); re-exposure and re-victimization are likely not only by the perpetrator, but by the culture itself.

Victims/survivors are often a "captive audience;" there is a significant difference in scrutiny and accountability within the military, which varies from branch to branch, as well as from unit to unit. Depending on the situation and where the incident occurred, scrutiny and accountability may limit the response of the victim, as well as anyone trying to support the victim. For example, if service members are stationed at a small camp or base where there are no other units or military support except that of their own chain of command, they may be more hesitant to come forward. A common statement made by victims is: "Did you see how they all acted together? Why would I ever believe they would care or do anything about this?" (This last statement was in reference to sexually harassing behavior or support of harassing behaviors by the leadership or higher-ranking members of the service member's unit.)

Geographic dispersion of members of the National Guard and Reserves creates yet another layer of complication for those members who have experienced MST. Service members who live within the community, often hundreds of miles from any military resources, often need to seek out their own help and support. The available resources, as well as ongoing support from these resources, is often directly related to where these service members and families live. This, as one can imagine, creates a huge inconsistency in the quality and level of support and care that can be provided to these victims/survivors of MST.

The VA and the Vet Centers (the Veterans Readjustment Counseling Service), who are charged with caring for service members after they are discharged from the military or from active duty status following deployment, are often the first place where a service member admits to victimization by MST. However, this may occur years after the incident. With complex trauma, positive resolution is more elusive and difficult. This can at least partially explain why a great majority of MST victims leave the military and the crimes against them go unreported. It is the authors' experience that in over 150 cases of MST, only one perpetrator was convicted by the military system—while the majority of victims/survivors have left the military system, even if they had always wanted to make the military a life career. This leaves victims in the position of spending years and even decades trying to resolve their MST issues without direct support from the DOD or the opportunity for resolution by assuring that the perpetrator pays the consequences. This might explain why each year, when Rasmussen conducts the MST group at a women's veterans' conference, more women sign up to attend and more women reveal an MST history that they have never talked about previously.

The effects of sexual harassment, assault and rape within the military are all the more devastating due to the fact that the military becomes one's family *and* community. Indeed, for some service members, it can be the only place where one's need for feeling a part of a community or a family is met. In addition to this violation of military values, there is a deep sense of betrayal that contributes to the complexity of the trauma, as well as the ability to recover from it.

It has been reported that women exposed to trauma show an increased risk for alcohol dependency issues, even if they are not experiencing some degree of psychological injury or demonstrated psychopathology, including symptoms that meet the diagnostic criteria for PTSD (Dryden, 2011). Coupling this information with the increase in use of alcohol or drugs to self-medicate following deployments and/or to avoid dealing with emotional issues in general helps to explain the rise in chemical dependency among service members and, more so, the difficulty faced by survivors in trying to heal.

Barriers to reporting MST

Barriers to reporting MST are varied. While several such barriers mirror those within the general population, other barriers are distinctive to the military setting and military culture. The first and most salient barrier for all victims/survivors is fear of harm. There is often a genuine fear and/or true threat that the perpetrator will harm the victim if they reveal the assault to anyone. And there is an underlying fear of embarrassment any time that sexual issues become a topic of discussion in any arena.

Denial is often the first response to any experience that is too difficult or painful to process. Rasmussen has found it necessary numerous times to educate the victim/survivor that she was, in fact, assaulted according to the legal definition. In one particular incident a young woman soldier was raped in a bathroom at the end of a party in a hotel room by a soldier who was 20 years older than she. Everyone had been drinking. After the incident was reported by her friend, she expressed confusion about her role in the incident, despite the fact that she had no attraction to this married man twice her age, or desire or inclination to have bathroom sex with him. She was unable to even say the word "rape" and never pursued charges. In fact, she volunteered to go to Iraq and did so at the point when the rape incident came to the attention of some of her family members and her military unit.

Alcohol and drugs are involved in a large number of MST situations. If victims/survivors are underage, there is a fear of being punished for using alcohol or drugs illegally, so they may hesitate to report. And in the military, aware-ness of such an incident can spread rapidly. Rasmussen recalls an incident that occurred on a military base at 3am. As the Sexual Assault Prevention and Response Coordinator (SARC), she received 12 calls on her cell phone before 10am about this incident. Victims/survivors may not report for fear of dam-age to reputation and career, i.e. not being promoted to the next higher rank, not being selected for various schools or training opportunities, and/or being denied preferred duty assignments and the like.

Many victims have reported that they were told not to say or do any-thing or they would cause problems for themselves and their units—in other words, to become victimized once again by the conspiracy of silence. And it is ingrained in military culture not to do anything that will bring a negative impact to one's unit, for fear of bringing additional shame to themselves and their fellow service members. The mission-first mentality is alive and well. Victims/survivors have reported being told they will have to leave their unit and cut short their own military careers if they report an incident. Worse yet, some are told, "If you report this, your whole unit will have to stay in Iraq or Afghanistan longer"—and of course, they all want to go home.

Sexual Assault Prevention and Response Program (SAPR): The military response to MST

In February of 2004, in response to increasing reports of MST from the Iraq theatre of operations and reported incidents at the Air Force Academy in Col-orado Springs, the then Secretary of Defense, Donald Rumsfeld, directed a review of all interventions and responses to victims of MST. Secretary Rums-feld ordered that a Care For Victims Task Force take a 90-day look at the response of the Department of Defense to sexual assault. Each of the services had developed their own policies and strategies for caring for victims; there did not appear to be a comprehensive, unified, or consistent approach to deal-ing with MST.

The Care for Victims Task Force recommended a number of approaches for improving assistance for victims and for prevention of sexual assault. The Joint Task Force Sexual Assault Prevention and Response program was assembled at this point in time to implement these recommendations. Sig-nificant among the recommendations was the initiative for development of a policy on MST for the DOD. One year later, JTF-SAPR (Joint Task Force for Sexual Assault and Prevention Response) created a policy and began imple-menting this in the field. This policy was unprecedented, as it covered MST in all of the services and brought about sweeping changes previously unheard of in the military arena. The most significant of those changes was the first-time policy of restricted reporting, which allows a victim of MST to confidentially report the crime and to obtain support and assistance without fear of reprisal or of military leaders learning of the incident.

The goals of this program at the outset were to guarantee care of the victim and to overcome all barriers to reporting. One of the first steps in the program was to establish a general definition of sexual assault and to begin a comprehensive DOD-wide education program concerning the definition and problem of sexual assault in the military. At the same time, the program provided training and support for system-wide sexual assault response coordinators (SARCs) to manage the program and unit victim advocates (UVAs) to support the victims. This created an environment that encouraged victims to come forward for help and support. UVAs were trained and mobilized down to the unit level—quite an undertaking for this massive organization. The army reserve alone trained thousands of UVAs.

In 2007, the next phase of the program was initiated. This focused on prevention and the responsibility of all members of the military to enforce prevention of MST. The program includes videos with vignettes which are shown to all military members, including discussions on how each person has a responsibility to recognize potential situations and to take an active role in preventing and stopping sexual assault in the military environment.

Male service members experiencing MST

At this point it is necessary to emphasize again that, although less prevalent, males both in and out of the military also experience sexual trauma. The SAPR training program reports that between one in eight and one in ten males are sexually assaulted at some point in their life. Sexual assaults on men are reported even less often than those on women. Added to the barriers that all survivors/victims encounter is the idea that a man should be able to fend off any attack and that if he is assaulted, then he must be homosexual. Finally, there is the frequent event of the victim having an erection due to the nature of the male physical response to stimuli; this often leads to questions about sexual orientation, adding yet another layer of shame onto the experience of having been raped. Emphasis during all training of SAPR program participants is that most sexual assaults against males are perpetrated by heterosexuals and are related to control, power and the need to shame another to feel better about themselves. The fact that a purely physical response happens in no way indicates any personal enjoyment or responsibility on the part of the person who is the victim to the crime.

Provider response strategies

Recognizing and responding appropriately to the devastating impact of MST

A mature, sensitive, informed and prompt response to the victim is an essential part of the training in the SAPR program. For this to occur, providers must be in touch with, and have their responses guided by, the full range of physical, emotional, psychological and social impacts that an MST victim/survivor experiences—the loss of control of their bodies and their physical and emotional integrity as they are assaulted, violated and made to feel more like an object than a human being.

Appropriately worded inquiries and responses

If there are no appropriately worded inquiries and responses, it becomes an unrealistic expectation for any victim/survivor of such an ordeal to be able to confide their worst nightmare to any caregiver or healthcare provider. For example, merely asking the question, "Why did you not report this earlier?" displays and clearly communicates a lack of sensitivity and understanding; indeed, it instead conveys a desire to avoid the full impact of the trauma the victim has experienced.

The horror, devastation and crippling effects of all forms of trauma can be buried or obscured within such terms as combat fatigue, operational exhaustion and PTSD. The same is true for MST when it is used to describe the violence and cruelty that perpetrators inflict upon other human beings. The term MST can mask and soften the full effects it attempts to communicate within the terms sexual harassment, sexual assault and rape. Hence, using terminology without an ability and willingness to attend to the full horror of what is subsumed under the term MST is clinically imprecise and may be further traumatizing to the victim/survivor. In fact, such an approach may promote the protection of the MST perpetrators or excuse the acts they committed.

Each and every provider must keep in mind, when responding to the victim/survivor of MST who is seeking help, that the blasé usage of such terms unfortunately also protects institutions and cultures at large. In addition, there will be further isolating of the person who was violated from his/her family, community, support and assistance. From the superior officer, nurse, primary service provider or investigative personnel, to the professionally trained therapist, sensitivity to and an understanding of this issue must be clear in all communications, so as to leave no doubt that MST is undeniably a criminal act and must not be tolerated under any circumstances. Until then, any person who has faced such an ordeal will never feel nor actually be safe or able to trust the provider, law enforcement officer, etc.

Safety first

If a service member presents in a crisis state shortly after the occurrence of MST, his/her safety and security becomes the first step in the process. This step is particularly crucial when the perpetrator is known to the service member or works/resides in the same unit or on the same military installation.

Regaining a sense of control

It is vital, when responding to a recent attack, that the victim is helped to regain a sense of control over her or his own life as quickly as possible. This is accomplished by explaining both the medical and the investigative processes to the victim/service member sand providing them with the choices and options which will allow them to make their own decisions and to assume control over a seemingly out of control situation.

Meeting immediate medical needs

Attending to the victim's immediate medical needs is essential. This includes tending to any physical injuries, a full physical examination, and the potential need for testing for sexually transmitted diseases. It must be borne in mind that seeking necessary medical care in a war zone frequently requires extensive planning and travel under dangerous and high-risk circumstances, so these factors need to be taken into account.

The victim's/survivor's support system

Also crucial is assisting with informing family and/or close friends of the assault—if and only if the victim chooses to do so—and then educating them about the immediate and urgent needs of the person who has just been sexually assaulted or raped. Such communication and information are essential to the establishment of an ongoing support system. In a war zone, this process is almost always fraught with many additional difficulties; the support systems for the person are usually not nearby or readily available.

Informing command

Informing the appropriate person in the service member's command is another issue that may require assistance and advocacy. The victim is the only person who should have the ultimate decision as to whether or not military leadership will be notified. The SAPR program is based upon the premise that all military leaders know and understand the complexities as well as the importance of their responses in MST cases.

And so, the assumption and hope that underlies the SAPR program and its approach to reporting is that, with the proper response and support, the survivor/victims will come forward—first to get help, which will then help them to be better able and willing to press charges, as well as to participate in the judicial process. This process eventually supports the healing process for the victim, unit, family, victim support systems and, finally, the military system. The absence of a proper response is in effect a direct encouragement *not* to report the crime and *not* to ensure that the appropriate legal process is undertaken and completed.

Most assuredly, one must consider that every action following an assault or rape is vital to facilitating the service member to learn and experience that help is available, that the world can behave in a caring manner, that the MST event is not representative of the world or the military as a whole, that there are more good and caring people than perpetrators and violent criminals, and that one can resume control over one's life. Such learning by the victim/survivor is critical if true healing is to take place.

Providers' early responses and restoring a sense of control

Once a report is made, intervention strategies include the immediate re-establishment of control over one's life and body, as demonstrated and experienced through the means by which providers respond to the crisis. This includes explaining evidence collection, the need for an interview to document the crime for future prosecution, laboratory testing, medical interventions and examination, and assuring safety and comfort. At each step of the process, caregivers and law enforcement/Military Police ask the victim/survivors for permission to proceed, and if they are ready for the next step, ensuring they remain in control of the process.

For example, a crisis worker asked a victim, who was obviously very cold and shivering, if she wanted a warmed blanket or if she wanted family or the Rape Advocate to come in to be with her, instead of undertaking these actions automatically. This may sound trivial, but any situation that allows the victim to make choices or gives some direction to caregivers is an opportunity to restore a sense of control. Zaglifa, as a victim advocate and emergency room crisis worker, has found that once victims feel more in control, they become active participants in the healing process and can become exceptional witnesses, more motivated to involve themselves in the process at this most devastating time in their lives.

Trauma centers and Department of Veterans Affairs MST services

If the location of the crime or the military base lacks a hospital facility with an emergency department, the service member will require transfer and escort to the nearest trauma center. It is there that a full sexual assault exam and evidence collection can be provided to meet the needs of the service member and to initiate any legal documentation process. Many trauma centers in the civilian sector offer specialized programs that include the use of specially trained nurse examiners, who conduct victim-sensitive examinations, evidence collection, counseling, advocacy and follow-up services.

In cases occurring overseas or in geographically dispersed areas, the challenge of providing care increases. Consider the case where a service member is raped in a war zone or while on deployment and requires medical and emotional follow up, but is stationed at a camp that is miles away from a medical facility. Would you want to be the service member who requests transport from the helicopter that may be out there saving lives or redirection of a convoy on a mission to get you the care you need? We think not—this would be in serious conflict with the "mission-first" mentality that prevails in the military culture, and even more so in a war zone.

In the case of MST involving a Reservist or Guard member not on active duty, the military may not have resources in their area; further, the Reservist or Guard member does not see his/her leadership more than perhaps two days a month. This results in the service member attempting to obtain care in the civilian sector and subsequent complications with communication and liaison with appropriate military officials.

Since Public Law 102-585 was enacted in 1992, healthcare and counseling have been mandated for women who encounter sexual harassment and assault. Also, services were expanded to include males, and past limitations were repealed so that mandatory, universal screening of all veterans, both male and female, is included.

VA MST programming.[1]

Each VA medical center across the country now has a Woman Veteran's Coordinator, as well as specially trained MST responders who provide comprehensive oversight and care for any military member or veteran who reports an experience of MST. The VA, in an unprecedented and indeed extraordinary policy shift, made the MST program the only program at the VA where even a service member without established veteran status can receive ongoing care for MST-related conditions. Compensation for a service-connected condition related to MST is also a possibility. As this book goes to print, increased education about working with and responding to victims of MST is being sanctioned for all VA employees.

Every VA facility has a designated Military Sexual Trauma Coordinator, who acts as a resource person and monitors the screening and referral process. The VA also offers a Continuing Medical Education Program on Military Sexual Trauma through the Veterans Health Initiative.

In response to all forms of military-related trauma that can occur (e.g. friendly fire incident, loss of a friend, witnessing mass casualties, handling dead bodies, to name a few), the VA has expanded treatment interventions to inpatient and outpatient care, co-occurring disorders, and military sexual trauma. Once a veteran responds positively to inquiries about a harassing or sexually assaultive experience, the veteran is referred for follow-up medical

---

1   See the VA website MST page (www.mentalhealth.va.gov/msthome.asp) which is dedicated to federal law and VA policy documents, as well as other resources relevant to MST.

and clinical assessment and treatment, if requested or indicated. The VA offers inpatient, residential and outpatient programming for veterans who have experienced sexual assault and rape across the country and at every VAMC. This includes programs for male victims.

Challenges in arriving at an accurate differential diagnosis

Treatment must include dual diagnosis programming for PTSD and co-occurring alcohol and drug use and abuse disorders that frequently occur secondary to a major trauma. Williamson & Mulhall (2009) indicated that 40 percent of homeless female veterans have reported sexual assault in the military. This fact supports the intervention strategy of providing housing and financial/employment services as a necessary part of any program addressing sexual assault and rape. Clinical assessments include a complete trauma history, an exploration of any childhood physical and or emotional sexual abuse and/or neglect, and any other traumas that are part of the veteran's past.

The differential diagnosis can be further complicated by a veteran having served in a combat zone, increasing the possibility of combat-related trauma. From Vietnam onward, wars have lacked any distinguishable foe or clear battle lines, resulting in a threatening environment where there is no safety and anyone is a potential enemy, including women and children. This requires the service member to maintain a constant state of hypervigilence and hyperarousal. Going "outside the wire" is no longer a pre-requisite to being exposed to combat-related trauma, as forward operating bases receive regular mortar, rocket and RPG (rocket-propelled grenade) and small arms fire attacks. Any service member traveling in-country is at risk for exposure to Improvised Explosive Devices (IEDs) and any number of forms of ambush.

It is more difficult to focus time and energy on a therapeutic intervention when a person suffers from the sequelae of PTSD, in addition to superimposed MST. For example, a service member victim/survivor of MST may also have experienced a childhood trauma or prior combat trauma during or after one or multiple deployments. Post-trauma symptomology can include poor sleep, depressed moods, extreme distractability secondary to hypervigilance, suicidal thoughts, chemical abuse, homelessness, health issues, unemployment, and related financial stressors. The provision of support or the resolution of a specific crisis, such as a serious illness or death in the family, allows the veteran to acquire a sense of stabilization and room to develop self-care skills. However, this is only one element of the treatment that is necessary. Specific treatment intervention protocols will be described in a later section.

Conducting assessments and other pre-therapy dynamics and issues

Assessments

As stated earlier, assessments must be conducted in a highly sensitive manner and free from professional terminology or jargon. It is also helpful to inform service members or veterans that they are in control of the session; they should be instructed that they do not have to answer a specific question if they do not feel comfortable doing so and that they can cease the interview at any time during the interview process. Their comfort and sense of control over the session is fundamental to working as a team. This respect for and sensitivity to the person must be genuine; it is essential to establish and improve rapport to facilitate the therapeutic conduct of more detailed histories, as well as increasing the possibility that the veteran will return for future visits.

There are self-report measures and structured interviews that may be of great value in conducting the appropriate inquiry with an MST victim/survivor. Included in the list published in the *Iraq War Clinicians Guide* (National Center for PTSD, 2004, p. 69) are three very useful instruments: (1) the Sexual Experience Questionnaire by Louise Fitzgerald— the most widely used measure of sexual harassment; (2) the Sexual Experience Survey by Mary Koss—a self-report measure designed to assess unwanted sexual experiences, including those associated with substance use; and (3) the National Woman's Study Interview by Heidi Resnick and her colleagues—which asks specific questions about a variety of unwanted sexual experiences. However, there is still a need for further scientific inquiry for the purpose of developing specific evidence-based protocols to intervene and treat service members and veterans who have experienced sexual assault and/or harassment in the military or within the wartime theatre.

Pre-therapy dynamics and issues

Prior to initiating any treatment intervention, there are a number of pre-therapy issues that require careful consideration. Much like the crisis response, these include establishing a safe and supportive environment, developing a therapeutic relationship with clear and consistent boundaries and addressing any crisis-related or survival issues.

Engagement in an evidenced-based therapy usually requires a time commitment and weekly attendance in therapy sessions. This could prove difficult for a service member who continues to have military obligations, redeployments, etc. A service member who has recently returned from a deployment has all of the normal readjustment issues in reintegrating into society, family, home, job, school, etc., often placing personal needs on hold for this time. In addition, the necessary establishment of a trusting relationship can be difficult to attain following the betrayal the victim has experienced within the military environment. This is especially so if the MST occurred in a combat zone, where a service member will often have closer bonds with their battle buddy, wing man, Marine and so on than with his/her own family.

The issue of control, as mentioned earlier, is a vital issue and it confronts the therapist from screening and assessment through intervention and therapy. Trauma includes the loss of control over oneself and a sense of complete helplessness. A therapist taking control of what occurs in a therapy session can duplicate that very sense of loss of control from the trauma itself. This requires the therapist to work with the veteran in a very respectful, therapeutic alliance in order to facilitate the development or re-establishment of a sense of trust and safety.

Open-ended questions which validate service members—both male and female—who have experienced harassment, assaults and rape, and the use of non-technical language all serve the development of a safe environment where a person can sense and experience re-establishment of control. There is a very delicate balance to achieve between fostering a sense of control and encouraging a person to confront fears, face and discuss traumatic memories, and find a way to no longer find it necessary to avoid reminders of the actual traumatic situation that occurred—or a situation similar to or reminiscent of the trauma. This allows the achievement as well as more control over the trauma and its widespread effects, a sense of safety and security, as well more control over his/her lives in general.

Female versus male therapists

Selection of a therapist is a critical issue when it comes to caring for veterans who have experienced MST. Clinically speaking, there are pros and cons to the selection of a therapist by gender. However, this again can become another control issue that is best left up to the veteran, while providing support during this decision-making process. Both female and male veterans often choose a therapist of the opposite gender.

A female victim establishing a safe and trusting relationship with a male therapist who consistently exhibits firm boundaries, a sense of equality, sensitivity, and good communication skills, can be a powerful corrective experience. On the other hand, a female therapist can provide a positive role model, demonstrating how a woman can be strong and assertive without requiring the protection of a man to function adequately and to self-protect. Male veterans may have difficulty facing another man while trying to sort out why the assault occurred and questioning their own masculinity and how they are being perceived by the male therapist.

It is the standard policy of the Office of Mental Health Services that VHA facilities are strongly encouraged to offer veterans being treated for conditions related to MST the option of being assigned a same-sex mental health provider, or an opposite-sex provider if the MST involved a same-sex perpetrator (U.S. Department of Veterans Affairs, 2012, p. 40).[2]

MST therapeutic intervention strategies

Pre-trauma-focused therapy interventions and motivational interviewing

During a period of stabilization and prior to the establishment of formalized therapy, stress management, relaxation training, breathing retraining and grounding skills can be very useful tools to offer the veteran early in treatment. "The provision of psycho-education about the intervention and incorporation of motivational enhancement processes—both at the outset [or prior] to treatment, as well as throughout treatment—has proven especially valuable in promoting veteran participation and interest in evidence-based psychotherapies for PTSD" (Karlin et al., 2010). This can help build a person's ability to attain self-regulation and self-soothing abilities, which may enhance his/her ability to take full advantage of an Evidence-Based Therapy (EBT). Seeking Safety (Najavitis, 2002), a cognitive-behavioral treatment for comorbid PTSD and substance abuse, is another example of a potentially effective intervention for veterans who have experienced MST—its effectiveness has been demonstrated with sexually assaulted civilian women (Hyun, J. K., Pavao, J. & Kimerling, R., 2009).

Motivational Interviewing (MI) is an intervention that has great utility when implemented with other treatments when resistance to treatment is very high. "It is a collaborative, not a prescriptive, approach, in which the counselor evokes the person's own intrinsic motivation and resources for change" (Miller and Rollnick, 2002). MI incorporates open-ended questions, affirmations, reflections and summaries. Given the need for the victim/survivors to maintain a sense of control, this intervention can be quite helpful when they are very avoidant and become defensive when the benefits of EBT are shared with them. However, "skills training does not yet have a sufficient evidence base for clients whose use of adaptive coping strategies should be strengthened before beginning a course of trauma-processing or in response to residual symptoms following a course of trauma-processing therapy" (Institute of Medicine, 2008).

---

2 See also the MST resource page of the VA website, which is dedicated to U.S. law and VA policy documents relevant to MST (www.mentalhealth.va.gov/msthome.asp).

Eye-Movement Desensitization Reprocessing, Cognitive Processing Therapy and Prolonged Exposure

There are many therapies and models specific to the treatment of PTSD but not necessarily specifically developed and validated for MST per se. For example, there are cognitive therapies that modify the relationship between thought and feeling, identify and challenge inaccurate/extreme negative thoughts, and develop alternative and more logical/helpful thoughts. Three trauma therapies in particular rise to the surface by virtue of being evidence-based and sufficiently researched, as well as proven to be highly effective with a number of, but certainly not all, rape victims (Foa et al., 2009). These include Eye Movement Desensitization Reprocessing (EMDR), Cognitive Processing Therapy (CPT) and Prolonged Exposure (PE). All three share the common feature of employing an exposure component in which the victim/survivor is subjected to aspects of the original trauma in some way. EMDR accesses a disturbing image within the traumatic event, solicits the experience of body sensations associated with the disturbing image, identifies an aversive self-recurring cognition that expresses what the patient "learned" from the trauma, and identifies an alternative positive self-recurring cognition. CPT and PE possess a cognitive-behavioral base.

Taking advantage of the latest research regarding the development of evidence-based therapies, in the face of an expected 20 percent of both men and women returning from combat zones with PTSD, the VA developed two training initiatives to train and certify therapists in cognitive-behavioral exposure-based protocols. These include CPT (Resnick, Monsoon & Chard, 2007) and PE (Foa, Hembree & Rothbaum, 2007). The CPT initiative began in 2006 and was closely followed by the PE initiative in 2007. As of 31 May 2010, the VA provided training to more than 2,700 VA mental health staff in the delivery of CPT or PE, with some staff trained in the provision of both therapies (Karlin *et al.*, 2010). "Randomized controlled studies (RCTs) of Exposure Therapy (ET) have demonstrated its efficacy in female victims of sexual and non-sexual assault, motor vehicle accidents, male combat related trauma, war refugees, and mixed trauma populations" (U.S. Department of Veterans Affairs and Department of Defense, 2010).

CPT identifies and challenges problematic thoughts/beliefs, focuses on "stuck points" and has the patient write/read aloud a detailed account of the traumatic event. PE has four steps: (1) Education; (2) Breathing Re-Training; (3) In Vivo or Real Life Practice; and (4) Talking Through the Trauma. In addition to confronting and processing the index trauma or most anxiety provoking event and repeating the imaginal exposure on tape and listening to the tape daily, PE also allows the person through the in vivo exercises to systematically practice the reduction of avoidant behaviors that act as reminders of or are similar to the actual trauma, but contain no inherent threat to the person. For example, for a female victim who avoids any intimacy with her partner and all males in public, an in vivo exercise would ask her to practice standing in a very public place, such as a mall, or choose the male checker in the supermarket, and repeat these activities until her anxiety level no longer rises to the point where she has to leave. This is referred to as habituation.

Having a range of treatment interventions available is a significant benefit to MST victims/survivors. Although therapists may have a preference for a particular treatment intervention, such as those described above, again, the authors stress that it is vital to allow the victims/survivors control over their lives. And discussing a choice of therapies, after describing each, is consistent with empowering the service member or veteran.

Research is lacking for a specific treatment designated for sexual assault and rape in the military and/or in a combat zone—CPT and PE were originally developed to address civilian sexual assault and rape victims (Resick & Schnicke, 1993; Foa and Rothbaum, 1998). EMDR, CPT and PE were all found to be effective by both the VA and the DOD (see U.S. Department of Veterans Affairs and Department of Defense, 2010; Foa *et al.*, 2009).

Closing

In conclusion, despite the fact that the DOD and VA have significantly increased their oversight and resources in support of caring for victims and preventing Military Sexual Trauma, the road ahead remains a long one. The vast majority of perpetrators remain in the military without consequences, while victims/survivors are left to fight the system to obtain the care they so desperately need. In addition, MST victims/survivors remain at high risk for suffering the lifelong sequelae from experiencing complex trauma at the hands of some of their military comrades, those whom they have trusted with their lives.

Even with experienced therapists who are sensitive to military culture and trained in evidence-based therapies, the healing process is disrupted and sometimes blocked when the response to the assaultive behavior is ignored, discounted, or dismissed. Both authors have heard story after story of service members and veterans being even more angry and traumatized due to the lack of response to the assault itself or to the victim/survivor. Instead, in many cases, responses were more supportive of the perpetrator.

This is not to diminish in any way the primary goal of addressing the index trauma itself. However, there is the absolute need to recognize how crucial the initial response to and progression of the investigation can be to the restoration of a sense of safety, the willingness to report and the healing process. The response to an assault is not therapy—but it certainly needs to be therapeutic and not re-traumatizing.

The intent of this chapter has been to document the problem of MST as well as to help professionals and the public at large to become aware of the additional trauma service members experience when they are betrayed by their battle buddies, who often are closer to them than their own families. Relationships forged in the military at large and in combat zones in particular are more powerful than almost any if not all other social connections. When this bond is betrayed in an environment that one cannot escape, or in which one cannot exercise the same freedoms that civilians take for granted, the damage can be significantly more complex and harder to understand and support outside of military culture.

It is a tragedy that there are so many service members who are subjected to MST and who are unable to sleep or tend to their personal needs in safety; who prefer to volunteer for hazardous duty, such as riding on convoys, because they feel less at risk chancing IEDs than some of their military counterparts, and/or who otherwise do not feel safe and cared for, even while still in uniform. This is not the military that service members had envisioned when they enlisted to serve their country.

Serving your country "in harm's way" is not supposed to mean the risk of harm from some of your very own fellow military service members. It is not fair, or just, or right; indeed, it is a travesty. The authors hope that this brief introduction to MST and the programs to support and assist those experiencing MST will result in those on a healing journey being provided with more hope and resources; and that insights and ideas have been provided to improve programming for and responses to all who may experience this most devastating and complex trauma.

LTC (RET) Cynthia Rasmussen, RN, MSN, CANP retired in 2011 from the army reserve having served 23 years as a Mental Health Nurse. She was mobilized for six and a half years to active duty as Director and Psychological Health and Sexual Assault Response Coordinator for the 88th RRC/RSC, serving service members and their families nationwide. She received her bachelor's and master's degrees from Marquette University, Milwaukee, Wisconsin and currently works as an Adult Nurse Practitioner for the Veterans Health Administration (ltcrazz@yahoo.com).

Chris Zaglifa, MSW, LCSW SAC, has worked in the field of violent crime, crisis intervention, sexual assault and domestic violence, inpatient psychiatry, emergency room crisis work, and adolescent and adult AODA treatment. He is a social worker at the Wausau OPT Clinic and the Tomah VAMC, Wisconsin, and has worked with combat veterans, specializing in complex PTSD, dual diagnosis and evidence-based therapy (czaglifa@gmail.com).

References

American Psychiatric Association (2000). *Diagnostic and Statistical Manual of Mental Disorders, IV-TR*. Washington, DC: American Psychiatric Association.

Courtois, C. A. (n.d.) Understanding complex trauma, complex reactions and treatment approaches. Gift from within PTSD resources for survivors and caregivers. Retrieved from http://www.giftfromwithin.org/html/cptsd-understanding-treatment.html

Department of Defense (2008). Sexual Assault Prevention and Response Program Procedures. Department of Defense Instruction (Number 6495.02, June 23, 2006, Incorporating Change 1, November 13, 2008). Retrieved from http://www.sapr.mil/media/pdf/directives/DODI649502p.pdf

Department of Defense (2011). Department of Defense Annual Report on Sexual Assault in the Military: Fiscal Year 2010. Sexual Assault and Prevention Response Office (SAPRO). Retrieved from http://www.sapr.mil/media/pdf/reports/DoD_Fiscal_Year_2010_Annual_Report_on_Sexual_Assault_in_the_Military.pdf

Dryden, J. (2011, February 14). *Trauma increases risks for alcohol problems in women.* Washington University in St. Louis Newsroom. Retrieved from news.wustl.edu/news/pages/21890.aspx

Foa, E. & Rothbaum, B. (1998). *Treating the Trauma of Rape. Cognitive-Behavioral Therapy for PTSD.* New York, NY: Guilford Press.

Foa, E., Hembree, E. & Rothbaum, B. (2007). *Prolonged Exposure Therapy for PTSD: Emotional Processing of Traumatic Experiences. A Therapist's Guide.* New York, NY: Oxford University Press.

Foa, E., Keane, T., Friedman, M. & Cohen, J. (Eds.) (2009). *Effective Treatments for PTSD: Practice Guidelines from the International Society for Traumatic Stress Studies* (Second Edition). New York, NY: Guilford Press.

Foster, L. & Vince, S. (2009). *California's women veterans: The challenges and needs of those who serve.* California Research Bureau, California State Library. Retrieved from www.library.ca.gov/ crb/09/09-009.pdf

Hyun, J. K., Pavao, J. Kimerling, R. (2009). Military sexual trauma. *PTSD Research Quarterly, 20*(2), 1–8. Retrieved from http://www.ptsd.va.gov/professional/news-letters/research-quarterly/V20N2.pdf

Institute of Medicine of the National Academies (2008). *Treatment of Posttraumatic Stress Disorder: An Assessment of the Evidence.* Washington, DC: National Academies Press.

Karlin, B., Ruzek, J., Chard, K. M., Eftekhari, A., Monson, C., Hembree, E. A., Resick, P. & Foa, E. (2010). Dissemination of evidence-based psychological treatments for posttraumatic stress disorder in the veterans' health administration. *Journal of Traumatic Stress, 23*(6), 663–673.

Miller, W. & Rollnick, S. (2002). *Motivational Interviewing* (Second Edition). New York, NY: Guilford Press.

Najavits, L. (2002). *Seeking Safety: A Treatment for PTSD and Substance Abuse.* New York, NY: Guilford Press.

National Center for PTSD (2004). *Iraq War Clinician Guide* (Second Edition). Department of Veterans Affairs. Retrieved from www.ptsd.va.gov/professional/pages/treatment-iraq-vets.asp

Resick, P. A. & Schnicke, M. K. (1993). *Cognitive Processing Therapy For Rape Victims: A Treatment Manual.* Newbury Park, CA: Sage Publications.

Resnick, P., Monsoon, C. & Chard, K. (2007). *Cognitive Processing Therapy.* Washington, DC: U.S. Department of Veterans' Affairs.

U.S. Department of Veterans Affairs. (2010). *Demographics*. Retrieved from www. va.gov/VETDATA/docs/Demographics/5l. xls

U.S. Department of Veterans Affairs and Department of Defense (2010). *VA/DoD Clinical Practice Guideline for Management of Post-Traumatic Stress*. Retrieved from www.healthquality.va.gov

U.S. Department of Veterans Affairs (2012). *VHA Handbook 1160.01*. Retrieved from http://www1.va.gov/vhapublications/ViewPublication.asp?pub_ID=2498

Williamson, V. & Mulhall, E. (2009). *Invisible wounds: Psychological and neurological injuries confront a new generation of veterans*. Iraq and Afghanistan Veterans of America Issue Report, January 2009. Retrieved from *http://iava.org/files/IAVA_invisible_wounds_0.pdf*

11 Veterans involved with the criminal justice system: Clinical issues, strategies, and interventions

Emily Simerly

Across from me in my office is a strapping 23-year-old combat veteran. We're deep in the belly of a prison, where he is serving ten years for vehicular homicide, a result of severe over drinking and then driving as if he were escaping an ambush. He is somber—far beyond reflective. The import of his actions weighs heavily on him. He has a primary diagnosis of PTSD (APA, 2000) and Polysubstance Dependence. Alcohol was his drug of choice, but anything would do.

I ask him what, so far, is the biggest difference for him between being in the military and being in prison. He starts with things that are the same—structure, discipline, officers who yell at you, the routine, the lack of sanitation. These are comfortable for him. Yet the most compelling thing for him is this one difference: in the military, the people in the bunk next to you could be trusted with your life. They would do anything they could to keep you safe. In prison, he indicates, no one can be trusted, so that instead of being able to relax, he has to be on guard all the time. Any camaraderie is false, and there is no community of support.

I tell him that some of the symptoms of his diagnosis could actually be exacerbated in prison. Hypervigilance in prison is a good idea, just like it was in theater. Being in a situation where he could be hurt or killed is be the same as in theater—only it is prison. I tell him that prison staff try to keep the peace, but years of decreasing budgets sometimes result in there not being enough officers for the number of prisoners. I try to educate him quickly on things not to do, worried he might fall prey, even given his skills, stature, and experience. All the while I know that he will not have the exoskeleton that was provided by his warrior buddies and the military to help him cope and have a sense of safety. He is alone in this theater.

Incarcerated veterans are not a new phenomenon. Returning combat veterans, though, with their particular constellations of physical and behavioral injuries, are at particular risk for interfacing with the criminal justice system (CJS). That the CJS is complex, sometimes capricious, sometimes arbitrary, with the justice outcome of committing a crime dependent on many variables, makes it all the more difficult to navigate.

This chapter is a primer on the special problems faced by combat veterans when they return home, a brief description of the CJS, and what resources are in place—resources that can make all the difference in outcome. In this chapter, the term "combat veteran" includes all who have served in war zones in various capacities, including, for example, medics, Reserves and National Guard and female veterans, who have the capacity for additional stressors and who are also treated for these in women's prisons.

The rationale for a chapter about these factors is that many clinicians, military and non-military, as well as civilians and military personnel, know little about the CJS or what to do if they encounter it—let alone about the distinctive circumstances and dynamics of incarcerated veterans, such as risk factors, common triggers and the role of substance abuse.

The setting

Fact: So far, approximately 2.3 million Americans have served in Iraq and Afghanistan, but this discounts the thousands who served in other conflicts—in Vietnam and since then. Although that sounds like a large number, only about 1 percent of the American populace has served overseas. Most Americans cannot even define OEF or OIF. Even when Operation Enduring Freedom and Operation Iraqi Freedom are explained, the result is often a glazed expression. I have asked about these acronyms in conversations with many civilians from all walks of life, and I cannot remember a single one knowing what they stood for. Not one. This indicates a powerful need for psychoeducational training for clinicians, at the very least, as well as the public in general —groups that are usually grossly unfamiliar with military culture and military cohesion.

Fact: Of the 1.6 million inmates now incarcerated in state and federal prisons, on any given day, 9.4 percent of these are veterans. On any given day, another 780,000 veterans are in jail. The statistics should cause alarm to people who have benefited greatly from these former military personnel.

Fact: Of the veterans who are incarcerated and who have honorable discharges or discharges under honorable conditions, 80 percent are jail inmates, 78.5 percent are state prison inmates and 81.2 percent are federal prison inmates (CMHS National GAINS Center, 2008). These percentages make it clear that the vast majority of veterans incarcerated were not derelict persons who happened to join the military. They are people who were discharged honorably for the time they served in the military (and sacrificed for us). Given the stressors facing military personnel in theater, one could hypothesize that a high ingroup percentage of those statistical groups listed above were combat veterans.

Before specifically discussing in more detail factors concerning combat veterans involved with the CJS, it is important to provide a context for what constitutes a crime, a brief overview of the CJS and the differences between jails and prisons.

CRIMES

All crimes fall into the categories of either misdemeanors or felonies. Felonies usually result in imprisonment. Crime categories include violence towards persons, animals or property, substance abuse or possession, and public disorder. State law codes vary, as does their implementation, but in general, misdemeanors include public trespassing, DUI (Driving Under the Influence), possession of marijuana of less than an ounce, prostitution, hiring a prostitute, and crimes of a similar level. Felonies are more serious than misdemeanors and include possession or trafficking in drugs, aggravated assault, murder, vehicular homicide, robbery, rape, child or elder abuse, kidnapping, domestic violence, and the like.

Federal and state criminal codes introduced in the 1970s criminalized behaviors that are often due to drug and alcohol use. Combat veterans from Vietnam on have faced a greater chance of arrest and incarceration because of these new statutes. Included in these statutes are opioid medications that are often necessary for the treatment of pain, one of the primary results of combat injuries. A tragic recurrence of the vast numbers of homeless and incarcerated Vietnam veterans over the years has become an increasing possibility for the new combat veterans. All the stakeholders working towards the care of veterans need to interface thoroughly and often with each other, especially the CJS. Prisons have long been closed systems and now need to and in fact are working towards collaborative care for veterans (Drug Policy Alliance, 2009).

The criminal justice system[1]

Remember that in interactions with the CJS, "you will pay on the front end or you will pay on the back end. And the back end is longer than the front." Education regarding options is paramount.

The arc of the criminal justice system is the same for everyone. In the most simple yet broad terms, the path follows this route: criminal/risky behavior (from speeding on a motorcycle to carrying a concealed weapon) that eventually comes to the attention of law enforcement → arrest → jail → plea bargain or trial/conviction → probation or prison → parole or probation → freedom.

Phenomenologically, this arc is actually concave. If a baseline of what has been normal behavior for a particular combat veteran is pictured as a straight line, each of the stops along the way involving criminal behavior and punishment represent the deterioration of a person's behavior and life. If the inmate

---

1　This section is written from my experience with the criminal justice system.

is able to use what is available in prisons to improve and add skills, then the end of the arc should at least return to baseline. For those who "get it," prison can be a radical learning curve and the convict returns to society in better form than at the time of pre-entry.

It has also been my experience that many of the men (and in some ways the women) who end up in prison are alive because they went to prison. Their behaviors and lifestyles pre-arrest were leading to a mortal dead end, through either violence or overdose. Mental health treatment in jails and prisons is a right guaranteed by our Constitution to all who are incarcerated and who require assistance. Of course, incarceration removes an inmate's ability to seek care at his or her own discretion, though it has been well adjudicated that this care be made available to inmates.

Jails are not prisons[2]

Note especially that jail and prison are two very different entities, even though the general public uses them interchangeably and without knowledge of the differences. Jails are indicated for those who have been arrested, but not convicted. They are usually run by local sheriff's departments. Deals and bargains are typically made with lawyers, prosecutors and judges.

While a person is in jail, there are practical factors that make dealing with the arrest charge difficult. Visitation and phone calls can be limited. Mail takes longer for security reasons. The court date is not known. Arrestees have been known to wait in jail for two years before going to trial. Overwhelmed public defenders have little time to do a thorough jobs of representing their clients. If the arrestee would rather just move the process forward, he or she can engage in a plea bargain. This typically means pleading guilty to a lesser charge, but then having a criminal record wherein guilt has been admitted. Charges of armed robbery are often "plea bargained" down to robbery, for example, which brings a lesser sentence and an earlier chance for parole.

Families of veterans (and of most other civilians) are usually unaware of these issues, and criminal attorneys do not come cheap. Families may frequently be on an emotional roller coaster and placed in a state of financial hardship due to the loss of the arrestee's income. Additional costs are incurred in time off from work for visitation and supplying money or goods (through proper channels). Families often feel conflicted about their arrested and incarcerated family member, having stood by them through the worst of times but also feeling betrayed that they were not careful enough to stay out of legal trouble.

Prior to trial or a plea bargain, the sentence for the crime is discussed. Some crimes carry mandatory sentences. If the combat veteran can obtain

2 This section is also is written from my experience with the criminal justice system.

an advocate who knows the court system, he or she will be in an immensely better position. Other factors include the context surrounding the crime, petitions for leniency and unpredictability regarding the amount of time the combat veteran will be in jail before transfer to a permanent prison after sentencing. Also, there is mental preparation, which includes an identity shift from warrior to inmate.

Most combat veterans are not aware that their warrior status means something to many involved in the CJS. To some, it is, shall we say, "off-putting." Many retired veterans become correctional officers. Some of these veterans harbor negative or at least conflicted feelings about a combat veteran who has been arrested.

Prisons

Once convicted, a person is sent to prison to serve the sentence for the crime committed. Many unknowns are part and parcel of prison life. Prisons are vastly overcrowded everywhere. For a convict in jail awaiting prison, there is no chance to select the preferred prison or location. It is not practical or even possible to put each prisoner where he or she wants to go, which is usually close to home.

Additionally, a prisoner may be shipped off to another prison at any time without notice, disrupting communication and relationships that have been established, which decreases their sense of stability. In many states, prison staffs typically do not know if a prisoner is a combat veteran. Inmates whose families do not send them money (typically accomplished through a central account with the state departments of corrections) either use only state-issued items or learn the art of bartering in a prison "economy." Bartering can be dangerous, but most inmates do this routinely.

Prisoners can also receive disciplinary reports (for example, for committing a crime in prison), which usually place them in the segregation area, with decreased privileges. Gangs are found in many prisons and are often formed along racial lines. These gangs are very dangerous and account for many of the murders that occur in prison.

Counterintuitively, most prisoners feel victimized by the CJS. Most prisoners did commit the crimes for which they have been sentenced, but the specifics of their circumstances, which most prisoners focus on and obsess about, are frequently different from what was stated in the courtroom. Think of a warrior who served in Iraq or Afghanistan, who saved lives and helped the Iraqis improve their living conditions. This often means nothing in court or in prison.

Role reversal: From veteran to prisoner

We play many roles in our lives; in fact, we are frequently defined by them: parent, CEO, teacher, child, soldier, psychologist, fireman, Marine, veteran, airman, drug addict, alcoholic, inmate, convict. Service members are accustomed to being a part of the large, tight-knit family of the military. When a person strays from that family into the criminal justice system, the disruption of roles is disastrous. This journey from revered American service member to scorned American convict can be alarmingly rapid. To add to the misery, once involved in the CJS, extraction can be slow and fraught with roadblocks and failures. It also results in vast costs in terms of disruption of family and belonging, emotions, money, sense of self, self-esteem, and change of status in the community (both military and civilian).

The list of negatives is endless, with none so damaging as the harm to the family. Many families have stood by the men and women who have gone to theater to fight or assist in the war process. To have them disappear again—this time into a prison—is almost unbearable. And there is no income from a veteran on "criminal deployment," unless he or she receives disability income, when a portion of the disability payments are sent to the family. One thing that is similar is that, once again, the family has to be concerned about the safety of their loved one.

Striking parallels and differences between deployment and prison

Striking parallels between military deployment and imprisonment exist, as well as striking differences. Prison is an involuntary commitment, similar to being drafted. Heads are shaved, uniforms issued. Personal effects are removed. A sort of "basic training" is undertaken upon intake into the prison system.

Prisoners mark time and are often bored. The lucky ones are classified into some sort of work "detail." Most states pay inmates very low wages; a few pay nothing for work duties performed. Privacy is minimal, and the loss of connection with the civilian world remains demoralizing. At the very least, veterans are familiar with the deprivation and austerity that comes with prison life. They learn quickly that they must unlearn trust and brotherhood. Every move and act, exchange of goods, every favor, everything becomes currency in the prison economy.

The self-identity shifts for warriors can be mentally depleting, and more treatment is unmistakably needed for these persons with two histories while behind bars.

Confounding risk factors for combat veterans

There are many stressors that trouble combat veterans returning from deployment. Family reintegration, life at home looking the same but not being the same, issues that occur when one has broken cultural moral values—even if out of necessity—during combat, challenges regarding employment, and feeling like an alien after returning from theater are all part of the constellation of a most difficult re-entry. Some stressors, however, are more likely to lead a veteran to interface with the criminal justice system. There are five risk factors to keep in mind so that prison can be avoided (Simerly & O'Hara, 2009): combat-related stress, environmental triggers, co-occurring mental health diagnoses, substance abuse and traumatic brain injury.

Combat-Related Stress

Case example: Corey

Corey came in for his monthly behavioral change session (we do not call it therapy, at his request). He was in a "stew" after having been "chewed out" by one of the correctional officer sergeants. Corey had committed a minor but important infraction and suffered the consequences. I happened to know the sergeant well and knew that he was a former combat veteran himself. Neither Corey nor the sergeant knew the history of the other. Power always trumps in prison and the sergeant had the power.

The behavioral session that day consisted of going through each of Corey's internal reactions. The most difficult one was his flashback to a firefight in Afghanistan, where the least little thing can mean the difference between life and death. The strongly tied shoelace on one of his boots had caught on the metal clip of the strongly tied shoelace of his other boot, so that his feet were essentially tied together. He was the closest to a buddy who was wounded and had made the move to run out to drag the wounded Marine out of harm's way. Instead, he went down hard on the rocks and had to figure out why. The wounded Marine was shot again as a consequence. He did not die, but Corey was "chewed out" by his superiors for such an "idiot" mistake.

When the correctional sergeant confronted him for a somewhat minor infraction, it didn't matter that lives were not involved or that he was no longer taking enemy fire. This event "threw" him into a flashback, which brought intense shame and guilt about the error he had made. I assess him at every session for suicidal thoughts or plans. I tell him during every session that I cannot help a dead Marine. He always smiles at that, but still he does not go a day without the guilt over his actions during that firefight. This guilt is so deeply agonizing that he hangs on to life in hope of relief only by a shoelace.

After Corey returned stateside, he learned not to drink because this was the quickest way to his demons. Unfortunately, one night at a bar, drinking non-alcoholic beer with some friends, a woman behind him popped a balloon, intending to play a joke on her waitress friend. Corey's brain reacted to that sound with a survival response and, besieged by his experience of instant intrusive memory, he turned, in less than a split second, to punch the woman in the face so hard that he broke her jaw and almost broke her neck. Seven years for aggravated assault. He could have received many more years, but the woman requested leniency for him.

Combat comes with its own set of variables that place those who have participated in it apart from the rest of us. Unfortunately, those same variables are ones that propel a veteran into the crosshairs of law enforcement. The drive to continue the adrenalin rush of the extreme heightened awareness that comes during combat does not diminish or disappear for many veterans. This drive is manifested in risk-taking behaviors such as driving at high speeds in any type of vehicle (motorcycles being the most dangerous) or carrying firearms (with or without a concealed weapons permit). There is also a sense of not knowing who the enemy is, leading to nightmares and interrupted sleep.

The need to protect the self continues in the brain, whether or not the "threatening" person is a law enforcement officer. And when police confront such a person, their primary objective is and should be to protect public safety. Thus, the continuation of the survival response post-deployment and the aggressive behavior that often accompanies post-combat stress can be a set up for disastrous circumstances for returning combat warriors (see Chapter 7).

Environmental triggers

Case example: Ishmail

Ishmail had survived two year-long deployments, occurring in close temporal proximity. He suffered a back injury and was treated by the VA. He was in despair because he could not continue to fight for his country. Due to his pain, both psychic and physical, he took more and more prescribed opioid prescription drugs. He was searching for a state of mind that could be called peaceful. He also walked the city at night, clearing his mind and dissipating some of the deleterious effects of combat.

He was walking by a building that was falling down due to disrepair. Out of the corner of his eye he saw a movement. The streetlight shadow made the creature moving look much bigger than it was in reality. Quick as a flash, he pulled out his weapon, his constant companion, and shot at the rat. Six times. Enough to make residents of lofts in the area call the police.

Ishmail was not even sure what the police wanted when they pulled up near him. In a lucky break, he told police he was the shooter, but that he had thought the rat was a terrorist. In his opioid-induced state, he was little more than coherent, though less anxious than he may have been otherwise. He said the police thought he was either "crazy" or "on drugs," but did not see him as a threat to them since he was cooperative.

He received a two-year sentence for carrying a firearm without a licence and possession of narcotics (he would take the pills out of the bottle and take them indiscriminately as he felt the need for them, thus using them illegally). In court, his combat history was noted and the judge used discretion to offer a shorter sentence, provided Ishmail attended substance abuse treatment upon release. Ishmail's sentence was considerably more lenient than those that occur in many other court proceedings, as it certainly was imposed by an enlightened judge.

Most of us who have not been in combat go about our daily routines without serious reactions to the onslaught of stimuli in everyday life. Typically, we do not have severe startle reactions when a car backfires nearby, a baby in a restaurant lets out a sudden and unexpected wail, or the smell of rancid road kill flows into the car, or at the sight of a building being razed into a tumble of concrete and rebar. A returning warrior, though, frequently has immediate and often severe negative reactions to these triggers (see Chapter 7): the car is suddenly a gunshot, the baby is one who is caught in gunfire, the road kill brings back the smell of rotting human flesh and the building pulls the warrior back in time to the war scene itself. Such flashbacks often are precipitated by hypervigilance and startle reactions to what otherwise would be normal events for most individuals. Mistakes in perception occur that can place the returning combat veteran at risk of run-ins with the police and commissions of crimes that were never intended.

Overreactions to what most of us perceive as common occurrences place a person in the spotlight. Persons who are behaving erratically and unpredictably are frightening, especially if they possess a firearm(s). People fear such persons, often rightfully so. As the usual first responders, police in the face of danger and with little information regarding the context of the situation will act first and ask questions later—as should be the case. Police are often considered warriors on the home front, and they will act accordingly. And this, combined with particular stressors perceived as threatening and a combat veteran's history and honed survival instincts, can result in behaviors and interactions that bring the veteran into the CJS.

Co-occurring mental health diagnoses

Case example: Mike

Mike joined the Army to "be someone." Born into the middle of a pack of nine children of an upper middle class Catholic family, his experience of childhood was one of neglect. His thoughts of himself were negatively oriented. He hoped the Army would help him stand out and be respected. But in his family, no one else had even considered a career in the military. Their minimizing of his choice aggravated his constant, angry rage. To his credit, he was able to transform that anger into a will to be the best he could be and the most respected man in his unit, which he came to be out of sheer determination.

One day, though, he was too close to an IED that exploded, and his left hand was blown off. His attempts to use a prosthetic successfully were hampered by his depressive cognitions and anger.

His family seemed to have an "I told you so" attitude about his loss, and he felt very much alone and alienated, distant from his family and the Army buddies who had so respected him. He managed to find a girlfriend, however, and this cheered him greatly. She was impressed that he had been a combat veteran and showed him off to her friends and family, which he took as a sign of respect. As relationships go, this one started off with a bang and with great hope for Mike, but when his girlfriend stopped returning his phone calls and wouldn't answer her door, he became both despondent and irate; another failure, more aloneness and another rejection.

He began to stalk the young woman. With his war-honed skills, he knew how to show up suddenly and would be aggressive towards her. Later, when she got a restraining order against him, he ignored this. He ended up in prison for aggravated stalking and carrying a concealed weapon without a permit; a six-year sentence with no parole because the judge perceived him as a continued threat.

Unlike some of the other combat veterans turned inmates, he was not scornful of the CJS. He said that eventually he probably would have killed her in a fit of rage, and he knew he needed the help he was now receiving in prison.

Typically, a co-occurring mental health diagnosis refers to substance abuse/dependence in combination with another Axis I (clinical disorders and syndromes) disorder (APA, 2000). It is my experience that with returning combat veterans, other Axis I disorders, either diagnosable or with symptoms that are subclinical, often co-exist. This makes the clinical picture, and thus the treatment picture, more complex and lengthy.

PTSD is not given as a diagnosis or condition for every warrior returning home, however. Around 20 percent of returning veterans have significant symptoms of PTSD and other psychiatric disorders (Hoge *et al.*, 2004; Seal *et al.*, 2007). The brain possessed by the human organism is much the same as that of our ancient ancestors. In other words, part of our brain is very primitive, even referred to as reptilian. It responds to fear, alarm and danger much the way our ancestors did thousands of years ago. We are still beings susceptible to an accumulation of brain chemicals in the service of survival and to to the sudden discharge of those chemicals. Stress exacerbates existing conditions and causes others (see Chapter 7).

Each combat veteran is different: some respond to re-entry and its stressors with hopelessness and depression, some may have had experiences (and/or some genetic predisposition) that precipitated or exacerbated psychosis. The best guess etiology of schizophrenia is the neural diathesis-stress model, an interaction of some genetic component of the person with a stressor that turns on this component. The theater of war provides an unsurpassed experience of stress.

Depression often begets irritability and psychosis begets bizarre behavior. Even without a PTSD diagnosis, returning warriors are at risk for behaving in ways that may engage law enforcement. Sometimes neighbors, with a little bit of knowledge, may become fearful of a post-deployment veteran. Fear is a powerful motivator for "calling in the big guns," and even kind and compassionate neighbors and friends may call the police when confronted with behavior that is frightening to them.

Additionally, not all who served in combat zones came into the military as perfectly formed and raised human beings who passed through all the developmental stages with flying colors. It is my experience that those with pre-existing Axis II disorders (personality disorders) will have a harder time adapting when they come home as they have deficient skill sets to cope with what has happened to them and all to which they were exposed in the wartime theater.

With PTSD and a co-occurring personality disorder, a veteran can appear as a "common criminal" to those charged with protecting the peace at home. And, in fact, no "co-occurring personality disorder" is needed for this to occur. The behavior of a heavily drunken person with a gun and an attitude is enough to place law enforcement in an engagement-ready stance and frame of mind.

Substance Abuse[3]

Case example: Henry

It was a straightforward case of drinking too much, being at the wrong place at the wrong time, and being angry with the wrong person. Henry was at a private party that had gotten out of hand. A few beer kegs, a long line of full liquor bottles, and the hot summer sun had contributed to a wild time.

When law enforcement arrived to encourage the crowd to cool down, Henry took it upon himself to tell the officers "where to get off," including the order to get off his friend's private property. Others at the party were growling, too, but Henry's love affair with alcohol made him turn into an aggressive, suddenly temporarily deaf and drunk man.

When the officer took Henry's arm to steady him, he took a direct shot at the officer's face. Suddenly, Henry was on the ground looking up at an officer with a bloody face. Obstruction of a law enforcement officer would probably be the only charge Henry would have received, except for the punch to the face. He ended in prison for aggravated assault on a law enforcement officer—10 years, no parole. He is still spending many hours, he tells me, thinking about how the next ten years could have been so different, "if only ..."

---

3 The information regarding substance abuse is from my experience and readings over the years.

In my experience, the problems that rise out of substance abuse for returning warriors cannot be overstated. The use of alcohol to decrease stress occurs in civilians and usually leads to little more than a disinhibition of behavior and very poor decision making. The frontal cortex goes to sleep and the emotional brain takes over, with no wiser mind preventing it. Inebriated people are unpredictable and police quite rightly worry when someone behaves erratically or impulsively. Drunk drivers frequently do not drive well or safely and a DUI charge will have numerous ramifications. Likewise, other substances, especially those that distort perception, can become a powder keg ready to ignite. These are also illegal, resulting in additional charges.

Traumatic Brain Injury

Case example: Sean

The injury Sean had sustained was not very noticeable to others, except for unexplained and sudden rages and responses that were out of line with situations encountered. Sean had been told many times that the area of his brain that had been most damaged was the area that managed his emotions and, subsequently, his behavior. His difficulty with newly acquired information had hampered the psychoeducational process, but he continued to work at it. His mother was doing all in her power to help him, including daily sessions to keep his learning active.

One day, with his best friend, Sean was discussing OEF and what it was like, and his friend casually said he was angry about the war because of what it had taken from Sean. In response, Sean immediately jumped up and began screaming aggressively at his friend. Then he went outside and took his wood-chopping axe to his friend's car. He turned around to go after his friend, but the door to the house was locked. He had just broken a window to crawl in, when he heard the sirens and saw the sheriff's car pull into the driveway. This sudden turn of events and the appearance of authority seemed to bring some distant memory of his military chain of command, and he put the axe down.

His friend declined to press charges, but the prosecutors felt Sean needed consequences for his behavior and a message not to behave that way again, so the state pursued the charges and the insurance company wanted justice. Sean received a felony criminal damage to property charge and was ordered to pay considerable restitution upon release on parole or probation.

Sadly, very little treatment is available in prison for persons suffering from head injuries of any kind, and so Sean was constantly besieged with perceived insults from officers. The consequences of those altercations kept Sean in segregation on a regular basis. Even if TBI was understood, prison is not a place where many exceptions are made. Sean told me that his greatest regret was disappointing his mother. His friend's car was repaired and he and Sean remained friends, exchanging letters back and forth between prison and the free world.

In OEF and OIF, the signature injury is mild traumatic brain injury (mTBI), i.e. concussion resulting from the impact of explosions from IEDs or other types of explosive devices Chapter 7). In an explosion, sound waves enter the ear and other bodily openings, causing powerful compressions and contusions to the brain. Traumatic brain injuries (TBIs) have been a curse upon many a combat veteran. Damage to the brain can have an untold number of outcomes, from memory loss, to the loss of a sense of self, to slowed thinking and even having to learn to walk and talk again. The road back to health is an arduous one. But military personnel have a get-the-job-done attitude, which is one of the positive characteristics in terms of recovery and rehabilitation.

The problem with many head injuries, especially mTBI, is that its effects are often unobservable or difficult to detect based on the behavior of the injured person, not least because those suffering from the effects of these brain injuries tend to hide the changes in their abilities. They want to be whole again, to fit in, so can't let go for a moment of the constant effort required to speak correctly and with seeming ease, to find the right word. This leads others (including law enforcement) to believe the warrior really does not have any residual problems stemming from brain injuries sustained in the wartime theater— "the warrior doesn't really have a problem." In its milder forms, mTBI is probably the war injury that is the least understood by the public.

Impact on the family

The impact of deployment versus the impact of incarceration

When a unit is being deployed and the families are overwhelmingly distraught and frightened, it is not unusual for others in close proximity to understand and appreciate their fears. And scenes on the web and on television showing deliriously happy families welcoming their loved ones back home from deployment bring up joyful feelings for all of us. As strong and cohesive as many military families are, at these times, emotions burst forth.

Those who have had a loved one deploy to a combat zone, whether friend or family, know the experience of waiting a long time to exhale. Only when the loved one returns and can be seen and hugged does that exhale burst forth. Often, with so many tasks to take care of at home while the service member is deployed, families do not even know they have been holding their breath until the moment of reunion. These same families, most often, have had good networks of support while their loved ones were deployed. The military is its own resource network, and the National Guard and Reserves can also call upon other non-deployed members and family members of the deployed (typically, the Family Readiness Group or "FRG") to help address needs back home.

When a loved one is arrested, the reaction is opposite to that described above. The family becomes stigmatized and alienated. Household compositions that were restructured during deployment because of the service member's absence become restructured again—only for very different reasons. Very different feelings are elicited, no matter how strong and intact the family system. Going through the trajectory of the CJS is arduous at best. Incarceration disrupts both marital and parent–child relationships and changes the family's relationships with others such as friends and extended family (Travis, McBride & Solomon, 2005). The parent not arrested, assuming there are two parents, is now the head—probably again—of a single-parent household.

A single-parent family with the other parent being deployed is honorable and often a magnet for assistance and caring. A single-parent family with the other parent in prison is a starkly different story; the members are placed in a stigmatized position. For children, both short- and long-term separation from their parents profoundly affect the stages of development characteristic of childhood, and the achievement of developmental tasks (ibid.). Having to tell a child that mom or dad is in prison is a terrible task—especially when the parent had previously been viewed as a hero or heroine who did the honorable task of serving his or her country.

The information black hole

When a parent is arrested, families are instantly dropped into a black hole of little or no information and/or misinformation. Jails and the personnel who work there are not working against the families; like prisons, the VA, and other large public institutions, jails are overcrowded beyond compare. Prison and jail staff try to do what they can in the face of increasing needs and chronically decreasing budgets. Families, therefore, face an uphill battle to obtain information and to stay in contact with their incarcerated loved ones.

Severely restricted access

Access to the outside world while deployed is complicated, but can be fairly regular. By contrast, prisons heavily control access to the outside world, with the mission of protecting the public. Visits are only allowed on specific days and inmates may only make collect calls to family through a prison vendor, which is extremely expensive. Some prisons allow visitation only through Plexiglas, thus not allowing touch between family members. For children especially, walking through a razor-wire-wrapped entrance into a caged prison is frightening. Having correctional officers scrutinize visits (watching for signs of tension or exchange of contraband) can foster fear of authority figures for these children. Other inmates in visitation may be sex offenders or some other type of violent offenders or simply be odd looking in some way, causing yet further anxiety in children and parents.

Post-deployment versus post-incarceration re-entry

When an inmate is released from prison, at least in some states, they receive one set of clothes, an ID card, a check for $25, and a bus ticket wherever they want to go. There are no waving flags, such as the family is accustomed to when their loved one returns from deployment. There is just the quiet family in the parking lot, waiting to welcome their loved one home.

Post-release, depending on the court's requirements, can be expensive, with the levying of fines, restitutions, classes, parole or probation and other fees—all causing additional financial strain. Moneys that need to be directed towards caring for the children and family are still diverted by the results of the crime. And former inmates will have a difficult time getting a job, still eliciting distrust and fear, even though they have served their time. Role reversal of the parents may occur, with more confusion for the children. On the other hand, many children and families are resilient, perhaps in part because of their loved one's military service and their adaptation to deployment. And this is the best case scenario for the released combat veteran—going home to a loving family and the reunited family unit, working hard to adjust to yet another new world—one that also requires bravery.

The good news

Following in the footsteps of drug treatment courts and courts that assist the mentally ill, many veterans' courts have been implemented across the nation. These courts generally handle misdemeanors or some felonies that can be reduced to misdemeanors charges. Mitigating factors are provided so that court personnel have a veteran's war service at their disposal in order to make their decisions more fair and just (see Veterans Court, 2010).

State services

The departments of corrections in each state have available, on their public websites, a handbook entitled Guidebook for Incarcerated Veterans (Department of Veterans Affairs, n.d.). It was prepared by the VA and includes many pieces of information to assist prisoners with various VA services. Various states have also published their own similar guidebooks for this population. State bar associations have come to recognize the necessity of training their attorneys in order to assist veterans. This is a vital resource to be considered. Some attorneys work pro bono, especially if they are veterans themselves.

U.S. Department of Veterans Affairs outreach/services

A few of years ago, a new VA service area was initiated, with the focus on "justice-involved veterans." Every state and every VA Veterans' Integrated

Service Network (VISN) has at least one contact person to assist veterans with legal problems. In addition, this group assists veterans not just with legal problems, but with civil issues as well, such as divorce or other issues that require legal expertise and assistance. For more information visit www. va.gov/HOMELESS/VJO_Contacts.asp

The VA has also created a Healthcare for Reentry Veterans (HCRV) program (www1.va.gov/homeless/docs/reentry/09_fl.pdf) and maintains a national identification hotline, regionalized for verification of veterans' status. This will be particularly helpful in veterans' courts and perhaps immediately after arrest as well.

Veteran support groups

Veteran support groups abound. Most veterans would much prefer to have a veteran advocate accompany them to the courtroom as a veteran buddy, perhaps even a veteran buddy ex-inmate who can help prepare them for the difficult road ahead. Vietnam veterans have, in many cases, shown a stalwart desire to assist other veterans, even those whose service came long after their tours of duty (see, for example, Vietnam Veterans of America at www.vva. org). This reflects a generosity of spirit that was sorely lacking in the American public when they returned home from the War in Vietnam.

Recommendations

Despite monumental efforts to put programs in place to offer combat veterans support, much more can be done. Below are some ideas for increasing the chances of intervening with warriors in time to keep the damage to a minimum (Simerly & O'Hara, 2009), looking chronologically at points for intervention:

- Provide a card to each veteran to place in his or her wallet that lists mental health contact information used by the veteran and instructions for the veteran upon arrest. Family members should be aware of the existence of this card.
- Provide veterans and their families with universal training by military and veterans' service agencies on legal issues/pitfalls/rights related to arrests.
- Provide education and training for local and state law enforcement officials, corrections wardens and officers, attorneys, and legislators, so that the dilemma the veteran is facing is not experienced singly. Instead, all parties should work collaboratively.
- Distribute VA Hotline ID numbers to local and state jails, law enforcement agencies, departments of corrections, attorneys, and veterans and their families.

- Ensure there is universal screening by defense attorneys, jails and prisons for a military service history, traumatic experiences and service-related conditions, especially PTSD and mTBI, with obtained information to be verified by the VA as necessary.
- Increase the number of VISN contacts for veterans to avoid the increased likelihood of them "falling through the cracks," particularly as the VA and departments of corrections are working beyond full capacity.

Any program must have a passion for good outcomes. Accomplishing the tasks and provisions mentioned above would unquestionably improve the futures of our veterans and their families. This is one of the most powerful means of showing continued respect for their service and sacrifice. We would hope for stronger networks within communities, especially the National Guard and Reserves. This way, the negative social and fiscal impact would certainly be decreased. With enhanced efforts upon re-entry, recidivism could be reduced for warriors who have been appropriately supported.

Resources

It is very good news indeed that the number of resources available to justice-involved veterans is increasing on a regular basis. One need only contact a few of these to reach many, as most of them are inter-connected. A combat veteran and his or her family need not, and indeed should not, go through his or her dilemma alone. Here is a sample of useful websites:

- **Care for the Troops.** Dedicated to the mental health of returning troops and their families, this website, created by Peter McCall, provides information and details on training available to families, clinicians, congregations and community leaders (www.careforthetroops.org).
- **Family and Corrections Network** provides numerous links and specialty information regarding grants, legal assistance and government agencies (www.fcnetwork.org).
- **Fedcure** provides information and links to resources regarding incarcerated veterans (http://fedCURE.org).
- **Incarcerated Veterans Consortium** provides a range of services in support of incarcerated (and formerly incarcerated) veterans and their families (http://incarceratedveteransconsortim.org).
- The website of the psychologist Ken Pope offers numerous resources for military persons and their families, and a myriad of general resources for clinicians and non-clinicians (http://kspope.com/torvic/war.php).
- **Military One Source** provides direct referrals to mental health professionals without cost and without fear of records being provided to the military (www.militaryonesource.gov).

- **National Coalition for Homeless Veterans** provides information and links regarding both homeless and incarcerated veterans (www.nchv.org/incarcerated.cfm).
- **Open Inc.** This organization is the original work of Ned Rollo, a former offender who has written down-to-earth and must-have pamphlets about imprisonment and re-entry. This is especially helpful for families (www.openinc.org).
- **Vietnam Vets of America.** This website provides information for and on behalf of incarcerated veterans (www.vva.org/incarcerated_vets.html).
- **Volunteers of America Website.** Comprehensive program designed to assist incarcerated veterans in reentry; a must-visit website (www.voa.org/Get-Help/National-Network-of-Services/Corrections).
- **Washington State Department of Veterans Affairs.** Particularly active, comprehensive services for incarcerated veterans (www.dva.wa.gov). Includes a guidebook for incarcerated veterans (www.dva.wa.gov/PDF%20files/IncVetHandbook.pdf).

Conclusions

The three most important factors in successful outcomes to jail and imprisonment are family, family, and family. Having loyal friends increases the likelihood the warrior will survive the myriad of inherent difficulties. Knowing a judge who is familiar with the trials and tribulations of service members may be considered more than a "lucky break" in this endeavor. Judge Advocate General (military) attorneys can be especially helpful in these cases. An extended network of fellow service members, family, friends and acquaintances increases the chances of good outcomes exponentially, given the concept of six degrees of separation.

Veterans interfacing the legal system, or their family members, should not hesitate to use the web to find judges and other veterans' court personnel. Resources include their local VA and the VA hotline, where they can ask for the VJO (Veterans Justice Outreach) Coordinator for their area. They will also know the particular judges a veteran is likely to encounter. These experts have a wide variety of resources available that veterans may not have. Even if veterans do not have much in the way of human resources or criminal knowledge, there are many formal and grass roots organizations that will assist and support this specialized group of veterans in need (several are identified in the above list).

Closing

In spite of the good news and an increasing number of resources for and concerning incarcerated veterans, there is still a substantial shortage of resources and a gross lack of awareness of the nature and extent of the problem of veterans involved with the CJS. Unfortunately, not nearly enough governmental agencies, other resources, service organization, officials of the CJS, clinicians or members of the public seem to find it relevant to address the significant problem of veterans involved with the CJS (a problem that in many cases is directly related to combat experiences and their aftermath) and the collateral damage inflicted on such veterans' families. "If anyone in this country deserves a second chance, it is a combat veteran" (Carr, n.d.).

Emily Simerly, Ph.D, is a clinical psychologist. She worked for 20 years in mental health units at Patton State Hospital in California and currently works at state prisons in Georgia. She has worked with maximum security and Death Row inmates as well as inmates in Special Management Units. She has surprised herself completely with the deep enjoyment, privilege and reward she has felt working with these disenfranchised populations and with veterans involved with the Criminal Justice System (emilysimerly@comcast.net).

References

American Psychiatric Association (APA) (2000). *Diagnostic and Statistical Manual of Mental Disorders* (Fourth Edition, Text Revision). Washington, DC: American Psychiatric Association.

Carr, B. (n.d.). Quote on Veteran Courts homepage by The Honorable Judge Brent A. Carr, Veterans County Criminal Court No. 9, Tarrant County, Fort Worth, Texas. Retrieved from www.veteranscourts.webs.com

CMHS National GAINS Center (2008). *Responding to the needs of justice-involved veterans with service-related trauma and mental health conditions: A Consensus report of the CMHS National GAINS Center's Forum on combat veterans, trauma and the justice system.* Retrieved from http://gains.prainc.com/pdfs/veterans/CVTJS_Report.pdf

Department of Veterans Affairs (n.d.) *Guidebook for Incarcerated Veterans.* Retrieved from http://www.fedcure.org/information/VA-IncarceratedVeterans.shtml

Drug Policy Alliance (2009). *Healing a Broken System: Veterans Battling Addiction and Incarceration.* New York, NY: Drug Policy Alliance.

Hoge, C. W., Castro, C. A., Messer, S. C., McGurk, D., Cotting, D. L. & Koffman, M. D. (2004). Combat duty in Iraq and Afghanistan, mental health problems, and barriers to care. *The New England Journal of Medicine, 351*(1), 13–22.

Seal, K. H., Bertenthal, D., Miner, C. R., Saunak, S. & Marmar, C. (2007). Mental health disorders among 103,788 U.S. veterans returning from Iraq and Afghanistan seen at Department of Veterans Affairs sacilities. *Archives of Internal Medicine, 167,* 476–482.

Simerly, E. & O'Hara, C. (2009). Combat veterans in the criminal justice system: Losing their freedom after fighting for ours. Presentation at the Force Health Protection Conference, Albuquerque, New Mexico, August 2009.

Veterans Courts (2010). Comprehensive website and clearing house for Veterans Treatment Courts news and resources. Retrieved from www.veteranscourts.webs.com

Part 3

Civilian populations impacted by war

12 Iraqi civilians and the recycling of trauma

Alexander Dawoody

The land known in modern times as the nation of Iraq has a very long and rich history. Unfortunately, it is also in Iraq that some of the most grievous and extensive sufferings in human history have taken place, endured from an early age and continuing to date. This chapter briefly examines the political turmoil that gave rise to Saddam Hussein and his Baath regime, the genocide against the Kurdish people, the two Gulf Wars of 1991 and 2003, the sanction period of 12 years in between these two wars, and the sufferings endured by all Iraqis as a result of these atrocities.

Selectively, I provide my own experience of growing up in Iraq and enduring some of these atrocities. This experience is a microcosm of a larger picture that reflects the sufferings of an entire population, caused by internal and external conflicts, and resulting in a problem of epic proportions. I will also describe the paucity of psychological and counseling resources and the cultural barriers to such; the reliance on family support networks that themselves are traumatized; public manifestations of exaggerated emotional display; and political processes that normalize the institutions of fear and repression (such as security and intelligence). Trauma becomes recycled through socially and politically re-emphasized rituals, and there is a retardation of opportunities for healing. Finally, there is a description of how healing can take place even in the context of a country that has such a trauma-saturated history and ongoing turmoil and repression.

Iraqi social groups: A source of blame and fragmentation

The following is a brief description of the remarkably varied ethnic, cultural and religious groups that comprise the Iraqi people. This description is provided as a context for understanding how diversity in Iraq complicates and exacerbates trauma between and amongst various social groups. In the United States, another country of multiple ethnic and religious groups, diversity is a source of strength. Members of all socio-economic groups consider themselves Americans and take pride in such identity. Many homes have the U.S. flag decorating their front yards or porches. During times of crisis, Americans of all walks of life come together to help one another and overcome difficulties as one nation, such as after Hurricane Katrina and 9/11. This sense of unity and identity, however, is missing in Iraq. There are no Iraqi flags decorating residents' homes. During crisis, each group blames the other without a sense of unity. Most Iraqis (here this term is used as a matter of reference, not as an actual sense of existential identity) pride themselves on belonging to ethnic and tribal groups and religious and sectarian sub-groups, rather than to the collective umbrella called Iraq.

The ethnic groups are the Arabs, Kurds, Turkomans, Assyrians, Chaldeans, Armenians and Jews. These groups are further divided into sub-groups along religious lines, which are then further divided along sectarian lines. Collectively, however, they are categorized based on tribal affiliations; there are more than 150 different tribes and nearly 2,000 clans in Iraq (MacFarquhar, 2003).

The Arabs are the largest group. They migrated to Iraq from the Arabian Peninsula in search of water prior to Islam and their population increased after the Islamic conquests in 644 (Marr, 1985). The word "Arab" itself is an Iraqi invention given to the nomadic tribes by the Assyrians, meaning "people of the desert" (Simmons, 1994). Most Arabs in Iraq are Shiites, constituting 55 percent of the population, followed by the Sunnis, which constitute 25 percent of the population. Iraqi Shiites are of the Twelve Imamates' order. This sect follows the teachings of 12 generational descendants of the Prophet Muhammad (Newman, 2000). The Sunnis do not subscribe to these beliefs and follow the orthodox teachings of the Prophet and the Quran. They do so based on interpretations by four orders, the Shafie, Malikie, Hanbali and Hanafi. Most Sunnis in Iraq are of the Shafie order. There are also some Sufis and dervishes who have mystical rituals similar to the Jewish Kabbalah and Buddhism (Al-Mufid, 2004). A percentage of Iraqi Arabs are Mandwees, a small community that lives along the Tigris and Euphrates and follows the teaching of John the Baptist.

The second largest group is the Kurds, with a population of nearly 15 percent. They arrived in northern Iraq (as well as northwestern Iran and southeastern Turkey) as part of the Indo-European migration waves around 2000 BC. Except for a few fiefdoms in their early history, the Kurds were often under foreign domination. Because of this, they developed resiliency in fighting their conquerors, while benefiting from the rugged terrain of their mountainous homeland. Kurdish society is historically plagued with internal tribal divisions, which contribute to their weakness. Religiously, most of them are Sunnis along with some Shiites, Christians and Jews. A small minority of the Kurds call themselves Yazedies. The remaining 5 percent of Iraqis are Turkomans, Assyrians, Chaldeans and Jews (Tripp, 2007).

The Christians in Iraq are largely divided into two groups that consider themselves as being the original inhabitants. The first group is the Assyrians, the descendants of the Assyrian Empire in Nineveh (current-day Mosul in northern Iraq). They pride themselves on their language having been spoken by Jesus Christ. The second largest Christian group is the Chaldeans. They are the descendants of the Chaldean Empire in Babylon (Gotlieb, 1981).

During the Islamic Caliphates, such as the Umayyads, Abbasids, Fatimids, Ghaznavids, Seliugs, Safavids, Mughals and Ottomans, a period that extended from 661 to the Second World War, the Christians were treated fairly as long as they paid taxes to the state (known as *Jizya*). They continued to enjoy peaceful coexistence with the Muslims during the Ottoman period. However, persecution escalated once the Ottoman Empire began to disintegrate to the degree that oppression against the Assyrians, for example, reached a level of genocide. Subsequently, there was a protection of their religious rights until 2003. At that time, the Shiite militias and Al-Qaeda terrorists began targeting Christian churches, communities and places of business. As a result and due to repeated suicide bombings, many Iraqi Christians were killed and thousands fled.

The Jews are another ancient community in Iraq and contributed to the development and advance of Iraqi arts, science and culture. After the creation of the State of Israel in 1948, Iraqi Jews were randomly targeted by mobs and their homes were often ransacked or destroyed. As a result, many of them had to migrate to Israel in order to escape persecution. Those who remained behind had to conceal their religious identity up until 2003.

The Baath regime

A series of power struggles resulted in the Baath Party succeeding in taking over political power in Iraq, first for a short period between February and November 1963 and later for a longer period from July 1968 to March 2003 (Morris, 2003). The Baath's policies aimed to "re-engineer" Iraqi society and mold it to fit within its ideology. The consequences were more repression and persecution, which added to an already traumatized society—as illustrated by my personal experiences, described next.

I was only 8 years old when the Baath Party seized power. At the time, I was living with my family in the small Kurdish town of Khanaquine. The city had a refinery and a major oil field. Instead of this bringing wealth, as is the case with oil-producing areas in other parts of the world, it brought agony. A Kurdish town possessing oil meant resources that could be utilized for Kurdish autonomy, a concept that was prohibited by the central Iraqi government. Because of this, the city resembled an occupied town. Military presence was everywhere.

On a bright Friday afternoon in March 1963, I was playing soccer with my friends in the playground between my house and the elementary school. Suddenly, my father's little Russian Moscovitch automobile passed by. He was driving and a soldier was sitting in the back seat, pointing his rifle to the back of my father's head. After a short detention, he was released from a military prison on the condition that his job as a physician had to be relocated to a remote clinic in the marshes of southern Iraq. A week later, a truck was carrying our furniture to the city of Omarah in southern Iraq. Omarah was two hours' distance from the marshes, where the clinic was located. My father's arrest and subsequent deportation was caused by an accusation by a security informant, who claimed that my father was smuggling medicine to the Kurdish fighters. With him being in the marshland, the possibility of sending medical supplies to the Kurdish fighters was remote.

All our neighbors in Omarah were Shiite Arabs, except for one who was Christian. One thing that I noticed and disliked about my Muslim neighbors was their treatment of their Christian neighbor. When the Christian neighbor visited them, for example, the Muslim hosts put on their best hospitality face. However, once the Christian neighbor left, the hosts took the utensils that the Christian used and washed them while repeating versus from the Quran. When I asked some of them why they did so, they replied, "because they are Christians and considered *'najis'* in our religion." Najis means "dirty." I knew that this had nothing to do with Islam—how can a person be dirty simply for having another religious belief?

The Kurdish quest for autonomy

On 11 March 1970, the Baath government reached an agreement with Kurdish fighters to grant the Kurds full autonomy within Iraq by 1974. Because of this agreement, many Kurdish citizens who had been deported by the government to outside the Kurdish region were permitted to return. This included my father. This four-year period, however, was designed not to craft a suitable formula for the Kurdish autonomous region, but to change the ethnic demographics of the two oil-producing Kurdish cities of Khanaquine and Kirkuk in order to carve them out of the Kurdish region. Kurdish residents in both cities were either bussed to concentration camps in southern Iraq or deported to Iran. In their stead, Arab residents were brought in and given free housing. The consequence of this *"Arabization"* policy was resumed conflict between the Kurdish fighters (known as the Peshmarga) and government forces, although limited to Khanaquine and Kirkuk instead of the entire Kurdish region. Each passing night was filled with the non-stop sound of AK-47s, composing a symphony of fear and intimidation for the local residents. As time passed, we became accustomed to the sounds. When there was a night without bullets penetrating the silence of the sky, it felt as though something was missing. Fear became a familiar phenomenon despite its discomfort.

In March 1974, the Baath party announced its promised autonomy law for the Kurds, excluding the oil-rich cities of Kirkuk and Khanaquine from the autonomous region. Full-scale fighting between Kurdish Peshmarga and Iraqi forces erupted in April 1979, with daily bombings of Kurdistan (Dawoody, 2006).

I was, at this time, sharing a house with seven other students while studying at the University of Basra in southern Iraq, with four of us living on the second floor and the other four on the first floor. It was time for the final exams and we were occupied with preparation. Late one particular night, I heard the sound of someone storming the house. One of my friends yelled from below, "They are here!"; a clue indicating that the Mukhabarat were there and that I needed to jump from the window and escape for my life. I did exactly that, running for an hour until I arrived at the train station. I took the night train to Baghdad and arrived in the morning. From Baghdad I took a minivan to Erbil in Northern Iraq. I wanted to go to Khanaquine and say goodbye to my family, but it was too risky to do so.

I arrived in Erbil, not knowing where to go or where to stay. The city was a ghost town, with almost everyone fleeing to join the Kurdish uprising in the mountains of Kurdistan. Then I remembered one of my classmates telling me that he had an uncle who owned a teahouse in Erbil. I was able to locate it. After staying overnight in a local hotel, I caught a ride with a tea-smuggling jeep that was arranged by the teahouse owner, and arrived at the nearest Peshmarga checkpoint. From there, I went to the city of Qalat Diza and joined other Kurdish university students who were waiting for the beginning of a new academic institution in liberated Kurdistan. Two weeks later, as I was walking with my new colleagues on the main street of Qalat Diza, the sky roared with the sounds of two fighter jets. The Soviet-made MiGs were flying so low that I could see the needles in front of their cockpits. The bombardments started with napalm carpet-bombing of the entire city. Parts were severed from running bodies by pieces of shrapnel and hot iron. The most frightening sight was a headless body coming toward me before it collapsed.

I took off to the nearby mountains along with a few other students. After several days of walking on muddy, rugged terrain, we arrived at the Kurdish uprising's headquarters. Thousands of people were amassed there, awaiting resolution of their affairs. After a few days of waiting, un-bathed, unshaven, tired and constantly itching because of the lice that had penetrated my clothes while I slept on the crowded floor of the local mosque, I finally met with a committee that was in charge of assigning tasks to new recruits. Instead of being welcomed to the front, I was ridiculed for leaving Qalat Diza. The ridicule escalated when I refused the assignment of joining a battalion of Peshmarga to fight the advancing Iraqi army. Although I supported the Kurdish plight, I was against violence of all kinds, and could not bring myself to kill another human being under any circumstances. So, I was assigned the position of news broadcaster on radio Kurdistan. During this entire time and until the collapse of the uprising in March 1975, I slept in a small mud room in a village that was tucked away in a valley, concealing the radio station. There were no facilities to care for personal hygiene or to prepare and eat a proper meal. Daily bombardments by Iraqi MiGs were ongoing. Witnessing and reporting death became part of my new vocabulary.

In March 1975, the Kurdish uprising collapsed due to the Algiers Accord between the Shah and Saddam Hussein (Khadduri, 1978). The Shah promised to stop aiding the Kurds, while Saddam promised to expel the Ayatollah

Khomeini from Iraq. About 70 percent of the Peshmarga surrendered to the Iraqi Army. Some remained in the hills of Kurdistan to continue fighting and about 30,000 crossed the border to Iran to join an estimated 100,000 to 200,000 civilian refugees (Ghareeb, 1981).

The life of a refugee

Like many other Kurds, I became a refugee in Iran and lived in a tent camp along with thousands of others near the Iraq–Iran border for nearly six months. My personal experience illustrates prototypical experiences of the life of Iraqi refugees. I was getting weaker with each passing day, caused by malnutrition and post-traumatic stress. I went to the camp's clinic and obtained a bottle of vitamin syrup in order to help me boost my strength. I drank the bottle at once to speed up the process, but the reaction of muscle spasms caused my jaws to twitch left and right involuntarily. Those who witnessed this, mostly uneducated farmers, thought I was possessed. They lifted me up on their shoulders and took me to the tent of a clergyman (mullah) so that he could cast the demons out of me. I fell asleep during this episode, while watching him praying over my head. It did not matter to me what he was doing. I was too tired and too weak to object or comment, and just wanted to rest. A few hours later, I woke up without symptoms. The locals heralded this as a religious triumph and asked me to kiss the mullah's hand and thank him for his miracle. They were angered when I walked out without doing as they asked. I spent the remaining days in my tent, until the Iranian government decided to disband the camp and ship us, in military trucks, to different Iranian cities.

I arrived at the city of Somaa Sera in northern Iran, along with a dozen other Kurdish refugees. We were housed in an abandoned school building. The rest of the refugees were given larger classrooms because they were married and had children. I was the only single person among them, so I was given the small janitor's room. No food was provided for nearly a week. Luckily, the families had brought some rice with them from the camp and they shared it with me.

After two months of working for a local contractor, I was accepted at the University of Tehran. I left Somaa Sera in order to attend language classes and learn Farsi (the official language of Iran) in Tehran before fall classes began. I was placed in a tent in the middle of a park in northern Tehran that was equipped with a cot and cooking utensils. After completing the language course, classes started in September of 1976. Then, I was relocated to the center of the city and given a room on the third floor of a condemned building. I attended Fine Arts classes at the University of Tehran, but most classes in all colleges were empty. Students were gathered outside in the yard, shouting anti-Shah slogans and renouncing the regime. I remained with a few other Iranian students in the skeleton classrooms, attempting to focus on my studies amidst the loud, disrupting shouts of demonstrators outside—before joining them.

Torture and political imprisonment

Again, I offer my own personal experiences to illustrate the political imprisonment and torture that have been experienced by countless Iraqis. I was asleep in my room on the third floor of the condemned school building, when I was awakened by two men in civilian clothes who took me with them to an Iranian-made Paykan vehicle that was parked outside the building. I sat in the back seat of the car next to a third man, while the other two returned to the building and came back with my letters and notebooks. One of them drove the car and the other two sat in the back, each on one side of me, sandwiching me in the middle. They first pushed my head down toward my knees and then blindfolded me as the car left the paved road, heading toward outer Tehran on a dirt road. Shortly after, the car stopped and I was escorted to the inside of a concrete compound after passing through many gates and armed men. Inside an empty room, a soldier lifted off my blindfold, handed me a blue prison uniform and placed my clothes in a bag. I was once again blindfolded and escorted to another building, which housed several cells lined up on each side of a long and narrow corridor. I was placed in a cell, the blindfold was removed, then the solid iron door shut. There was only a thin mattress on the concrete floor, a plastic bowl and a spoon. A small window was located near the high ceiling, through which I could see the the sky change from day to night.

I stayed in that cell for a month without being interviewed or questioned. Once a day the iron door was opened in order to fill my plastic bowl with carrot soup. A soldier was entrusted with the task of pouring the soup from a large cauldron with a shovel. There was no shower room or facilities for shaving. To use the toilet, I had to knock on the door and await my turn. Time moved very slowly, seemed almost to be at a standstill. I marked the end of each day on the door with the tip of the spoon. Fear was paralyzing, especially as I was hearing the cries and agonies of other inmates in the adjacent cells.

After a month had passed, I was escorted to an interrogation room by the notorious SAVAK, the Shah's secret police. I now learned that I was imprisoned in the infamous Aveen torture camp. For the next five months I endured various methods of torture that ranged from beating to electric shocks, hanging upside down from a ceiling fan, and having my fingernails pulled out.

Five months later, the torture suddenly stopped. Two men arrived at my cell wearing light blue jackets with UN insignia attached to the left pockets. They asked me about my ordeal. Shortly after their visit, a military court decided to release me, on the condition that I leave Iran within 48 hours or be surrendered to Iraq. I was granted asylum in the United States after a short stop in West Germany and arrived at JFK Airport on 29 September 1977.

War and genocide

In 1979 the Shah was overthrown by an Islamic revolution led by Ayatollah Khomeini. At the same time Saddam Hussein became President of Iraq

(Henderson, 1991). In September of 1980, he invaded the western part of Iran (Freedman, 1995) and the Iraq–Iran War started. It continued for eight years. One of the most reprehensible of Saddam's actions during this time was his campaign against the Kurds, known as Al-Anfal—a twisted reference to a verse in the Koran. In February 1988, Iraqi forces cleared areas of Kurdish residents through massive bombardments of chemical weapons and high explosives, followed by sweeps that often killed anyone left alive, and then razing to the ground anything left standing (Pollack, 2002). A month later Saddam attacked the Kurdish town of Halabcha with several varieties of chemical weapons, killing at least 5,000 residents. When the campaign ended in 1989, some 200,000 Kurds were dead, roughly 1.5 million had been forcibly resettled, and huge swaths of Kurdistan had been scorched by chemical warfare (Dawoody, 2006).

To salvage his economically devastated regime, Saddam invaded the tiny oil-rich country of Kuwait on 2 August 1990. His actions prompted a military response by the United States and its allies. Desert Storm was launched in January 1991 to expel Iraq from Kuwait. For 42 days, the allied forces bombed both Baghdad and the Iraqi army in Kuwait (Pitt & Ritter, 2002). Some of the bombs and missiles missed their targets, destroying private homes and killing 2,278 civilians (Simon, 2003).

Shortly after Saddam's defeat in Kuwait, an uprising broke out against his regime in the Shiite south, followed by another one in the Kurdish north. These uprisings were encouraged by President George H. Bush when he called upon the Iraqi people to rise up and push Saddam aside. Unfortunately, the president left the rebellious Iraqis at the mercy of Saddam's Republican Guard (Dawoody, 2006).

As of 1991 and for the next 12 years, Iraq was placed under heavy UN-imposed economic sanctions that punished Iraqis more than the regime. Due to these sanctions and the breakdown of systems to provide clean water, sanitation and electrical power, nearly 5,000 Iraqi children died each month as a result of diarrhea and acute respiratory infections. This overall toll, according to a UNICEF report, was 1.2 million (RUPE, 2003).

I was unable to find out what my family was experiencing during this time, since I was unable to contact them, except for once in 1977 after arriving in the United States. I sent a letter to my father to inform him that I was well. The letter, however, was intercepted by Iraqi secret police, as it had an American stamp on it, and he was arrested by the Mukhabarat and tortured once a month as punishment for my "crime against the state." When he grew older and too frail to stand torture, my youngest brother volunteered to take his place. This continued until they managed to escape from Iraq by hiding in the back of a truck shortly before 2003. They first lived in a refugee camp in Jordan before becoming refugees in Sweden. In 2004 I was able to see them for the first time since I escaped from my university in Basra.

Not only had my immediate family suffered, but also my relatives and friends. For example, in 1997, my aunt was attacked in her home by a group of thugs, known as the Sanction Generation, who stole her gold necklace, severed her head with a knife and left her lifeless body on the floor.

The second Gulf War, known as Operation Iraqi Freedom, began in March 2003, when U.S. forces occupied Iraq (Dawisha, 2009). On 9 April 2003, the regime of Saddam Hussein collapsed. I despised the criminal regime of Saddam Hussein because of the atrocities it had committed against millions. The demise of such a regime was both a hope and an inspiration. However, the senseless killing of thousands of Iraqi civilians during and in the aftermath of the war removed any sense of joy from my heart and replaced it with bitter agony and hurt.

Today's Iraq is plagued by civil unrest, sectarian violence, terrorist acts and nearly one million civilian deaths (Iraq Body Count, 2010). This is in addition to an inept Iraqi administration, marred by corruption, incompetence, waste, nepotism, tribalism and sectarianism (Lendman, 2010). Terrorism, in the form of kidnappings and suicide bombings, are becoming daily occurrences in Iraq (Sobel, Furia & Barrett, 2010). One of those who was kidnapped in 2004 was my cousin. His kidnappers asked his wife for a large sum of money and gold in exchange for his release. When she was unable to come up with the ransom, she found his body a few days later on a street corner in Baghdad with a hole in his head made with an electric drill.

The future of an artificial state and continuing trauma

Iraqi nationalism did not materialize, despite 80 years of the nation state's enforced efforts to assimilate the conflicting groups and sub-groups within the fabric of Iraqi society. The lack of "national identity" and a unified sense of belonging to a motherland further reinforced the ethnic, religious, sectarian and tribal divides. For a country plagued by division, trauma and lack of unifying elements, where can it go from here and what does the future hold for its people?

It is fruitless to predict the future, since many interplaying factors will alter the various possibilities and morph them in unexpected directions. Instead, it is best to examine trends and then assess possible short-term outcomes.

The first outcome is the continuation of the current structure with the central government emerging as a coordinator, while regional governments grow more autonomous. Within this scenario, violence will continue as both a social and a political language to suppress the varying conflicting segments within the artificial mosaic, while benefiting groups in power or seeking power. Trauma will continue to be recycled and experienced on individual or societal levels.

The second outcome is Iraq becoming a satellite state of neighboring Iran, especially once the United States has completed pulling its military presence from the country. Iran is already exercising its influence over Iraqi internal affairs and foreign policy, through either the Iraqi central government or the various competing ethnic and sectarian militia and political groups. The complete hegemony of Iran over Iraq, however, will intensify an already fragmented society and advance the sense of hopelessness and pessimism while fostering dependency. Opportunities for therapeutic intervention will decrease, with the focus instead being greatly on meaningless religious ceremonies and mass hysteria. Fear will replace the faint hope for healing. The adaptation of assimilation will become the enforced mantra for the emerging situation, which, by itself adds to the recycled trauma.

The third outcome is the nation state of Iraq disintegrating into completely autonomous (or independent) regions, based on ethnic and sectarian affiliation. Iraq may continue to exist, but only symbolically. This probability is perhaps the best remedy to marginally treat centuries-long recycled trauma by, hopefully, facilitating more positive inter-group dynamics within each autonomous region. Yet, it is also the most dangerous, as it will invite new suffering of subsequent reactions to emerging new traumatic events caused by internal and external conflicts. The internal conflicts may be generated by warring sub-groups within the larger group to sustain gains. There is also the problem of dealing with or relocating ethnic, religious and sectarian pockets of populations that do not neatly fit within the autonomous region. The external conflicts may arrive through foreign interventions by countries that feel vulnerable to the impact of this scenario on their own interests or that will seize the opportunity to invade and forcibly absorb one or more autonomous or independent regions.

Trauma and healing in Iraq

When someone dies in Iraq, whether young or old, due to natural causes or to an atrocity, the funeral sessions are always portrayed with exaggerated displays of grief and sorrow. People from distant neighborhoods arrive at the funeral sessions in order to engage in the public drama. These dramas serve as ventilations, both to grieve current deaths, but also to allow a traumatized nation to further attempt to cope with cumulative recycled generational and chronically unhealed trauma. Women weep loudly, tear their clothes, wear black attire for 40 days and paste their heads with mud, while men cry and refuse to shave for the same duration. Such dramatic events may aid in dealing with the immediate sense of loss, but in reality, they camouflage a much deeper sense of hurt and hopelessness caused by years of recycled trauma.

I remember my mother rushing from one funeral event to another, engaging in exhausting marathons of grief, often for people that she did not know. This sense of self-imposed torment is magnified annually during the Arabic lunar month of Moharam. During the first ten days of Moharam (known as Ashora), Iraqi Shiites, for example, take to the street to publicly beat themselves with iron chains and swords to commemorate the martyrdom of Imam Hussein, the Prophet Mohammad's grandson, who was killed in 680. Outsiders would be baffled by such a massive degree of self-inflicted torture, involving continuous masochistic rituals that involve millions.

Expression of public exaggerated grieving and grief as ventilation can also be seen in Iraqi arts and folklores, including songs, plays and fairy tales. One example is Iraqi fairy tales produced during Iraq's golden Abbasid period, such as the legendary One Thousand and One Nights. Comparing such magical stories with those after the Mongol invasion and the subsequent decline of the nation of Iraq, one can identify the traces of pain in the emerging stories, reflecting a traumatized people yearning for help within some form of healing. Often, these yearnings take on an inadequacy of absurdity, as hopelessness takes hold and Iraqis find in jokes a vehicle for rationalizing feeling and masquerading hurt through satire and humor. Humor, in effect, along with exaggerated expression of grief and a sense of greatness, take the place of therapy—especially when mental health therapy is taboo. Victims, as such, mask their suffering with an unbending toughness as a way to shy away from expressing emotional distress due to a trauma. They will, otherwise, be considered weak by society and ridiculed by their peers and families. Indeed, traumatized individuals are taught from early childhood to mask their pain and suffering within a harsh facade, to rely on their family support network and to exploit social events such as funerals and religious ceremonies or absurdity in order to vent. And the availability of intact and healthy family networks is greatly diminished due to the historical and ongoing cycles of trauma that afflict an entire nation.

Throughout my entire adult life in Iraq, I did not see a single office for a counselor or therapist. The subject, although taught in most Iraqi universities, is utilized merely as an academic exercise. Clinical psychology, on the other hand, is practiced in specialized public institutions devoted to individuals with severe mental illness. In Baghdad, for example, there is one hospital for psychiatric treatments of severe mental illness in the district of Shamaaya. Individuals with less severe mental illness or developmental disabilities are cared for by family members.

When I was in Khanaquine in northern Iraq, I remember two adults who were living there with their family. Both were disabled, one (named Kamal) with a mental disability and the other (named Yehya) with a developmental disability. Everyone in the city, however, welcomed them as part of the community. It made sense for people, themselves suffering from masked trauma, to be kind to the disabled with unmasked sufferings. In a recent portrait of the city's prominent people by a local artist from Khanaquine, both Yehya and Kamal were included as iconic figures in the city.

In governance, however, the provision of care is different. The absence of a cultural acceptance of counseling and therapy has contributed to the manifestation of a governmental system that is devoid of institutions of care. Instead, the few that did exist were institutions of brutality, such as prisons and torture camps to parallel the pain exhibited by the public's tormented psyche. When such government-induced pain exceeds the inherited trauma, the public starts to ask for and demand other solutions through mass demonstrations or armed revolts. The result is a schizophrenic trajectory of tormented behavior, cycling between "being trapped in victimhood" and "causing victimhood." Self-pity and self-grandiosity become exchanged metaphors and personal manifestations, reflecting an untreated hurt and a socially prolonged and recycled trauma.

One wonders how it was possible for only one person, Saddam Hussein, to rule and inflict pain on an entire population for 30 years if he was not aided by his own countrymen to cause victimhood to themselves. One also wonders how is it possible for the same people who were rescued from Saddam's brutality to once again invite another psychopath, the Shiite cleric Muqtada Al-Sadr, to re-inflict the pain on them. This author suggests that the answer to these questions regarding the people of an entire nation can be understood, at least partially, by parallels to the Battered Woman Syndrome (a woman ending her relationship with an abusive man, only to engage once more in a relationship with another abusive man) and go on to the dynamics involved when a victim subsequently becomes a perpetrator. Unless true healing can take place, a forced dependency relationship with the perpetrator remains binding, unresolved grief and rage become projected onto others, the vicious recycling of self-inflicted suffering will continue and traumatized victims will keep on inviting torment into their lives and/or will perpetrate such onto others.

Making the pomegranate bleed

During the cold winter nights in Kurdistan, Iraq, and while I was a young boy, my mother used to hand me and each of my siblings a red, ripened pomegranate. It was our preferred snack as we gathered around the kerosene heater in the middle of the room, sitting on a red Persian rug, drinking tea while listening to my grandmother's fairy tales. While everyone carefully peeled off the pomegranate's skin and ate the seeds by freeing them from the inner layers, I, on the other hand, squeezed the entire pomegranate with its skin intact, creating a ball of red juice inside the fruit and then sipping it through a small hole that I punctured in its skin. This way, I did not have to bother with the agonizing process of peeling and then freeing each single trapped seed. My way was much quicker, and a bit messier, as I always ended with red juice over my pajamas. This, of course, angered my mother; not because of the red stain on my pajamas that she had to wash out the next day, but because "I made the pomegranate bleed." Her advice was to respect life, regardless of its form, by bestowing on it the full integrity it deserved. A pomegranate, she claimed, was designed to be eaten by freeing its seeds, one by one. If nature intended for it to be a ball of juice, then it would have offered it to us as such.

I did not understand my mother's reasoning at the time and why she was concerned about such a tiny matter. Later I came to understand that it was the collective of these tiny matters that composed the album of life. If we are given a gift or entrusted with something, we ought to treat it with the integrity it deserves, instead of bleeding life out of it. Freedom is everything in life and we see its metaphors repeated in our experiences. With each action, we accentuate these metaphors. As with eating the seeds of a pomegranate, life is emphasizing enjoyment and nourishment as we consume the fruit. Yet, we can achieve that only if we have "freed" the seeds without desecrating them. With the act of freeing the seeds, in effect, we are enjoying freedom. If we instead "make them bleed," not only are we deforming beauty, but we are also depriving ourselves of the true meaning of life and turning into a pariah species that is foreign to what nature intended.

My mother's simple message can also be translated into politics and the principle of good governance. A government's proper treatment of its people is similar to a person's proper treatment of a pomegranate. If a government treats its people by allowing each citizen the freedom she/he deserves and respecting the process of governance, then it benefits as a result by gaining strength, resources and energy. If a government, on the other hand, oppresses its people and make them bleed by depriving them of their liberties, then it will end up deforming, tormenting and killing its citizens. As a result, it will deprive itself of peace by turning into a pariah entity, foreign to those who had entrusted it with their lives, hopes and affairs. Sadly, this was the case with the government in Iraq as I was growing up.

This chapter is a short illustration of my personal experiences as I watched my country bleed and the lessons I learned. War, torture, imprisonment, repression, suppression, discrimination, and physical and emotional abuse are all different forms of hate and violence. The victims who survive deal with each ordeal differently as survival instincts take hold. Some victims may become jaded, others may become angry and pessimistic throughout their lives, and some may even become violent. The process of healing is long and unpredictable. As a society, we need to understand what victims of hate and violence have experienced and provide them with a support system without stigmatization in order to allow their wounds to heal and for them to become fully integrated into the society as productive citizens with their humanity and integrity affirmed. Each one of us deals differently with trauma. Some will take longer to heal, and some may never be able to overcome the trauma they have experienced. None, however, will forget what they had to endure, and they will never be as others who did not experience the same suffering. Thus, an essential element of their healing is for us to allow and facilitate them to regain their trust in humanity, build confidence in the goodness of mankind, and walk on their own in order to arrive at some sort of inner peace without judgment.

The millions of Iraqi victims of violence are not lesser beings because they have experienced trauma and recycled trauma in modern times and for generations past. They are not the guilty ones and should not be excluded from the human community, or ignored or forgotten. We need to embrace the victims of hate and violence, accept their wounds as ours, and allow them the opportunity to teach us how to be even more human by aborting the ill traits of inflicting harm on others for the sake of power. And we must appreciate the courage and strength it has taken to endure so much for so long.

Closing

It took me a long time to overcome the hurts and nightmares that I had experienced in my life from an early age. For years I used to wake up in the middle of the night screaming, sweating and often rushing to hide under the bed, thinking that war planes were dropping napalm on me. To date, I cannot sleep in a dark room because it reminds me of the places where I was detained and tortured. Instead, I must have some sort of light in my room while I am asleep, along with a plant or a small tree next to my bed to remind me that life is still safe and the hurt belongs to the past.

I was able to survive in large part because of the sense of safety I had created for myself inside my mind, along with the learning and love from my family and culture that enriched me. I was able to escape to a peaceful imaginary world and ignore whatever hurt I was experiencing simply by telling myself stories of a much more harmonious life. Perhaps it was my grandmother's stories during the long winter nights of my childhood that helped me learn how to become my own storyteller and hide in an imaginary safe place that cannot hurt me.

I do not hate those who inflicted pain on me, because that way the cycle of hate would continue and I could never heal. I believe in something greater than me that helped me to go on and endure, allowing me the strength to hear my faint whispers, comfort my soul, and slowly walk toward safety on my own. I was fortunate to come to safety in the United States in order to heal. I hope one day that Iraqis can have opportunities to live in peace and, through a genuine sense of safety, be able to overcome their long recycled agony and heal both as people and as a nation.

Putting my experiences into words is a healing process by itself, and I hope it can bring some closure and healing to others who went through the same (or perhaps have experienced even larger atrocities). I feel blessed for having escaped Iraq and to now be living in the most beautiful country in the world. It is the sense of safety that I experienced in the United States, provided by its institutions, laws, traditions and kindness of its people, that helped me to cross the bridge over past pain and the abyss of the torment that resulted from years of trauma in Iraq. I feel sad for those left behind, who continue to experience such trauma without any sense of safety or opportunity for healing, instead experiencing further agitation for abuse. Human suffering, I have found, is one and its language shares the same vocabulary. Only its variation from one place, individual or group to another differs. I am hopeful we can open up discussion, expose atrocities, and find common bonds for people throughout the world to connect in the awesome and noble process of healing so that we can all engage with the beating of the same universal heart that is called human consciousnesses.

I watch with sadness the daily torments of people throughout the Middle East, who endure unimaginable sufferings at the hands of their repressive governments—while hoping for freedom and a life that allows them to live without pain and suffering. Their faint whispers and increasingly shouted demands for safety and freedom are penetrating the silence of the night as the world is coming to their aid, echoing with one voice the need for an end to all forms of agony and for the bleeding of the pomegranate to stop once and for all. We need to empower this voice so that the whispers for peace, safety and freedom within each one of us will not die and healing can take place.

Alexander R. Dawoody, Ph.D., is an Assistant Professor of Public Administration at Marywood University, Pennsylvania, and received his Ph.D. in Public Affairs and Administration from Western Michigan University. He is a native of Iraqi Kurdistan who fled to the United States, escaping the Baathist government's genocide against the Kurds (adawoody@marywood.edu).

References

Al-Mufid, S. (2004). The journey of Imam Husain. In *Kitab Al-Irshad* (I.K.A. Howard, Trans.). Qom, Iran: Ansariyan Publication.

Dawisha, A. (2009). *Iraq: A Political History from Independence to Occupation*. Princeton, NJ: Princeton University Press.

Dawoody, A. (2006). Iraqi notes: A personal reflection on issues of governance in Iraq and U.S. involvement. *Journal of Public Voices, 8*(2), 4–42.

Freedman, L. (1995). *The Gulf Conflict, 1990-1991*. Princeton, NJ: Princeton University Press.

Ghareeb, E. (1981). *The Kurdish Question in Iraq*. Syracuse: Syracuse University Press.

Gotlieb, Y. (1981). Sectarianism and the Iraqi State. In Michael Curtis (Ed.), *Religion and Politics in the Middle East* (pp. 153–161). Boulder, CO: Westview Press.

Henderson, S. (1991). *Instant Empire: Saddam Hussein's Ambition for Iraq*. San Francisco, CA: Mercury House, Inc.

Iraq Body Count. (2010). Documented civilian death from violence. Retrieved from iraqbodycount.org

Khadduri, M. (1978). *Socialist Iraq: A Study in Iraqi Politics since 1968*. Washington, DC: Middle East Institute.

Lendman, S. (2010, April 28). U.S. legacy in Iraq: Torture, corruption and civil war. *Dissident Voice*. Retrieved from http://dissidentvoice.org/2010/04/iraq-today-afflicted-by-violence-devastation-corruption-and-desperation

MacFarquhar, N. (2003, January 7). Unpredictable force awaits U.S. in Iraq storied tribes of the Middle East devout, armed and nationalistic. *International Herald Tribune*, p. 2.

Marr, P. (1985). *The Modern History of Iraq*. Boulder, CO: Westview Press.

Morris, R. (2003, March 14). A tyrant forty years in the making. *New York Times*. Retrieved from www.nytimes.com/2003/03/14/opinion/a-tyrant-40-years-in-the-making.html

Newman, A. (2000). *The Formation of Twelver Shi'ism: Hadith as Discourse Between Qum and Baghdad*. Richmond, VA: Curzon Press.

Pitt, W. R. & Ritter., S. (2002). *War on Iraq, What Team Bush Doesn't Want You to Know*. New York, NY: Context Books.

Pollack, K. (2002). *The Threatening Storm: The Case for Invading Iraq*. New York, NY: Random House.

RUPE (Research Unit for Political Economy). (2003). *Behind the Invasion of Iraq*. New York, NY: Monthly Review Press.

Simon, J. (2003, June 13). War may have killed 10,000 civilians, research says. *The Guardian*. Retrieved from www.guardian.co.uk/world/2003/jun/13/highereducation.research

Simmons, G. (1994). *Iraq: From Sumer to Saddam*. New York, NY: St. Martin's Press.

Sobel, R., Furia, P. & Barrett., B. (2010). *Public Opinion and International Intervention: Lessons from the Iraq War*. Dulles, VA: Potomac Books Inc.

Tripp, C. (2007). *A History of Iraq*. Cambridge, UK: Cambridge University Press.

13 Afghan civilians: Surviving trauma in a failed state

Anna Badkhen

Farida

When Farida could no longer summon the energy to boil rice for dinner or pin laundry to the lines that sagged along the hand-slapped mud walls of her family compound, her husband drove her to Mazar-e-Sharif and checked her into one of the handful of Afghanistan's mental healthcare facilities: the pale blue, four-story Alemi Neuropsychiatric Hospital, a private clinic that greets its mostly illiterate visitors with posters that proclaim, in English and Dari: "No Health Without Mental Health" and "No Entry With Weapon."

Farida was twenty years old. Her days brought tidal surges of panic attacks. Her nights brought no sleep. Headaches tormented her. The shrill voices of her three small children sawed through her skull. She could not eat. Inside her farmhouse, Farida found no peace.

Outside, as always, was war. Farida was two years old when the mujaheddin who had fought off Soviet invaders drove Afghanistan's communist government out of Kabul, and the country plunged into fratricide. She was six when Taliban tanks rolled into Khanabad, her northern Afghan hometown of dusty poplar alleys. She was 11 when a series of American air raids pummeled the town, targeting Taliban fortifications; the bombings killed between 100 and 150 civilians (Huggler, 2001). Soon a ragtag mujaheddin army once more dragged its howitzers and tanks through town, executing in the streets the Taliban fighters who had not fled in time. Five years later, the Taliban were back. Ambushes waylaid NATO patrols. There were beheadings. A school for girls shut down. A roadside bomb killed the leader of a pro-government vigilante team outside his house.

Invasions and fratricides, genocides and insurgencies have concussed Afghanistan for millennia, mirroring the country's truculent tectonics. Clinging to the country's forbidding mountains and sun-scorched valleys, 30 million people eke out a living amidst the scars of generations of wars: ruins of cities sacked by Genghis Khan; imperial forts abandoned by the British; rusted hulls of Soviet tanks; bomb craters hollowed out by air raids during the latest, American-led invasion. Against this wretched backdrop, Afghans like Farida nurse their own internal, invisible scars: grief for loved ones lost to conflicts and rampant waterborne disease; fear that their next-door neighbors will kill their men and rape their women; and the gnawing knowledge that they are utterly alone, and that no government, foreign or their own, will do anything to protect them.

I met Farida in the spring of 2010. She sat in a stuffy third-floor room of the Alemi Neuropsychiatric Hospital on some rug-covered planks fixed to a metal frame that passed for a cot, her arms folded around her knees, and was rocking lightly. Her old flowered dress, now several sizes too large, hung off her wasted shoulders. Flies landed on her exposed, twig-like collarbones, explored her dry skin, took off. Farida just rocked. Her eyes stared dully upon the room's uneven, salmon pink walls.

Doctor Mohammad Nader Alemi, the clinic's owner and head doctor, glanced at Farida's chart: just as he'd thought—"Panic attacks and depression," he read. He noticed the persistent headaches. "And conversion." Most of Alemi's clients—the doctor had seen more than 4,600 in the six years since he had opened the hospital—were suffering from the same symptoms, all commonly recognized as manifestations of mental trauma. In fact, the most conservative estimates suggest that between 12 and 18 million Afghans—up to two thirds of the country's population—have, like Farida, withdrawn from the chronic war that is ravaging their country into the fog of war within their own minds. (Scholte *et al.*, 2004)

Afghanistan, PTSD, and the West

Before sitting down to write this chapter I googled the words "Afghanistan," "depression," and "post-traumatic stress disorder." The first page of search results painted Odyssean portraits of thousands of American war veterans: restless and explosively violent, battling internal monsters, incapable of making the emotional return home years after they have left the physical combat zone. By January 2011, by some estimations, one in five American veterans who had served in Iraq and Afghanistan—as many as 400,000 people—suffered from severe depression or post-traumatic stress disorder. The noxious bouquet of depression, panic attacks, psychosomatic pains, rage and sleeplessness had become the signature injury of the wars that have turned the term and its acronym, PTSD, into household words in the United States.

Occasionally, we see a news report about a veteran driven to violence by misfiring neurons in his brain. For the most part, though, war trauma abrades the minds of individual servicemen and women in private, and its destructive repercussions reverberate within tightly contained circles of the victims' immediate family and friends, overlooked by the rest of the nation.

Afghanistan and PTSD

But what happens when physical and emotional battlefields converge to bleed entire societies—failed states like Somalia or eastern Congo; sadistic dictatorships like Zimbabwe or Chechnya; lands recovering from fratricidal conflicts like Iraq or Uganda? What about countries that, like Afghanistan, have been eking out an existence amid unending violence for generations? Such trademark symptoms of individual war trauma as depression, hypervigilance and hyperaggression, when suffered collectively by entire nations, lead to those populations being envenomed with despair, sectarian and ethnic mistrust, desire of revenge and the widespread belief that violence is the ultimate solution to conflict.

In 2002, shortly after the Taliban government fell in Kabul, the Center for Disease Control and Prevention dispatched a research team to Afghanistan to study the prevalence of mental trauma among civilians there. As I write this, that nationwide survey remains the only modern comprehensive inquiry into the mental health of Afghans. The researchers found that 42 percent of Afghans suffered from post-traumatic stress disorder, and 62 percent exhibited signs of major depression (Scholte *et al.*, 2004).

How do such common prodromes of war trauma as anxiety, hypervigilance and mistrust stand in the way of peace and reconciliation? Here is one example: Afghan civilians feel so unsafe that many are resisting the 2006 order to disarm—a 2009 Gallup poll showed that two thirds of Afghans felt unsafe walking alone outside (English & Ray, 2010, p.2). Scores of Afghans have told me, in private, that they secretly keep their rifles stashed within easy reach: in shallow pits in their backyards; beneath some boards in the earthen floor of their houses; behind knotty rafters holding up clay roofs. One driver in northern Afghanistan's truculent jigsaw puzzle of ethnic alliances explained that his family owns enough rifles to arm an infantry squad. The man himself keeps a 9mm pistol, wrapped in a camel wool blanket, in his car. He said he felt threatened by government troops, police, Taliban, ethnic militias, and civilian neighbors who belonged to different ethnic groups—in short, by almost everybody who was not his kin. For this man, and thousands like him, a firefight remains just a perceived threat away.

In 2010, in a village about 30 miles south of Mazar-e-Sharif, I took lunch in a castle that presides over 15 acres of farmland that belongs to two brothers. I admired the 360-degree view of the valley through the tower's primitive castellations, from behind four-foot-thick walls. The brothers told me they needed the castle, built 60 years ago by their grandfather, to defend their women, their wealth, and their honor. I asked the farmers from whom they were defending themselves. They responded, in unison: "Everyone."

The feeling of hurt, betrayal, and injustice lingers among victims of post-traumatic stress disorder. In Afghanistan, many people bear grudges like badges of honor. One man, a Pashtun, told me in minute detail how ethnic Hazara gunmen killed his brother: at 4 o'clock, on a Thursday. The episode had taken place 15 years earlier. The man, a tribal elder with fingernails dyed orange with henna, then counted off out loud the 22 people he said Hazaras had killed in his village that year: "Khan, Ghazi, Qamalladin, Sakhedad, Matai, Abdul Rauf ..." In a Hazara hamlet a mile away, a Hazara elder, too, tallied his murdered tribesmen—killed, he said, by Pashtun gunmen: "Mohammad, Alivar, Haidar, Ghulam Sakhi, Nawruz…" As he recited the names, his grandchildren squatted around him. They will inherit the memory of these men's deaths, and the hatred that comes with it.

Pashtuns and Hazaras in northern Afghanistan share a blood-soaked history. The presence of Pashtuns in northern Afghanistan is the product of a 120-year-old state-sanctioned ethnic cleansing of Hazaras, the Shia Muslim minority who are believed to have descended from the armies of Genghis Khan, and who are traditionally shunned by other Afghans. As part of an anti-Shia campaign, the Afghan Pashtun king Abdur Rahman forcibly settled 10,000 Pashtun families north of the Hindu Kush in the 1890s.

In 1997, members of the Hazara Hezb-e-Wahdat party helped massacre 3,000 Pashtun Taliban soldiers in Mazar-e-Sharif. The following year, the Taliban, which was made up mostly of ethnic Pashtuns, mutilated, shot, and slit the throats of some 6,000 Hazaras in the city. In 2001, after helping expel the Taliban from northern Afghanistan, victorious Hazara militiamen whooped through Pashtun villages around the city in pickup trucks and on foot, slaughtering the men and raping the women. "In my father's house they gathered all the women in one room," one Pashtun woman told me. "We will never forgive these crimes. Until we die."

"Feelings of hatred and revenge, and the desire of acting on that feeling of revenge, directly affects the peacemaking process," Barbara Lopes Cardozo, the psychiatrist who oversaw the 2002 mental health survey in Afghanistan, and who has studied the mental health of civilians in such war-scarred geographies as Somalia, Uganda, and Kosovo, told me in 2011. "We found very high numbers for having those feelings of hatred and revenge—almost 80 percent—in Afghanistan."

Trauma begets trauma. Post-traumatic stress often spawns domestic violence, and Afghanistan is no exception. *Time* magazine's shocking photograph of Bibi Aisha, the 18-year-old whose husband had cut off her nose and both ears, became the face of Afghanistan's spousal abuse. While such horrific mutilations are not typical, violence inside Afghan homes is common.

Two thirds of Afghan children surveyed by British anthropologists in 2006 reported traumatic experiences (Panter-Brick *et al.*, 2009); two years later, the *Journal of Marital and Family Therapy* reported that more than half of Kabuli children said they had witnessed three or more different types of domestic violence (Catani, Schauer & Neuner, 2008). This means that millions of depressed, distraught, and easily enraged parents are raising a generation whose childhood is marred by extreme violence both outside and inside the home. The majority of the young men and women who will determine Afghanistan's future are growing up today with the understanding that nowhere is safe, seeing cruelty as the norm.

"People get used to using violence to settle their dispute, and it is difficult to find a way to unlearn those behaviors," said Peter Bouckaert, the emergencies director at Human Rights Watch, who has worked in war zones around the globe. "You end up with a warlord economy [that] is incredibly hard to break, and which does lead to a constant renewal of conflict—as it will in Afghanistan."

Protracted warfare, civilians and trauma

Interdependence between protracted warfare and mental trauma is not unique to Afghanistan. A few years ago, researchers examining the potential for reconciliation in northern Uganda—where the Lord's Resistance Army of the self-proclaimed messiah Joseph Kony has killed and mutilated more than 100,000 civilians and abducted tens of thousands into servitude—conducted a survey specifically designed to determine the emotional effects of violence on local residents. The idea was to look at mental trauma "in the context of people's exposure to violence and what their needs are … what their expectations are," said Eric Stover, one of the study's authors, who has conducted similar research in Cambodia, the Central African Republic, and the Democratic Republic of Congo to "try to understand where justice fits in with the needs of war-affected communities."

The study, published in the *Journal of the American Medical Association* in 2007, established that civilians who were suffering from post-traumatic stress disorder—about 73 percent of the Ugandans Stover and his colleagues surveyed—were "more likely to favor violent means to end the conflict" than civilians who were not (Vinck *et al.*, 2007).

Compared with the research into the effect of conflict on war veterans, studies of combat trauma among civilians are few. But for the last century the emotional toll of war on noncombatants has been mounting everywhere. During the First World War, when military physicians described soldiers' traumatic reactions to war as "shell shock" and "combat fatigue," more than nine out of ten war casualties were fighters. Today, the way we wage war is starkly more personal. Terrorism battlefields recognize no front lines. Vicious sectarian rampages pit neighbor against neighbor. Victims of genocidal campaigns often know their attackers by name.

In the most current conflicts, at least nine out of ten war casualties are believed to be civilians (Krippner &McIntyre, 2003). Communal psychological wounds—what medical anthropologist Arthur Kleinman has called "social suffering" (Kleinman, 1997)—permeate the lives of survivors scraping by in unimaginable poverty amid collapsed infrastructure, the common afterbirth of modern combat. According to the Centers for Disease Control and Prevention, between 30 and 70 percent of the people who have lived in war zones bear the scars of post-traumatic stress disorder and depression (CDCP, 2009). In some regions, the emotional cost of war is even higher: A 2008 United Nations survey found that one in nine Iraqi refugees in Syria suffered from depression, and one in eight suffered from post-traumatic stress disorder (UNHCR, 2008).

In the medical world, an understanding is growing that addressing mass war trauma may help advance reconciliation and peacebuilding.

And yet, the invisible wounds of entire societies remain largely unnoticed by us. The Afghans who suffer them are barely more than silhouettes stenciled against the Central Asian battlefield. "Everyone in Afghanistan has been mentally affected by war," Abdul Khodi Wahidi, an Afghan Health Ministry official, once told me. "Everybody needs help, and very few can get it."

Sordar

I met Sordar in Laghmani, a village of glaucous orchards and vineyards in Shomali Valley, just north of Kabul. It was 2004, perhaps the most hopeful year for Afghanistan since the U.S.-led invasion had begun. At the time, Laghmani bore the scars of the Soviet occupation and pitched battles in the 1990s between the Taliban and the Northern Alliance. Near the small vineyard owned by Sordar's family, a girls' school stood in ruins, its walls enclosing a rubble-filled crater left by a Taliban missile. The village fields, paths, and streams were a mosaic of red rocks that international de-miners had placed to mark the unexploded landmines buried there by Soviet soldiers and Afghan mujahedeen.

One such mine had claimed the life of Sordar's father, Mohammed Yusuf, in 1999. Three years later, another took the leg of his younger brother, Shakar. Sordar's family had never left Laghmani, not even when the front line ran right through the village. They did not have enough money to flee the fighting. Shakar—Sordar's crippled brother—told me about growing up during the decade-long Soviet occupation in the 1980s, when Afghan mujahedeen blew up Soviet tanks along the Old Road that runs through Laghmani. He told me about the 1990s, when Taliban and Northern Alliance forces pushed each other back and forth across the Shomali Valley, reshaping the front line several times a year.

From their position a few miles to the south, Taliban troops had shelled Laghmani regularly, keeping the villagers in constant fear. Throughout the shelling, Sordar, the oldest child, always did his best to take care of his siblings and help his father with the vineyard—150 gnarled vines of Thompson Seedless on a quarter acre of land that were the family's main source of income.

One early spring day in 1999, Sordar's father, a thick-boned man with a long beard, stepped on a land mine while tending the vineyard. He lost both legs, and shrapnel pierced his arms and neck. After 50 agonizing days at a hospital in Kabul, he died in Sordar's arms, of infection and blood loss. The young man brought the body home and buried his father in a small village cemetery near his family compound, marking the grave with a green flag, a symbol Afghans typically reserve for men who have died as martyrs.

"That was when Sordar stopped eating food," recalled Mohammad Agha, Sordar's youngest brother, a teenager when I met him. "He started to cry all the time. He didn't sleep well at night. He would go to our father's grave every day and cry there."

"He worried about the family a lot," Shakar said. "He worried about our mother. He was upset about our father. He was worried that we didn't have enough money. He worried about what would happen if the Taliban took over the village."

In 2001, around the time Northern Alliance militiamen, backed by the United States and reinforced by American air raids, marched on Kabul to expel the Taliban from power, Sordar, exhausted by war and grief, shut his eyes and dropped his forehead into the palm of his right hand. This is how he was when I met him: sitting in a chair propped up against the mud-brick wall of his family compound, his long, unkempt black beard concealing his strong chest, his right hand propping up his forehead, his eyes closed. He was 29.

On a bad day, Sordar would stumble into his spartan room and lock the door, often staying inside for three days in a row. There, he would lie on the corduroy-covered mattress and hold his face in his right hand, as if trying to pull together his disturbed mind, shattered, like his country, by perpetual warfare and loss.

Once a week, Sordar would ask for water or naswar, the smokeless tobacco Afghan men sometimes chew—a blend of tobacco leaves, calcium oxide, and wood ash. Sometimes, he would eat the food his mother served him. Often, he would "become wild," his brothers said. He would hurl rocks at visitors who entered his compound. He would beat anyone he could lay his hands on. He beat his tiny widowed mother, whose face bore scars and brown bruises from Sordar's heavy farmer's fists, and whose eyes were always wet with tears. He beat his two younger brothers, who struggled to feed the impoverished family. He pummeled his terrified two younger sisters if they addressed him or spoke too loudly. He would stop only after becoming exhausted. "He wants to escape from his pain," Shakar explained to me then. "It is too loud in his head."

In 2002, as Shakar was digging a canal to re-route precious snowmelt from the craggy Hindu Kush mountains into his vineyard, he stepped on another landmine. The blast tore off his left leg from the knee down. The only adult male in the family apart from Sordar, Shakar continued to tend the knotted vines. Every morning, he would limp out of his mud-brick compound and past the cemetery where a tattered green flag flew over his father's grave. Half skipping, half sliding awkwardly on his plastic prosthetic left leg, Shakar would cross the collage of red rocks that marked the antipersonnel mines buried along the bottom of a creek, then scramble up the stream's steep side to his vineyard to prune and water his crop. He would move carefully amid the red rocks the de-miners had placed over the mines they had found in his vineyard, all the while praying he did not step on the mines they may have missed. An estimated ten million landmines still tick in Afghanistan's soil, the lethal crop that has replaced past harvests of rice, wheat and almonds: enough to kill or maim a third of the country's entire population, children included. Just 20 pounds of pressure are enough to detonate an antipersonnel mine. Generations of Afghans have grown up with this grim computation in the back of their mind.

Sordar's wrecked psyche was not as graphic a consequence of war as the demolished buildings or the minefield that had claimed the life of his father. But minefields, eventually, painstakingly, can be cleared of explosives. Orchards can be replanted, canals redredged, buildings rebuilt. Post-war effort still focuses largely on rebuilding the infrastructure damaged in the fighting. Treating the invisible wounds of conflict has been "the poor orphan of a development policy in post-war societies, because of resources," said Stover, who is the director of the Human Rights Center at the University of California, Berkeley, and the former head of Physicians for Human Rights.

My own PTSD

My own post-traumatic stress disorder was born in the minefields of Afghanistan. I first went there in 2001, to write about the U.S.-led war for the *San Francisco Chronicle*. None of my previous travels to the outskirts of conflict in the former Soviet Union had prepared me for the relentless grief of women who had been raped, village after village, by ethnic militias; for the savage absurdity of fratricide that unraveled in valleys aglitter with bullet casings; for the poverty so dire that mothers fed opium to their infants to stave off hunger; for disease—typhoid, dysentery, malaria, cholera—that lurked in every spoonful of rice, every cup of water; for the snap of a bullet—did it come from behind or ahead, and will there be more?—so close I could hear it break the sound barrier; or for the arbitrary horror of minefields. After I had learned to treat every stream, orchard, and pasture as a minefield, hiking in the dunes in New England seemed to me, for months, as appealing as sticking my hand into a pot of boiling oil. I still duck when Fourth of July fireworks go off: an idiotic, face-down plunge, one for each volley. In restaurants, I make sure I sit with my back to a wall. On many nights, dreams take me back to war; I take turns being the executed and the executioner.

I have reported from many conflict zones since then, and have returned to Afghanistan several times. But when I travel, I always know that, if I survive this particular journey, this stretch of a minefield masquerading as a road, I will get to leave. That in a few weeks, I will be in a safe place, maybe talking to my therapist. I will take long hikes to "walk myself into a state of well-being and walk away from every illness," like Søren Kierkegaard (Kierkegaard, Hong & Hong, 1978, p. 412). For my fellow travelers, my hosts in Afghanistan, such a luxury does not exist, and never has.

Healing a traumatized nation

How to help heal a nation that has been forged in millennia of almost incessant war? There is no such thing as the Marshall Plan for the mind. Most mental health professionals agree that war injures the psyche, but not everybody believes that the diagnosis of post-traumatic stress disorder, formally recognized by the American Psychiatric Association in 1980, can be applied to people from non-Western cultures, who may perceive and experience grief and shock differently. Weekly counseling sessions may be appropriate for a platoon sergeant from Arkansas, but may not be as helpful for a shepherd from the Hindu Kush.

Adapting Western-style therapy to the cultural context of patients

To be effective, cognitive therapy must be mindful of local traditions, warns Richard Mollica, a psychiatry professor at Harvard Medical School, who has developed a way of treating war-related mental disorders that adapts Western-style therapy to his patients' specific cultural context. Mollica is one of the pioneers of the notion that mental healing is essential for postwar recovery. "It is important to enlist traditional aspects of the society itself, such as its cultural and spiritual resources," writes the psychologist Steve S. Olweean (Krippner & McIntyre, 2003). In Afghanistan, Lopes Cardozo recommends combining counseling with practices to which war-affected communities traditionally turn for comfort: talking to an imam, for example, or visiting a shrine (personal communication, 2011).

One such shrine squats at the base of Zadyan Minaret, Afghanistan's oldest and one of the least known, whose intricate brickwork rises cylindrically 60 feet out of dun desert floor in Balkh Province. Beneath the shrine's vaulted, muqarnassed ceilings, pale lizards dart over folds of the heavy green velvet that shrouds a tomb believed to belong to Hazrat Saleh, a pre-Islamic prophet. An eerie, albino creeper sprouts from the wall near the door, the shrine's only source of light. Outside, knobbly roots of mulberry trees grab onto the side of a jade-colored, perfectly round pond.

Mohammad Yusuf, the eighth-generation keeper of the shrine, believes that its four-foot-thick walls are an infallible cure for *djinns*—emotional disorders that haunt many of the pilgrims who travel to this remote oasis, two hours by car on dirt roads from Mazar-e-Sharif.

"We put the crazy man in here. We lock the door. When the crazy man comes in, the *djinns* can't go inside with him," Mohammad Yusuf explained to me. The treatment—forced seclusion for several hours inside a windowless burial chamber—is mild compared to some. A 2009 article in the *Christian Science Monitor* describes another Afghan shrine that is believed to treat the mentally ill, the Mia Ali, where patients remain chained to the walls for weeks, living on bread and black pepper amidst their own waste (Arnoldy, 2009).

Lesser shrines—fenced, coffin-sized ziggurats, painted green and aflutter with shreds of shiny cloth—sparkle along country roads and hillsides like jewels. Pilgrims come to kneel or lie prostrate next to the metal palisades, seeking delivery from the *djinns* that bedevil them. On some roads, a traveler can pass by half a dozen such shrines during an hour-long drive.

"Receiving them with empathy"

Afghans seeking more conventional cognitive therapy have fewer choices. In early 2011, the sum total of the clinics in the entire country had only 200 beds between them for mental health patients. Twenty of these beds were at Alemi Neuropsychiatric Hospital in Mazar-e-Sharif. I visited the hospital in 2010; at the time, the Taliban resurgence that was sweeping across northern Afghanistan had spared this regional capital. But just in case, a pair of ram's horns protruded from the eaves of a police station two blocks east of the hospital, to protect the building and its occupants from danger and evil spirits. At a checkpoint a mile or so to the west, police officers searched all cars and trucks headed into the city. Across the street from the hospital, a morbid caravan of disemboweled Soviet armored personnel carriers rusted in a garbage-clogged ditch.

Inside the clinic, an underpaid team of two psychologists, five psychiatrists, four nurses, a pharmacist, and a lab technician, armed with generic equivalents of Zoloft, Paxil, Lithonate, and Prozac from Iran, India, and Pakistan, treated about 100 patients daily.

The first time I visited the hospital, two dozen or so men and women sat quietly on rows of fold-out chairs and on the tiled floor of the lobby, waiting for their appointments. Most of them had traveled to Mazar-e-Sharif from other provinces, journeying for days on unpaved roads that tick with landmines and bristle with ambushes. Most were battling symptoms that often accompany mental trauma: unexplained fatigue, panic attacks, abiding headaches, chronic stomach pain. For most, the $3 the hospital charged for a consultation—let alone the $20 per night for inpatient treatment—was a week's wages. The visitors would sit in this lobby for a week or longer to pay this small fortune. A typical wait at the clinic lasted ten days.

"Our facility is not sufficient for their needs," doctor Alemi said, in the precise English he had learned as a medical student at Kabul University in the 1980s. "You have to have social workers, psychiatrists, social psychologists, psychotherapists, psychiatric nurses. We do not have psychotherapists. We do not have psychiatric nurses. I am sorry."

Doctor Alemi apologized constantly. He apologized for his hospital's lack of staff. For the perfunctory conditions at his inpatient ward, with its flies and its bare cots. For what he called, in English, his "paltry knowledge of English." He apologized not to anyone in particular, but, it seemed, to his own sense of rectitude. As he spoke, the lights in the clinic went out. Government power plants supply different Mazar-e-Sharif neighborhoods for several hours on alternate days, and on this day, the hospital's quota of state-issued power was up by noon. "I am sorry," Alemi said again, into the sudden midday crepuscule.

The doctor made rounds. He checked on Farida, watched her rock on her bed for a minute or two. He checked on an old woman curled up on a cot in the room next to Farida's. The woman's diagnosis was severe depression; she did not speak. He checked on Nuria, a 19-year-old whose mother had brought her from Jowzjan province, about 100 miles away. Nuria suffered from panic attacks: paint rollers of sudden, inexplicable, animal fear that made her think she was dying. She was hiding under a blue blanket, leaving visible only the pale soles of her bare feet. Her toes looked vulnerable.

"A lot of PTSD cases are coming here," Alemi explained. "We don't have a lot of staff. But we are able to listen to them. We are receiving them with empathy." The doctor's Afghan accent stifled English phonemes. He pronounced the last word "empty:" "We are receiving them with empty."

Anna Badkhen, a journalist, writes about conflict and people *in extremis*. She has reported from four continents and has traveled extensively in Afghanistan since 2001. She is the author of, most recently, *Afghanistan by Donkey*. Her other books, Peace Meals: *Candy-Wrapped Kalashnikovs and Other War Stories*, and *Waiting for the Taliban*, were published in 2010. (badkhen@gmail.com)" .

References

Arnoldy, B. (2009, December 15). Afghanistan mental health: Treatment caught between ancient and modern worlds. *Christian Science Monitor*. Retrieved from www.csmonitor.com/World/2009/1215/Afghanistan-mental-health-Treatment-caught-between-ancient-and-modern-worlds

Catani, C., Schauer, E. & Neuner, F. (2008). Beyond individual war trauma: Domestic violence against children in Afghanistan and Sri Lanka. *Journal of Marital and Family Therapy, 34*(2), 165–176.

Centers for Disease Control and Prevention (CDCP) (2009). *Mental health in conflict-affected populations: Fact sheet*. International Emergency and Refugee Health (IERH) Scientific Publications. Retrieved from www.cdc.gov/globalhealth/gdder/ierh/Publications/mentalhealth_affectedpopulations_pib.htm

English, C. & Ray, J. (2010). Latin Americans least likely to feel safe walking alone at night. Gallup poll. Retrieved from www.gallup.com/poll/144083/Latin-Americans-Least-Likely-Feel-Safe-Walking-Alone.aspx

Huggler, J. (2001, November 19). Carpet bombing 'kills 150 civilians' in frontline town. *The Independent*. Retrieved from www.commondreams.org/headlines01/1119-01.htm

Kierkegaard, S., Hong, H. V. & Hong, E. H. (1978). *Søren Kierkegaard's Journals and Papers, Part1: Autobiographical, 1829–1848*. Bloomington, IN: Indiana University Press.

Kleinman, A. (1997). *Social Suffering*. Berkeley, CA: University of California Press.

Krippner, S. & McIntyre, T. M. (2003). *The Psychological Impact of War Trauma on Civilians*. Westport, CT: Praeger.

Panter-Brick, C., Eggerman, M., Gonzalez, V., Safdar, S. (2009). Violence, suffering and mental health in Afghanistan: A school-based survey. *Lancet, 374*(9692), 766–767.

Scholte, W., Olff, M., Ventevogel P., de Vries, G.-J., Jansveld, E., Lopes Cardozo, B. & Gotway Crawford, C. A. (2004). Mental health symptoms following war and repression in eastern Afghanistan. *Journal of the American Medical Association, 292*(5), 585–593.

UNHCR (2008). Second IPSOS survey on Iraqi refugees (31 October–25 November 2007): Final results. Retrieved from www.unhcr.org/cgi-bin/texis/vtx/search?page =search&docid=4795f96f2&query=syria%20iraqi%20ptsd

Vinck, P., Pham, P. N., Stover, E. & Weinstein, H. M. (2007). Exposure to war crimes and implications for peace building in northern Uganda. *Journal of the American Medical Association, 298*(5), 543–554.

Part 4

Military and resiliency initiatives

14 U.S. Army combat and operational stress control: From battlemind to resiliency, debriefings, and traumatic event management

CPT Christian Hallman (OIF) and
MAJ Patrick Pischke (OIF)

This chapter is dedicated to the late Captain Christian J. Hallman, Army Officer, who died unexpectedly on 6 June 2011, while in the midst of co-writing this chapter. CPT Hallman served in Iraq between 2004 and 2005 with the 785th Medical Company, Combat Stress Control, and pushed the boundaries by utilizing alternative methods for treating combat stress. His colleague and co-author, Major Patrick Pischke, continued CPT Hallman's unfinished draft and expanded and finalized the chapter. We salute CPT Hallman for his service to his country, his family, and his many military comrades. He will certainly be missed.

The present day military approach to addressing combat stress in the combat theatre of operations is to deploy Combat and Operational Stress Control (COSC) companies/detachments to the war zone. These COSC units focus specifically on being the "first responders" to address mental health issues and psychological symptoms, with the ultimate goal of keeping the soldier in the fight and preserving the fighting force. These frontline mental health services must take into account the distinctive aspects of providing mental health services in a war zone so that they are able to offer a vital initial level of intervention that may be sufficient in and of itself or complement more extensive, long-term therapies to be completed stateside subsequent to redeployment.

This chapter provides a general overview of COSC functions as well as the distinct characteristics and challenges of providing mental health services to soldiers in combat regions. This will include the most common therapeutic interventions utilized by these specialized units: Traumatic Event Management (TEM), three types of psychological debriefings (defusings, critical event debriefings and battlemind debriefings), the Kuhlman Debriefing Model for processing grief, and Comprehensive Soldier Fitness (CSF).

Evolulution of military mental health services

One of the great paradoxes that has not changed over time is that sometimes, unfortunately, in order to obtain peace war must be waged. Throughout history, successful warfare tactics have primarily focused on troop numbers, equipment and the physical readiness aspects of war, with very little regard to mental health issues. Israeli Defense Forces (IDF) have been the notable exception.

The seminal contributions of the IDF model in treating combat stress casualties

Witztum, Levy & Solomon (1996) described the serious problems with combat stress reactions and chronicled the IDF therapeutic responses toward combat stress reactions during Israel's War of Independence (1948), the Sinai Campaign (1956) and the Six Day War (1967). Dr. Louis Miller, who was appointed Israel's first Chief Military Psychiatrist and pioneered combat stress control services for the IDF, led the establishment of treatment principles for combat stress casualties. The casualty first had to be placed close to the front lines in a situation similar to the one in which he "broke down", and then sent back to the front lines as quickly as possible. This involved the creation of a supportive group atmosphere, maintenance of an adequate level of activity, and referring to and treating psychiatric casualties as "soldiers" rather than as "patients" as much as possible (soldiers were required to perform maintenance and clean-up duties and to maintain their military identity, including continuing to wear uniforms). The IDF model for treating combat stress casualties is attributed, in part, to the successes of the Israeli Army in this endeavor. U.S. military mental health has adopted many of the pioneering and remarkably enduring principles and understanding of the IDF concerning etiology, intervention and prevention of military psychiatric casualties.

U.S. military mental health development

In previous wars involving U.S. Armed Forces, soldiers manifesting psychiatric symptoms were labeled as suffering from "battle fatigue", "shell shock" or "combat neurosis". During the Vietnam War, mental health support provided to soldiers involved two Army psychiatric teams, a small number of social work officers and even fewer psychiatrists deployed at the division level. Soldiers suffering from psychological symptoms were often considered "weak" or malingering by unit commands. Mental health assessments often considered presenting symptomology to stem from non-combat exposure factors, such as "pre-existing" mental health problems or reactions to issues occurring back home (Scurfield, 2004).

In 1980, strongly influenced by the substantial number of "delayed" and "chronic" psychiatric casualties from the Vietnam War, the American Psychiatric Association formally defined Post-Traumatic Stress Disorder (PTSD), categorizing it as one of the anxiety disorders (APA, 2000; Schiraldi, 2000). The gradual evolution of mental health service provision developed further within the military context to provide far greater mobility in the delivery of mental health services and in very close proximity to soldiers on the front lines.

Through analysis of the IDF front-line mental health treatment and principles, in addition to Vietnam and post-Vietnam military mental health efforts, the critical importance of treating combat and operational stress reactions (COSRs) became more readily apparent. The same held true for the essential need to maintain a psychologically fit military for ultimate combat readiness and effectiveness.

Selective literature review

One of the most stressful things that any person can endure is the range of traumatic experiences faced during war. *Combat* stress refers directly to those stressors inherent in combat operations and exposure to catastrophic events both on and off the battlefield, i.e. hand-to-hand combat, fire fights, mortar rounds, RPGs (rocket propelled grenades), IEDs (improvised explosive devices), recovery missions for collection of human remains, etc. *Operational* stress refers to those stressors secondary to battlefield and combat operational activities, i.e. working long hours with minimal sleep, lack of privacy, homefront stressors, fatigue from high mission tempo, etc.

In addition, the various types of combat and operational stress and traumatic exposure that arise during the course of wartime deployments are likely to be accompanied by other significant stressors, such as separation from family for lengthy periods of time, lack of comfort items in often extremely austere environments, and fatigue associated with the high and demanding operational pace of serving in the combat theater of operations. Most trauma victims in civilian life have a much higher probability of being removed—or being able to remove themselves—rapidly from traumatizing events and placed in safer environments. Conversely, those exposed to combat trauma are usually required to remain in the combat zone, hence lacking the feeling or perception of having reached a safe haven until the completion of their deployment and a safe exit from exposure to the trauma inherent in a war zone.

Recent research studies have reported the mental health effects on combat arms soldiers engaged in wartime operations. It has been reported that at least 17 percent of post-combat veterans suffer from depressive disorders and anxiety disorders, particularly PTSD (Hutchinson & Banks-Williams, 2006). In their study of infantry soldiers, Hoge *et al.* (2004) reported that the percentage of study subjects whose responses met the screening criteria for major depression, generalized anxiety, or PTSD was significantly higher after returning from duty in Iraq (15.6 to 17.1 percent) than after duty in Afghanistan (11.2 percent). (This, however, may have changed since the suspension of combat operations in Iraq in 2010.) A 12-member advisory team surveyed 756 soldiers in Iraq and found that 87 percent of them reported high levels of stress with respect to not knowing how long they would be deployed; 71 percent reported high levels of stress regarding length of deployment; 57 percent reported high levels of stress in response to separation from family; and 55 percent reported high levels of stress over the lack of privacy and personal space (Jewell, 2004). Adler, Castro & McGurk (2009) mentioned that between 20 and 30 percent of U.S. military personnel returning from combat reported significant psychological symptoms.

Early mental health intervention and frontline treatment principles

The combat stress literature addresses the importance of delivering early mental health treatment following traumatic events. Lutz (cited in Vesper, 2006) comments that evidence reveals that once veterans develop military-related PTSD, these symptoms remain chronic across their lifetime and are resistant to treatments that have been shown to be effective with other forms of chronic PTSD. Thus, it is vitally important to provide early intervention to reduce chronic impairments and psychological injuries in veterans. Significant findings include the discovery that providing soldiers with immediate psychological intervention close to the front lines increases the likelihood of sufficient recovery to return to duty (Bell, 1995). The psychologist Viktor Razdvev, who studied combatants during the war in Chechnya from 1994 to 1996, recognized that if these individuals could be treated within two to three hours or no later than two to three days after suffering psychological trauma, the incidence of PTSD might be considerably diminished or even prevented (Thomas & O'Hara, 2000). MacDonald (2003) indicated that the concepts of proximity, immediacy and expectancy are widely relied upon in military psychiatry (see also Scurfield, 2006). These frontline treatment principles have also been associated with a higher rate of return to combat duty and a lower incidence of PTSD. The more recent version of these concepts is the acronym BICEPS, which stands for brevity, immediacy, contact, expectancy, proximity and simplicity (U.S. Army, 2009). These principles are described below as part of the soldier restoration process.

The controversy regarding psychological debriefings

Presently there remains controversy, in particular among civilian mental health practitioners and researchers, as to whether single-session psychological debriefings are as effective as once believed. Some believe that, in some instances, they may cause more harm than good. For example, they may "unnecessarily" expose other debriefing participants to trauma, interfering with natural healing processes and suggesting negative messages regarding recovery (Adler, Castro & McGurk, 2009). Conversely, there have been other studies and reports, such as those on New York law enforcement officers following 9/11, which strongly suggest that single-session psychological debriefings have been beneficial— although not necessarily sufficient— for a great number of those participating in such debriefings (Scurfield et al., 2003).

Several studies of military populations have described the benefits derived from providing mental health services, such as psychological debriefings, to individuals who have experienced traumatic events. Pischke & Hallman (2008) surveyed 396 soldiers in Iraq following the completion of a Critical Event Debriefing (CED) and found that the majority of participants (n=273) either agreed or strongly agreed that the CED was helpful. Other positive effects have been reported from similar interventions that involved military populations (Eid, Johnsen & Weisaeth, 2001; Shalev *et al.*, 1998). Other studies of civilian populations have also reported positive effects from the provision of debriefings (Jenkins, 1996; Burns & Harm, 1993; Robinson & Mitchell, 1993).

There remain divided beliefs between mental health professionals regarding the benefits of single-session psychological debriefings. However, it is the authors' impression that group-centered psychological debriefings within the military setting are very congruent with military culture and appear to be particularly meaningful for participants. There is a continued and significant need for further research in this area —particularly with military populations in military settings.

Currently, there is a higher level of awareness of the tremendous significance of treating mental health symptoms, not only after warfare and following redeployment, but also during combat operations. This has resulted in the creation of Combat and Operational Stress Control (COSC) teams as one of the primary mental health assets deployed to the wartime theater.

Combat and Operational Stress Control

The Army's response to the vital need for addressing combat and operational stress reactions (COSRs) in theatre is to deploy COSC units to the wartime theater to ensure that soldiers suffering from stress reactions can be treated rapidly, so that they may be returned to duty as soon as possible. COSC units are comprised of psychiatrists, psychologists, social workers, occupational therapists, psychiatric nurses, and mental health specialists. Under supervision, mental health specialists conduct clinical interviews, assist with the care and treatment of soldiers with COSR or psychological problems, and counsel military personnel on outpatient bases.

These behavioral health professionals and paraprofessionals are trained to provide mental health services in combat regions and in addition must also meet all standards for soldier warrior tasks. Such tasks include weapons qualification, satisfying Army physical fitness requirements and conforming to other military cultural norms and expectations, such as the ability to deploy to combat regions for lengthy periods of time. Behavioral health officers must be credentialed through the Army in order to provide mental health services while serving in the military; this is equivalent to state board licensing procedures for mental health practitioners in each specialty area. There are typically different theoretical approaches and a diversity of experiences within each discipline. Regardless of education and training, all mental health professionals are required to complete formal COSC training prior to deployment.

The COSC training capitalizes on the widespread experiences and levels of expertise of each practitioner, incorporating these talents and skills into a team approach to be utilized for combat and operational support in war zone regions. COSC teams are involved in a multitude of activities and services, including walkabouts (informal contact while making one's way around in-theater military installations on foot), individual counseling, group debriefings, psychoeducational behavioral health classes, command consultations, command climate surveys and psychotropic medication management.

Military Traumatic Event Management (TEM)

TEM (U.S. Army, 2006) involves the utilization of trained behavioral health service members—both enlisted mental health technicians and mental health professionals (officers)—to employ brief mental health interventions. These interventions are a means of minimizing impairments secondary to combat and operational stress, strengthening mission capability by treating soldiers experiencing psychological symptomatology or symptoms of combat/operational stress, and preserving the fighting strength of military operations as a "force multiplier." TEM incorporates a flexible set of interventions and support activities utilized in response to potentially traumatizing events (either individually or organizationally with respect to military units) and to promote post-traumatic growth.

COSC companies and detachments

COSC companies/detachments are divided into teams when deployed and dispersed throughout the combat theatre of operations. The battle roster for COSC detachments is usually comprised of approximately 40 soldiers, while COSC companies are typically slotted for 80 soldiers. COSC companies also contain soldiers who perform in support roles, such as mechanics, personnel technicians and cooks. Both COSC companies and detachments are comprised of both Prevention Teams and Restoration or Fitness Teams.

Prevention Teams

Prevention Teams typically consist of three to five mental health personnel: a behavioral health officer who serves as the Officer in Charge (this can be a psychologist, social worker, psychiatrist, prescribing nurse practitioner, or occupational therapist) and a Non-Commissioned Officer in Charge, in addition to mental health specialists of varying enlisted ranks. The primary focus is outreach to various units and the provision of psychoeducational classes, suicide awareness education, homecoming and reintegration briefings, psychological debriefings, command consultations (meeting with leadership of other units to discuss COSC services), leadership training, administration of command climate surveys (surveying soldiers to obtain information about trends pertinent to attitudes and morale) and individual counseling. Prevention Teams typically remain mobile and frequently travel with combat arms, combat support and combat service support units on convoys or via air assets (typically Blackhawks or Chinook helicopters) to remote areas of the wartime theatre on a rotational basis.

Fitness or Restoration Teams

The next echelon of mental health care are the Fitness or Restoration Teams, which provide more extensive multidisciplinary care. Each COSC Restoration site consists of approximately 20 COSC members ideally and usually does not have the mobility of smaller Prevention Teams. Soldier restoration is accomplished using the principles of BICEPS and the Five Rs (discussed below), which are tailored to the needs of the soldier, and is conducted as close to the soldier's unit as possible.

Soldier restoration process

The process of soldier restoration involves several steps, which include screening; assessment; psychological, psychiatric and COSC interventions; reintegration/coordination; and movement of soldiers to more advanced echelons of care as necessary.

Screening

Adequate medical screening and treatment must first be accomplished upon entry to restoration programs. Minor medical conditions can be treated during a routine sick call. Soldiers entering restoration programs should be comprised only of hold cases that require continuous medical and/or behavioral health evaluation and observation due to potential disruptiveness that may worsen or become emergent over time (see U.S. Army, 2006, Chapter 8 for a full discussion of COSC triage). Tending to and restoring physiological status (such as sleep and hydration) is always a priority before initiating treatment for mental disorders.

Assessment and intervention

Initial evaluation and subsequent COSC/behavioral health interventions depend upon the severity of the COSR or other mental health issues and to what degree these interfere with the soldier's ability to function on mission. More in-depth assessments are conducted only after the soldier's physiological status has been stabilized.

Reintegration

When soldiers begin to respond to treatment with demonstrated improvements, interventions are modified towards reintegrating them back into their units. COSC staff must coordinate with other available resources to assist in this process and to assure ongoing follow-up interventions as necessary (see U.S. Army, 2006, Chapter 10).

Frontline treatment principles

There are six primary COSC treatment principles, identified by the acronym BICEPS, which stands for Brevity, Immediacy, Contact, Expectancy, Proximity and Simplicity (see U.S. Army, 2006, Chapter 1).

Brevity

Initial rest and replenishment at COSC facilities located close to the soldier's unit should last no more than one to three days. Those requiring further treatment are moved to the next, higher level of care. Since many require no further treatment, military commanders expect their soldiers to return to duty (RTD) rapidly,

Immediacy

It is essential that COSC measures be initiated as soon as possible when operations permit. Interventions are to be provided as soon as symptoms become apparent.

Contact

The soldier must be encouraged to continue to consider him/herself as a warfighter, rather than a patient. The chain of command remains directly involved in the soldier's recovery and RTD. The COSC team coordinates with unit leadership to determine the soldier's level of performance prior to the onset of COSR or other more serious mental/behavioral health problems. Whenever possible, representatives of the unit or messages from the unit to the soldier are encouraged in order to reinforce the absolute need for that solider to return to duty as a valued member of the unit. The COSC team coordinates with the unit leaders, through unit medical personnel or chaplains, to assure rapid reintegration once the soldier returns to his/her unit (U.S. Army, 2009).

Expectancy

The individual is explicitly informed that he/she is reacting normally to extreme stress and is expected to recover and return to full duty in a few hours or days. It is essential for each soldier to be informed that his/her reactions are normal responses to extraordinary wartime stressors and that their comrades in arms both want and intend them to return. Due to the bonding process that typically occurs between military personnel, such communications are thought to have a powerful and positive impact. Additionally, expectations for performance excellence and equivalent treatment as an integral member of that soldier's unit must be conveyed (U.S. Army, 2006).

Proximity

Soldiers requiring observation or care beyond the unit level are evacuated to facilities in close proximity to, but separate from, medical or surgical patients at the battalion aid station (BAS) or medical company nearest their unit. As a last resort, soldiers who cannot continue their mission and require more extensive intervention are transferred to military hospitals in theater or undergo medevacuation out of theater to Landstuhl Regional Medical Center in Germany. In most cases, these soldiers are ultimately returned to military treatment facilities in the U.S. and do not return to duty in the wartime theater. Combat and operational stress reactions are often more effectively managed in areas closest to the soldier's parent unit. Rapid, frequent maneuver and continuous operations require COSC personnel to be innovative and flexible in designing interventions which maximize and maintain the soldier's connection to his/her parent unit. (See U.S. Army, 2009 for additional information.)

Simplicity

This principle specifies the need to use brief and straightforward methods to restore physical well-being and self-confidence. These include the Five Rs:

- Reassurance of normality;
- Rest (respite from combat or break from the work);
- Replenish bodily needs (such as thermal comfort, water, food, hygiene, and sleep);
- Restore confidence with purposeful activities and contact with the parent unit; and
- Return to duty and reunite soldier with his unit. (See U.S. Army, 2006 and U.S. Army, 2009 for additional information.)

Specific interventions include (U.S. Army, 2006): medication management and monitoring; one-to-one suicide watches (Buddy Watch Program); comprehensive psychological and occupational therapy assessments; and educational interventions, such as anger or stress management, or sleep hygiene classes. Soldier restoration activities include psychological and psychiatric consultation, rest, relaxation, and treatment as necessary for a speedy RTD

(U.S. Army, 2006). The primary goal of COSC is to provide rapid, readily accessible mental health/combat operational stress control interventions in order to keep the soldier in the fight. Despite the highly demanding, exceedingly stressful combat environment, leaders can expect more than 95 percent of the soldiers who receive COSC services to be retained and returned to duty (U.S. Army, 2009).

Challenges faced by COSC units

It is the experience of the authors and other military providers that there are many challenges faced by COSC units while they are conducting their varied missions. These include the dangers and uncertainties of living and operating in the battle zone and continued stereotypical biases regarding receipt and provision of mental health services. Behavioral health professionals are certainly not immune to their own stress reactions, home-front issues, or the endless additional hardships associated with family separation for lengthy periods of time. Living conditions are usually very basic, cramped and without privacy in extremely austere environments, particularly throughout many areas of Afghanistan. COSC units increase their effectiveness when there is collaboration with other mental health and medical health care workers in theatre, including brigade mental health assets such as psychologists and social workers, mental health technicians, Unit Ministry Teams (chaplains and chaplains' assistants), and medical professionals of varying specialties and disciplines.

Working in concert with collateral assets in other commands, however, can be difficult at times due to opposing views, differing treatment philosophies, high mission tempo and competing demands. Deployed behavioral health professionals have the distinct advantage of experiencing the adversities of harsh deployment conditions first hand, as they are typically co-located with the very units they support. This lends itself to opportunities for significant rapport-building with other soldiers of all ranks and military occupational specialties, though this may require a tremendous amount of effort in terms of overcoming the stigma of treatment and being permitted entry into the culture of combat arms units. It has been the experience of this author (MAJ Pischke) that some commands tend to minimize the necessity of COSC services within the larger context of their own specific missions, until these services become desperately needed in the aftermath of mass casualty events and loss of life. It is vital to promote an appreciation and complete understanding of COSC services as combat multipliers for maximizing and conserving the fighting strength.

Psychological debriefings and Traumatic Event Management (TEM)

One of the most valuable therapeutic interventions utilized by COSC units is the group psychological debriefing. "The term 'debriefing' is used to describe both single-session psychological interventions for stress-related casualties led by mental health workers and sessions administered to rescue workers and military forces following missions in which catastrophic life events have occurred" (Knobler et al., 2007).

Although there are several different types of psychological debriefing, they all contain similar elements: a structured group discussion designed to review a stressful experience (Adler, Castro & McGurk, 2009), as well as similar phases such as *introduction, event discussion, reactions to events* and *teaching* phases. The primary goals of the debriefing process are to prevent and mitigate traumatic stress reactions, to promote and accelerate the recovery process, to enhance unit cohesion and camaraderie, to restore function, and to maintain and improve soldier welfare (U.S. Army, 2006).

The term "psychological debriefing" includes an umbrella of several different types of model, the varying theoretical approaches of which are described in this chapter. All of these models are best understood within the unifying framework of Traumatic Event Management (TEM) currently utilized by COSC units.

Traumatic Event Management (TEM)

The primary objective of TEM is to promote readiness, both on and off the battlefield. TEM is readily adaptable to individuals brought together by Potentially Traumatizing Events (PTEs) and is conceptualized as an ongoing process or series of interventions across a continuum of military operations. TEM blends with other COSC functional areas to create a flexible set of interventions specifically focused on stress management for units and soldiers/military personnel following PTEs (U.S. Army, 2006).

It is commonplace for soldiers to endure multiple traumatic events throughout deployment. This is in great contrast to most traumatic events experienced by civilians; usually, civilians are placed in safe or nurturing environments relatively quickly after experiencing traumatic events. On the other hand, soldiers typically remain in the combat zone long after exposure to multiple traumatic events (deployments are characteristically 10 to 14 months in length).

Conducting interventions in groups lends itself to efficiency in that within a one-hour time frame, one soldier can be treated during a one-to-one consultation, whereas a platoon size or similar group of 20 to 30 individuals can participate in group debriefings (Adler, Castro & McGurk, 2009). The group modality is also consistent with military culture, which is very group or small-unit centered and counters the stigma of individuals being "singled out" as in need of psychological interventions. It is also significant to note that TEM is not considered therapy or a substitute for psychotherapy.

The three most common types of psychological debriefings utilized by military mental health or COSC personnel are defusings, critical event debriefings and battlemind debriefings.[1]

Defusings

A shortened version of a debriefing, utilized within eight hours of a traumatic event, is referred to as a Defusing Model (Mitchell & Everly, 2003). The goals of a defusing include: (1) mitigating the impact of the event; (2) accelerating the recovery process; (3) assessing of the need for psychological debriefings and other mental health services; and (4) reducing cognitive, emotional and physiological symptoms. The defusing model involves efforts to afford a safe environment in which participants may vent their stressful experiences and express their feelings within a supportive structure.

It is important to include two or more mental health personnel, preferably one clinician and one or more mental health technicians, to guide the defusing process and provide increased observation of the group at hand, and to provide supplementary individual interventions as needed. For example, if during the defusing procedure a soldier leaves the group, mental health personnel might join that soldier to provide individual support. It is also advantageous for a chaplain to participate in defusings in order to provide spiritual and faith-based support to those members who value religious beliefs. Most group members will participate in and appreciate prayer led by the chaplain during times of great hardship. Chaplains are also frequently trained and experienced in the use of TEM (see Purinton, 2012 and Chapter 17 in this volume).

The Defusing Model facilitates discussion by asking opened-ended questions, such as: "Who can explain what happened?" or "What did you experience?" or "Are you angry/sad/grief-stricken?" Defusings are typically completed in a shorter duration of time in comparison to other psychological debriefing models and are more challenging to conduct, as group members are often highly traumatized directly after experiencing catastrophic events. Defusings may be particularly uncomfortable for group leaders, as there are characteristically more lengthy periods of uncomfortable silence. An effective technique is to practice what is referred to as the "ministry of presence". The focus here is not so much about what is said, but about active listening and availability for support.

CASE EXAMPLE

The authors were present at a defusing that was conducted hours after seven soldiers of a National Guard infantry unit were killed in Iraq in January of

---

1 The descriptive information on defusings and critical event debriefings is taken from Mitchell & Everly (2003).

2005. The incident involved a tank that hit a roadside bomb (IED), killing the occupants upon impact. The convoy traveled back to the FOB and shortly afterwards, the traumatized soldiers were brought to a room for a defusing. An Army General spoke to the group, offered condolences and stated: "I don't know what to do in this situation, but I will turn it over the experts who know what to do."

The defusing was later assessed as being successful in minimizing the negative impact of this traumatic event. There was a strong sense of guilt among group members, as many expressed feelings that they had failed to bring their comrades back home as promised. It appeared that the defusing experience helped them to confront such feelings and to realize how beneficial it was to share their common experience with peers.

It has been the perception of this author (MAJ Pischke) that losses in National Guard or army reserve units can be particularly devastating. Often Guard or Reserve unit members live and grow up in the same communities, know one another's families and can easily be triggered with loss and survivor guilt by coming into contact with family members of the deceased upon the return home.

Critical Event Debriefing (CED)

The CED is a psychological debriefing model utilized in both military and civilian sectors. It is based upon the seven stages of a Critical Incident Stress Debriefing (CISD), often referred to as the Mitchell Model (Mitchell & Everly, 2003). It is employed primarily to process traumatic events within a structured group process.

> The recommended time frame for a Critical Event Debriefing is 48 to 72 hours. The CISD begins with an *introduction* of team members and the CISD process; this is followed by a statement of expectations, goals and "rules of engagement". Participants are then guided through a process of sharing recall of actual events in chronological order (facts), their *thoughts* about the traumatic event, their emotional *reactions* to the most traumatic aspects of the event, *symptoms of physical and psychological distress* they may be experiencing, the *teaching* phase in which participants are reminded that what they are experiencing are normal responses to exceedingly abnormal situations, as well as education about normal reactions and positive coping strategies and provision of information regarding follow-up services; and lastly, *re-entry* (clarifying ambiguities and preparing for termination, to include encouraging a level of acceptance of their individual and shared responses, unit cohesion, and camaraderie. (Mitchell & Everly, 2003).

The CED differs distinctly from the Defusing Model, in that the CED group model is a formalized structure that invites all group members to contribute to the group process. The Defusing Model, on the other hand, is a less formalized process that must be conducted within hours of the traumatic event. The waiting period of 48 to 72 hours for CEDs allows individuals who experienced the traumatic event ample time for "shock reduction" (U.S. 785th Medical Company, 2004).

It is the authors' experience in the war zone that it is important for participants to be physically comfortable and seated in a circle so that all can view each another. The group location should be in a quiet area, with optimal confidentiality—although this arrangement can be challenging in a combat theatre of operations. It is ideal to limit the group size to no more than 15 members. However, this is often not possible due to unavailability of mental health assets, and mission demands. If the duration of the CED is excessive, attention span and involvement may diminish quickly. A good general rule is not to allow the CED to exceed the one and a half hour point due to the fading attention span of participants as well as consideration of the command's time demands and usually high mission tempos. It has been the experience of the authors that if the group has more than 15 participants, it is recommended that the larger group be divided into two smaller groups, which can be conducted simultaneously if a sufficient number of group leaders is available. Only those service members who were directly involved with the traumatic event should participate in the CED. The inclusion of a chaplain may add tremendous value. As in all psychological debriefings, it is highly preferable to have two trained group leaders (U.S. 785th Medical Company, 2004).

It has been this author's (MAJ Pischke) experience that trauma survivors usually obtain positive affirmations from other participants and can utilize the group to correct false expectations and distorted belief systems. They also frequently harbor erroneous beliefs, such as that they could somehow have prevented the traumatic event from occurring or changed the outcome. It is common for group members to express anger over the traumatic event or associated losses; therefore, group leaders must be careful not to personalize angry comments or feelings that are expressed. Instead, it is important for group leaders to allow angry group members to ventilate their feelings within the group, and to monitor and redirect thoughts, all of which may be necessary if anger levels escalate to a severely high and dysfunctional level. It has been the perception of the authors that allowing group participants to express frustrations within the debriefing can be beneficial to help prevent subsequent escalation to an intolerable level of emotional deregulation during military operations.

The CED begins an internal healing process that is not expected to be fully accomplished after the group process is concluded. Group leaders should refrain from feeling discouraged if participants appear to be feeling no better than they were before the debriefing began. The healing process is internal and often difficult to measure objectively. Psychological symptoms typically subside over time, but the recovery process may be expedited with the CED process (Mitchell & Everly, 2003). A metaphoric view for the CED intervention is that of a large magnet within the group that collects distressed thoughts and feelings from group participants as they openly reveal their individual experiences of the traumatic event in a place considered safe and secure, both physically and emotionally.

CASE EXAMPLE 1

This author (MAJ Pischke) experienced a rather unforgettable CED conducted for a transportation company in Iraq in 2004, which clearly reflects the particular utility of such an intervention in the military setting. Although there were no casualties, the convoy was hit with an IED, which brutally startled several soldiers who were in close proximity to this life-threatening explosion. The debriefing group consisted of approximately 20 soldiers who were very angry and divided against each other. Members of the group began shouting at each other and half the members of the group walked out of the debriefing. Shortly afterwards, the First Sergeant ordered everyone back to the CED group, which picked up where it had abruptly ended. The CED group finally resumed and was completed after strenuous work by the group leaders to preserve the group's integrity.

After the group, I was very disappointed, believing that the debriefing process was a complete disaster. However, afterwards, it became apparent that although the course of the debriefing was marked by disruption and discord, the CED was very beneficial in allowing group members to express, without fear of reprisal, their frustrations and to process their thoughts within a facilitated and supportive group structure.

During the final stages of the CED, the group leader should specifically designate where additional mental health services can be obtained. It must also be mentioned that group leaders will be available following the debriefing to respond to individual questions and concerns. It is most helpful to distribute flyers or business cards to remind group participants of follow-up treatment options and additional support services. The *teaching* phase of the CED model (Mitchell & Everly, 2003) should include positive affirmations to group members, who are usually distressed, feel defeated and, most often, have been psychologically wounded by the experience of a traumatic event. It is recommended that group leaders offer positive statements to the group, reminding them that they are doing an excellent job in performing their mission, which is ultimately one of the most challenging jobs in the world. It is always appropriate to display gratitude in these statements. The teaching phase of the CED should also emphasize the importance of self-care and buddy care (U.S. 785th Medical Company, 2004). Group participants should be reminded that whatever their experience, theirs are normal reactions to exposure to extremely abnormal situations and that over time, most unpleasant symptoms typically subside.

It has been the experience of the authors that it is also good practice to slow the pace of the group during the final *re-entry* phase as a means of encouraging group participants to add final comments. By fostering a calm and supportive atmosphere throughout the CED, it is increasingly probable that group members will disclose inner, personal feelings with less hesitancy.

CASE EXAMPLE 2

This author (MAJ Pischke) was present at a CED conducted with Army firefighters in Iraq in 2004, all of whom were involved in a particularly gruesome mission to recover the bodies of Iraqi National Guard (ING) members. This involved a convoy that was struck by a series of "daisy chain" roadside bombs, which burned their bodies beyond recognition. A soldier who was extracting the dead bodies from the vehicles laughed and joked while performing this hideous task. Other soldiers were angry with him for his seemingly unacceptable behavior. During the debriefing, this soldier apologized for his behavior. He explained that he was so deeply disturbed by this assignment that he was only able to endure with the use of "gallows humor". The group accepted the soldier's apology and the unity and cohesion of the group were restored.

Battlemind debriefings

Another debriefing model created and implemented by the U. S. Army in 2007 is known as the Battlemind Debriefing Model. The stages of the time-driven battlemind psychological debriefing are: (1) Introduction; (2) Event; (3) Reactions; (4) Self and Buddy Aid; and (5) Battlemind Focus (Adler, Castro & McGurk, 2009). This type of model differs from other psychological debriefings in that it emphasizes a simpler and briefer identification of the most severe aspects of traumatic events, rather than a detailed, individual reconstruction of the traumatic event and chronological reconstruction of critical events (ibid.). There remains considerable controversy, however, as to whether the battlemind debriefing process is effective, neutral, or even potentially harmful (ibid).

An important feature of this model is a focus on self-care, buddy aid and resiliency, rather than concentrating on distressing psychological symptoms such as anxiety, excessive fear, depression and grief (ibid.). The focus also tends to be upon individual strengths and utilizing them to establish more effective coping modalities. Battlemind principles have been integrated as part of the block or routine training for *all* components of the Army, regardless of deployment status. Hence, this model is considered less stigmatizing for recipients, in contrast to the historical and stereotypic notion that those seeking mental health or COSC services are somehow weak or defective (ibid.). This model is also is designed to promote unit cohesion through reliance upon military training, promoting resiliency, and watching out for one another as "buddies" (ibid.). Like the other psychological debriefing models, it is important to provide group members with information regarding follow-up services and availability of mental health personnel to provide one-to-one support/consultation following the debriefing.

Kuhlman model

The Kuhlman Model is a bereavement debriefing model developed by the 785th Medical Company, Combat Stress Control, based out of Fort Snelling, Minnesota. This model addresses the emotional pain and trauma associated with the death of a comrade and assists with the emotional grieving/healing process (Scurfield, 2006). This model has many similar features to a memorial service and allows group participants to experience a full range of emotions surrounding grief and loss. Group participants are given full latitude to engage in storytelling about the deceased, often with elements of humor and irreverence, as a means of reminiscing about and memorializing their fallen comrades. These stages comprise the unique qualities of the Kuhlman Model. The education component of this model includes a review of both common reactions experienced after significant loss and of the Kubler-Ross five stages of grief and loss (denial, anger, bargaining, depression and acceptance) (U.S. 785th Medical Company, 2004). The group size for this model can be quite large, as it does not require verbal input from all participants. Unlike many other critical event debriefing models, this model is designed to include everyone acquainted with the deceased, rather than only those individuals directly involved with a specific traumatic event.

The Kuhlman Model is fairly easy to conduct and usually well received by groups, especially when introduced as a means to pay tribute to and honor the fallen. There are six stages (U.S. 785th Medical Company, 2004). We will use the fictitious name of "Johnny" to describe them:

- *Factual:* Where were you when you heard about the death? Talk about this.
- *Factual:* What are some of the traits that you liked most about Johnny/ what did you most like about Johnny?
- *Factual:* What are some things that annoyed you about Johnny? This brings out the humanity of persons—i.e., that no one is perfect—and delivers some levity and laughter.
- *Reaction:* How did you first feel when you heard about Johnny? How do you feel now? How do you feel now that Johnny is not returning (normalize, validate, educate)?
- *Action:* How can we pay tribute to Johnny's memory? How can we show honor and respect for Johnny's life and the sacrifices he made?
- *Action:* Tell us a story about Johnny (preserving, sharing the memories, storing memories collectively, sharing organizational history).

As with other debriefing models, the Kuhlman Model should be presented by a small group of trained professionals, or at the very minimum two mental health providers. Chaplains can be a valued resource when dealing with issues pertaining to life and death matters from a religious perspective. Group facilitators can provide helpful suggestions during the later action stages of the debriefing, such as proposing that the unit send cards with personal messages to the families of the deceased, signed by all unit members, or that memorials be constructed in the company area with pictures and symbols to honor the fallen. Finally, consistent with other debriefing models, it is imperative to provide education regarding follow-up mental health services and to be available at the conclusion of the debriefing.

CASE EXAMPLE 3

A Kuhlman Debriefing was conducted with Charlie Company in the aftermath of an IED incident in which three soldiers were killed in the Kandahar Province of Afghanistan in the winter of 2010. Due to the very high optempo (operation tempo) and mission demands, the command made the decision to mandate attendance for the entirety of the unit, whether on scene or not. Anger was palpable throughout the room and each soldier elected to "pass" when encouraged to speak. The decision was made by the group leader to transition to the Kuhlman Model in order for these grieving soldiers to memorialize their lost comrades. This altered the group temperament and allowed the participants to move past their anger, to freely reveal the impact of their losses individually and to generate a powerful sense of camaraderie (Platoni, personal communication, 2011).

Comprehensive soldier fitness (CSF) and resiliency training

The latest trend in mental health application within the U.S. Army focuses primarily on comprehensive resiliency training. In contrast to traditional approaches and the use of the various models of psychological debriefings described above, CSF is proactive. This model provides strategies for improving resilience for all members of the Army prior to the onset of negative stress reactions (Cornum, Matthews & Seligman, 2011). The CSF approach is holistic in nature and is intended to promote the ability to respond to a wide variety of traumatic events by developing personal inner strengths. Cornum, Matthews & Seligman (2011) outline the four-pillared paradigm, modeled after a similar approach to physical fitness and technical proficiency:

- *Assessment:* In combination with physiological measures obtained twice a year by means of the Army Physical Fitness Test (APFT), a Global Assessment Tool (GAT) measuring psychological fitness is administered when new recruits enlist in the Army. Reassessments occur at appropriate intervals (every two years or between 120 and 180 days following contingency operations) and follow soldiers throughout their military careers. The GAT will thus track the psychological fitness of the entire Army.

- *Universal Resilience Training*: Progressive training in techniques to improve resilience in self and subordinates, beginning at initial entry (for both officers and enlisted soldiers), in order to build resilience at every level of the Army.
- *Individualized Training*: On the basis of their performance on the GAT, training in different aspects of resilience (emotional, social, family, or spiritual) is available to soldiers, both through actual training protocols and through virtual training protocols documented within the Army's Digital Training Management System (DTMS).
- *Trained Master Resilience Trainers (MRTs)*: Soldiers with advanced training in building the mental, emotional, and physical skills for maintaining and enhancing resilience will become teachers of resilience throughout the Army (ibid.).

Resiliency training concentrates on a present-centered model as opposed to a trauma-centered model. Teaching soldiers how to recognize and replace distorted thought patterns with positive ones is crucial for addressing problems such as anger or depression. Mindfulness meditation skills are being adopted as useful techniques, specifically to keep the mind in the present moment, focusing upon the senses of sight, sound, hearing, touch and smell and thought patterns in the "here and now" (Mizuki, 2012). This meditation technique can be helpful in confronting survivor guilt and other aspects of an unforgiving and self-critical mind. Progressive muscle relaxation and diaphragmatic breathing exercises are other very useful tools that can easily be taught and practiced in combat zones. Guided imagery/guided visualization techniques are also very effective in improving the psychological state of mind.

Any of these skills can be very beneficial when practiced routinely. Once soldiers on the front lines experience success with these therapeutic tools, their efficacy becomes self-evident and assists soldiers through deployment if practiced regularly. These tools may also be beneficial during the difficult post-deployment and reintegration period as service members return to the home front and readjust to their civilian lives.

Spirituality and faith

Chapter 17 of this volume is dedicated to discussion of the role of chaplains in the war zone. Suffice it to say here that it is important to note that the danger element of combat and the quest for many soldiers to seek divine protection often paves the way for faith-based services. Hence, the Unit Ministry Team

(UMT) (consisting of at least one chaplain and one chaplain's assistant) is a vital supplement to and partner of the provision of COSC interventions.

Closing

Combat and Operational Stress Control (COSC) teams in the theatre of operations are a most valuable resource to commands, as well as to individual service members. Early mental health interventions on the front lines of the battlefield are critical to the enhancement of rapid psychological recovery following a traumatic event in order to maintain the fighting force. Time, safety factors and availability of mental health/COSC services are greatly affected by mission constraints, as well as working with service members who are usually embroiled in high operational tempos in often volatile and unpredictable wartime environments. On most occasions when considering the cost-benefit analysis, the benefits of COSC and of psychological interventions very clearly outweigh any potential of harm that might be done through provision of such services and interventions (Seligman & Fowler, 2011).

The military mental health service system continues to evolve, with lessons learned from past and present day military experiences (Scurfield, 2006). The goals for mental health have been the same over the years; however, the methods of providing these services have changed. It is essential to be cognizant of the unique aspects of providing mental health services in combat regions, such as the obvious ready access to weapons. With the prolonged combat operations that were waged in Iraq and continue to be waged in Afghanistan, along with the rapidly escalating suicide rates within all branches of the Armed Forces, there is no better or more compelling time than now to invest in the training of mental health providers who are willing to serve their country by going into battle with America's finest. The embedding or inclusion of COSC personnel and services within combat arms/combat service support units in the wartime theater is unquestionably one of the most valuable forces in promoting survivorship on the battlefield, not only for the duration of military service, but long after its conclusion.

CPT Christian J. Hallman, Ph.D. (10 January 1970–6 June 2011) was an Army Health Care Recruiter based in Bloomington, Minnesota until his untimely death. He served with the 785th Medical Company, Combat Stress Control, in Iraq from 2004 to 2005, where he specialized in relaxation therapy, guided imagery, and meditation to treat combat stress casualties.

MAJ Patrick Pischke, MSW, LICSW is a social work officer with the 785th Medical Detachment, Combat Stress Control, with over 17 years of military service, including two deployments to Iraq. He is employed at the VA Medical Center in Minneapolis, Minnesota as an out-patient mental health provider specializing in work with PTSD including trauma-centered therapy, couple and group therapy and teaching psychoeducational classes (Patrick.pischke@ us.army.mil).

References

Adler, A. B., Castro, C. A. & McGurk, D. (2009). Time-driven battlemind psychological debriefing: A group-level early intervention in combat. *Military Medicine, 174*(1), 21–28.

American Psychiatric Association (APA) (2000). *The Diagnostic and Statistical Manual of Mental Disorders IV-TR*. Washington, DC: American Psychiatric Association.

Army Publications (2009). *FM 6-22.5: Combat and operational stress control manual for leaders and soldiers*. Retrieved from www.apd.army.mil

Bell, J. L. (1995). Traumatic event debriefing: Service delivery designs and the role of social work. *Social Worker, 40*(1), 36–43.

Burns, L. & Harm, N. J. (1993). Emergency nurses' perceptions of critical incidents and stress debriefing. *Journal of Emergency Nursing, 19*(5), 431–ß436.

Cornum, R., Matthews, M. D. & Seligman, M. E. P. (2011). Comprehensive soldier fitness: Building resilience in a challenging institutional context. *American Psychologist, 66*(1), 4–9.

Eid, J., Johnsen, B. H. & Weisaeth, L. (2001). The effects of group psychological debriefing on acute stress reactions following a traffic accident: A quasi-experimental approach. *International Journal of Emergency Mental Health, 3*, 145–154.

Hoge, C. W., Castro, C. A., Messer, S. C., McGurk, D., Cotting, D. L.& Koffman, M. D. (2004). Combat Duty in Iraq and Afghanistan, Mental Health Problems, and Barriers to Care. *New England Journal of Medicine, 351*, 13–22.

Hutchinson, J. & Banks-Williams, L. (2006). Clinical issues and treatment considerations for new veterans: Soldiers of the wars in Iraq and Afghanistan. *Primary Psychiatry, 13*(3), 66–71.

Jenkins, S. R. (1996). Social support and debriefing efficacy among emergency medical workers after a mass shooting incident. *Journal of Social Behavior and Personality, 1*, 477–492.

Jewell, L. (2004). Army releases findings of first-ever soldier well-being study in combat arena. Army News Service. Retrieved from https://webmail.us.army.mil/ Attach/Soldier%20well-being%20study0325%20(2).htm

Knobler, H. Y., Nachshoni, T., Jaffe, E., Peretz, G. & Yehuda, Y. B. (2007). Psychological guidelines for a medical team debriefing after a stressful event. *Military Medicine, 172*(6), 581–585.

MacDonald, C. M. (2003). evaluation of stress debriefing intervention with military populations. *Military Medicine, 168*(12), 961–968.

Mitchell, J. T. & Everly, G. S. (2003). *Critical Incident Stress Management (CISM): Basic Group Crisis Intervention* (3rd ed.). Ellicott City, MD: International Critical Incident Stress Foundation, Inc.

Mizuki, C. (2012). Mindfulness with service members and veterans. In R. M. Scurfield & K.T. Platoni (Eds.), *Healing War Trauma: A Handbook of Creative Approaches*. New York, NY: Routledge.

Pischke, P. J. & Hallman, C. J. (2008). Effectiveness of critical event debriefings during Operation Iraqi Freedom II. *The United States Army Medical Department Journal*, July–Sept, 18–23.

Purinton, C. (2012). Chaplains in the military. In R. M. Scurfield & K. T. Platoni (Eds.), *Healing War Trauma: A Handbook of Creative Approaches.* New York, NY: Routledge.

Robinson, R. C. & Mitchell, J. T. (1993). Evaluation of psychological debriefings. *Journal of Traumatic Stress, 6*(3), 367–382.

Schiraldi, G. R. (2000). *The Posttraumatic Stress Disorder Source Book: A Guide to Healing, Recovery, and Growth.* Los Angeles, CA: Lowell House.

Scurfield, R. M. (2004). *A Vietnam Trilogy. War Trauma and Post Traumatic Stress: 1968, 1989 & 2000.* New York, NY: Algora Publishing.

Scurfield, R. M. (2006). *War Trauma: Lessons Unlearned From Vietnam to Iraq.* New York, NY: Algora Publishing.

Scurfield, R. M., Viola, J., Platoni, K. & Colon, J. (2003). Continuing psychological aftermath of 9/11: A POPPA experience and critical incident stress debriefing revisited. *Traumatology, 9*(1), 31–57.

Seligman, M. E. P. & Fowler, R. D. (2011). comprehensive soldier fitness and the future of psychology. *American Psychologist, 66*(1), 82–86.

Shalev, A. Y., Peri, T., Rogel-Fuchs, Y., Ursano, R. J., Marlowe, D. H. (1998). Historical group debriefing after combat exposure. *Military Medicine, 163*(7), 494–498.

Thomas, T. L. & O'Hara, C. P. (2000). Combat stress in Chechnya: "The equal opportunity disorder". *Army Medical Department Journal.* Retrieved from http://fmso.leavenworth.army.mil/documents/stress.htm

U.S. Army (2006). *Field Manual FM 4-02.51: Combat and Operational Stress Control.* Retrieved from www.fas.org/irp/doddir/army/fm4-02-51.pdf

U.S. Army (2009). *Field Manual FM 6-22.5: Combat and Operational Stress Control Manual For Leaders & Soldiers.*

U. S. 785th Medical Company (2004). *785th Medical Company (CSC) Knowledge Book: "Find the Balance," Operation Iraqi Freedom '04.* Fort McCoy, WI: Print Shop (54656).

Vesper, J. (2006). *Healing Traumatic Stress, PTSD and Grief: Practical & Effective Treatment Strategies.* Eau Claire, WI: PESI.

Witztum, E., Levy, A. & Solomon, Z. (1996). Lessons denied: A history of therapeutic response to combat stress reaction during Israel's War of Independence (1948), the Sinai Campaign (1956) and the Six Day War (1967). *Israel Journal of Psychiatry and Related Science, 33*(2), 79–88.

15 Enhancing resiliency through creative outdoor/adventure and community-based programs

LTC Valvincent Reyes, USAR, OEF-A

Exposure to high-risk factors in the protracted, 11-year Global War on Terrorism requires service members and veterans to discover new and innovative ways of adapting after their return to society. This has created the need for these combat veterans, their families, the Department of Veteran Affairs, veteran service organizations, and community-based medical and behavioral healthcare agencies to identify and maximize their coping skills. Resiliency—the ability to overcome stress and trauma—can be achieved using a set of skills, knowledge and abilities that is now being utilized by some outdoor adventure and community-based programs to create innovative and individualized reintegration services for our redeployed veterans. This chapter will document how resiliency skills are integrated in these outdoor adventure and community-based programs to expand options for successful community readjustment.

Background

With combat operations in Afghanistan now extending into their eleventh year and the withdrawal of forces from Iraq after eight years of fighting having been completed, our country must face the responsibility for the healing of our warfighters and their family members. Multiple deployments, lack of adequate psychological reset from combat stress; less than a year of "dwell" time between deployments, preventing the proper reunification of family relationships; and the horrific effects of the enemy's IEDs have produced devastating consequences. A 2008 RAND Corporation study reported that 18.5 percent of combat veterans deployed to Afghanistan and Iraq suffer symptoms from either PTSD or depression (Burnham et al., 2009).

Service members suffer severe physical wounds, including the "signature" injuries of the war in Afghanistan and Iraq: Traumatic Brain Injury (TBI), amputation, blindness and burns. These physical wounds require specialized medical and behavioral healthcare. After medical stabilization, the wounded warrior experiences psychological distortions of body integrity and competency, requiring a bio/psycho/social approach and follow-up care in the community. According to a 2010 report by the American Legion, 10,848 service members deployed to Afghanistan and Iraq have been wounded in action, with 1,552 having suffered traumatic amputations (Williams, 2010).

Advanced combat trauma medical care and tactical body armor in combination have created a 90 percent survival rate, the highest in the history of warfare (ibid.). The VA Office of Public Health and Environment Hazards (2010) reported that of the veterans who enrolled for VA services, 150,000 have been diagnosed and treated for PTSD, 115,000 for depression and 50,000 for substance abuse.

When we look at ways for a service member to adjust back to community living, we focus on three major spheres: family, work and education. When examining psychotherapeutic approaches, the scientific literature shows that veterans are likely to be given a diagnosis of mental illness and that problems within the veteran's psyche need to be addressed (Caplan, 2011). Most veterans do not need to be labeled mentally ill, but rather need assistance to come to terms with their distorted belief systems and their losses, and to discover personal meanings from their exposure to war trauma.

Many do not complete counseling. They instead search for various alternative treatments to help them to restore personal meanings, develop self-efficacy and adapt back into society. This chapter describes one such alternative approach: innovative outdoor/adventure programs which promote healing and reintegration for service members and veterans by focusing on psychological resiliency factors. Resiliency skills are of importance to Operation Iraqi Freedom (OIF), Operation New Dawn (OND) and Operation Enduring Freedom (OEF) veterans[1] and their family members, as these promote emotional well-being with a personalized, strength-based approach and serve to reduce the stigma of seeking mental health services during the reintegration process.

As therapists, we recognize that exposure to the combat zone is a transformative experience that can contribute to both post-deployment stress and post-traumatic growth. For the service member who found the experience of combat and the aftermath challenging and not yet overwhelming, the result can be personal growth. The clinical imperatives for therapists are to assist the veteran in searching for personal meanings, resolving conflicting belief systems, and the implementation of the individual's learned resiliency skills. This therapeutic focus encourages the vertern to adapt to overcome the physical,

---

1 OIF includes U.S. military personnel who served in Iraq between 20 March 2003 and 31 August 2010; OND includes U.S. military personnel who have served in Iraq from 1 September 2010 and marks the official end to Operation Iraqi Freedom and combat operations by U.S. military personnel in Iraq; OEF includes military personnel who served in Afghanistan and other military actions as part of the Global War on Terror—this includes Afghanistan (OEF-A), Guantanamo Bay, Cuba (Joint Task Force-GTMO), Philippines (OEF-P), Horn of Africa (OEF-HOA), Pankisi Gorge (completed in 2004), Trans-Sahara (OEF-TS), Caribbean and Central America (OEF-CCA) and Krygystanzstan (completed in 2004).

emotional and psychological challenges that lie ahead. Encouraging the veteran to be resilient within an otherwise difficult healing process creates meaning and purpose.

Resiliency for service members returning from deployment and their families

Recovery from a physical wound, post-deployment stress, or both requires a service member's ability to regenerate from traumatic experiences and find a sense of personal meaning after redeployment back to mainstream society. Resiliency is defined as "the process by which people manage not only to endure hardships but also to create and sustain lives that have meaning" (Van Hook, 2008). A resilient person has the capacity to exercise self-efficacy within three levels of influence: the individual, family and community.

Factors that contribute to *individual* resiliency point to self-efficacy skills. Self-efficacy can be defined as "self-worth," based on the ability to establish an internal locus of control of the self and one's environment (ibid.). The five resiliency skills that contribute to self-efficacy on the individual level are: (1) discovering a new sense of purpose and meaning in life; (2) developing realistic self-appraisal skills; (3) the ability to maintain positive social relationships; (4) the ability to use problem-solving skills and positively cope with crisis in everyday life; and (5) physical fitness—an individual-level, evidence-informed factor defined by Meredith *et al.* (2011) as "bodily ability to function efficiently and effectively in life domains."

The first resiliency skill the veteran learns is to maintain hope in discovering a new sense of purpose and meaning through suffering. The veteran who desires to psychologically adapt and overcome combat zone-related trauma maintains a sense of optimism about the future. After one returns home, one maintains an open and flexible attitude to meet the challenges of community reintegration. The second skill is self-appraisal—the ability to process information, recognize positive alternatives to challenging situations and develop positive expectations based on one's realistic knowledge of personal strengths. The third skill impacting individual resiliency is the ability to communicate and develop mutual support with others. The combat veteran has already learned the military value of group cohesion and come to rely on the Battle Buddy System.

The Battle Buddy System is of paramount importance to understanding military culture and the experience of being in the military, offering a crucial dynamic to attend to as part of community reintegration and readjustment. It is the friendship, camaraderie and emotional support provided between two or more service members, within the same military unit, usually within a combat zone environment. The emotional support engendered within the relationship improves work performance and team concept, and is the major source of encouragement to overcome stressful military-related situations. Consequently, the application of the Battle Buddy System or team orientation, along with clear communication and mutual collaboration, is a key ingredient towards the completion of any mission during the adjustment phase to societal living.

The fourth skill that contributes to individual resiliency is the ability to problem-solve and utilize positive behavioral or emotional coping skills to overcome a situational crisis. Returning to a civilian environment can create a situational crisis when the service member experiences a stressful life event, such as marital, financial, employment or parent–child problems. For example, during the course of a year-long deployment, a platoon leader maintains military discipline among the unit members by issuing verbal orders. However, the same platoon leader, now redeployed back home as a father, encounters a situational family crisis when his 13-year-old daughter rebels in response to his verbal orders to keep her room clean. His ability to resolve the conflict is dependent on many factors, including the previous and current levels of communication between father and daughter, parenting skills, and advice and emotional support from his spouse and other family members. Another example is dealing with traumatic amputations and severe wounds caused by IEDs, which impel OIF and OEF veterans during the reintegration phase to re-evaluate their self-concepts, rely on a network of social supports, redefine their body image and rebuild their physical capacities through disabled veterans' adaptive sports programs.

There are four resiliency factors at the *family* level: (1) The emotional support, sense of love, intimacy and togetherness shared between family members; (2) Communicating, sharing information and problem-solving family reunification issues together (Van Hook, 2008); (3) Involving family members in collaborating to develop coping mechanisms to assist the veteran in managing combat trauma reminders; and (4) Developing adaptability of family roles and family member responsibilities. The task in adapting to transitions in the military is the re-alignment of each family member's roles, which is important in the normalization of family life following a deployment.

Factors at the *community* level that promote resiliency include providing veterans with connections to individuals who provide caring, mentoring relationships within the community. For example, connecting veterans with other veterans who have adapted to civilian life and can serve as positive role models or putting them in touch with coaches, teachers, business owners and/or social workers. Other factors which encourage resiliency are community collaborations with Vet Centers (Readjustment Counseling Service, U.S. Department of Veterans Affairs), Veteran Service Organizations or support groups that offer programs which expose participants to knowledge, problem solving and coping skills. Finally, and perhaps most importantly, is the provision of opportunities to work cohesively within an organization that encompasses shared goals in an institution of higher learning, place of employment, or community service agency. Veterans can benefit from the opportunity to mutually collaborate with civilians or fellow veterans at work, at school or in any organization that provides a sense of group cohesion and resurrects the belief that they belong to something bigger than themselves (Meredith *et al.*, 2011).

Resiliency, outdoor/adventure programs and their special relevance to service members and veterans

Creative "out-of-the-office" programs offer veterans the opportunity to practice resiliency skills, challenge their distorted belief systems, encounter "in vivo" experiences which restore self-efficacy, and receive support from civilian mentors, caring individuals and volunteers. Outdoor adventure activities also provide veterans with the chance for transformational post-traumatic growth. Their participation in outdoor adventures allows them to translate their combat survival belief systems (i.e. "I will make the world a safer place"), values (i.e. unit cohesion) and skills (i.e. cautious driving over roads interspersed with IEDs) into successful civilian, community-oriented belief systems (humanity), work completion (persistence) and skills acquisition (love of learning) (Seligman et al., 2005).

There is a special relevance that outdoor and adventure-based interventions have for service members and veterans. Persons who are or have been in the military typically are outdoor and adventure-oriented through their military training and subsequent experiences while on active duty. Many of them, early in life and into their adulthood as civilians, have been exposed to rewarding outdoor recreational activities, including camping, fishing, hiking and hunting. In addition, the special bond among military personnel that is engendered in small military units can be replicated to some degree through participating in outdoor adventure-based programs with other veterans.

Brief history of models of outdoor therapy

A number of programs for outdoor adventure therapy have evolved over time. The first was the Recreational Service set up by the Veterans Administration (VA) under the Rehabilitation Medicine Service Office. In 1946, Therapeutic Recreation was developed into a specialized field by the VA, in recognition of the fact that the veteran's healing and recovery from trauma relied on the interdependence between the physiological, psychological and social needs of the individual (Mansfield, 2008).

One of the first adaptive sports programs that the VA developed after the Second World War was adaptive basketball for combat-disabled veterans. Adaptive sports programs take their name from disabled veterans, who adapted their remaining physical abilities and skills to master recreational sports. In relation to basketball, veterans adapted their abilities to the court by wheeling themselves around, passing the ball to each other, shooting baskets and scoring points. More recently, the VA has sponsored various adaptive sports and has teamed up with Disabled Sports USA to provide adaptive skiing clinics for disabled veterans with traumatic injuries, PTSD and TBI. Groups of veterans from Wounded Warrior programs across the country will travel to local mountain slopes to learn how to handle ski poles with prosthetic limbs, fit into a wheelchair-like mono chair to ski and use stand-up skis with twin handheld mini-ski outriggers (Stannard, 2009). Disabled veterans master the physical demands of skiing from the shorter to the longer runs, producing a sense of exhilaration and a resurgence of feelings of control and competency. During the 1980s, several of the VA inpatient PTSD programs utilized outdoor activities to enhance therapeutic benefits for participating veterans. For example, the specialized inpatient unit at Northhampton, Massachusetts, pioneered taking veterans out on Outward Bound hiking and rappelling activities. Additionally, the American Lake VA (Tacoma, Washington) and the Augusta (Georgia) VA specialized inpatient units conducted Outward Bound courses for disabled veterans that integrated hiking, river rafting, camping and rappelling with debriefing sessions during and following the courses (Hyer *et al.*, 2004).

The American Lake VA specialized inpatient PTSD unit also pioneered utilizing therapeutic rides in Army helicopters to enhance the more traditional individual and group therapy conducted on the hospital ward (Scurfield, Wong & Zeerocah, 1992; Scurfield, 2004). Finally, an extension of outdoor and adventure-based interventions for Vietnam veterans with war-related PTSD involved taking a PTSD therapy group of veterans back to Vietnam (Scurfield, Root & Weist, 2003; Scurfield, 2006). Since then, other veterans have returned to former battlefields on their own or as part of groups of veterans in their quest for further healing.

Currently, the VA sponsors or partners with various year-round outdoor/adventure disabled sports programs. They include the following: Saddles for soldiers and Heroes for Horses—horseback riding; Winter Sports Clinic—cross-country snowmobiling, adaptive ice hockey, skiing and snowboarding; Summer Sports Clinic—rock climbing, surfing, kayaking, sailing and scuba diving; Golden Age Games—track and field events for disabled veterans aged 55 years and older; and Creative Arts Festival—art, drama, and music competitions for disabled veterans (E. Rule, personal communication, 2011).

Types of outdoor adventure programs

There are a variety of outdoor or adventure-based programs. Their mission is to offer disabled veterans a wide range of outdoor activities. Matching the veteran with potential outdoor activities will require staff to determine what the veteran is capable of doing with existing adaptive equipment, as well as what activities the veteran may be capable of doing with modifications to existing equipment. These programs offer walking, mountain biking, cross country all-terrain vehicle riding, outdoor shooting, mountain climbing, fishing, rafting, canoeing, kayaking, jet skiing, water skiing, para-sailing, snow shoeing, cross-country skiing, snowmobiling and sleigh riding.

This chapter will describe several types of outdoor adventure programs utilized with veterans: Ocean Therapy, Paralyzed Veterans of America: Shooting Sports, VA-Sponsored Disabled Veterans Scuba Project, Warrior Transition Unit-sponsored disabled sports programs and the Pathway Home Residential Program. There will be a description of each intervention followed by a discussion of associated treatment implications. It is important to note that participation in an outdoor adventure-based activity or program might be the only therapeutic activity with which a service member or veteran may be involved. However, when very significant PTSD or other psychiatric or disabling physical conditions are present, it is strongly recommended that participation in outdoor/adventure-based activities be accompanied by concurrent involvement in some kind of more traditional psychotherapy to help optimize the therapeutic goals.

Ocean Therapy

A unique outdoor program that focuses on resiliency skill-building is Ocean Therapy, a surfing program established for the Wounded Warrior Battalion at Camp Pendleton, California. It was founded in 2008 by Carly Rogers, an Occupational Therapist, long-time Los Angeles County Lifeguard, and Program Director/Board Member with the Jimmy Miller Foundation, a non-profit disabled sports and preventative mental health program set up in 2005 and originally designed to teach physically disabled and "at-risk" youth to surf. Ocean Therapy is based upon the philosophy that surfing is a socially acceptable alternative to self-destructive, risk-taking behaviors. It is a year-round, two-day-per-month program for Marines diagnosed with PTSD and/or TBI or amputees assigned to the Wounded Warrior Battalion at Camp Pendleton. Volunteers and lifeguards teach these Marines on a one-to-one basis how to have successful surfing experiences. The one-to-one coaching relationship between the volunteer and the Marine is characterized by supportive encouragement and identification of the Marine's strengths and abilities. The surfing program is taught on the beach at Camp Pendleton, on the Pacific coast. In between surf lessons, mentors/surfers lead discussion groups on self-efficacy themes (Rogers, personal communication, 2010).

The key elements of the Ocean Therapy Program are:

- Two training sessions in which the veteran is taught a three-step "standing up process"—learning to lift oneself up, maintain balance, and hold steady on the board—in addition to safe riding practices.
- Three discussion groups on reintegration issues including transitions, motivation, goal-setting, and recreation as a tool for coping. Groups are led by Rogers and scheduled between surf lessons.
- Implementation of substance abuse and calming strategies, using the themes of Leadership, Identity, Resource Acquisition (Connection) and Social Engagement.

- Use of a "task analysis" by the surfing mentor to help the veteran adapt and to stand safely on the surfboard to achieve a successful ride.
- Constant feedback provided by surfing mentors on the individual's attained surfing skills to reinforce the transfer of self-efficacy to activities of daily living.
- Trusting, caring, coaching relationship between surfing mentor and Marine, characterized by clear and open communication.

Treatment implications

The clinician can readily find uniqueness within this program through the teaching of resiliency skills during the group discussion process. When discussing Leadership, the group leader translates warrior skills familiar to the OIF and OEF veteran by contextualizing the discussion in military terms. For example, the group leader may use the term "Battle Buddy" to explain the sense of trust and mutual cooperation required between the surfing volunteer and the veteran in order for a successful ride to occur. Also, the clinician helps the group to identify military leadership skills that transfer into positive coping skills in civilian life. These include assertiveness, clear communication, goal-setting and anger management.

To foster Resource Acquisition, the group leaders help veterans to identify vocational, educational and recreational community-based services that will help them to access productive community engagement. With Social Engagement, participants will be able to distinguish key aspects of social opportunities within the community, which aid them in feeling affiliated with family, peers or other community members. For example, many OIF and OEF veterans desire higher education to gain entry to employment. By focusing on the search for educational resources, the clinician can encourage the veteran to seek education as a means for an improved quality of life.

Further, the clinician can take from this program the concept that he/she is helping to create a living laboratory (in the ocean) for the veteran to practice self-efficacy skills. The OIF or OEF wounded warrior is struggling to redefine his/her body image and is searching for personal meaning and redefined physical competencies. The surfing volunteer is a guide who encourages the veteran to participate in an "in vivo" exposure, which provides the opportunity to adapt the physical endurance and motor skills required to surf. This creates in the veteran an improved self-concept and a newfound sense of self-efficacy. Afterwards, the surfing volunteer discusses the experience of re-adaptation of skills with the veteran to acknowledge and associate positive emotions with moments of post-traumatic growth.

Paralyzed Veterans of America: Shooting Sports

Paralyzed Veterans of America (PVA) is a private, non-profit, 501(c)(3) national veteran service organization that provides disabled veterans with spinal cord injuries and other diseases with benefits services, advocacy, medical research and adaptive sports programs. Based in Washington, DC, the organization has served thousands of disabled veterans from 34 chapters located in all 50 states for 65 years. Its adaptive sports programs include bass fishing, billiards, bowling, handcycling, and wheelchair racing. Of special importance to OIF, OEF and OND veterans is its shooting sports program. PVA sponsors year-round trapshooting competitions, shooting at clay targets. Also, along with the Outdoor Recreation Heritage Fund, PVA co-sponsors deer hunting expeditions (Paralyzed Veterans of America, 2011). During the hunt, the veteran is paired with a mentor who provides guidance on safe shooting stances and positions, wears protective personal gear and is outfitted with corporate-sponsored adaptive shooting equipment. The highlight is the camaraderie between the mentor and the veteran, born of the shared rigors of the outdoor hunt. After the hunt is completed and the deer is shot, the veteran usually experiences a sense of accomplishment, improved self-efficacy, new friendships and a renewed appreciation for the great outdoors.

Treatment implications

The successful completion of the hunt brings about an increased sense of success and mastery. The physical rigors and durability required of the disabled veteran in the completion of the mission lead to a perception of renewed personal strength—which was previously required during active duty—and improved self-esteem. The veteran, familiarized with weapons in the military, becomes reacquainted with their shooting skills without the experiences of killing and maiming that accompanied shooting during combat—this helps to bring about a renewed sense of personal competency. Many veterans developed early in their lives a love of outdoor recreational activities such as camping, hiking and hunting. PVA-sponsored deer hunting expeditions allow them the opportunity to reconnect with nature and re-experience a place of relaxation and peace. The bond with the mentor creates an interrelatedness that helps to de-condition any negative associations to war trauma that the veteran holds with regard to weapons.

The Disabled Veterans Scuba Project

The mission of the VA Sponsored Disabled Veterans Scuba Project is to teach a 12-week certification course in scuba diving to veterans with quadriplegia, double amputations and PTSD. Its current class consists of both male and female disabled veterans from the Long Beach and the West Los Angeles Veterans Administration Medical Centers in California. A 501(c) non-profit corporation, founded in 2008 by Nicolas Coster at the Challenges Foundation, Disabled Veterans Scuba Project established a collaboration with the Spinal Cord Injury Unit at the Long Beach Veterans Administration Hospital and the Pain Management Clinic at the Loma Linda Veterans Administration

Hospital to teach scuba diving and ocean sailing (M. Paisley, personal communications, 2011). The course is conducted at the National Guard's Joint Forces Training Base, in its Olympic-sized swimming pool, in Los Alamitos, California. There are two segments: the classroom, where instruction in diving theory and safety procedures are taught; and the pool, where diving equipment is worn and instructors coach scuba diving skills application. Resiliency skills taught include the following: (1) Problem solving—for example, veterans are provided instruction in calculating nitrogen levels using a diving table; (2) Communication skills—student veterans are encouraged to clearly communicate and rely upon a diving buddy; (3) Study skills—veterans are expected to learn diving theory and procedures using focus, memorization, math calculation and utilization of basic reading skills; (4) Veterans learn self-discipline. They are expected to attend four-hour weekly training sessions, requiring intense physical strength and exertion. Of high importance to student veterans is the mentoring provided by Melvin Paisley, a civilian real estate professional, OIF combat veteran and retired Army officer. He is a positive role model who encourages the adaptation of their military skills to successful community adjustment.

Treatment implications

Swimming and diving allow veterans the opportunity for stress management training. Water encourages the relaxation response in veterans and leads to a decrease in anxiety-producing and stressful thoughts. One can feel hyper-aroused at the beginning of class but calm by the end of water training.

Diving theory class improves cognitive functioning with a diving instructor who encourages veteran students to use memorization and calculation skills to remember diving times and water safety procedures. Scuba diving improves self-efficacy and a sense of competency in disabled veterans who are amputees, as they can maximize the use of their remaining limbs by lifting heavy oxygen tanks, wearing diving equipment and diving safely.

The mutual collaboration involved in scuba diving with a diving buddy encourages a sense of high morale and group camaraderie. The sense of reliance between veterans to ensure the safety of one another approximates the Battle Buddy system they depended on in the combat zone, leading them to feel a strong bond of peer support.

Warrior Transition Unit-sponsored disabled sports programs

Warrior Transition Units (WTUs), co-located in both Army and Navy Medical Centers, are designed to provide treatment, rehabilitation and case management services to injured OIF and OEF Veterans. The mission is to provide supportive services from battlefield evacuation to return to duty or transition to veteran status in the community. These service members have sustained injuries such as PTSD, severe burns, physical disfigurement, traumatic amputations, traumatic brain injury, spinal cord injury, visual impairment, blindness and strokes (AW2, n.d.). WTU treatment staff include the family members of the service members in the treatment planning as a means to provide direct family support and to increase the opportunities for successful family and community reintegration following discharge. They have also developed adaptive sports and fitness programs for the injured personnel assigned to these units. Ongoing programs are designed to enhance service members' rehabilitation, improve their physical fitness and enhance their quality of life.

These WTU programs have been developed to promote the return of injured service members to a healthy, active lifestyle, with a schedule of activities being offered multiple days per week at each installation. Activities offered include: basketball, swimming, sitting volleyball, spinning, archery, walking/running, strength and conditioning skills training and skiing. Additionally, The U.S. Olympic Committee (USOC) Paralympic Military Program has provided post-rehabilitation support and mentoring by teaching adaptive sports techniques and offering access to sports clinics and camps in the service members' hometowns. An innovative expansion of this program is the Warrior Games, in which injured service members from all branches of the Armed Services participate in annual Olympic-style competitions. Another original approach that includes an emphasis on resiliency is the use of sponsored tours of historical battle sites in Rome for service members and their families. The tours of battle sites involving early Roman soldiers have provided learning opportunities for service members to reflect on the courage and endurance necessary to survive early Roman battles (Roman Empire, n.d).

Treatment implications

Clinicians are acutely aware that injured service members are learning to take responsibility for their lives again, and are gaining skills in self-efficacy to promote their return to duty or to transition to veteran status in the community. Clinicians helping injured OIF and OEF veterans may use individual counseling interventions, which focus on an individual, strengths-based approach. The importance of this is that the injured service member is taught to identify and maximize key individual strengths that lead to self-acceptance, improved self-care and greater independence.

The Pathway Home

The last type of outdoor/adventure-based program is embedded as one component within the comprehensive array of services provided at a residential treatment center for OIF and OEF veterans. Thus, this is an example of how outdoor/adventure-based programs can be offered not as a "stand-alone" intervention, but as complementary to a more inclusive treatment approach. The Pathway Home is a non-profit, residential treatment home located in Yountville, California, designed to treat veterans of Afghanistan and Iraq who suffer from Post-Traumatic Stress Disorder, Traumatic Brain Injuries, Combat-Related Stress and other post-deployment adjustment problems. Pathways was founded by Fred Gusman in 2007, who previously served as Director of the PTSD Training Program at the Palo Alto Veterans Administration Medical Center. He is himself a veteran and works as a social worker (Gusman, personal communication, 2011).

The Pathway Home is innovative for three reasons: First, the treatment staff look at exposure to trauma within a developmental perspective. A developmental family history is conducted on each veteran/resident to assess what age-appropriate coping skills were learned during critical developmental milestones over the course of their life events. Using a balance between evidence-based practice and alternative/holistic treatment approaches, the veteran is provided with resiliency skills training based on maximizing individual strengths. The clinician explores the veteran's set of traumatic experiences over their lifetime, and trauma work is focused upon numerous and complex PTSD symptoms, utilizing intensive individual and group therapy sessions. This contrasts with the traditional therapeutic approach offered by the VA, wherein an evidence-based practice is used to work on only one specific issue throughout the course of a residential treatment stay. The developmental approach of trauma work and the program's flexibility mean that veterans are allowed to reside in Pathways longer than in VA residential treatment programs. This treatment approach also addresses the veteran and his/her family relationships. The veteran is given the opportunity to engage in couples and family therapy, allowing for the reunification of the family members with sessions for communication-building and conflict resolution.

Second, there is the use of alternate holistic modalities such as yoga, family dinners, bowling and fly fishing to assist the veteran in developing competencies. Yoga encourages skill building in pain management and development of relaxation skills. The deep breathing techniques required in yoga teach the veteran countermeasures for hypervigilance and irritability, deconstructing automatic responses wired from the combat zone and encouraging relaxation. Participation in fly fishing helps to develop patience, endurance and the use of fine motor skills.

Third, Pathways encourages its veterans to participate in community-based activities and volunteerism. Veterans attend family dinners with families outside the program, exercise at the local fitness center and bowl at the neighborhood bowling alley as a way to increase their sense of community belongingness. This helps to counter the belief system and perception of many redeployed veterans that civilian communities maintain a distance from and lack of understanding about their adjustment issues. Attending dinners with families and bowling in local alleys provides the veteran with exposures to guided "in vivo" systematic desensitization experiences in a real world setting. And interacting with civilian members in positive ways restructures the veteran's belief systems so that they see themselves as valued and acknowledged by civilian society.

Fourth, there is the use of new technologies, including texting and podcasts, to reach out to graduates of the program and ensure positive outcomes in their community readjustment. The texting program system, developed through a contract with Live Wire, enables the Pathway clinical staff to monitor their graduates' progress in the community by providing a daily text message requesting feedback as to how they are coping. If the veteran graduate responds by saying that they are in trouble, a message is sent back to alert treatment staff and their "Battle Buddies." This early warning texting system allows for the treatment staff to provide preventative interventions designed to head off potential cases of relapse in the community. Often, text alerts have enabled treatment staff to contact local veteran outpatient clinics to interface with veteran graduates who have admitted themselves for emergency mental health assessments. Treatment staff have, in the past, consulted with outside providers and transferred important clinical information about the veteran graduate, leading to a successful resolution of an otherwise difficult crisis situation.

Treatment implications

The value of the Pathway Program to the clinician treating veterans is in the approach of developing an individualized treatment plan using the balance between evidence-based practice and holistic/alternative healing modalities. With the combined use of evidence-based practice and holistic/alternate therapeutic interventions, the clinician can assist the veteran to cognitively reframe their distorted belief systems. With holistic approaches such as progressive relaxation techniques, the clinician can guide the veteran in counterconditioning the anxiety response when their thought processes are consumed with anxiety-producing thoughts.

Second, with regard to those veterans who have served multiple deployments in OIF or OEF, the clinician must be versatile in his/her treatment modalities in order to assist the veteran in processing multiple layers of unresolved PTSD symptoms. It is importance for the clinician to use a developmental model in order to explore with the veteran the chronological sequence of traumatic experiences over the course of his/her lifes. Collaboratively, the veteran and clinician can sort through the trauma work involving early childhood trauma, pre-military stressful life events and combat-related trauma to help the veteran identify unresolved issues, expose feelings and develop positive coping skills.

Third, and most effective, is the activation of new meanings derived from reconnecting the veteran with their significant other and family relationships. The provision of couples and family therapies allows for a template of family relational and communication skills that couples and families can use as a guide to transition the veteran back from combat skills to couples and family living skills.

Fourth, the clinician can assist the veteran in reconnecting with community citizens, which may readily contribute to social competence. OIF and OEF veterans often feel disconnected from mainstream society, which has largely been unaffected by the war. The clinician can mitigate this isolation by encouraging participation in volunteer activities that approximate soldiering skills, such as volunteering for a local Red Cross first aid training program. Volunteering with a community organization can increase the veteran's opportunities for positive social interaction and encourage the development of a belief that the world is a safer place.

Closing

This chapter has described innovative outdoor/adventure and community-based agencies that use resiliency skills approaches to promoting healing and reintegration. The individual levels are: discovering a new sense of purpose and meaning in life; development of realistic self-appraisal skills, the ability to maintain positive social relationships and the ability to use problem-solving skills to positively cope with crises in everyday life; and physical fitness. The family levels are: family communication; family coping mechanisms; and adapting to transitions. Community levels are: connections with individuals, community collaborations and working cohesively with others.

In view of the above resiliency skills, this chapter proposes that innovative outdoor/adventure and community-based programs are therapeutic supplements for evidence-based practices for service members and veterans. Cognitive-behavioral therapies are utilized with veterans to reduce combat-related anxiety, increase daily functioning, decrease negative self-talk and enhance coping abilities. In therapy, the clinician assists the veteran in constructing and implementing both imaginal and "in vivo" exposures to feared negative consequences; records, reviews and processes the responses; and provides feedback to facilitate improvement. The clinician is a personal resiliency coach who combines cognitive-behavioral therapy with an innovative outdoor/adventure program to challenge fearful self-talk and confront feared negative consequences, using "in vivo" exposures in an acceptable, non-stigmatizing approach. For example, a veteran who has avoidance behaviors related to traumatic associations with a firearm can participate in the deer hunt sponsored by the Paralyzed Veterans of America Shooting Sports Program. He/she can learn from an incident-free hunt to be de-conditioned from the intensity of feared negative consequences, that fear schemas can be replaced with more reality-based schemas and that confidence in coping with irrational fears can be improved.

Also, resiliency skills can be used to teach positive coping strategies in individual therapy sessions. The clinician can combine an individual therapy session for depression with the evidence-based practice of teaching the service member/veteran "problem-solving skills and how to positively cope with crisis in everyday life," which is a resiliency skill taught in Ocean Therapy.

In addition, clinicians can incorporate family-level resiliency skills in couples and family therapy sessions. Families often realign their family roles to accommodate a loved one with a traumatic amputation or physical injury. Resiliency skills included in programs such as Pathways and Warrior Transition Units focus on the teaching of emotional support, family communication and family coping skills in couples and family therapy, both of which encourage family reunification and strengthen bonds.

Further, clinicians can develop a preventative mental health training seminar for redeployed service members, veterans and their family members based upon resiliency skills identified earlier at the individual, family and community levels. These can be packaged as decompression seminars for service members and their families, conducted within 30 days of their redeployment from the combat zone or reintegration into the community. These preventative mental health seminars provide safe learning environments in which clinicians lead discussion groups that focus on the learning of stress inoculation skills.

Finally, it is very important to note that there are a number of service members and veterans who are resistant, if not unwilling, to utilize more traditional office-based mental health interventions or for whom such traditional interventions provide a limited level of healing. For such veterans, the special attraction of outdoor/adventure programs can provide a very appealing alternative or supplement for them to consider.

In conclusion, innovative outdoor adventure programs offer OEF, OIF and OND veterans and their family members treatment approaches that appeal to their learned military values of group cohesion and physical fitness. This stigma-free combination of treatment approaches, using personalized coaching of resiliency skills and adaptive outdoor/adventure sports equipment, offers survivors of combat trauma an emotional/physical fitness approach to multiplying strengths. The determination and resiliency learned in the military before the trauma can be identified and re-adapted for overcoming and healing traumatic injuries through innovative outdoor/adventure and community-based programs that enhance community reintegration skills.

LTC Valvincent Reyes, LCSW, worked as a coordinator and faculty member teaching military field education at the University of Southern California military social work and veteran services program for three and a half years. He is a former medical company commander and a social work officer who served for more than 23 years in the USAR, including deployment in Combat Stress Control (Afghanistan). He has worked extensively with PTSD and MST and was OIC of post-shooting debriefings and counseling services after the Fort Hood shooting in Texas majval@sbcglobal.net

References

Army Wounded Warrior Program (AW2) (n.d.). In *Wikipedia*. Retrieved from http://en.wikipedia.org/wiki/Army_Wounded_Warrior_Program

Burnham, M. A., Meredith, L. S., Tanielian, T. & Jaycox, L. H. (2009). Mental health care for Iraq and Afghanistan War Veterans. *Health Affairs, 28*(3), 771–782.

Caplan, P. J. (2011). *When Johnny and Jane Come Marching Home*. Cambridge, MA. The MIT Press.

Mansfield, J. (2008). *A Clinical Perspective History of Recreation Therapy*. Retrieved from www.recreationtherapy.com/history.ht

Hyer, L., Boyd, S., Burke, S., Scurfield, R. & Smith, S. (1996). Effects of Outward Bound experience as an adjunct to inpatient PTSD treatment of war veterans. *Journal of Clinical Psychology, 52*(3), 263–278.

Meredith, L., Sherbourne, C., Gaillot, S., Hansell, L., Ritschard, H., Parker, A. M. & Wren, G. (2011). *Promoting Psychological Resilience in the U.S. Military*. RAND Center for Military Health Policy Research. Retrieved from www.rand.org/content/dam/rand/pub

Paralyzed Veterans of America (2011). *Get Sports*. Retrieved from www.pva.org/site/c.ajIRK9NJLcU2E/L

Roman Empire (n.d.) In *Wikipedia*. Retrieved from http://en.wikipedia.org/wiki/Roman_Empire

Seligman, M., Steen, T., Park, N. & Peterson, C. (2005). Positive psychology progress: Empirical validation of interventions. *American Psychologist, 60*(5), 410–421.

Scurfield, R. M. (2004). *A Vietnam Trilogy. War Trauma and Post Traumatic Stress: 1968, 1989 & 2000*. New York, NY: Algora Publishing.

Scurfield, R. M. (2006). *Healing Journeys: Study Abroad with Vietnam Veterans*. New York, NY. Algora Publishing.

Scurfield, R. M., Wong, L. E. & Zeerocah, E. (1992). An evaluation of the impact of "helicopter ride therapy" for inpatient Vietnam veterans with war-related PTSD. *Military Medicine, 157*(2), 67–73.

Scurfield, R. M., Root, L. P. & Wiest, A. (2003). History lived and learned. Students and Vietnam veterans in an integrative study abroad course. *Frontiers. The International Journal of Study Abroad, IX,* 111–137.

Stannard, M. (2009, March 15). Amputee vets learn more than skiing. *San Francisco Chronicle*. Retrieved from www.sfgate.com/cgi-bin/article.cgi?f=/c/a/2009/03/14/MNKJ16E7Q4.DTL

VA Office of Public Health and Environmental Hazards (2010). *Analysis of VA Health Care Utilization among Operation Enduring Freedom (OEF) and Operation Iraqi Freedom (OIF) Veterans.*

Van Hook, M. P. (2008). *Social Work Practice with Families: A Resiliency-Based Approach*. Chicago, IL: Lyceum Books.

Williams, D. (2010, July). *Healing the physical injuries of war*. Veteran's Affairs Subcommittee on Health. Presented before the United States House of Representatives.

16 Artreach: Project America and other innovative models in civilian–military partnering

Christopher A. Morley, Susan M. Anderson and Christiane C. O'Hara

In order to wholly and holistically serve our military personnel, their families, and our military veterans in their ongoing sacrifices and transitions to home, communities must engage and build bridges among all Americans, both military and civilian. This rallying of relationship between military and civilian communities can be considered a "Circle of Healing" (Scurfield, 2006), which includes initiatives and partnerships established through public, private, non-profit, volunteer, corporate, veteran, and civic networking. This chapter illustrates the capacity of creative civilian programming, which can lead to local, statewide, national, and international partnerships to benefit the mental health and well-being of military personnel, veterans, their families and communities affected by war.

The ArtReach Foundation' is an example of how one person's vision led to the establishment of ArtReach: Project America, which uses the creative expressive arts to serve military personnel and veterans, their families, and their professional providers. Founded in 1999, ArtReach has contributed to the expansion of the Circle of Healing through the non-profit development and implementation of The ArtReach Model'. This model is a uniquely designed program which integrates multiple creative and expressive arts interventions (art, drama, movement/dance, music, and creative writing) in portable, cost-effective group workshops. Each workshop is led by a licenced and certified therapist, who establishes a "safe space" through setting boundaries, providing guidelines, and modeling behavior that immediately establishes emotional security and non-judgment amongst workshop participants, accomplishing this primarily through the use of metaphorical exercises. ArtReach also relies upon a unique Train-the-Trainer program that can build rapid expansion of programs through a community-based empowerment approach. To discuss how ArtReach and other community-based organizations achieve success, this chapter will describe: (1) the ArtReach Model' and methodology; (2) ArtReach domestic and international projects; (3) Cultural adaptation of the model to an initiative serving our United States military personnel, their families, and their supportive providers; (4) ArtReach local, regional, national, and international partnerships that promote community responsiveness to traumatized persons; and (5) other important novel civilian initiatives that complement and/or partner with government-driven programming.

The creative arts therapies

Creative arts therapies—or expressive arts therapies as they are often called—and meditation have traditionally been implemented and researched as discrete units of therapeutic intervention with traumatized individuals and groups. Peer reviewed, published studies have demonstrated that exposure to individual modalities (e.g. art alone or music alone) can alleviate symptoms of brain injury, physical illness, pain, stress and, more recently, combat and deployment-related stress, post-traumatic stress (disorder), and mild traumatic brain injury (mTBI). For example, research has demonstrated that art therapy is an effective intervention for adults and children with traumatic brain injury (David, 2000), dementia (Wood, 2002), pain management (Sexton-Radek, 1999; Trauger-Querry & Haghighi, 1999) and trauma (Anderson, 1995; Rothenbert, 1994). Guidelines have been published for art therapy interventions with combat related post-traumatic stress (Collie et al., 2006). Dance therapy research has demonstrated similar effectiveness with schizophrenia (e.g. Nagpal & Ruta, 1997), neurological insult (Berrol, Ooi & Katz, 1997), eating and body image disorders (De Tommasi, 1999; DuBose, 2001; Krantz, 1999), developmental disability (Reinemann, 1999), breast cancer (Sandel et al., 2005), psychiatric disorders (Koch, Morlinghaus & Fuchs, 2007; Stewart, 2009) and depression (Jeong, 2005). Dance groups have been demonstrated to improve overall physical condition in an elderly population (Hui, Chui & Woo, 2009) and dance and Tai Chi have demonstrated a significant positive effect on arthritis patients (Marks, 2005).

Music therapy research demonstrates efficacy for patients with brain injury (Knox & Jutai, 1996; Purdie, 1997) and stroke (Nayak *et al.*, 2000), attention deficit disorders (Pratt, Abel & Skidmore, 1995), pain (Good *et al.*, 2001; Presner *et al.*, 2001), immune disorders (Dileo Maranto, 1992) and physical trauma (Tanabe *et al.*, 2002). Creative writing therapy, in which patients write about traumatic experiences in either poetry or prose, has been demonstrated as a therapeutic tool across diverse clinical populations (Lepore, 1997; Pennebaker, 1997; Smith *et al.*, 2005; Smyth, 1998). Meditation, deep breathing, and mindfulness-based stress reduction research has demonstrated a significant contribution to reducing heart rate, anxiety, distractibility, and other symptoms of stress across medical and traumatized populations (Davidson *et al.*, 2003; Kabat-Zinn, 2003; Reinemann, 1998).

Drama therapy research has been demonstrated as an effective intervention with veterans diagnosed with combat-related post-traumatic stress (James & Johnson, 1997), as well as with the other populations described above (Landy, 2007, 1994; Jennings, 1994). Finally, participation in therapeutic groups has been shown to accelerate coping with the adjustment to significant life change

(Pennebaker, Colder & Sharp, 1990; Pennebaker & Francis, 1996; Petersson *et al.*, 2000). It is also effective with veterans diagnosed with post-traumatic stress disorder (Kanas, 2005; Schnurr *et al.*, 2003). While earlier research using integrated expressive therapies was demonstrated to be effective in the treatment of addictions (Johnson, 1990), this research is in its infancy. It holds promise in light of the body of research in each of the expressive arts therapies, and those calling for bridging expression in treatment (Robbins, 1997). In summary, the creative arts therapies

> offer considerable benefits to clients who have not fully benefited from traditional verbal therapies. It seems consistent with a holistic approach, an appreciation of mind–body integration, that these therapies would have a legitimate place in the treatment of mental health disorders, and may occupy an essential role in the treatment of trauma. (Crenshaw, 2006)

The ArtReach Model®

The ArtReach Model® incorporates four central components:

- Immersion of participants in homogenous, small groups for one to five consecutive days in a *workshop* format;
- Creation and maintenance of a *safe space* by at least two co-leader trainers who have completed the multi-phase, ArtReach Train-the-Trainer program;
- Work *in metaphor* using the creative arts to access participants' creativity and imagination, while protecting their deeply personal material and avoiding potential re-traumatization or vicarious trauma; and
- *Integrated use of creative expressive arts*, including art, drama, movement/dance, music, and creative writing, with incorporation of deep breathing, meditation and visualization in seamless transition from one modality to another.

Each of the creative art therapies and meditation demonstrate their individual contributions to healing and recovery from physical and emotional trauma. However, the ArtReach Model *incorporates all of these modalities* and invites participants to explore several mediums within a single workshop. This format allows participants' fluid movement from one creative art experience to another, minimizing negative responses to any single approach (e.g. "I can't draw" or "I don't write well"). The model encourages both mental and physical shifting: from internal (me) to external (us); silence (art, writing) to sound (music, reading aloud); and sitting (meditating, speaking) to moving (stretching, mirroring movements, dancing). When group members work within the creative arts around one or more themes selected by Trainer Leaders, this process holds trauma "in metaphor"—that is, in an image or idea that safely contains that which is too painful to directly access. This distancing and containment of trauma creates a place in which no individual participant needs to directly speak of or consciously access their memories. They can reframe their trauma in metaphor, perhaps "tell" pieces of their story, try new behaviors through guided experiences with each of the expressive arts, or connect with others in the safety of the small group.

When these modalities are integrated into an ArtReach workshop, together they contribute to the *creation of a safe space*, sufficient for each participant to move, meditate, imagine, create art, write, act, make music, and experience the power and personal meaning of metaphor in the presence of other participants. This integrated process contributes to building self-awareness without the requirement of discussing the specifics ("details") surrounding one's trauma(s). To best illustrate the process, art and poetry examples are presented below.

Generated within an hour into an ArtReach workshop, a combat veteran's drawing of himself as something in nature, which emerged during group guided meditation and visualization, depicts him alone, separate, a black spot in the universe—entitled "Black Hole in Sky."

Another combat veteran wrote a metaphorical poem during a free-form writing exercise about his individual artwork. The poem, written to develop and transform his metaphor from art to words, conveys powerful feelings within the metaphors of metal and ice:

Figure 16.1 "Black Hole in Sky." Used with permission.

I am the metal who shields all that
I'm supposed to protect
I am the boxer who keeps getting up no matter
how many times I get
knocked down
I am ice, I feel no pain or emotions.

Now I am worn out, I want to
protect but I'm too weak, I want
to get up but I can't,
I want to feel but I don't know how.

—Hugo Patrocinio, USMC (Ret.)

In each of the above cases, as in all ArtReach workshops, participants were invited, but not required, to display their art or read their creative writing aloud. Both the above combat veterans chose to share their work with the group. As is testament to the growth and building of group cohesion within the single workshop format, a group poem was scribed at the end of a workshop. This poem was created by having each participant speak one phrase that resonated from the day. The poem's metaphors speak of shared sorrow, hope, trust, and commemoration of that (and those) left behind. It also touches on a theme that emerges frequently in ArtReach workshops that often goes untouched in other therapeutic milieus: the aspects of the sacred (sanctuary, spirit) elements of healing.

The sacred space within—our journey
Finding the courage to write a new chapter
I see myself in the reflection pool in the sanctuary of the heart
Walk with me
There are no walls to keep us apart
Our hearts have to be together
Refreshed in the sweet waters of the river
Seeing inside the hollow places in my soul
It's OK to let in the light
Reaching out to help and to be helped
To let the light shine in the darkness
Blue
Time and space allow for this voice
Live in the layers of the sacred
We can do this together in the present
Trusting in the moment and what's beyond the moment
Gone, but never forgotten.

—Group poem, ArtReach Project America Veterans
and Clinicians Workshop, March 2009

This exercise in group poetry illustrates the bond which is created amongst group members during the ArtReach workshop process. It also demonstrates the power of risk-taking within the safe space. Risk-taking in the presence of others invites participants to engage in new experiences with others; to laugh and cry together. It allows for building trust with others. It aids accessing individual and group imagination, creativity and humor (known to often be buried or shelved during and after experiencing a traumatic event). Each of these experiences enhances healing and connection within a small community, opening up possibility and hope for participants.

The language of the model is normalizing ("we can laugh, imagine, play"), inclusive ("we are all in this together") and emphasizes individual and community health, rather than the isolation and stigmatization associated with mental illness (being a "patient" with "mental problems"). The message of ArtReach groups is one of connectedness and group empowerment ("we are not in this alone, we will take small risks, wonder together, and grow stronger"). ArtReach groups, through the use of training, workshops and retreats, move warriors, families, and civilians into a community-driven public health model of holistic care. This differentiation in language parallels recent efforts to promote mental health within the entire community and to encourage preventive health and wellness skill building.

ArtReach training programs and workshops are designed to match the culture, conditions, level of training, and resources available to professionals and clients in their local environments. ArtReach selects and trains indigenous professionals (educators, mental health workers, creative arts therapists, etc.) of a targeted population in order to build capacity and promote expansion. Thus, this Train-the-Trainer process selects and provides local trainers who are familiar with the local culture, arts and traditions, and who are best able to serve their own consumers.

The ArtReach Foundation, Inc.: Origin and international and domestic projects

ArtReach: Projects Bosnia (2000–5), Katrina (2005–6), Lebanon (2006–8), Jordan (2008–Present)

The ArtReach Foundation® was a response to one person's recognition of the need for healing among survivors of the Bosnian War (1992–1995). ArtReach launched its first international project in 2000—ArtReach: Project Bosnia—to address war trauma associated with human rights violations and ethnic cleansing. The initial goal was to train Bosnian educators and counselors in the use of art activities as emotionally reparative interventions to promote mental health and healing of traumatized Bosnian children. In 2001, the United States Army partnered with ArtReach to assist in the transport of five tons of arts supplies from Hunter Army Airfield, Georgia to Eagle Base,

Tuzla, Bosnia, following which the Army convoyed those supplies in-country. This humanitarian act marked ArtReach's first military–civilian partnership. Workshops were conducted with regional educators from over 100 government schools over a five-year period as a commitment made by ArtReach to the Bosnian national government.

During these years, ArtReach built what would become its global training standard and model, which now incorporates and integrates art therapy, drama therapy, creative writing, dance, music and movement. It also demonstrated the power and necessity of partnerships among non-profit and government agencies, businesses, educators, clinicians, and volunteers. Completion of the five-year pilot showed the sustainability of ArtReach training as a model that is culturally adaptable to global regions with traumatized populations. Finally, the pilot demonstrated the capacity to develop and implement a non-profit international program solely on private donations.

The development and replication of the success of the Train-the-Trainer model evolved from subsequent ArtReach domestic and international projects with civilian adult and child populations impacted by natural disaster (Katrina) and war (Lebanon, Jordan). Project Katrina was established in 2005 to serve children and families suffering from the effects of trauma as a result of natural disaster (Hurricane Katrina) and who were displaced into Arkansas and Georgia. As in Bosnia, this project emphasized the use of creative arts within educational settings to promote healing of children. In addition, ArtReach professional teams also trained boys' and girls' club staff members working with these children using the model.

In 2006, ArtReach established the ArtReach Institute to replicate the Train-the-Trainer model used in Bosnia with educators in Lebanon, who subsequently trained an additional 150 educators from the region. This was the first ArtReach community-replicated intervention by indigenous educators to benefit school children and refugees suffering from war-related violence and displacement.

ArtReach: Project Jordan began with an invitation from His Royal Highness, El Hassan bin Talal of Jordan to help address the growing needs of Jordanian educators and NGO workers serving displaced Iraqi youth and their families. Jordanian educators were facing an influx of resettled Iraqi children who were being admitted into public schools and/or residing in refugee camps (Weiss Fagen, 2009; Rozokhi *et al.*, 2006; UNICEF, 2011). Most of these refugee children were functioning in a "survival mode" and experiencing overwhelming uncertainty and instability (Weine *et al.*, 2004). ArtReach conducted its first workshops in Jordan in 2008. In 2010, with the support of the King Abdullah II Fund for Development, and partnerships with the Jordan Museum, Jordan National Gallery, Royal Society of Fine Arts Jordan, and the Olive Tree Initiative, ArtReach launched its Middle East Institute. ArtReach is now an officially registered Jordanian NGO, continuing to build its local presence to train educators and health care professionals to promote healing, empowerment, and peace.

ArtReach: Project America (2009–Present)

The ArtReach Foundation's volunteers, professionals and clinicians have served in both international and domestic programs incorporating the model for well over a decade. During this time, United States military personnel have faced their own war trauma (Bisson et al., 2007; Levy & Sidel, 2008; Tanielian & Jaycox, 2008). Their families, children and healthcare providers have also faced secondary trauma, commonly associated with exposure to and support of Wounded Warriors (Figley, 1995). In early 2009, the founder of ArtReach, who has multi-generational family ties to the military, recognized the need to initiate a new ArtReach domestic project to serve the public health needs of military communities—military personnel, former combat veterans, their families, and their healthcare providers—experiencing combat stress, post-traumatic stress, stressful transitions (often related to deployments) and provider compassion fatigue and burnout (Valent, 1995).

As ArtReach is headquartered in Georgia and because of the state's high rate of deployments, Georgia was identified as the location to initiate a pilot project to test the cultural adaptability of the ArtReach model to our military personnel and veterans. The model offers an intervention that matches our U.S. military's move toward a public health model, while offering a complementary intervention (creative and expressive arts in groups) for those already in individual mental health treatment. ArtReach workshops, held in community settings for families and clinicians, as well as military personnel, also provide an alternative for military personnel who wish to avoid stigmatization, change in status, and removal of security clearances that may follow their admission of need/request for help to deal with the stressors of repeated deployments and/or combat.

In its first three years, ArtReach: Project America produced Trainer Teams of creative and expressive arts therapists, licensed mental health professionals, and veterans. ArtReach workshops have been conducted for active duty military and veteran populations suffering from combat stress, post-traumatic stress, traumatic brain injury, and illness. From the beginning, ArtReach: Project America recognized the vulnerability of family members and military service providers to secondary trauma, and has conducted workshops for families and providers. The need to adapt the ArtReach model across generations and degrees of trauma was also essential in program development as older veterans approached ArtReach for healing from war trauma.

As the model was adapted specifically for ArtReach: Project America, it was expanded to include veterans from earlier and current wars as Veteran Peer Trainers. Their inclusion has assisted in the rapid building of trust in the team by this traumatized population, enhancing a sense of safety and camaraderie ("I've got your back" or "I understand"). Their participation as trainers along with non-veteran or civilian trainers mirrors the possibility of reconciliation among veterans and civilians, listening, forgiveness, and long overdue welcoming home of veterans who have been caught in anger and silence.

It also offers an opportunity for disabled or retired veterans to continue their service to their comrades. In the words of an ArtReach trainer and Purple Heart recipient:

> Never in my life did I think I would be doing this kind of work… art never really played a big part in my life. I was never a guy who wrote poems, or painted, or acted in plays. After these workshops I feel like a weight has been lifted off my back. I don't have to exactly tell all the things that have happened, but with the metaphor, they get out. I am part of the team working directly with other veterans.… This is a way for me to stay connected and still serve the military, other veterans, Americans.

The intergenerational connections among veterans who need to heal from combat can best be illustrated through a six-foot-long mural created by veterans from the Vietnam War, the Gulf War, and Operation Iraqi Freedom, all of whom participated in an ArtReach Project America workshop. Their mural, entitled War Panorama, includes words of war as well as images of fire, smoke, chaos and camaraderie that civilians can only imagine.

In addition, spouses and adult family members of veterans are also in training to serve as co-leader trainers for military spouse, couple and family workshops. Families have their own experiences of fear, loss and sacrifice. This trainer program expansion to include military family members will build capacity and enhance a rapid multiplier effect (ergo, the ability to gain multiplicative expansion through community integration) which is much needed from a public health perspective due to the numbers of our military personnel, veterans, families and communities in need of healing.

As military mental health personnel cannot meet the current and projected needs of our troops needing post-deployment interventions, civilian professionals and veterans will need training in culture-specific military

Figure 16.2 "War Panorama." Six-foot mural completed by OEF/OIF/Vietnam veterans. Used with permission.

trauma. Training for participation as a trainer in ArtReach: Project America is conducted over several phases. It requires the completion of multiple experiential workshops and training modules. These modules include trainer self-awareness, ethics, military culture (including the impact of deployment and combat on families as well as military personnel), group leadership, creative arts interventions, and symptoms and consequences of post-traumatic stress, traumatic brain injury, secondary trauma and burnout.

In conducting workshops, ArtReach Trainers have recognized the specific vulnerability not only of military personnel who have been repeatedly deployed in combat conditions, but also first responders in theater and in hospital settings: medics, nurses and physicians, behavioral health staff and chaplains (Hayes, 2009; Levy *et al.*, 2011; Stewart, 2009). These groups, in particular, need complementary treatment options, such as ArtReach workshops, in order to maintain the resilience, energy and capacity to continue their ongoing Force Health Protection endeavors. Figure 16.3, entitled Metaphor in Clay Containers, illustrates the forms that were generated by a group of military mental health providers when each was given clay to work with in freeform fashion until an object emerged. Note that several containers and an anchor represent metaphors that emerged among these caretakers.

This metaphor of what a container represents is a powerful, multi-layered issue for military first responders, chaplains and mental health providers.

Figure 16.3 "Metaphor in Clay, Containers." Used with permission.

Trainers have also seen the value of workshops and retreats for military families, in particular Wounded Warrior Families and families of repeatedly deployed personnel. These opportunities give families time to reconnect to one another, to witness one another's imaginations at work, to partner in play, storytelling, art, drama, music, movement, and dance, and to create positive memories. The ArtReach collaboration with the Fort Gordon Warrior Transition Battalion (WTB) has led to the Fort Gordon Warrior Transition Battalion Family Retreat Model (Clow *et al.*, 2011), an example of a military–civilian partnership that incorporates multi-dimensional programming (ArtReach, Military Chaplain Strong Bonds program), cross-disciplinary faculty (ArtReach: Project America Trainers, Operation Military Kids volunteers) and an integrated workshop agenda (outdoor team building, recreational activities). ArtReach trainers collaborate with retreat staff to incorporate metaphor into family introductions (for example, choosing a nature name for the retreat), conduct rituals around the campfire, encourage creative writing, and lead family storytelling. The Fort Gordon WTB model balances the Mind-Body-Spirit-Heart health of families and promotes the core messages of "we are not alone" and "we can still have fun"—themes shared by ArtReach.

A major program goal of ArtReach: Project America is expansion to all military installations, Guard and Reserves Units, and Veterans Administration Medical Centers. The model's portability, inexpensive materials, Train-the-Trainer multiplier effect, and workshop structure all serve to enhance attendance by military personnel, families and clinicians who are short on time and avoidant of mental health diagnoses and clinics. To accomplish this goal, research protocols are in development to demonstrate the efficacy of the work not only with at-risk groups (including traumatized veterans, families and providers) but also with military personnel prior to deployment as a means to provide emotional tools for self-awareness, decompression and communication during and after deployment.

To develop its vision and fund its research and training, ArtReach: Project America has developed a large network of referrals, funders and creative arts initiatives. Varied and diverse partnerships from Kiwanis International to Georgia Shakespeare Company to the Atlanta Public Library, in addition to the many private donors and foundations, have made ArtReach programming successful. This cooperative and multi-disciplinary network builds the capacity and success of ArtReach: Project America. It also helps to inform civilians at local, regional and national levels of our U.S. military's growing needs. This expansive network encourages ongoing partners to respond in ways specific to their unique skills, time, and finances. These partnerships demonstrate to military personnel and families that they are appreciated and are being offered thanks, services and assistance in return. This, in itself, is a form of ritualization, which many current veterans and service practitioners feel has been lost over time. Rituals have been described as a means of personal and social transformation, giving back to an individual after trauma/loss a sense of power, meaning and direction (Clarke, 2008). As a nation, we must restore rituals of acknowledgement and create opportunities to build healing. In the words of a veteran who attended an ArtReach Conference in July 2011:

> The Welcome Home ritual you conducted for all of us veterans at the end of the day was the first time in the six years since I left the service that I have been publicly thanked for my service. It meant a lot.

In addition to the many agencies that work together to enhance the work of ArtReach, the foundation's Board of Directors and many volunteers add to its capacity to educate civilians. Despite the continuing belief that most civilians remain unaware and unconcerned about the strain on our military personnel from repeated deployments and long wars, many civilians seek opportunities to use their skills and time to contribute to the health of the military community and the community at large.

As a component to the overall ArtReach global mission, ArtReach: Project America is indicative of the partnerships that build lasting bridges between populations, encourage ownership and empowerment within communities, and impress upon those communities the need for responsiveness to underserved groups. Partnerships maximize our resources and skills and provide that important link between military and civilian communities.

Research directions: The future of interventions like ArtReach

Integration of the creative and expressive arts therapies into formalized professional curricula is now in a period of dramatic growth: several graduate programs offer advanced degrees in creative arts therapies; the International Expressive Arts Therapy Association was founded in 1994 (www.ieata.org); and an annual international Expressive Arts Summit was initiated in 2010 (www.summit/expressivemedia.org). Following the National Institutes of Health official designation of three primary creative arts therapies (art, music and dance) as complementary to standards of clinical care (Pratt, 2004), research has expanded from efficacy only, to include more program-oriented objectives such applicability and scope. The limits of capability, applicability and adaptability are new foci within creative arts therapy research.

As a leading example of the use of combinatorial therapy, the ArtReach model matches this research trend in its emphasis on ethnographic relevance (i.e. how its intervention programming can be adapted both in format, culture and scope). A central research question that ArtReach targets is: to what degree, and under what circumstances, can creative arts therapies demonstrate positive outcomes for their participants? Research has, until recently, been limited to collecting anecdotal evidence via structured post-workshop interviews (Kempler & Davidson, 2008) and structured participant pre-, post- and follow-up measures using Likert Scale ratings and qualitative analyses of responses to open-ended questions (ongoing internal ArtReach program evaluation). As a public health program for health and healing using creative arts, ArtReach continues to build its capacity for scaling program scope and portability. Through partnerships with research institutions, creative arts interventions like ArtReach continue to develop more rigorous, evidence-based practices. Such research can demonstrate that structured use of the creative arts therapies in clinical settings may increase the capacity, resilience and well-being of our military personnel, their families, their healthcare team and communities at large. The first National Summit on Arts in Healing for Warriors, held in Bethesda, Maryland in late 2011 and sponsored by the Society for the Arts in Healthcare, is an indicator of hope for more collaborative efforts on behalf of our military personnel and veterans in the future.

Other civilian/military partnership models

Creative arts models: Theater

Theater of War is a New York-based production sponsored by Outside the Wire, LLC, a social impact company that uses theater and a variety of other media to address pressing public health issues, such as combat-related psychological injury. Theater of War Artistic Director, Bryan Doerries, and Producing Director, Phyllis Kaufman have staged dramatic readings of Sophocles' plays, including Ajax and Philocetes, for more than 30,000 military personnel and civilians at military sites under a contract with the Defense Centers of Excellence for Psychological Health and Traumatic Brain Injury. Pre-selected panel members, then the audience, participate in a "town hall" discussion following the presentation. These performances aim to increase awareness of post-deployment psychological health and the challenges faced by service members, veterans, their caregivers and their families. Theater of War has partnered with regional theaters/universities to expand its audience to more civilians and regionalize its performances. This initiative includes collaboration with the United Service Organization (USO) and support from The Stavros Foundation.

Creative arts models: Film and television

Filmmakers have produced fiction and documentary films that can have a wide impact on civilian audiences. For many, these are their primary connection to the impact of war. Recent fictional films include *Hurt Locker* (2010) and *The Messenger* (2009). Documentary films include *Restrepo* (2010) and *The War Tapes* (2006). The mini-series *Generation Kill* (2008), based on a journalist's recollections of the U.S. Marine invasion of Iraq in 2003 (Wright, 2004), brings modern American military combat into civilians' homes through cable television. *Taking Chance* (2010) illustrates the impact on a Marine of accompanying home the body of a fellow Marine killed in action. Such films, and the yearly GI Film Festival in Washington, DC, serve to expand dialogue between civilians and veterans on what war trauma means, and how to define communal responsibility in healing the wounds of war.

Creative arts models: Writing

Troops and veterans have been writing about war experiences for centuries. In 2004, The National Endowment for the Arts initiated Operation Home-coming, a writing project for troops and family members for instruction in writing their stories, thoughts and feelings about deployment, separation and other war-related issues in real time. With the support of The Boeing Company, and cooperation of the Department of Defense, distinguished writers at military installations in the United States and Europe conducted 50 writing workshops. When invitations were extended to those who participated to submit their writing to be considered for publication, Operation Homecoming directors received over 10,000 pages of submissions, ultimately publishing 100 edited stories in Operation Homecoming (Carroll, 2006). Such writing continues to be encouraged through such efforts as The Legacy Project (war-letters.com). The Legacy Project is a nationwide volunteer effort to collect and preserve veterans' letters and emails. Along these same lines, the Veterans Writing Project (veteranswriting.org), a non-profit based in Washington, DC, offers war writing seminars and workshops for veterans, by veterans.

Regional efforts to encourage writing include Warrior Writers, a grassroots group "that provides tools and space for community building, healing and redefinition for veterans of the Global War on Terror" (Warrior Writers Project, 2011). Its Veterans and Community Conference: Coming Home through Art and Dialogue, held in 2011, expanded its vision to include visual arts and drama. These efforts encourage direct storytelling and allow for reframing of war experiences, two critical elements of healing from war trauma, through creative writing and other forms of artistic expression. They parallel key elements of healing from war trauma that define The ArtReach Model.

Creative arts models: Competitions

Local, regional and national competitions are held in specific creative arts domains, such as photography, painting and poetry. One such competition is the National Veterans Creative Arts Competition and Festival. This competition begins with local-level competitions through Veterans Administration Medical Centers, ultimately leading up to the national festival, held in a different location each year. The purpose of this competition is to recognize veterans for their creative accomplishments and to educate and demonstrate to communities throughout the country the therapeutic benefits of the arts.

Each year, up to 3,500 veterans enter the competition and more than 100 receive invitations to exhibit their place-winning artwork, music, dance, and dramatic or original writing selections.

Collaborative networking models: State, business, research and community

State and regional networking efforts are emerging to connect military personnel and civilians with resources. The Georgia Paving the Way Home for Veterans Initiative, for example, is a network of state agencies, Veterans Administration representatives, military personnel, nonprofits, mental health professionals, faith communities, and other interested parties which has identified several targeted goals for the state to coordinate efforts to meet the needs of our military and veteran families. Local and regional businesses in some communities have initiated the "Round Table" concept of monthly meetings to network supportive services and meet the needs of veterans returning to the community. Examples include the Atlanta Business Round Table (initiated by a U.S. Marine), and corporate projects/foundations/funding partnerships such as The Lockheed Foundation. Research collaborations have also been initiated that educate civilians about the needs of our veterans and raise funds for research while they are viewing sports and entertainment. The Red Sox Foundation, supporting research on traumatic brain injury, combat trauma, and other military-related injuries was one of the first such collaborations with several research facilities in Boston.

Community-based models: Veteran, civic and faith

Community-based organizations have long supported our veterans, and Veterans Service Organizations such as the Veterans of Foreign Wars, American Legion and Patriot Guard continue to be a place of welcome and safety for our newest veterans. In addition, other groups often have veteran members who encourage initiatives for their brethren in need:

- Kiwanis Rotary and other civic groups sponsor camps and offer grants to nonprofits serving our veterans.
- Initiatives that coordinate faith community education and programs to welcome veterans have begun to expand. One example, Care for The Troops (www.careforthetroops.org), engages and trains faith communities in how to be military friendly.
- Organizations such as 4H, through land grant universities, have developed programs such as Operation Military Kids at local and state levels to benefit military children. These programs offer camps, Hero Packs and other supportive services.

Social media, websites and technology

Social media offers veterans a way to stay in touch with each other after their service has ended. Such support can be instantaneous and possible from great distances. Social media outlets such as Facebook and Twitter, with their capacity for micro-blogging and rapid information/photo sharing, have changed fundraising efforts for veteran groups, as well. Additionally, most organizations now connect veterans to other veterans through national websites. For example, Iraq and Afghanistan Veterans of America, Vietnam Veterans of America and the Wounded Warrior Project can connect veterans, galvanize them for political and social action, and offer support and resources. Veterans, military families, and civilians can communicate through websites and blogs, building networks for specific needs, e.g. military child needs (Military Child Education Coalition, www.militarychild.org), expressive arts options (www.artreachprojectamerica.com) and job searches (www.herohealthhire.org, www.vetjobs.com). Expanded technology also allows wounded and ill veterans to participate in telemedicine programs (communication with medical personnel via cell phone or webcam). Finally, military and military-friendly organizations have made available smartphone applications, which help military personnel to manage stress and the coping process (e.g. TATRC, www.patriotoutreach.org).

Closing

ArtReach: Project America represents a community-oriented resiliency initiative that expands the Circle of Healing and provides a de-stigmatizing intervention to military personnel, families, and providers. It offers an alternative health intervention that can be implemented within or outside of mental health settings, the latter removing the stigmatization of psychiatric diagnoses in military medical records. For those already receiving mental health treatment, it offers a complementary intervention, using metaphor work to reconnect to self, others, and community after war.

ArtReach: Project America and other innovative public health interventions can and do make a considerable difference in the healing process of our military personnel and their families. There continues to be a divide, however, between our military and civilian communities, especially with regard to ideas and techniques for building community-level cooperation. Both military and civilian partners must work together to bridge that gap through reframing our stories, building community, accessing our imaginations, and finding our paths to our best selves. The Circle of Healing resides within oneself and one's family, and families reside within communities. Healing communities will strengthen us individually, as a nation, and as a world.

Christopher A. Morley, MPH, is a Board Director with The ArtReach Foundation, Inc.® He served nine years in the United States Marine Corps before working in the field of international trauma and completing his MPH at Emory University, Atlanta. His areas of interest include global health research, clinical trial study design and global project management, specializing in global mental health. As a veteran, he recognizes the public health needs of our combat veterans and their families (Christopher@artreachfoundation.org).

Susan M. Anderson founded The ArtReach Foundation, Inc.®, an international non-profit dedicated to children and adults recovering from the trauma of war, violence or natural disaster, in 1999. Ms. Anderson initiated ArtReach:Project America in 2009 in response to the mental health needs of U.S. military personnel, veterans, their families and their professional providers. She was recently was selected as 2011 Purpose Prize Fellow by Civic Ventures for her work as a social innovator (susan@artreachfoundation.org).

Christiane O'Hara, Ph.D., is a retired neuropsychologist who serves as Co-Chair of ArtReach: Project America for The ArtReach Foundation, Inc.˚ She is a Red Cross volunteer and a Consulting Psychologist in the Functional Recovery Program at the Traumatic Brain Injury Clinic, Dwight David Eisenhower Medical Center, Fort Gordon, and with the USO Georgia. She has three sons, one of whom serves in the United States Army (coseifring@bellsouth.net).

References

Anderson, F. E. (1995). Catharsis and empowerment through group clay work with incest survivors. *Arts in Psychotherapy, 22*(5), 413–437.

Berrol, C. F., Ooi, W. L. & Katz, S. S. (1997). Dance/movement therapy with older adults who have sustained neurological insult: A demonstration project. *The American Journal of Dance Therapy, 19*(2), 135–160.

Bisson, J., Ehlers, A., Matthews, R., Pilling, S., Richards, D. & Turner, S. (2007). Psychological treatments for chronic post-traumatic stress disorder: Systematic review and meta-analysis. *British Journal of Psychiatry, 190*, 97–104.

Carroll, E. (Ed.) (2006). *Operation Homecoming: Iraq, Afghanistan, and the Home Front, in the Words of U.S. Troops and Their Families.* New York, NY: Random House.

Clarke, J. J. (2008). Ritual: A mythic means of personal and social transformation. Dissertation, Pacifica Graduate Institute, Santa Barbara, California. UMI 3318838.

Clow, S., Storey, R., Vicars, C., O'Hara, C., Brown, B. (2011). *Fort Gordon Warrior Transition Battalion Family Retreat Model.* Presentation at DOD/USDA National Military Family Resilience Conference, Chicago, Illinois.

Collie, K., Backos, A., Malchiodi, C. & Spiegal, D. (2006). Art therapy for combat related PTSD: Recommendations for research and practice. *Art Therapy: Journal of the American Art Therapy Association, 23*(4), 157–164.

Crenshaw, D. (2006). Neuroscience and trauma treatment. In L. Carey (Ed.), *Expressive and Creative Arts Methods for Trauma Survivors.* Philadelphia, PA: Jessica Kingsley Publishers (pp. 21–38).

David, I. R. (2000). An exploration of the role of art as therapy in rehabilitation from traumatic brain injury. *Dissertation Abstracts International: Section B: The Sciences and Engineering*, 60(8-B), 3894.

Davidson, R. J., Kabat-Zinn, J., Schumacher, J., Rosenkranz, M., Muller, D., Santorelli, S. F., Urbanowski, F., Harrington, A., Bonus, K. & Sheridan, J. F. (2003). *Alterations in brain and immune function produced by mindfulness meditation. Psychosomatic Medicine*, 65, 564–570.

De Tommasi, V. (1999). Dance movement therapy (DMT) and eating disorders: A possible method of approach. *Methods of Research and Clinical Experience*, 6(12), 129–145.

Dileo Maranto, C. (1992). Music in the treatment of immune-related disorders. In R. Spintge & R. Droh (Eds.), *Music Medicine*. St. Louis, MO: Barcelona Publishers (pp. 142–154).

DuBose, L. R. (2001). Dance/movement treatment perspectives. In J. J. Robert-McComb (Ed.), *Eating Disorders in Women and Children: Prevention, Stress Management, and Treatment* . Boca-Raton, FL: CRC Press (pp. 373-385).

Figley, C. (Ed.) (1995). *Compassion Fatigue: Coping With Secondary Traumatic Stress Disorder In Those Who Treat The Traumatized*. London: Brunner-Routledge.

Good, M., Stanton-Hicks, M., Grass, J. A., Anderson, G. C., Lai, H. L. & Roykulcharoen, V. (2001). Relaxation and music to reduce postsurgical pain. *Journal of Advanced Nursing*, 33(2), 208–215.

Hayes, M. (2009). *Compassion Fatigue in the Military Caregiver*. U.S. Army War College, Carlisle Barracks, PA. Strategy Research Paper.

Hui, E., Chui, B. & Woo, J. (2009). Effects of dance on physical and psychological well-being in older persons. *Archives of Gerontology and Geriatrics, 49*, e45–50.

James, M. & Johnson, D. R. (1997). Drama therapy in the treatment of combat-related PTSD. *The Arts in Psychotherapy, 23*(5), 383–395.

Jennings, S., Cattanach, A. Mitchell, S., Chesner, A. & Meldrum, B. (1994). *The Handbook of Drama Therapy*. New York, NY: Routledge.

Jeong, Y. (2005). Dance movement therapy improves emotional responses and modulated neurohormones in adolescents with mild depression. *International Journal of Neuroscience, 115*, 1711–1720.

Johnson, L. (1990). Creative therapies in the treatment of addictions. *The Arts in Psychotherapy, 17*, 299–308.

Kabat-Zinn, J. (2003). *Mindfulness-based interventions in context: Past, present and future. Clinical Psychology Science Practice, 10*, 144–156.

Kanas, N. (2005). Group psychotherapy for patients with chronic trauma-related stress disorders. *International Journal of Group Psychotherapy, 55*(1), 161–165.

Kempler, B. & Davidson, M. (2008). Research and evaluation of ArtReach JOHUD & Lebanon Workshops. Unpublished Manuscript.

Knox, R. & Jutai, J. (1996). Music-based rehabilitation of attention following brain injury. *Canadian Journal of Rehabilitation.* 9(3):169–181.

Koch, S. C., Morlinghaus K. & Fuchs, T. (2007). The joy dance: Specific effects of a single dance intervention on psychiatric patients with depression. *The Arts in Psychotherapy, 34*, 340–349.

Krantz, A. M. (1999). Growing into her body: Dance/movement therapy for women with eating disorders. *The American Journal of Dance Therapy, 21*(2), 81–103.

Landy, R. J. (1994). *Drama Therapy: Concepts, Theories, and Practices* (2nd Ed.). New York, NY: Charles Thomas.

Landy, R. J. (2007). *The Couch and the Stage: Integrating Words and Actions in Psychotherapy.* New York, NY: Rowan and Littlefield/J. Aronson.

Lepore, S. (1997). Expressive writing moderates the relation between intrusive thoughts and depressive symptoms. *Journal of Personality and Social Psychology*, 73(5), 1030–1037.

Levy, B. S. & Sidel, V. W. (2008). The Iraq War. In B. S. Levy & V. W. Sidel (Eds.), *War and Public Health.* New York, NY: Oxford University Press (pp. 243-263).

Levy, H. C., Conoscenti, L. M., Tillery, J. F., Dickstein, B. D. & Litz, B. T. (2011). Deployment stressors and outcomes among Air Force chaplains. *Journal of Traumatic Stress*, 24, 342–346.

Marks, R. (2005). Dance-based exercise and Tai Chi and their benefits for people with arthritis: A review. *Health Education*, 5(105), 374–391.

Nagpal, M. & Ruta, A. M. (1997). Joy in schizophrenia through dance/movement therapy. *American Journal of California Alliance for Mental Illness*, 8(3), 53–55.

Nayak, S., Wheeler, B. L., Shiflett, S. C. & Agostinielli, S. (2000). Effect of music therapy on mood and social interaction among individuals with acute traumatic brain injury and stroke. *Rehabilitation Psychology*, 45(3), 274–283.

Pennebaker, J. W. (1997). Writing about emotional experiences as a therapeutic process. *Psychological Science*, 8, 162–166.

Pennebaker, J. W. & Francis, M. E. (1996). Cognitive, emotional, and language processes in disclosure. *Cognition & Emotion*, 10, 601–626.

Pennebaker, J. W., Colder, M. & Sharp, L. K. (1990). Accelerating the coping process. *Journal of Personality and Social Psychology*, 58, 528–537.

Petersson, L. M., Berglund, G., Brodin, O., Glimelius, B. & Sjoeden, P. O. (2000). Group rehabilitation for cancer patients: Satisfaction and perceived benefits. *Patient Education and Counseling*, 40, 219–229.

Pratt, R. R. (2004). Art, dance, and music therapy. *Physical Medicine and Rehabilitation Clinics of North America*, 15, 827–841.

Pratt, R. R., Abel, H. H. & Skidmore, J. (1995). The effects of neurofeedback with background music on EEG patterns of ADD and ADHD children. *International Journal of Arts Medicine*, 4(1), 24–31.

Presner, J. D., Yowler, C. J., Smith, L. F., Steele, A. L. & Fratianne, R. B. (2001). Music therapy for assistance with pain and anxiety management in burn treatment. *Journal of Burn Care*, 22(1), 83–88.

Purdie, H. (1997). Music therapy in neurorehabilitation: Recent developments and new challenges. *Critical Reviews in Physical Rehabilitation Medicine*, 9(3/4), 205–217.

Reinemann, D. (1998). ROM dance: A treatment for symptoms of depression and anxiety in adults with mental retardation. *Dissertation Abstracts International: Section B: The Sciences and Engineering*, 60(3-B), 1051.

Robbins, A. (Ed.) (1997). *Therapeutic Presence: Bridging Expression and Form.* London: Jessica Kingsley.

Rothenberg, E. D. (1994). Bereavement intervention with vulnerable populations: A case report on group work with the developmentally disabled. *Social Work Groups*, 17(3), 61–75.

Rozokhi, A. H., Taha, I. K., Taib, N. I., Sadik, S. & Gasseer, N. A. (2006). Mental health of Iraqi children. *The Lancet*, 368, 838–839.

Sandel, S., Judge, J., Landry, N., Faria, L., Ouellette, R. & Majczak, M. (2005). Dance and movement program improves quality-of-life measures in breast cancer survivors. *Cancer Nursing, 28*(4), 301–309.

Schnurr, P., Friedman, M., Foy, D., Shea, M., Hsieh, F., Lavori, P., Glynn, S., Melissa Wattenberg, M. & Bernardy, N. (2003). randomized trial of trauma-focused group therapy for posttraumatic stress disorder. *Archives of General Psychiatry, 60,* 481–489.

Scurfield, R. M. (2006). *War Trauma: Lessons Unlearned from Vietnam to Iraq.* New York, NY: Algora Press.

Sexton-Radek, K. (1999). Interplay of art making practices and migraine headache pain experience. *Headache Quarterly: Current Treatment and Research, 10*(4), 287–291.

Smith, S., Anderson-Hanley, C., Langrock, A. & Compas, B. (2005). The effects of journaling for women with newly diagnosed breast cancer. *Psychooncology, 14*(12), 1075–1082.

Smyth, J. M. (1998). Written emotional expression: Effect sizes, outcome types, and moderating variables. *Journal of Consulting and Clinical Psychology, 66,* 174–184.

Stewart, D. W. (2009). Casualties of war: Compassion fatigue and health care providers. *Medsurg Nursing, 18*(2), 91–94.

Tanabe, P., Perket, K., Thomas, R., Paice, J. & Marcantonio, R. (2002). The effects of standard care, ibuprofen, and distraction on pain relief and patient satisfaction in children with musculoskeletal trauma. *Journal of Emergency Nursing, 28*(2), 118–125.

Tanielian, T. & Jaycox, L. H. (Eds.) (2008). *Invisible Wounds of War: Psychological and Cognitive Injuries, Their Consequences, and Services to Assist in Recovery.* Santa Monica, CA: RAND Corporation.

Trauger-Querry, B. & Haghighi, K. R. (1999). Balancing the focus: Art and music therapy for pain control and symptom management in hospice care. *Hospice Journal, 14*(1), 25–38.

United Nations Children's Fund (UNICEF) (2011). *Humanitarian Action for Children: Building Resilience.* New York, NY: UNICEF. Retrieved from www.unicef.org/emerg/files/HAC2011_EN_PDA_web.pdf

Valent, P. (1995). Survival strategies: A framework for understanding secondary traumatic stress and coping in helpers. In C. R. Figley (Ed.), *Compassion Fatigue: Coping with Secondary Traumatic Stress Disorder in Those Who Treat the Traumatized.* New York, NY: Routledge Press (pp. 21–50).

Warrior Writers Project (2011). Retrieved from www.warriorwriters.org

Weine, S., Feethham, S., Kulauzovic, Y., Besic, S., Lezic, A., Mujagic, A., Muzurovic, J., Spahovic, D., Zhubi, M., Rolland, J. & Pavkovic, I. (2004). Bosnian and Kosovar refugees in the United States: Family interventions in a services framework. In K. E. Miller & L. M. Rasco (Eds.), *The Mental Health of Refugees: Ecological Approaches to Healing and Adaptation.* Mahwah, NJ: Psychology Press (pp. 263-293).

Weiss Fagen, P. (2009). *Iraqi Refugees: Seeking Stability in Syria and Jordan.* Institute for the Study of International Migration, Georgetown University and the Center for International and Regional Studies, Georgetown University School of Foreign Service in Qata. Retrieved from http://www12.georgetown.edu/sfs/isim/Publications/PatPubs/Iraqi%20Refugees.pdf

Wood, M. (2002). Researching art therapy with people suffering from AIDS-related dementia. *Arts in Psychotherapy, 29*(4), 207–219.

Wright, E. (2004). *Generation Kill.* New York, NY: G. Putnam & Sons.

17 Military chaplains' roles in healing: "Being here and there"

LTC (RET) Charles Purinton (OEF-OIF)

Blessings on your work!
Charles M. Purinton, jr

This chapter is written to increase understanding of the opportunities for creative healing of traumatic experience through spiritual growth. This is accomplished, in part, by describing the role of a chaplain in the military and the personal experiences of the author as a military chaplain. On the one hand, the spiritual origins that influence this writing lie in the author's early New England Protestant Christian traditions of the northeastern United States. On the other hand, the author's spiritual origins lie in the continuing ageless creation of the world. My career as a military chaplain required me to work within the established authorities of both religion and the Armed Forces. These authorities are the familiar customs, laws and culture of our nation. This career also required me to work in spiritual places I had only been able to read about in textbooks, books and journals on ethnology and anthropology, as well as theology and psychology. What was ancient and academically interesting became present and intimately powerful for coping and healing. An example of this personal experience was the spiritual presence and communication of a totemic relationship, which will be described later. First Nations peoples have always lived this way. What scholars call "primitive" or "legend" became remarkably contemporary living to me.

This chapter is intended to encourage the professional counselor to accept the veteran without predisposition, and to utilize spiritually and religiously infused therapeutic interventions in order to support the veteran in achieving a more familiar and normative world view. From the ruination of broken expectations, hopes and faith, soldiers and veterans can use spiritually informed services provided by chaplains to promote individual and family healing, performance and promise. While the services described here were provided within the role of a military chaplain, there is considerable relevance for any care provider who wishes to inform their practice with service members or veterans with relevant religious and spiritual understanding and knowledge.[1]

---

1   Editors' note: For a very moving account by a chaplain who served in the Vietnam War and who helped to design the VA Vet Center Program, see *Out of the Night: A Spiritual Journey of Vietnam Vets* by William P. Mahedy (1986).

The setting of the chaplaincy

What follows is a brief regulatory description of the Army chaplain, the Oath of Office, the Soldier's Creed and Army Values. These define the cultural imperatives of the soldier, the military family, and the spiritual milieu. For the purposes of this description, there is little significant difference between the several branches of the military. There can be significant differences, however, in military service practice, or religious beliefs and practices among chaplains. It is very important for care providers of any kind to understand that the qualifications and duties of a chaplain both receive and require the highest attributes of professionalism in our society. The roles of the Chaplain, Military Officer and Clergy are among the top ten most respected professions in the United States (Van Riper, 2006). However, the challenges of providing spiritually and religiously informed services as a chaplain in the military can result in perceived shortcomings of individual chaplains; such perceived shortcomings need to be understood within the context of the relational responsibilities of individual chaplains, those service members seeking such services, and the challenges of the chaplain's personal situations.

Chapter 3 of *Army Regulation 165–1* (Chief of Chaplains, 2010) describes the status, roles, and responsibilities of chaplains. It is imperative to more fully appreciate some of the essential segments of these regulations that pertain to professional and educational qualifications and the distinctive role of military chaplaincy: (1) Section 3–1.a specifies that the chaplain must have a divinity-related master's degree or equivalent and be "endorsed" by one of the approximately 200 religious denominations that have military members. Hence, by definition, the military chaplain is a "professional" and a member of a recognized religious denomination: (2) Section 3–1.b specifies that Army chaplains must have dual roles as both "religious leaders and religious support staff officers" and that a chaplain not only has rank without command, but will not bear arms. These restrictions are unique in the Armed Forces.

The above briefly describes some of the distinctive qualifications, status and role of military chaplains. In addition, it is particularly noteworthy to understand that in the military, the chaplain is *also* a Soldier (or a Sailor, Marine, Airman or Coastie). Therefore, the chaplain has dual orientation and obligations as both "a servant of God" and a dutiful soldier who has raised the right hand for the Oath of Office. Anyone making this commitment to the Armed Forces delivers this oath:

> I [name], do solemnly swear [or affirm] that I will support and defend the Constitution of the United States against all enemies, foreign and domestic; that I will bear true faith and allegiance to the same; and that I will obey the orders of the President of the United States and the orders of the officers appointed over me, according to regulations and the Uniform Code of Military Justice. So help me God.

The Chaplaincy is a profound and unique "dual allegiance." Since Chaplains are also soldiers, they are also required to learn and to live the principal elements of this solemn oath within the confines and culture of military life. This life is exemplified by The Soldier's Creed:

> I am an American soldier. I am a Warrior and a member of a team. I serve the people of the United States and live the Army Values. I will always place the mission first. I will never accept defeat. I will never quit. I will never leave a fallen comrade. I am disciplined, physically and mentally tough, trained and proficient in my warrior tasks and drills. I always maintain my arms, my equipment and myself. I am an expert and I am a professional. I stand ready to deploy, engage, and destroy the enemies of the United States of America in close combat. I am a guardian of freedom and the American way of life. I am an American soldier.

Upon entering the United States military, everyone in the Armed Forces learns the guiding values of their new and different culture. For example, the Army Values mentioned in the Soldier's Creed above are *Loyalty, Duty, Respect, Selfless Service, Honor, Integrity,* and *Personal Courage.* These Seven Core Values are learned in depth during Basic Training, memorized as the moral standard, and lived over and over again during military service. Each military service has its own set of Core Values like those above. Service oaths, creeds, and values form the mental and behavioral setting of their culture. The regulations, oath, creed, and values have the potential to bring with them problematic psychological and spiritual issues within the chaplain's roles, and between the tenets of respective faith groups, military regulations and policies, and the chaplain's care of military members. Soldiers often discuss these problematic issues with their leaders or with a chaplain. A follow-on discussion in a safe setting with another counselor may prove to be fruitful for understanding and healing.

Distinctive factors and issues surrounding the military chaplain's role

The booklet Turning to a Chaplain for Care and Support (Normile, 2011) offers a summary of what you can expect from a good chaplain: confidentiality; good listening skills; regular visits; support for individuals and families; linking individuals and families with staff; religious services, sacraments and prayer; and information regarding medical ethics questions, living wills, organ donation, and life support decisions. It also provides specific information regarding support groups designed to meet various needs of individuals and their loved ones. It is important to note that these practices and skills are primarily designed for civilian settings such as hospitals, hospices, and prison ministries. Each one has a military equivalent, however, and this list of civilian chaplains' services often becomes the natural expectation of soldiers who have never encountered a member of the clergy in any other setting. This is especially true in combat grief ministry in the military as this pertains to dealing with loss or death.

There are significant additions and caveats to add that are characteristic of the military chaplain's role which might challenge, confuse, or become an issue for the inexperienced, lower ranking person in uniform who may be in need of chaplain services. The first is the officer rank of the chaplain. This can be intimidating or alienating for the enlisted (non-officer) soldier, especially if they have had prior negative experience with officers. In particular, trust may be difficult to establish if the person is referred for a problem involving higher authority because the problem cannot be solved without personal engagement within this hierarchy. Because everyone is in the chain of command within a military unit, everyone works for the commander. The chaplain is a personal advisor to the commander and the soldier might have a problem with a supervisor who must also eventually answer to the commander. The chaplain explains that the soldier's expectation of confidentiality must be violated in order for the chaplain to successfully intervene with higher authority. The chaplain's professional credibility, as well as trust, is on the line, a situation not faced by a civilian counselor, who is not "on duty" with the client, and rarely intervenes with a supervisor at work. In extreme instances, soldiers may face a fellow soldier who is outraged and suicidal, and must be deprived of their weapon on the spot. Both the soldier and his/her peers could interpret this as the soldier's failure to perform the mission instead of recognizing it as an issue of personal and community safety. The weapon symbolizes protection of the identity of the soldier, and the means of defending all values. The challenge of the chaplain is to support and participate in this confiscation by a soldier's peers, and then strengthen the shreds of the soldier's sense of self-worth by identifying positive reasons for the soldier living with hope. These reasons are commitments familiar to any counselor: oaths, creeds, values, love of country, family, friends, and combat buddies. These conversations require considerable time, and involve a holy journey on the way to a safe behavioral health setting.

Another possible issue is that soldiers may find it difficult to reconcile or understand how military chaplains might be perceived to be in an inherently contradictory role, in which God or religious beliefs are perceived to be used to sanction or "bless" the military's role as a purveyor of death and destruction. This role may also contribute to common civilian misperceptions. The chaplain's role is not to take sides on issues (though some do), but rather to understand the nature and significance of the soldier's specific predicament. The chaplain's intervention strategy is to inquire about the soldier's "religious origins," much like inquiring about "family origins" in the secular setting. A person's church or denomination, or even a single judgmental statement from a peer, can develop doubt in a soldier's ethical or moral positions. Sometimes religious authors, mistranslations of scripture, positions and attitudes of teachers, or obligations of the religious calendar year can generate insoluble dilemmas resulting in distractions that can contribute to a soldier's mission failure and death on the battlefield. The chaplain compares the religious origins of doubt with the requirements of the present situation, uncovering potential ways of reconciliation from the reflections of the soldiers themselves. Reconciliation may simply be the recognition and acceptance of a problem that cannot be solved in the present. The affirmation of the soldier's personal concerns is often more significant than potential clinical issues. Simple affirmation of the problem presented is sometimes the most effective intervention that the chaplain or civilian provider can give.

These are examples of possible issues that a soldier or veteran might face in their experiences with a military chaplain. Any healthcare provider might do well to consider inquiring about these specific matters. Such issues as the role of, relationship with, communication patterns with, and attitudes and/or actions of the military chaplain might be remembered by the soldier or veteran and carried into the future, warranting further inquiry and discussion. The counselor may easily continue to be the incarnation of hope represented by the chaplain. With regard to this hopeful situation, two more examples illustrate provision of care in seemingly irreconcilable situations. The first is relationships with parents. Like no other system of authority, the military chain of command creates and fosters relationships between leaders and those who are led which unconsciously evoke, reinforce, or contradict relationships with parents. Family values, discipline and behavioral patterns are areas of discussion that provide potential opportunities for the counselor to aspire towards a constellation of forgiveness. The second example is combat death. To the soldier and veteran, any combat death may feel forever wrong, and be the source of any emotional or behavioral symptoms seemingly unrelated to the presenting issue. In this case, even though we know no one can raise the dead, the care provider can explore meaningful explanations and ways to affirm that the dead did not die in vain.

"Care provider" is not a noun to describe standing by; it is an action verb describing the sensitive application of healing power. This healing power is spiritual power for the chaplain, but healing power is available to every counselor. This power comes from self-awareness, education, clients, reading, and mentors of all kinds in the secular setting. In the religious setting, it comes from God.

One of the most common and caring actions of spiritual power for the chaplain is prayer, an expression of healing intent that galvanizes the inner will toward the best of directions in the face of the worst situations. Best and worst are value judgments, of course, and may even apply to the soldier or veteran finally joining the chaplain for counsel. As a chaplain, I receive the best value if the soldier offers a positive response to spiritual inquiry as part of the counseling process. I ask if the soldier would like a concluding prayer based on the counseling material. In combat, I identify and pray for a soldier's situation and focus on one meaningful concern. For a soldier in Ramadi, this was fear of going outside the wire, leaving the camp for the first time. Knowing he trusted me, I verbally identified the issue of his courage, prayed with him for courage and gave him a pamphlet about courage that was filled with advice and scriptural quotations. The soldier did his duty and never brought up the subject again. Before missions, in many platoons a soldier comfortable with spiritual leadership leads a group prayer. Again in Ramadi, I prepared "prayer kits" for the battalion's platoons, and this appeared to fulfill their needs for the remainder of the tour.

Prayer can also be an appropriate subject for discussion; not necessarily saying a prayer itself, but asking a question such as: "If you were to pray now, what would you pray for? What would this prayer mean? How and why would you pray?" Prayer is simply an intentional thought and action in the realm of holiness. I carry this intention around with me, and talk with God about my needs and hopes all the time. Framing my expectations is critical for a positive experience. I do not get myself into the depths of reflection or name things or developments that I personally want. Rather, for myself and others, I ask for successful resolution of a problem, blessings, forgiveness, healing, or the strength to meet whatever may come our way.

Another way of entering soldiers' spiritual lives is through the contents of "the little sacreds of the soldier," which they carry in their pockets or the liners of their helmets or their rucksacks, or use to decorate their sleeping area. I have used such "sacreds" myself. For example, prior to my deployment to Ramadi, Iraq in 2005 through 2006, I asked each member of my immediate family to choose a color for the threads of a woven tapestry I hung on my wall in my "hooch." This example highlights the high and positive significance of my family to me.

Another example of the "little sacreds of the soldier" is the touchstone in my pocket. The story of the touchstone begins early in my life, yet it came to mind on Thanksgiving Day in November 2010, when I began to write this very chapter. I was a Sunday School dropout. When I was a child avoiding Sunday School, I occasionally sneaked into the congregation during worship, much to the dismay of my usually proud mother. I heard the minister introduce sermons with words which are particularly meaningful to me because my primary means of service as a chaplain is through prayer. They were from the Biblical Book of Psalms (Psalm 19:14): "May the words of my mouth and the meditation of my heart be pleasing in your sight, O Lord, my Rock and my Redeemer."[2] I mention the prayer now because my touchstone is a little river rock I carry with me all the time. It remains in my pocket at all times, where I can readily touch, move and hold it with my fingers. This activity is both a

---

2 This and all following Bible quotations are from *The Holy Bible, New International Version* (1984). Colorado Springs, CO: International Bible Society.

response to stress and a repetitive comforting activity—a kind of prayer. Every "little sacred" has the potential to assist the healing of a soldier.

The rock in the Psalm and elsewhere in sacred texts is ordinarily a symbol for eternal strength, for a "steadfast" value or attitude. After a month or so of serving soldiers during times of heavy combat in Ramadi in 2005, I had several dreams of individual stones standing before me. They were "silently speaking," telling me they were supporting me. The dream experience reminded me of Jesus' statement in Luke 19:40 about the stones crying out if his disciples were silenced, as it seemed to be a spiritual communication.

As recently as July 2011, I dreamed about a "red hot living rock," just like the one I encountered in real time during my very first veterans sweat lodge in June of that year. At the invitation of Vietnam veterans, I entered the low dome tent of animal skins and blankets for an "experience." The leader invited prayers from the circle of people, and then began the introduction of large rocks that had been heating in a fire for hours. Through several stages of entrance and exit over a couple of hours, water thrown on these rocks created steam heat in the lodge. Prayer, song and musical instruments accompanied this profound purification ritual. If they desired, each veteran shared a personal statement. The sharing and physical purification creates a feeling of spiritual purification from the combat past. In the sweat lodge, these rocks were addressed as "Grandfathers and Grandmothers." Stones share the energy of millions of years. They reminded us, and remind me, of the eternal God always "being here and there" in the manner that I, as a military chaplain, steadfastly maintained my performance in this role and, as an individual, "stood fast" in the presence of so much blood and pain, and so many memorial services and grieving people.

I find that every soldier has his or her own war. With this simple perspective the care provider must disregard the platitudes of national patriotism (even the oath, creed and values), however meaningful they sometimes are, and accept the singular experience of the one whose boots were on the ground. Shock and evil happens, not just "shock and awe." You, the person listening, are the one called to accept the horrific as well as beautiful stories. After talking with a soldier, Jesus tells a crowd in Matthew 8:10, "never have I seen such faith" in all the nation. This kind of faith may be in the heart of the soldier or veteran you counsel, a faith directed toward you for healing. You do not need to agree with what the soldier or veteran has shared with you. For example, when a soldier shares guilt or justification, agony or satisfaction at taking the life of an enemy combatant, we must suspend our judgment of moral and ethical implications, as well as those personal belief systems related to killing. Many soldiers over the years have questioned me about the sixth of the Ten Commandments in the Biblical Old Testament Book of Exodus 20:13, which is often mistranslated as: "You shall not kill." The correct translation is: "You shall not murder." The distinction is critical, for murder is a crime, yet killing for the nation, homeland, or tribe is sanctioned by Biblical as well as most human law. Whatever transpires and is verbalized during the provision of spiritual counsel must be accompanied by the goal of improving relationships and planning for the healing of those soldiers in the counseling process.

Simplicity itself: What the chaplain brings

Chaplain John Feltz was another of the senior chaplains assigned to our command. We are comrades from different sides of the Christian fence (a picket fence, porous); myself a Protestant of the denomination United Church of Christ, he a Roman Catholic priest. I offer his example because our ministries start and continue from very different perspectives. They are basically acceptable to each another as long as soldier healing continues. Our very diversity is the greatest strength of our service together. The following extract was sent to me in September 2010 by Chaplain Feltz as his first response to my request to write about his chaplaincy. He summarizes the most important elements of his chaplaincy ministry in the Roman Catholic denomination:

> I believe a Catholic priest brings *many* things to our soldiers. First he brings the sacraments, especially that of the Eucharist (The Mass). So, no matter where the soldiers are, they feel connected to the Church throughout the world and to our Lord and His saving Grace. A priest also brings the beautiful sacrament of Confession or Reconciliation; this is especially helpful when the soldier is dealing with different stresses caused by guilt, real or not. This sacrament brings the soldier the power to begin the process of healing. I also believe the priest helps not only those Catholics who are out in the war zone with the sacraments, but also many of the other liturgical faiths who are looking to connect with their God via the outward signs of these sacraments, many of which have been used to celebrate when they are in garrison or at home. The term used by so many now for the chaplain (no matter what faith they might be)—"Father"—says it all. He is the person who makes them God's children through their Baptism, feeds them in the Eucharist, and forgives and lifts them up when they are hurting. And finally, the priest is the one who, as they are dying, is there to anoint and pray with them as they begin their journey home to God.

Chaplain Feltz's summary of his chaplaincy is what I call "simplicity itself," though some people might call it simplistic. I might call it simplistic too, if I had not seen priestly healing first hand in Ramadi. What follows is the story of "Soldier Joe," so called because of his many deployments and exceptional leadership (and, incidentally, his name really was Joe). Joe was a self-described "lapsed Catholic" who did not give his religion much thought and only told me of his church and status because I asked him. I visited him in his quarters because he had an infected toe, and was ordered by the medics to elevate his foot and not to report for duty. The medics and doctors tried everything to heal his toe for several weeks. When every attempt at medical healing had failed and Joe faced evacuation back to the United States, I confronted him. "Joe," I said, "the problem isn't your toe. The problem is you." He agreed, and asked for a priest Chaplain to visit him for the sacrament of Confession. The priest arrived, heard his Confession, the toe healed, and Soldier Joe returned to duty.

If only every problem could be solved with the application of prayer. Unfortunately, if a simplistic faith or moral stance is also inflexible, the shattering of that stance in combat may be the cause of combat post-traumatic stress. An example of such a situation is the irreconcilable moral dilemma described above of killing when the Bible says "Thou shall not kill." This example shows the significant reframing of a moral imperative through the correct translation and interpretation of a well-known law. Alternatively, as my experience will show, the acquisition of coping skills (with or without the therapeutic milieu) provides the conscious "faith stance" flexibility to continue positive growth in spiritual and religious life.

"Healing on the go" and the commitment to self-care

"Healing on the go" describes what the soldier in combat must do to perform, protect buddies and stay alive. Military field manuals describe chaplains, lawyers and medical personnel as "combat multipliers." This means that our personal influence exceeds the bounds of our personal presence. A technical metaphor would be the mechanic who finds and tightens the loose bolt that holds a tank tread together for successful movement. Unfortunately, this metaphor collapses when soldiers and care providers abuse coping mechanisms such as drugs, which create the appearance of healing. Sometimes the best delivery of spiritual and other therapeutic interventions "on the go" takes the form of a night of secure rest, maybe even sleep, or switching from computer to paper reading, or meditative yoga stretching instead of calisthenics. When the Chaplain tells a soldier to forget about God for a while and go to bed, the implications can be stunning and clear in the appropriate context.

My personal reactions to the traumatic stress of combat in Ramadi occurred in the camp's medical-surgical stations, morgue and memorial services. I am able to handle this past, so far, suffering only one symptom, which I can usually control; this is the tearful emotional response of grieving, triggered by certain music. Dealing with the almost daily and nightly bloody wounded, weekly dead and occasional mass casualty was part of my chaplain service and support to my battalion task force and the medical company. These units totaled well over 1,000 soldiers. This experience could have been disastrous to my chaplaincy had I not been open to new meaning far beyond my "early New England Protestant Christian traditions of the northeastern United States," mentioned in the first paragraph of this chapter.

I prepared myself in several ways for the demands and hardships I anticipated. I reworded a passage from the New Testament of the Bible into a Prayer
for the Spiritual Armor of God, and kept this prayer in my wallet. I used the
prayer in command ceremonies. My commitment to daily exercise included
group exercise three times a week. I read from a devotional book every day. I
practiced, as I still do, the spiritual discipline of Reiki meditation. These practices followed my commitment to abide by a combination of two scriptural
passages: the first from the Torah in Deuteronomy 6:5, and the second from
Jesus in the Gospel of Matthew 22:37. I formed a commandment for myself:
"Love the Lord your God with all your heart, soul, mind, and strength." Every
day I tried to practice each one of these ways of loving God as a means of supporting and caring for myself.

In Camp Ramadi I lived in a compound named "Hotel California" by
previous occupants. *Hotel California* is a popular song that was performed
and recorded by the Eagles in the late Seventies. The words describe a surreal
nightmare reported by a hotel visitor, who was told by the doorman at the
end of the dream that "you can check out, but never leave." This condition
of "checking out but never leaving" is a precise description of the soldier's
dilemma, stemming from the violence of combat. We can check out of the
combat zone upon redeployment home, but we never leave the experiences of
that place. "The mission never ends."

I spent many hours of prayer in the presence of medical emergencies,
during which some people thought I was not doing anything but standing
there. In actuality, I was "doing" several things. I was remaining at the sides
of stretchers with the wounded to be transferred to cots in the holding ward
or "packaged" for evacuation. I was witnessing surgeries for every conceivable
injury. I was walking the final march to the morgue—and began to notice the
ravens outside. After I prayed for the wounded and dead, I would see a raven
outside on the way, my way, to my next place. I then noticed the flock on the
roof of the medical headquarters. I also observed the flock over my compound
in the morning when I awoke, and how these birds migrated to the medical
company during the day, just as I did. Occasionally I paused to visit with a
raven outside the medical company, and eventually became oddly certain of
their support for me. When this feeling was no longer peculiar, but a virtual
certainty of great comfort to me, I wrote my wife, telling her that when a raven
appeared at the house, it would be representing me. It was only two days later
that she reported the arrival of a raven nesting in the tallest tree over our
home.

According to myth, the raven's primary reason for appearing is *transformation*—original and new creation. Transformation of the psychological self is a
necessary element for healing from the effects and symptoms of trauma or any
extreme stress. A soldier expects change, but the first requirement is openness
to this change; second is the need to adapt and "go with the flow" in creative
and responsible ways. A responsible approach, for instance, is to share pain

with buddies or find a counselor. Transformation was the task for my psyche and spirit—heart, soul, mind, and strength—in Ramadi. This transformation was the reforming and reframing of my traumatic emotional responses to the chaotic activities around me.

"New occasions bring new duties," as the old hymn says. New experiences also bring new coping opportunities, of which Raven was one. For this reason, when I am counseling a soldier after his or her own traumatic experience, I inquire about what is meaningfully different now, after this initial reflection together. What is odd or unfamiliar to the new, traumatized psyche will be an experience for the next beginning and an opening of the possibilities of personal change. This is the recognition and acceptance that violence to the soul occurred and the soldier lives for something yet to be, which is now only a strange thought or experience to support in its potential, with hope.

During my OIF deployment I became very close to the medical company commander and the executive officer (also the mortuary affairs officer), who were both male, and a female platoon leader. They provided me with profound emotional support in response to the spiritual support I provided them during painful incidents, and thus we became friends as professionals on the same team. One evening, as I lay on my cot reviewing the events of a day with them and marveling at this team of four individuals, I began to analyze us as parts of a whole. I had a flash of amazement as I realized that we met the traits and personalities of the four characters in *The Wonderful Wizard of Oz* (Baum, 1993). The Commander, very tall, athletic, assertive and protective, represented the Courage so desired by the Cowardly Lion. The Executive Officer, an overly reflective, pensive and colorful writer of letters, represented the Brain so desired by the Scarecrow. The Platoon Leader, a sensitive artist, represented the Heart so desired by the Tin Man. So who was Dorothy? I sought and found the meaning of the name Dorothy, which is daughter of God. I was Dorothy, child of God, the Chaplain.

These four types also represent the Heart, Soul, Mind, and Strength of the scriptural self-care that I lived by and required of my chaplain assistant and, later, the chaplains I supervised. It became an essential part of our daily tasks to engage in one activity in each of these realms every day, for the purpose of spiritual resilience. As examples of these activities, I communicated with home or my buddies for my Heart, performed Reiki for my Soul's harmony, read a daily devotional for my Mind, and trained physically for my Body.

Five years later, reading *Finding Oz* (Schwartz, 2009) during another deployment, I discovered that L. Frank Baum learned the philosophy of yoga from Swami Vivekananda during the World's Columbian Exposition of 1893 in Chicago. This great teacher delivered a set of meditations he called "The Four Yogas."

The first is the Jnana Yoga, a meditation pertaining to the meaning of one's brain to receive wisdom. The second is the Bhakti Yoga, about what it means for the heart to know compassion and devotion. The third is Karma Yoga, a meditation about gaining courage to take action. Finally, there is Raja Yoga, a meditation regarding serenity and the achievement of inner harmony.

(Schwartz, 2009)

Note how these four yogas match the four ways of spiritual self-care that I developed in Ramadi during the height of the war: the first, brain = mind; the second, heart = heart; the third, courage = strength; and the fourth, harmony = soul. I followed this challenge in my daily life and by conscientiously following this regimen, I was able to heal "on the go," enabling me to perform my chaplain service and support at the highest standards of professionalism.

"Being here and there": The ministry of presence

My strength in committing to durable self-care became the formula for spiritual resilience as I became the designated Chaplain member of the mortuary affairs team, another function of the medical company. I spent hours in the morgue supporting the team, in addition to performing other chaplaincy roles within the medical company, such as pastoral counseling, teaching, traumatic event management, encouraging sleeping on those rare occasions when the opportunity presented itself, awaiting the arrival of casualties, and "hanging out," being here and there, providing the ministry of presence.

"Being here and there" acquired significant connotations. After several deaths in my unit, as well as in numerous other units, deaths occurring either outside the wire or during hours of surgery trying to sustain human life against all odds, I spent a vast amount of time in the morgue with the mortuary affairs officer and others whose presence was necessary. They told me that my presence, as well as prayer for both the living and the dead, became vital for spiritual support. This presence was all they wanted from me in the darkness of day or night, more significant than food. Soldiers sometimes requested my counsel because they had "had contact" with their dead comrades who had been killed in combat. I helped them to interpret the experience, discover the meaning for themselves and affirm their spiritual as well as physical courage. After counseling on this subject, I would usually walk away alone to settle myself afterwards. Like the ravens seeking my attention, it became more and more evident that there was definite communication from the dead. Most of the time they were simply my companions, remaining with me for a while for their own comfort and solace.

On one memorable occasion after attending to a casualty who had suffered fatal injuries in his vehicle from an IED, I walked back along the road with this now spiritual soldier. It was late and dark. I had some apprehension. The only light came from the laundry truck, where a single soldier waited for his bag. I walked down to pick up my bag. He asked me how I was doing. I told him I had been minding my own business when I was called to the morgue, etc. He said, "I know exactly how you feel, Chaplain, because I work in the motor pool and I had to clean that vehicle today." This soldier had been minding his own business, too, and now had his own experience to share. These are the kinds of experiences to which soldiers are exposed that the care provider earns sufficient trust to hear. Sometimes the spiritual soldiers were distressed and confused, seeking guidance and wondering where to go and what to do. I would speak to them in my mind, praying and assuring them that they would be all right, giving them permission to go home. Learning these experiences personally enabled me to provide a level of pastoral care I otherwise would likely fear, dismiss or explain away.

Closing

These intense spiritual experiences are meaningful and profound, yet absent from the modern expression of my religion. They connect and harmonize the radical difference between the traditions of my culture and the ancient cultures still current today. No doubt my experiences are spiritually profound because this is my life, my study, my practice, and my training. Perhaps even more importantly, my own intense experiences have helped me to never doubt the experiences of any other soldier and also to maintain the attitude of helping soldiers to embrace their own experiences—to help them realize and appreciate how the connections that they draw are just as meaningful for them.

In other words, it is not for the counselor or the chaplain to judge the relevance of the connections. Rather, the role is to facilitate individual soldiers or veterans to investigate meanings for themselves in the context of their own experiences, dilemmas, hopes, and goals. If therapists are sensitive enough to recognize and receive these unusual ideas, perhaps they will recognize the sincere trust developing within the therapeutic relationship. It is through these experiences that I came to recognize, in new ways, the potential for spiritual healing among my professional friends, as none of us (like Dorothy and her companions) were "in Kansas anymore."

In conclusion, I advocate the challenge and opportunity of providing a wide variety of therapeutic approaches in the spiritual and religious realm, as well as the medical and psychological behavioral realms. Careful dedication to both tradition and the creative possibilities opened by traumatic events can produce successful treatment and healing. I emphasize that our perspectives outside the counseling relationship are meaningless unless we communicate with the raging unknown in the person facing us. At the end of the day, when I tell my earthly companions that it is all right to go home, this means to families, lovers and friends. Let us go home together with all our hearts, souls, minds, and strengths.

LTC(RET) Charles M. Purinton, Jr. graduated (1974) from the Andover Newton Theological School (M DIV). After several civilian parishes, he served as Chaplain, Vermont Army National Guard (1982 to 2011) the last 23 years full-time to retirement. He graduated from the Army War College (2003). His deployments include Battalion Chaplain, Ramadi, Iraq (2005-2006) and Brigade Chaplain, Bagram Air Field, Afghanistan (2010). His awards include two Bronze Stars (cmpurinton@gmail.com).

References

Baum, F. L. (1993). *The Wonderful World of Oz*. New York, NY: HarperCollins.

Chief of Chaplains (2010). *Army Regulation 165-1: Army Chaplain Corps Activities*. Washington, DC: Department of the Army.

Mahedy, W. P. (1986). *Out of the Night: The Spiritual Journey of Vietnam Vets*. New York, NY: Ballentine Books.

Normile, P. (2011). *Turning to a Chaplain for Care and Support*. St. Meinrad, IN: One Caring Place.

Schwartz, E. I. (2009). *Finding Oz*. New York, NY: Houghton Mifflin Harcourt.

Van Riper, T. (2006, July 28). America's most admired professions. *Forbes*. Retrieved from www.forbes.com/2006/07/28/leadership-careers-jobs-cx_tvr_0728admired. html

18 Afterword: A surviving spouse speaks

Beate Medina

Live every Moment
Beate Medina

The expanding circle of healing would be missing a very significant group of civilians who are sorely impacted by war if we did not acknowledge the surviving spouses of service members killed in action (KIA) and their families. When one considers the casualty figures for the wars in Iraq and Afghanistan (over 6,300 KIA) (U.S. Department of Defense, 2012) and the Vietnam War (58,193 KIA) (U.S. National Archives and Records Administration, 1998), the numbers whose deaths left behind widows and widowers is not insignificant. In addition, there are the partners who were not legally married. Perhaps most disconcerting is how "invisible" such surviving spouses are once the funerals have taken place and life returns to normal for most everyone else—while the surviving spouses (and extended families) have a lifetime of bearing and coping with such a traumatic loss.

We were committed to having a chapter in this book on surviving spouses. However, we were unable to find anything substantive in the mental health literature or any research studies whatsoever about surviving spouses and what happens to them. However, we were fortunate to have a professional counselor give us a lead to Beate Medina, a surviving spouse.

Beate's story serves a dual purpose. It introduces into the mental health literature a number of the critical dynamics, challenges, decision points and triumphs of at least one surviving spouse of a service member killed in action. Beate is also a counselor and has known a number of other surviving spouses; consequently, she has been able to insert thoughtful discourse about some of the variance that occurs among surviving spouses. We are honored to be able to relay SSG Oscar and Beate Medina's story to you

Raymond Monsour Scurfield
Kathy Theresa Platoni

My journey

I see life as a journey. It has been nearly eight years from the point of Oscar's death to writing this story. My journey with my husband when he was alive was actually around six years. I believe that now I am in a good place and I grew a lot as a person throughout those years. But still, there are moments when I get pulled down into deep sadness because of the love that I felt for my late husband and I believe he felt for me. And the sadness becomes deeper, because I have yet to find anything similar in another partner relationship. I do not expect the same, but hope for something similar—if you have had something good, you want something good again. Now I live with my feelings without shame; I do not accept or feel pressure from society telling me "how I should feel" by now.

I have met some wise people along my path (counselors, friends, veterans and strangers), and over time they have helped me to see that I have a choice: to move forward or to stay stuck in my feelings and in the past. Oscar was my soul mate and I know he would have wanted me—and his military comrades—to move forward.

We were stationed in Hawaii when Oscar deployed to Iraq. His unit was the A Co 84th ECB (H)—Engineering Combat Battalion (Heavy). If you had known Oscar, you would agree that he loved the Army, his job and those he worked with as a mechanic with the combat engineers. He always stood up for his soldiers. I learned over time, and especially after his death, how great an impact he had had on his soldiers and others. I clearly remember from the beginning of our relationship Oscar telling me: "Don't ever make me choose between you and the Army, because you will lose." I admired his dedication to his job and to his country. I know I would not be able to give up what he gave up and what most of our soldiers give up for us.

Casualty notification and reaction

When the service member is seen as a partner, best friend or soul mate—as Oscar was for me—and his/her heart stops beating in the war zone, another heart breaks thousands of miles away.

Receiving the death notification

A military Casualty Notification Officer (CNO) and a military Chaplain have the difficult and necessary task of bringing news in-person to give the official condolences. This is very meaningful, especially realizing that in former wars, widows and widowers received the news through a telegram. I don't remember very much about the death notification. When I saw the two soldiers in Class A uniforms, I did not connect them right away with the worst. I was one of the wives that did not worry about my service member not coming back. Hey, Oscar had had twelve years in service and several deployments to places like Somalia, Bosnia and Kosovo, and I knew he was good at his job. Why worry? But you cannot predict what is on your path of life, like this notification and the bad news it communicated. When I heard the condolences, I wanted to convince them that they were talking about the wrong person—not my husband. I really wanted to know what had happened to Oscar, but they said they did not know exactly and that my CAO (Casualty Assistance Officer) would help me with this question. I remember that the two soldiers asked whether I wanted someone with me, but I did not. I needed time for myself. I also decided that it was the Army's role to call my mother-in-law because I did not have a close relationship with her and neither did Oscar; he was raised by his grandmother.

I do not remember how long they spent with me, but it was long enough that when they left I was able to feel comfortable alone. So I spent the night by myself with our two dogs. I could not sleep. I tried to take in what just happened. My world ended at this point. That night I wrote a letter to the soldiers in Iraq. For them this nightmare started so much earlier. It was so important for me to let them know that I did not blame any of them for what happened. In my heart I know Oscar would have taken a bullet for any of his soldiers—rather him than anybody else. That night was neverending.

Whose funeral is it?

The next day finally came, and with it came my biggest help throughout this hard time—my CAO. He was my support with all the arrangements and paperwork; he was "my soldier's voice." The most important statement my CAO gave to me was actually a question: "Whose funeral is it?" This statement became my mission. It was not my funeral and it was not the funeral of Oscar's family. It was Oscar's funeral.

I sat down and tried to remember what Oscar and I had discussed. Yes, we had talked about death, and what we wanted. Looking back, I am glad we did. I remember we had had this conversation here and there, even about if one of us would be terminally ill and about life support, etc. I knew that some of my decisions about the funeral and burial, and arrangements about who was going to get what money would make some people mad, especially his family, but oh well. It was about Oscar at this point and he had no voice. Believe me, all these decisions were hard decisions and I had to stand my ground, because Oscar's family wanted some things done differently. They also asked about the SGLI (Servicemembers Group Life Insurance) money, which was the last thing on my mind at this point. I knew that Oscar had divided the SGLI and his family knew it too. I thought, "Oscar is not even buried yet and it's about money?" This was something I could not understand. My communication to his family broke up.

I am so glad that my CAO always stood by me and never challenged my decisions. I am glad Oscar's best friend, who he considered his big brother, supported these decisions. I listened to his opinion and it gave me the strength to do what Oscar would have wanted. Oscar wanted to be buried in a National Cemetery, but he also wanted to be close to his grandmother, who is buried in Florida. It was difficult for me, but I fulfilled his wishes. When I die, I hope that someone will do the same for me.

The funeral

The funeral was huge. So many people came, which showed what kind of person Oscar was. A friend even took Oscar's motorcycle up to the site. Oscar put so much work and detail into his bike and he was out riding the island "with his boys" as often as possible. To see his bike at the funeral meant the world to me. And strength was something I had to come up with every day, again and again. I feel very blessed, looking back, that I had so many good people around me—especially my CAO being on my side and giving me the support that I needed.

I have just one regret about the funeral. I know that during such a difficult time, many other surviving spouses have had regrets about things that were said or not said, done or not done. I truly wish I could turn back time to one particular moment. Oscar's half-brother, who was serving at that time in the Air Force, tried to call me and I did not pick up the phone. It was at the time when my mother-in-law had her viewing and the family was told that nobody else could see Oscar but his birth mother, his son from his first marriage and me (as was Oscar's wish). I was scared that if I picked up the phone, everyone who called or came would want to see Oscar and that it would become impossible to stay true to his wishes. So I ignored the ring of my phone. I regret and apologize for not picking up the phone and listening.

Once the house is empty

After the funeral and everyone had left, and my brother had gone back home to Germany, the house became empty—or at least that's how I perceived it. I started realizing how important Oscar was for my life and how much I had oriented my life around him and his career. All my plans were crushed; my life was crushed. I started to get mad—no, I became really angry and enraged. I aimed my feelings straight towards the source that I blamed for everything: God. I can even say that my anger with him started with my receiving the death notification. I remember that I could not pray with the chaplain, because I felt it would not have been honest. I asked him to pray in my place. I started having very serious conversations with God—some of which included yelling, screaming, pouting, crying, etc. Believe me, I cried my eyes out and sometimes there was no stopping. Shopping, at work, or driving—tears just poured from nowhere. I hate to cry in public, but after a while I stopped caring who was around me or where I was. What sense did life make now? What was to happen to all the plans we had made? What was I to live for? Why was I alive? In my eyes there was no future, just this black hole.

I did not want to live anymore. The wish to be dead was present almost every day for many days. And throughout these past seven years, the thought of death has visited me here and there. I started praying that God would take my life and reunite me with Oscar. But God did not answer me, and so I started making plans to end my life. I put a lot of effort into planning my suicide so that it would look like an accident. I thought that my family would have it easier that way. Riding my motorcycle, the cliffs of Oahu, the bridge of H3, the street curves—all would make it so simple. And I would die doing something I love: riding my bike. Two things were holding me back: first, my belief that if I committed suicide I would not end up in the same spirit world as Oscar, who died a hero; and second, I was scared that I would survive my attempt.

Making friends with death

Over the last seven years I've made friends with death. There were hours I spent having thoughts about death and an afterlife. I tried to acquire as much knowledge as possible. I adjusted my belief system to what I needed it to be and what made me most comfortable—because at the end, we just do not know what awaits us. With all the adjusting of my belief system, I can say today that I am not scared of death anymore. This was a very long process.

Heartache is a special pain

The journey of life can take different roads: some are country roads with beautiful sites of nature; some are city streets with stop lights, or even rush-hour traffic jams. Some travel is with company, some is alone. Sometimes the journey goes uphill, sometimes downhill. There might be complications or even the feeling of being caught in a dead end. Perhaps the worst thing is when on your journey the road collapses underneath as if from an earthquake—which is what happened when Oscar was KIA. You end up in a deep dark hole, where it is pitch black. You can't see or hear anything. It is like the world comes to an end. War widows/widowers who lose the love of their life will feel just like this.

On the other hand, there are war widows/widowers who see their marriage as having been much more of a "business agreement"; they describe the road they are on very differently. And there is another group, which is often forgotten, who survive the death of a partner KIA—those who were not legally married at the time of the service member's death. This group is even more disconnected from help in facilitating their special grief, cut-off from military resources and from receiving government benefits. Thus, they experience not just the loss of their loved one, but also that their relationship to their service member is not recognized and validated.

When the pain starts

The pain starts at notification. Many surviving spouses say that they don't have the words to describe this feeling. Many widows and widowers try to cut themselves off as their way of responding to the pain. In the beginning it seems like no one understands, because the death of a spouse KIA is such a distinctive traumatic event. And yes, most of us look for others who might have a similar pain. Some find it in other widows and widowers; some find it in our veterans, when they come back from the war zone; some find it in family or church—and some will never find it.

A profound discovery

Along with many widows and widowers, I found myself struggling with difficult questions: How can I honor my deceased spouse? How can I keep his memory alive? How can I move forward and not betray my late husband? What is expected from me by society? How can I honor my war hero with my behavior? There can also be profound discovery in this process: sometimes you have the feeling you have to choose between moving forward and keeping a memory alive.

What makes this heartache particularly difficult for those of us who have lost the love of our life is that many other people seem reluctant or unwilling to talk about the deceased service member. When a grandfather dies, or a mother, or any other relative, typically their memory is kept alive by remembering the person and "talking story" about them. In the case of the deceased service member, as time goes on, others stop talking about him/her, as if they want to erase the memory in order for the surviving spouse to be able to move forward—and perhaps as a way that *they* can move forward. Actually, many of us carry the burden by ourselves. Some of us move forward pretty quickly to the next partner, hoping that we can fill the void. And some of us take a very long time to move forward, because we want to make a point about how important the lost love is for us. Finally, there are some who will never move on.

I know very well about this struggle—a struggle I fought for over seven years. At this point I want to thank all the soldiers who knew Oscar, who came forward at some time following his death and "talked story" with me. They helped me immensely in my healing process. Additionally, I was able to gradually achieve a balance—Oscar remains a part of my life and I will always remember him; he will always have a place in my heart, but I am also allowed to move forward. Nobody else but Oscar's military buddies could have given me that initial permission and freedom, and this helped me to give myself that permission. I hope that other surviving spouses will have a similar experience with their spouses' military buddies, but this can't happen when the surviving spouse and/or the service members are unwilling to contact each other.

Grieving

As a survivor going through the stages of grief, the literature can give a false impression that you go from one stage to the next and that once you enter a new stage, the previous stage is over. I found myself bouncing around from one stage to the other, and sometimes I'd experience more than one stage at the same time. It is hard, painful and frustrating to feel that I'd started to accept things and then to suddenly burst into tears at the sight of a flag at half mast or when I have my hand over my heart during the playing of the national anthem. Some widows/widowers get stuck in one of the "stages" and put guilt/blame on others and themselves. Some widows/widowers find themselves blaming the president and/or congress for starting the war, or God, or the existence of war, or the military, or themselves. Some blame their spouse for having been in the military in the first place. Eventually, many of us also realize that there is no time frame on grief, especially when our service member died in war—and even more so when the same war is still going on. Some widows/widowers find themselves taking on "military pride and bearing" to do "justice" to their loved one. It would be considered "weak" to show feelings in the military culture; therefore effort is put into "staying strong" for each other.

Every journey is different. Even so, I have found that many surviving widows/widowers are very private and might not share their stories easily. Hence, they tend to be "invisible" and are not considered by many to also be casualties of war. And so their voices often go unheard.

The Casualty Assistance Officer

I learned that the Casualty Assistance Officer (CAO) is a different person to the Casualty Notification Officer (CNO). The CNO sees the survivor only once—to give the initial condolences and offer support. The CAO will take over after the CNO leaves the home. Also, the CAO is a military service member and is assigned to the surviving spouse for as long as CAO assistance is needed. The CAO works closely with the Casualty Assistance Office.

I am grateful that I had two Casualty Assistant Officers (CAOs): one at Schofield Barracks on Oahu, Hawaii and the second one at Fort Hood, Texas, after I made my final move to Killeen. I am grateful for both CAOs and the assistance and help they gave me that was so needed during this overwhelming time. To my CAO in Hawaii I give the credit for having helped me through the most difficult decisions. He also helped me to organize all the information that came in. Without his help to start and organize the binder that holds together vital information about benefits and resources, I would not be where I am at now.

I have to say that the government and U.S. Army really took care of me and are still taking care of me. Many rules have changed over the years for the good, but even thinking back to what was there for me originally, it feels like it was/is plenty. Conversely, there are a number of widows and widowers who complain that they are not given what they deserve. "What they deserve?" Maybe it's an attitude. In my case, I was not expecting anything, because I did not serve in the U.S. Army—my late husband did. I am not a gold star—my late husband is the gold star of the banner. So everything I received and still receive is a blessing in my eyes.

There are very substantial monetary and other benefits that surviving spouses can be eligible for (see U.S. Department of Veterans Affairs, 2011; U.S. Military Survivor Benefits, 2011). The CAO has the very difficult duty of dealing simultaneously with the bureaucracy involved and the emotional side of the widow/widower and other family members. The CAO is vital in assisting and helping the survivor to receive benefits. My CAO was a blessing; he was more clear in his thinking and able to give me factual explanations about the paperwork. He also helped me to fill out the many required forms. The CAO can accompany the survivor to all necessary appointments and to difficult situations like the return of the service member's body, the memorial service, the funeral, etc. S/he will be there whenever the survivor needs them as long as it is within the military rules and regulations. Also, survivors find themselves under the influence of the opinions of family, friends and others; very quickly the CAO might need to be in the role of providing a "soldier's voice" concerning such decisions as the question of military honors, national cemetery versus civilian cemetery, etc. The CAO is also very valuable when it comes to keeping track of appointments. Survivors often find themselves in a "fog" and unable to access their short-term memory. The CAO can be an enormous help with noting down decisions and helping the survivor to remember.

Often the CAO is the connection to military life. Spouses who supported their loved ones in the military career have adapted to the military lifestyle, like I did. Now they are concerned about how fast they might become "cut off." Having a military person helping the surviving spouse through the difficult times gives the spouse the feeling of being cared for and still being a part of military life. The CAO can also help the spouse to connect with his/her soldier's unit. The command of units normally reaches out to the survivor, but sometimes the survivor, as I did, wants to exchange stories with the veterans who served with their loved one. However, I know that some veterans might not want to face the surviving spouse or are at a point where they can't face the survivor.

Many surviving spouses do not live near a military base and hence many resources and services are not nearly as accessible to them. Of course, all the benefits and resources do not bring the lost loved one back, but they help immensely to get back on two feet; and most war widows/widowers are thankful for what they receive. Even so, money can go fast if not managed wisely. During such time of grief it is very hard to focus and to stay on track, and surviving spouses need to be careful about making sure they find people who can give them good advice.

Using resources to heal and grow

As already mentioned, we are all different; therefore our ways of healing are different. Many try to deal with their grief by themselves—especially widowers—and do not want to be marked as having a "problem." And yet, are not loss and grief a "normal" part of life? But we do not expect the love of our life to die and a hero of society to die. Some seek the comfort of other widows and widowers. There are many organizations like SOS (U.S. Army, Survivors Outreach Services, 2011) and TAPS (Tragedy Assistance Program for Survivors, 2011) that offer grief camps, survivor groups, individual counseling and/or other support, such as having get togethers.

When participating in the peer support groups that are offered, I have found that there are too many professionals who feel that they need to "set us straight" or "tell us their mind" or "give us advice" because we are the widows/widowers of a fallen hero. Also, there seems to be the unspoken rule, "you don't disagree with a surviving spouse of a fallen hero." But the silent voices of many would like to have the support to be able to contradict the ones that are just there for their own benefit, or who think they are "privileged," or who simply accept being told by a therapist or some group members how to feel, how to act, and especially how assistance is judged. To all the behavioral health professionals dealing with us, please help us to be able to use our own inherent abilities so that we are better able to think and see more objectively.

Another approach is individual counseling. It is my experience (and I've heard this from other survivors too) that the greatest challenge is to find the right person. If you are still on a military base, the professionals might have experience with helping surviving spouses of partners KIA. If you are off base, this can be a significant challenge. What is important is to keep an open mind and trust the professional. On the other hand, it is essential to give yourself permission to switch counselors when you feel a particular professional will not be able to help you anymore.

Resources outside the military

I tried to be a part of some of the non-military resources in my search to find some comfort after Oscar's death. However, what I experienced was nagging against the military and government and what seemed like attempts to get me angry with them as well. These organizations seemed to try to keep you in grief and anger, instead of helping you to grow.[1] I know that not all non-government resources are like that. Many are very important for some surviving spouses, and I respect the organizations that the editors mention below.

---

1 Editors' note: We very much respect Beate's experience. On the other hand, we would be remiss not to mention as an example one private resource that Raymond Scurfield has had very positive contacts with. This is the American Widow Project (http://amerianwidowproject.org), established by Taryn Davis, the widow of a spouse KIA in 2007. Taryn and the AWP have received several civic awards in recognition of their work. The AWP website is "built to house ideas, stories and advice" and identifies resources. Also, there is a very moving DVD available about four surviving spouses as well as a 24-hour hotline staffed by surviving spouses (1-877-AWP WIDOW).

But I never was nor will I be angry with the military or the government, and I found more comfort in going to and participating in what was provided for veterans—like the healing seminars offered by Soldier's Heart.

Rituals and acknowledgment

Talking to other widows/widowers, it seems that both keeping old rituals and developing ones are helpful in getting to the next step in grieving a loved one. For example, children can play a big role in this and are an advantage, because they will hold adults to continuing certain established rituals, like Christmas. In addition, there is the need to incorporate new rituals into the established ones. Examples of new rituals include hanging special ornaments on the Christmas tree that acknowledge the lost loved one, or developing new rituals concerning how to leave and enter the home. I have also found that acknowledgement of the deceased partner and the relationship the surviving spouse and deceased partner had is very important. When you meet with other survivors and get to know them, many will admit that they "still talk to" their loved ones. Some state that there are whole conversations going on in their heads, in which they make up or imagine their loved ones' answers. And some even write to their loved ones.

Connection to service members: A give and take

The surviving spouse and the service member's extended family experience a loss, but so do the veterans connected to the fallen soldier. All of these people have needs and ways of dealing with grief, and those need to be respected. All of these people have faces and hearts and each person might have a different reaction to her or his loss and different ways to do what is needed in their healing process.

Many of us war widows/widowers find comfort in the connection to veterans, because the pain we see in veterans seems so similar to our own pain. It seems like someone understands what is going on inside of us and hopefully we can give the same in return to the veteran. Sometimes a bond becomes established even before the unit returns home from deployment. Emails and/or letters go back and forth. And some of these veterans are our friends through former barbeques or other get togethers. On the other hand, we know that our deployed service members do not have the time or the circumstances to be able to fully grieve; they still have to concentrate on the mission. Therefore, some veterans decide to stay quiet. This leads to difficult questions: Should war widows/widowers attend the homecoming of the returning unit that our spouses KIA belonged to? Are we going to "spoil" the happiness of others? Some of us have gone to the homecomings and all the ones I talked to were glad that they made this step—including me. It was the first step to share feelings and to acknowledge each other's loss.

Those who have taken the steps to reach out often have some incredible experiences. Stories are exchanged and the widow/widower hears the perspective of the veterans and the "truth" about their loved one's death. This may seem like pouring salt in the wound, but sometimes pain is necessary in order to heal. But not just the incident that caused the death is shared; many other memories are shared from before and throughout deployment. For widows/widowers this fills a void, especially when family and friends have stopped talking about our deceased service member. And so, veterans and war widows/widowers can find each other, connect and laugh and cry together. Many state that the sharing of those moments is very healing and takes them a step further along their grief process.

While listening to all of the stories about our fallen service member, we widows/widowers sometimes find ourselves hearing that some veterans feel guilty about what happened, that somehow they feel at fault for not having been able to prevent the death of their battle buddy. These are moments when we can help immensely by assuring the veterans that we (the surviving spouses) do not hold the battle buddies responsible or think they were at fault. It is my experience that most widows/widowers do not blame their late husband's/wife's comrades for their death. On the other hand, some surviving spouses seem to need to find someone to blame and are extremely angry: at the battle buddies, the military, family members who encouraged or supported a military career, and even at the deceased for choosing to be in the military.

Having experienced this deep connection, there was the day when I decided that as much as Oscar's soldiers were there for me to ease my pain, I wanted to help ease the pain of the soldiers. Because I went for counseling, I knew how helpful or unhelpful counseling can be. My first counselor was at the hospital. I went a few times, but he always tried to get facts, and facts weren't what I needed. So I stopped counseling. Later I met a chaplain who offered to talk with me. And even though I was still mad at God, I went. This chaplain did not make it about God, but about life. It was more about the process, not the content. I took his words in and, believe it or not, the day came when certain words became translated into my life's journey. I realized how important it was for him to be there to hold my hand, but to let me take the direction I needed to go in. This is what I wanted to be for others.

My relationship with Oscar now

Many people do not understand my relationship with Oscar now. When I speak of Oscar or share memories, people ask me, "When are you going to move on?" It makes me so mad. When it is your partner who was KIA, somehow it is different to losing a sibling, a parent, or a grandparent. It feels like people expect you to just forget about him. Take everything down and hide what are reminders of him.

But Oscar is a part of my life, he has a place in my heart and he always will. Having him and his memories as a part of me will not exclude me having a partner again one day. With all the expectations aimed at me, I had a period where I had a shrine for Oscar; and another period where I put everything about Oscar away. Now I have found balance in my eyes. Oscar has a corner in my home—and will always have a place in my heart.

Paying it forward

There was a time when I felt I was just "taking," so I was excited to be able to volunteer at military-related resources; this helped me to feel like I was still a valuable part of my military family. I volunteer for the Army Family Team Building and, when possible, volunteer for the Army Family Action Plan and the Casualty Assistance Officer Training as a guest speaker. And I am very happy that after a long road of practice and internships, I am working for the U.S. Army as a Civilian Behavioral Health Therapist. The reason is very simple: the military is and always will be my family. They understood and still understand me the best when it comes to my feelings about Oscar, his life and his death. They are the ones that put me back on my two feet and helped me to become independent. I feel that I especially owe Oscar's comrades. His soldiers are the who are not scared or reluctant to talk about him. I also realized when Oscar's soldiers came back, that they carried pain similar to mine. I saw myself in their eyes. Therefore it was very important for me to make the connection. This made me decide to go to all the homecomings of the 84th and to do a luncheon for the soldiers of the convoy Oscar died on. And with the 84th there was another widow whose soldier died in the same convoy as Oscar. We were able to come together on the first year anniversary of their deaths. The 84th soldiers put up a memorial stone in front of their battalion. It is still there and I know that soldiers still visit it every year in honor of their two fallen comrades.

In retrospect

Oscar's death made me grow. It pushed me to do things and strive for things I would have not done otherwise. I was able to become the person I am now. I have grown so much in the past seven years, because of the way Oscar died and the experiences that followed. I learned so much about him and about being a soldier than I otherwise would have been able to. It helps as a counselor, because I know I connect to soldiers on a different level than others can. Often in our world the mind is addressed, but we forget the mind's connection to the body and the spirit. I have found that the process is sometimes more important than the content. I also believe and have experienced that it is not always the therapist's place to know what is going on. We are just a tool, someone holding a hand until the person finds their path.

Oscar's legacy

Oscar's legacy has become very important to me—and to others. For a very long time I thought I was the only one remembering him, and I tried very hard to tell Oscar's story and talk about him as much as I could. Over the years, I learned that Oscar touched many lives and that his memory is kept alive. For example, the high school Oscar went to in Chicago named their drill after him. I sent them some of Oscar's military things for display, because I thought it would be an awesome place for such a display, instead of them collecting dust in my home. One soldier who had served with Oscar gave me a remembrance bracelet that I still wear. This bracelet made it possible for me to take off my wedding band. I also received a remembrance bracelet from Oscar's soldiers in Hawaii and I shared that with Oscar's son, Danny. And there is this wonderful story of a family who saw a remembrance field full of flags with fallen soldiers' names—including Oscar's. They contacted me and told me their story and wanted to know about Oscar.

Closing

I hope that I have not only told Oscar's and my story but also shown how diverse the grief of surviving spouses can be and given insight into the extensive help we receive from the government and also from many non-profit organizations. I also hope I've shown that, while war widows/widowers receive benefits, this does not guarantee they will heal from the tragic loss they have experienced. Finally, I hope I've shown that our veterans still need our help. We have not done enough to acknowledge their service.

We all have the ability to make sense and meaning out of certain experiences, and this is especially true concerning the traumatic loss of a partner to war. I have not covered everything about what it is to be a surviving spouse, but I hope I have given readers some insights. Surviving spouses of service members are also casualties of war and both need and deserve recognition and support in their healing journeys.

Beate Medina, MS, LPC, LMFT is the widow of SSG Oscar Medina, who was KIA in Iraq in 2004. She was born in Germany and is now a naturalized U.S. citizen, living in Leander, Texas. Beate is a U.S. Army Behavioral Health Therapist at Fort Hood, Texas, specializing in "bringing our veterans back home," integrating alternative therapies into traditional behavioral health therapies. She also volunteers for the Army community and is a guest speaker for the Army Casualty Assistance Officer training (Beate.medina@hotmail.com).

References

Tragedy Assistance Program for Survivors (TAPS) (2011). Retrieved from www.taps.org

U.S. Army (2011). Survivor outreach services. Retrieved from www.myarmyone-source.com/FamilyProgramsandServices/SurvivingFamilies/SurvivorOutreach-Services.aspx

U.S. Department of Defense (2012). U.S. casualty status. Retrieved from www.defense.gov/news/casualty.pdf

U.S. Department of Veterans Affairs (2011). Survivors benefits. Retrieved from www.vba.va.gov/survivors

U.S. Military Survivor Benefits (2011). Retrieved from www.military.com/benefits/survivor-benefits

U.S. National Archives and Records Administration (1998). Statistical information about casualties of the Vietnam War. Retrieved from www.archives.gov/research/military/vietnam-war/casualty-statistics.html

Epilogue

There is no one or handful of clinical interventions or healing approaches that is the end-all treatment modality that is equally appealing to, appropriate, or sufficient for all or even most service members and veterans. This belief is the inspiration for writing our second book, *Healing War Trauma: A Handbook of Creative Approaches* (Routledge, 2012).

It is understandable that governmental agencies want to emphasize and train their staff in very select approaches that have strong empirical/research support. These approaches are almost entirely verbal/cognitive and office-based, e.g. manual-driven cognitive-behavioral approaches. Indeed, one of their major strengths—that both practitioner and client are held to adherence to a very formalized and prescriptive set of intervention procedures—is also a great shortcoming.

Such approaches are not appealing to a large number of veterans who do not want to participate in cognitive-behavioral "exposure-based" approaches, or who enter such treatment and then drop out before completing the treatment protocol, or who complete such protocols and find yet further healing is desired and needed. Many clinicians also find that such approaches restrict if not stifle their ability to utilize their idiosyncratic, intuitive and creative clinical acumen to "start where the client is" and tailor interventions to the distinctive if not unique characteristics, dynamics and strengths of both the client and the clinician. Finally, there are inherent limitations in who (clients and clinicians) is attracted to such approaches in the first place, and what the range of therapeutic benefits might be.

There is a whole other world out there that says there is much more to the damage that has been incurred by service members and veterans from their war experiences than their *DSM-IV-TR*-defined PTSD symptoms. For example, that war has inflicted serious psychological, social, moral and indeed physiological pain and injury—such as the impact on self-identity and self-esteem; alienation; loss of belief in our country and its institutions, and of religious and spiritual beliefs; and physiological stasis and existential malaise. Furthermore, there are many avenues of intervention that tap into and stimulate the creative, expressive, movement/body/actions, existential, social and religious/

spiritual aspects of war survivors and that validate and affirm their wartime and readjustment experiences. A very small sampling of such approaches have been included in this book.

However, there is a much broader range of healing dimensions that can be tapped and stimulated by a number of wonderful approaches that reflect the marvelous array of individuality, creativity, innovativeness and healing energy of the clinicians and providers who practice and offer these approaches to our wounded warriors. And this is what *Healing War Trauma* is all about.

Healing War Trauma and *War Trauma and Its Wake* are two separate but related books. Together, they offer a gateway to innovative and creative knowledge and experience that reflects the impressive array of authors that have contributed to both books. All of the authors are dedicated to understanding and helping our service members and veterans in their healing journeys—and we presume that you are too, having chosen to read this book.

We thank you so very much, from the bottom of our hearts, for joining us and our service members and veterans, their families and supporters, and being part of this expanding and creative circle of healing on behalf of those so willing to lay down their lives.

Ray Scurfield
Kathy Platoni

Index

4H 297

Abdur Rahman 234
About Face program 58
acupuncture 99, 168
addiction 98–9, 101, 161–3, 165, 285
Afghanistan 231–41; civilian population
  of 12, 231–41; and post-traumatic
  stress disorder 232–5, 241; Soviet
  invasion of 231
Afghanistan conflict 1, 4, 5, 7, 10, 32, 12,
  14–15, 25, 32, 56, 59, 63, 66, 72, 73,
  90–1, 95, 97, 114, 123, 134, 135, 156,
  172, 173, 178, 194, 197, 199, 231, 236,
  262, 264, 278, 317
aging process 17
Air Force Wounded Warrior Program
  141
alcohol 46, 92, 96, 97, 99, 177, 184, 193,
  195, 203–4
alcohol treatment programs 9, 101
alcoholism 101, 103
Algiers Accord 219
Al-Qaeda 217
American Legion 297
American Red Cross 138
American Revolutionary War 31, 70
amnesia 22, 23
amputations 134, 139, 142, 148, 267, 268,
  270, 274, 275, 277
amygdala 117–21, 124–6
anger 23, 24–5, 42, 45–6, 99, 114, 115,
  119, 150, 163, 164, 201–2, 204, 226,
  227, 232, 253, 263, 274, 320
anti-Vietnam War protests 54

anxiety 17, 40, 59, 84, 93, 114, 115–16,
  124, 146, 162, 237, 279, 284
anxiety disorders 26, 246, 247
Armour, Vernice 70
Army Family Action Plan 328
Army Family Team Building 328
Army Force Regeneration (ARFORGEN)
  cycle 36, 39
army media 44
Army National Guard (ARNG) see
  National Guard
Army Nurse Corps 71
army reserve see U.S. Army Reserve
army reserve recovery care coordinators
  35
Army Reserve Warrior and Family
  Assistance Center 35
Army Strong Community Centers 35
army values 37, 304, 305
ArtReach Foundation 13, 283, 285–98
arts, use of in healing 13, 129, 272,
  283–98
arts competitions 296–7
attention deficit (hyperactivity) disorder
  101, 284
Ayatollah Khomeini 219–20, 221

Baath regime 215, 217–18
"battle buddies" 3, 20, 45, 65–6, 143,
  165–6, 168, 190, 260, 269, 274, 276,
  279, 327
battered woman syndrome 226
battlemind 25, 245, 260–1
Belgian Congo 90
bereavement 94, 261, 317–29

BICEPS principles 248, 251, 252–3
blame 11, 19–21, 216, 323, 327; self- 4, 10, 19–20, 323
body image disorders 284
bonds (between service members) (*see also* camaraderie) 4, 6, 17, 24, 45, 63, 141, 143, 157, 186, 190, 253, 271, 276, 288
Bosnia 54, 288–9, 318
Bosnian War 288
bracelets (hero/remembrance) 7, 329
brain 115–23, 161, 201, 204 *see also* traumatic brain injury
Branch Davidians 55
breast cancer 284
Brown, Edmund Gerald, Sr. 54
burn patients 134, 139, 140, 144, 148, 267, 277
burnout 60, 290, 292
"burying" of memories 22, 25
Bush, George H. 222
Bush, George W. 62, 63

camaraderie (*see also* bonds between service members) 17, 24, 106, 157, 253, 255, 257, 262, 271, 275, 276
Cambodia 90, 235
Canadian Forces 12, 90–108
Canadian Forces (CF) Member Assistance Program 90, 97
Canadian Veteran Adventure Foundation 90, 102–7
Care for the Troops 209, 297
Care for Victims Task Force 178
caregivers 145–52, 180, 182, 295
Casey, George W., Jr. 55
Central African Republic 235
chaplains 13, 25, 135, 137–8, 140, 254, 256, 258, 263–4, 292, 303–15, 318, 327; rank of 306
Chechnya 233, 248
child abuse 9
child development 39
child neglect 9
children 78
citizen/warriors 31–50; dual role of 37–8
Civil War (American) 70

civilian community, opinions of 41
civilian–military partnerships 13
cognitive-behavioral therapy 12, 14, 92, 99, 101, 107, 129, 166, 187–8, 331; evidence-based 14
cognitive processing therapy (CPT) 99, 188–9
cognitive therapy 239
Cold War 57
combat, impact of 14, 80
combat death 307
Combat Action Badge 72
combat multipliers 311
Combat Operational Stress Control (COSC) 13, 245, 249–56, 261, 264
combat and operational stress reactions (COSRs) 249
combat stress 4, 7, 45, 60, 61, 84, 184, 236, 267; post-traumatic 115, 123–4
community building 152
community service centers 10
compassion fatigue 60, 290
Comprehensive Soldier Fitness (CSF) 245, 261–3
concussion injuries 113–131
Congo 232, 235
coping mechanisms 40–1, 86, 164, 166, 270, 278, 279, 280, 298; maladaptive 103, 311
cortex 117–20, 124, 129, 204
counseling 9, 25, 40, 46, 239, 250, 268, 303, 306, 310, 315, 327, 328
creative arts therapies 284–8
creative writing therapy 283, 284, 285–7, 289, 293, 296
crimes 195
criminal justice system 193–211
Croatia 92, 108
Cuba 32, 268n1
cultural diversity 80–3, 85
cultural shock 44
Cyprus 90, 95, 96

Dallaire, Romeo 91–2
dance therapy 284, 289, 293, 294
debriefing 6, 8–9, 10, 11, 60, 66, 92, 245, 248, 250; battlemind 25, 245, 260–1; bereavement 261–2; critical

event (CED) 245, 249, 257–60;
  psychological 254–5
decompensation 1, 101
decompression 90, 95, 96, 293
deep breathing 128
deer hunting 275, 280
defusings 245, 256–7
dementia 284
Department of Defense 8, 11–12, 53, 55,
  150, 164, 168, 173, 177, 189, 296
Department of National Defence
  (Canada) 90, 93, 94
Department of Veterans Affairs (VA) 8,
  11–13, 35, 46, 48, 64, 66, 69, 73, 82,
  83–4, 94, 148, 150, 152, 173, 174, 176,
  183–4, 188, 189, 200, 206, 207–8, 271,
  273, 275, 278, 293, 296; Washington
  State 210
depression 26, 45, 60, 93, 97, 114, 115–16,
  124, 127, 139, 140, 146, 158, 162, 163,
  203, 232, 233, 235, 240, 247, 260, 263,
  267, 268, 284
Descartes, René 120
Desert Storm 54, 222
"desertion", guilt over 2
developmental disability 284
Disabled Veterans Scuba Project 273,
  275–6
disasters 56, 67; man-made 16; natural
  16, 25, 54, 58, 175, 289
disfigurement 144, 149, 151, 277
dissociation 99
dissonance 159
divorce 35, 57, 62, 77, 208
djinns 239
domestic abuse/violence 35, 195, 234
"Don't Ask, Don't Tell" (DADT) 83
drama therapy 281, 284, 285, 289, 293
drug treatment programs 9
Duerk, Rear Admiral Alene B. 71

Eagles, the 312
East Timor 90
eating disorders 284
education 48, 151–2
Egypt 90
Eisenhower, Dwight D. 54
electroencephalography (EEG) 100

empathy 19, 241
Employment Partnerships of the Armed
  Forces 35
endorphins 161–2, 167
evidence-based therapies 14, 185–7, 278
expressive arts therapies *see* creative arts
  therapies
eye movement desensitization
  reprocessing (EMDR) 188, 189

Facebook 298
family advocacy programs 9
Family and Corrections Network 209
family dynamics 78, 146, 206, 210, 307
Family Readiness Groups (FRGs) 145
family service centers 10
family therapy 94, 100
Faubus, Orval 54
Fedcure 209
Female Engagement Teams (FETS) 72
fight or flight response 118–19, 128
film 295–6
financial concerns 17, 47, 65, 66, 83, 146,
  184, 207, 270
Finding Oz 313
First Nations peoples 303
First World War 54, 71, 235
Five Rs 251, 253
flashbacks 99, 162, 199
folk-wisdom 17
Fort Hood shootings 4–7, 64
Four Yogas, the 313–14
Frankl, Viktor 18

Gates, Robert M. 56
gender discrimination 80, 84
gender equality 71, 80
genetic factors 123
Genghis Khan 231, 234
Georgia Paving the Way Home for
  Veterans Initiative 297
Global War on Terror(ism) 54, 56, 72,
  113, 114, 267, 268n1
glucose metabolism 123
God 20, 138, 141, 304, 306, 307–313, 320,
  327
"going crazy" 24, 44
"going inside the box" 40–3, 45, 46, 49

"going outside the box" 43–5, 47, 49
good governance 227
Good Guys Marine Fund 150
Grenier, Stéphane 93
grieving 225, 261, 262, 309, 311, 322–3,
   326
group therapy 94, 98, 99, 100, 107, 265,
   272, 278
Guantanamo Bay 32, 268n1
guided imagery 263
guilt 2, 10, 19, 86, 99, 120, 141, 145,
   159, 199, 257, 309, 310, 323, 327;
   abandonment 41–2; survival 4–5, 141,
   164, 263
Gulf War I 8, 9, 10, 40, 44, 54, 57, 72, 73,
   215
Gulf War II 215, 223
Gulf War on Terror 157

habituation 188–9
Haiti 54, 90
Hays, Brigadier General Anna Mae 71
Hazaras 233–4
headaches 114, 115, 116, 124–5, 127, 131,
   231
healing 4, 13, 16, 19, 21, 35, 127, 182, 189,
   190, 215, 224, 226–9, 238–9, 268, 281,
   287, 289, 294–5, 308–9, 310, 315, 322,
   329, 332; circle of 12–13, 27, 47, 283,
   298, 317, 332; spiritual 303, 315
"healing on the go" 311
healing power 307
hippocampus 124
Hoefly, Brigadier General E. Ann 71
holistic approach 127–8
homelessness 35, 84, 85, 184
"Hotel California" 312
humour 225, 226, 260, 288
Hurricane Katrina 24–5, 55, 57, 216, 289;
   positive outcomes of 25
Hutus 91
hyperarousal 114, 117–18, 121, 124,
   127–9, 131, 184, 276
hyperthermia 123
hypervigilance 108, 184, 193, 201, 233,
   237, 278

Imam Hussein 224

immune disorders 284
improvised explosive devices (IEDs) 4,
   10, 61, 114, 117, 141, 142, 144, 184,
   190, 202, 205, 257, 262, 267, 271, 314
Incarcerated Veterans Consortium 209
incest 175
Individual Ready Reserve 41
injured, the *see* wounded/injured, the
injuries: classifications of 137; range of
   139
insomnia 114, 116, 124, 125, 127, 131,
   146, 162, 167, 232
"internal deficits" 18
Iran 220–4
Iraq 215–29, 233; arts in 225; Christians
   in 216–17; civilian casualties in 223;
   civilian population of 12, 215–29,
   289; future of 223–4; and Iran 223–4;
   Jews in 216, 217; and national identity
   223; peoples of 216, 224; sanctions
   against 222; Shiite militias in 217;
   Shiites in 216; Sunnis in 216
Iraq and Afghanistan Veterans of
   America 298
Iraq–Iran War 222
Iraq Star Foundation 151
Iraq War 1, 7, 10, 12, 14–15, 18, 25, 32,
   46, 53, 56, 59, 62, 63, 66, 69, 72, 73–4,
   75, 81–2, 114, 123, 135–6, 156, 172,
   173, 174, 178, 194, 197, 215, 249,
   256–7, 259, 264, 268n1, 278, 308–9,
   310, 311, 314, 317, 318–19
irritability 114, 115, 116, 119–20, 124,
   203, 278
Israel 217
Israeli Defense Forces (IDF) 246
Israeli War of Independence 246

jail 194–7, 206, 208–10
Jensen Suicide Prevention Peer Protocol
   (JSP3©) 167
Jesus Christ 309, 312
Joint Task Force for Sexual Assault
   Prevention and Response 178
Jordan 289

Kent State University shootings 54–5
Kierkegaard, Søren 238

Kiwanis Rotary 297
Kony, Joseph 235
Korean War 17, 54, 71, 91, 94, 172
Kosovo 54, 59–61, 63, 65, 234, 318
Kuhlman Debriefing Model 245, 261–2
Kurdish autonomy, fight for 217–20
Kurdish people 216; genocide against
   215, 222
Kuwait 54, 174, 222

Lebanon 289
Legacy Project, the 296
"Little Rock Nine" 54
logotherapy 18
Los Angeles riots 55
loss 3
Lozen 70

major depressive disorder (MDD) 97, 99,
   103, 233, 247
"malingering" 17–18
Marine Corps 1–3, 32, 72, 81, 140–4,
   159–60, 199, 273–4, 295–6, 297
Marine Corps Wounded Warrior
   Program 141
marital/family therapy 100
marriage 65, 67, 77, 270
massage 99, 100, 129, 147, 168
Maslow, Abraham 86
medical model 127–8
medication 115–16, 125, 127, 146, 162,
   165, 200, 253
meditation 128, 166, 195, 263, 284, 285;
   Reiki 312, 313
memory problems 114–15, 117, 124–6,
   131, 150
mental health 10, 26, 31, 47, 75, 92, 95,
   97, 144, 164, 225, 264, 268, 283, 288,
   317; of Afghans 232–3, 239–40, 247,
   249
mental health services 7, 8, 10, 58–60,
   85, 92, 166, 186–8, 196, 231, 240, 245,
   246, 249, 254, 256, 264, 281, 291
mental instability 18
mentoring 149–50
migraines 125
mild traumatic brain injury (mTBI) 78,
   113–31

military culture 31–2, 49, 80, 85, 98,
   175–8, 183, 189–90, 194, 249, 255,
   269, 292, 323
military families 11, 34, 36, 38–40, 48
Military Family Resource Centres 90,
   97–8
military intervention strategies 13, 14
Military OneSource 34, 209
military psychiatry 2
military service 21; risks of 26
military sexual trauma 12, 19, 70, 75,
   78–80, 84, 85, 172–90; and complex
   trauma 175–7; definition of 174;
   extent of 173; reporting of 177–8, 180
Moharam 224–5
mood issues/disorders 26, 116–17, 124,
   125, 127
Motivational Interviewing 166–7, 187
"moving on" 22, 322, 327
Muqtada Al-Sadr 226
music therapy 283, 284, 285, 289, 293,
   294

national "amnesia" 11
National Coalition for Homeless
   Veterans 210
National Guard 12, 33, 53–67, 73, 152,
   164, 176, 183, 194, 205, 209, 256–7,
   276, 293; changes in 58–; origins of
   54, and reintegration 64–5; role of
   54–7; at war 57–8
National Woman's Study Interview 185
Navy Nurse Corps 71
Nazi death camps 18
neurofeedback (NFB) 90, 100–2, 107
neurofeedback training (NFT) 100
neurogenesis 124
neurological insult 284
neuroscience 100, 122
neurotransmitters 122
nightmare re-scripting 99
nightmares 162, 200, 228, 238
Northern Alliance 236
Nurse Corps 71

Oath of Office 304
Ocean Therapy 273–4, 281
Open Inc. 210

Operation Desert Shield 57
Operation Desert Storm 39, 56, 57
Operation Enduring Freedom (OEF) 10,
    32, 56, 66, 73, 90, 138, 194, 204, 205,
    268, 270, 274, 275, 277, 279, 280, 281
Operation First Response 150
Operation Homecoming 296
Operation Iraqi Freedom (OIF) 7, 10, 18,
    32, 56, 65, 67, 70, 73, 138, 194, 205,
    223, 268, 270, 274, 275, 277, 279, 280,
    281, 291, 312–13
Operation Mend 151
Operation New Dawn (OND) 12, 73,
    268, 275, 281
operational stress injury 93
Operational and Traumatic Stress
    Support Centres (OTSSC) 94–5
Operational Stress Injury Social Support
    (OSISS) 90, 93–5
Ottoman Empire 217
outdoor adventure activities 271–81
Outward Bound courses 272

pain 22, 45, 46, 108, 115–16, 124, 125,
    141, 195; chronic 139, 140, 162, 163,
    167; emotional 23, 25; management of
    278, 284; psychological 17, 108, 161–2
panic attacks 231, 232, 240, 241
Paralyzed Veterans of America:
    Shooting Sports 273, 274–5, 280
parenting 270
Pashtuns 233–4
Pathway Home program 273, 277–81
Patriot Guard 297
patriotism 48
Pearl Harbor 48
peer relationships 2
peer support 43, 49, 62, 76, 83, 85, 93–5,
    102, 156, 166, 167–8, 276, 325
perfectionism 156, 163
Persian Gulf Wars *see* Gulf War I and
    Gulf War II
personality disorders 203
Pitcher, Molly 70
plastic surgery 151
plea bargaining 195–6
polysubstance dependence 193
positron emission tomography 123

post-concussion symptoms 115–17, 124,
    127, 130
post-trauma symptoms 18, 184
post-traumatic growth 3, 66, 271, 274,
    328
post-traumatic stress/post-traumatic
    stress disorder (PTSD) 11, 12, 13, 17,
    18, 23, 26, 46, 66, 69, 74–5, 79, 81n2,
    84, 92, 94, 97, 98, 99, 101, 104, 108,
    123–4, 127, 130, 134, 139, 150, 164,
    177, 180, 184, 187–8, 203, 209, 220,
    232, 234, 235, 239, 241, 246, 247–8,
    267, 268, 272, 273, 275, 278, 279, 284,
    285, 292, 311, 331; as survival mode
    23
post-war recovery 1, 14
prayer 307–9, 311
prison/prisoners 193–211; and
    combat-related stress 199–200; and
    environmental triggers 200–1; and
    families 205–7; and mental health
    diagnoses 201–3; and substance
    abuse 203–4
prisoners of war 17
Project Katrina 289
prolonged exposure therapy 66, 99, 101,
    107, 188, 189
Protestantism 303, 311
psychiatric breakdowns 1–2; timing of
    1, 22
psychiatric disorders 11, 13, 202, 284
psychological interventions 9, 249
psychological services 45, 59, 92, 102,
    224, 240, 254–5
psychosis 1, 202–3
psychotherapy 129, 166, 186–7, 255, 273,
    331
psychotic breaks 1
psychotropic medication 23
Puritan work ethic 37
Purple Heart 148, 150, 291

quadriplegia 275
qigong 128

racial discrimination 80–1, 84
racism 81–2
rage *see* anger

rape 174, 177, 179–82, 184, 189, 195, 234, 238
readjustment (post-conflict) 7, 10, 11, 12
reconstructive surgery 151
reintegration 13, 24, 36, 43–4, 45, 47, 53, 64–5, 73–4, 83, 84, 85, 95, 96, 107, 114, 164, 185, 198, 250, 252, 267, 268, 270, 277, 281
relationship issues 34, 35, 42, 47, 62, 65, 75–7
religious beliefs 32, 42, 159, 216–18, 220, 224–5, 256, 262, 303–10, 312, 331
religious dimensions of service 13, 20
reserve warriors 12
resiliency 13, 14, 48, 142, 164, 216, 260, 263, 269, 274, 276, 280, 281; spiritual 314
resiliency initiatives 13, 25, 27, 298
resiliency training 262–3, 280–1
returnees 9–11, 114–15, 118, 131, 193, 198, 201, 232, 267
revenge 233, 234
Rhodes, Jim 54
ritualization 293
Rochester riot 54
Rockefeller, Nelson A. 54
Roman Catholicism 310
Round Table model 297
Rumsfeld, Donald 173, 178
Rwanda 91

sacrifices "in vain" 3
Saddam Hussein 215, 219, 221–3, 226
Sartre, Jean-Paul 120
Saudi Arabia 54
SAVAK 221
schizophrenia 1–2, 201, 284
scuba diving 273, 275–6
Second World War 17, 18, 38, 44, 48, 71, 91, 94
September 11 2001 attacks 48, 59, 67, 173, 216
sexual assault 79, 172–4, 189; definition of 174, 179, 180, 183, 184, 185, 187, 188; on males 179, 184
Sexual Assault Prevention and Response Program (SAPR) 172, 173, 179, 181
Sexual Experience Questionnaire 185

Sexual Experience Survey 185
sexual harassment 53, 79, 174, 176, 180, 183, 185
sexually transmitted diseases 181
Shah of Iran 219, 221
shame 10, 91, 99, 159–60, 178, 199
"shell shock" 235, 246
signature wounds/injuries 13, 138, 205
Silver Star Families of America (SSFOA) 150
social media 298
social networks 17
social suffering 235
soldier restoration 251
Soldier's Creed 37–8, 45, 304, 305
Somalia 54, 91, 232, 234, 318
Sophocles 295
Spanish-American War 71
spirituality 13, 95, 98, 128, 152, 256, 263–4, 287, 303–15, 328, 331–2
sports programs 271–2, 275
spouse KIA (Killed-In-Action), loss of a 317–29
STARBASE program 58
stigma 43, 50, 92–4, 156, 165, 205, 227, 254, 255, 288; against suicide 159–61
strengths approach 3
stress 3, 43, 46, 50, 62–3, 115–16, 121, 124, 125, 131, 146, 165, 166, 201, 284; age-related 17; combat 4, 7, 45, 60, 61, 84, 144, 199–200, 245–7, 278, 284; family 42; management of 187, 253, 255, 276; operational 90, 93–5, 127, 245, 247; relationship 35, 42; traumatic 8, 116
stress control 60; combat 4, 60, 64; combat/operational (COSC) 62, 245, 249–56, 261, 264
stress disorders 92 *see also* post-traumatic stress disorder (PTSD)
stress hormones 123, 128
stress reduction techniques 127–9, 284
stressors 26, 31, 39–40, 42, 59, 66, 77, 81n2, 130, 146, 157, 164, 165, 175, 184, 194, 198–9, 201, 247, 253
stretching 128
stroke 277, 284

Strong Bonds program 34, 140–1, 293
subcultures 31
subordinate abuse 19, 75
substance abuse 22, 23, 96, 99, 103, 163,
    165, 177, 184, 187, 195, 200–1, 203–4,
    268, 311
substance abuse programs 9, 35, 99, 101,
    201, 273
Sudan 90
Sufis 216
suicidality 12, 35, 45, 99, 156–69, 184,
    199, 321; and ACE training 166;
    chronic 157–8; and community
    support 165–6; definition 156;
    dynamics of 157–8; ideation of 156,
    158–9; and peer support 166–8;
    prevention of 156; psychobiology of
    156; and psychopharmacology 156;
    and stigma 156;
suicide 35, 45, 60, 63, 65, 84, 91, 156–69,
    253, 321; awareness of 250; and
    perfectionism 163; psychobiology
    of 161–2; rates of 157, 165, 264; risk
    factors for 156, 163–5; stigma against
    159–61
suicide bombings 121, 217, 223
surviving spouses 12, 317–29
Swami Vivekananda 313–14
SWAN 83
sweat lodges 309

tai chi 128, 284
Taliban 6, 231, 233, 234, 236, 240
Team Lioness 72, 74
telemedicine programs 298
television 295–6
Ten Commandments 309, 311
terrorism 32, 54, 56, 59, 60, 72, 113, 114,
    217, 223, 235, 267
text alerts 279
thalamus 118
Theater of War 295
therapeutic relationship 22, 100, 185,
    315
Third Location Decompression (TLD)
    Program 90, 95
"time heals all wounds" myth 10–11,
    16–17

tinnitus 115, 139–40
torture 221; self-inflicted 224–5
totemic relationships 303
touchstones 308
Train-the-Trainer programs 283, 285,
    288, 289, 293
transformation 312–13
trauma 3, 7, 19–27, 66–7, 91–2, 99, 101,
    102, 107, 108, 148, 180, 186, 188,
    189–90, 215, 224–7, 232, 234–5,
    256, 263, 268–9, 278, 284–6, 290;
    behavioral 17; childhood 184, 279;
    denial of 19, 22–3; detachment from
    22–3; dysfunctional adaptation to
    22–3; emotional 17; and forgetting
    22; gender-based 18; inpatient
    treatment programs for 98–9; and
    "moving on" 22; myths regarding
    16–26; outpatient treatment of
    99–100; positive outcomes of 24–5;
    psychological 79; race-based 18;
    recycled 227; secondary 292; sexual
    12, 19, 70, 75, 78–80, 84, 85, 172–90;
    vicarious 285; war-related 10, 14, 17,
    123, 188, 233–6, 239, 247, 268, 275,
    279, 281, 289, 290, 297
trauma recovery 4, 86
trauma survivors 16–17, 20, 22–4, 80,
    258, 281
trauma "trigger" myth 17–18
traumatic brain injury (TBI) 12, 13, 69,
    79, 134, 139, 150, 164, 204–5, 267,
    272, 277, 278, 284, 292, 297; mild
    (mTBI) 78, 113–31, 205, 209, 284
Traumatic Event Management (TEM)
    245, 250, 255–6, 314
traumatic threats, myths regarding 19
Troop Program Units 41
trust 20, 21, 23, 25, 26, 82, 104, 186, 189,
    193, 198, 237, 306; of authorities 10;
    building of 99–100, 288
Tutsis 91
Twitter 298

Uganda 233, 234, 235
UN Security Council 90
UNEF 90
unemployment 35, 57, 74

United Nations peacekeeping missions
90–2, 103
UNFICYP 90
UNPROFOR 90
U.S. Air Force 32, 71
U.S. Army Reserve 31–50, 53, 67, 73,
164, 176, 179, 183, 194, 205, 209, 257,
293; demographics of 32; and family
programs 34, 36, 49; minorities in 32,
82; and reintegration programs 34;
and relationship education 34; units
of 32–3
U.S. Code 79; Title 10 31, 61; Title 38 79
U.S. Navy 32, 71

VA *see* Department of Veterans Affairs
Vegetius 62
"Vet Centers" 150
veteran support groups 208
veterans 12–14, 17, 93–4, 102–7, 113,
157, 165, 168, 185, 189, 232, 248, 267,
268–81, 283, 289, 307, 309, 322, 327,
331, 332; and arts therapy 283–7, 290,
291, 293–8; and the criminal justice
system 193–211; and discrimination
21, 81n2; female 69–70, 73–86,
194; financial assistance for 150;
incarcerated 193–211; LGBTQ
82–3, 84; and MST 174; and positive
outcomes 24; post-service traumas
of 21–7; recreation for 102–7, 151;
services for 1, 10–13, 69–70, 92–108,
183, 208–9; resources for 209–10,
271–81, 298
Veterans Affairs Canada (VAC) 93, 94,
107
Veterans Benefits Administration (VBA)
84
Veterans' Charter (Canada) 98, 107
Veterans of Foreign Wars 297
Veterans' Integrated Service Network
(VISN) 207–8, 209
Veterans Justice Outreach 210
Veterans Writing Project 296
Vietnam Vets of America 210

Vietnam War 1–2, 7, 15, 17, 33, 44, 48,
53, 54, 64, 81n2, 138, 140, 172, 184,
194, 246, 247, 291, 317; women in 71
visualization 285; guided 263
volunteerism 278, 280, 328
Volunteers of America 210

Waco Siege 55
Warrior Ethos 37–8
Warrior Games 277
Warrior Transition Units (WTUs) 276–7,
281, 293
Warrior Writers 296
Watts Riots 54
websites 298
well-being 97, 152, 166, 238, 253,
283, 295; emotional 165, 268;
psychological 60, 62
wilderness therapy 90, 102
Women Accepted for Volunteer
Emergency Service (WAVES) 71
Women Air Force Service Pilots
(WASPS) 71
women warriors 12, 32, 53, 69–86, 194
Women's Army Auxiliary Corps
(WAAC) 71
Women's Army Corps (WAC) 53, 71
Wonderful Wizard of Oz, The 313, 315
workaholism 22
World War II (*see* Second World War)
wounded/injured, the 3, 5, 12, 35, 60, 64,
90–1, 102, 104, 124, 134–52; female
144–5
Wounded Warrior Project 138, 151, 272,
273, 289, 293, 298
Wounded Warrior Transition Unit 141,
143

Yellow Ribbon Reintegration Programs
34, 64–5, 150, 152
yoga 128, 147, 278, 311, 313
Youth Challenge program 58
Yugoslavia (former) 90, 91, 108

Zimbabwe 233